MARK WILSON'S
CYCLOPEDIA
OF MAGIC

A COMPLETE COURSE

RUNNING PRESS
PHILADELPHIA · LONDON

Printed in the United States of America

Library of Congress Cataloging-in-Publication Number 94–74318

ISBN 1–56138–613–8

Jacket design by Toby Schmidt
Jacket photography by Weaver Lilley
Compiled by Carolyn and Peter Caprioglio
Edited by Liz Kaufman
Interior design by Ruthie Thompson

This book may be ordered by mail from the publisher.
Please include $2.50 for postage and handling.
But try your bookstore first!
Running Press Book Publishers
125 South Twenty-second Street
Philadelphia, Pennsylvania 19103–4399

TABLE OF CONTENTS

ABOUT THE AUTHOR...
MARK WILSON

Mark Wilson has performed magic for more people than any other magician in the 3,500-year history of the art. During his successful career over the past 30 years, Mark Wilson has shared his wondrous magic with the world in many ways:

♦ Starred in the first weekly network magic series, *Magic Land of Allakazam*, which aired for two years on CBS, and for three years on ABC networks; six *Magic Circus* specials; *Magic of Mark Wilson* syndicated series; four HBO Magic Specials; *Magic of China, Children of China, Mr. Magic* syndicated specials; and many more.

♦ Developed international programming, including television specials for the NHK, NTV, and ASAHI Japanese networks and for Korea, Canada, Hong Kong, Australia, Great Britain, and People's Republic of China. Wilson's U.S. productions have aired throughout South America, Europe, Southeast Asia, Pacific Rim countries, and elsewhere.

- Authored *Mark Wilson's Complete Course in Magic*, the most popular book of magic instruction in history with over 300,000 copies published.

- Served as creative consultant and supplier of magic to countless television series, such as *Columbo, Simon and Simon, Love Boat, Circus of the Stars, Perfect Strangers, Dear John,* and *The Odd Couple.*

- Instructs Hollywood's top stars in the performance of magic. Past and present celebrity students include Cary Grant, Tony Curtis, Peter Falk, Bill Bixby, Jackie Gleason, Cher, Johnny Carson, Burt Reynolds, and many others.

- Prepares entertainment packages for many of the world's finest theme parks, world's fairs, expositions, and major corporations worldwide.

- Most notably, in 1980 Mark Wilson was the first foreign magician to perform on mainland China since the founding of the People's Republic of China. He is the world's most honored magician, with *two* prestigious "Magician of the Year" awards and the "Master's Fellowship" from the Academy of Magical Arts. He has also won the "Superstar of Magic," "Magician of the Decade," and "Lifetime Achievement" awards.

ACKNOWLEDGMENTS

The contents of this book do not represent the efforts of only two, three, or a dozen individuals; rather, they represent all those magicians of the past and the present who have labored so diligently to create, perfect, and present the Art of Magic.

Just as a stalagmite, buried unseen in a dark cave, builds from tiny drops into a towering structure, so has our Art increased through the centuries, shrouded in a like darkness of secrecy which remains a prerequisite to its growth.

With this book, you will join the ranks of those who have learned these inner secrets—and you must acknowledge and respect those whose contributions we enjoy. *Acknowledge* by being aware of the countless hours of study, work, and practice that have been expended by the magicians of the past to create our Art. *Respect* the magicians of today by never revealing any of these hard-earned secrets.

This, then, is the grateful acknowledgment of this book: *to the Magicians of all times and places,* for their countless contributions to the Art of Magic.

INTRODUCTION

Welcome to my wonderful world of Magic. You're about to enter a mysterious and fascinating realm in which you'll learn some truly baffling illusions. *Mark Wilson's Cyclopedia of Magic* includes more than 200 magic tricks carefully selected, written, and illustrated to provide you with a complete course for learning the art of magic.

For most of the tricks, you'll find detailed information on:

♦ EFFECT—what the spectator will see; the mystery or miracle, as performed by you, the magician

♦ SECRET AND PREPARATION—the props you'll need, and the secret of how tricks work

♦ METHOD—clearly illustrated, step-by-step instructions on how to present tricks to an audience

♦ COMMENTS AND SUGGESTIONS—extra tips and ideas that will help you make tricks even more amazing and entertaining

The secrets to good magic tricks are quite simple. So don't judge a magic trick by its secret—judge it by its effect on the audience. To ensure a captivating effect, it's important that you remember these rules whenever you perform:

- ◆ NEVER REVEAL THE SECRET. If you reveal how a trick is done, the mystery, the excitement, and the magic are gone and the entertainment value lost.

- ◆ NEVER REPEAT A TRICK FOR THE SAME AUDIENCE. When you do a magic trick for the same audience a second time, they will know what to expect and they will be more likely to "catch on" to the secret.

- ◆ ALWAYS PRACTICE BEFORE YOU PERFORM. By taking the time necessary to rehearse tricks, you will build self-confidence, which will dramatically enhance your performance before an audience.

As a magician, you'll appear to make the impossible happen. There aren't many people who can pull this off. So practice and perform your magic well, and you'll make the magic fun for yourself and a rare treat for your audience!

If you'd like to learn more about magic and take the next step in exploring our wonderful art, please write to me.

Happy Magic!

Mark Wilson

Mark Wilson
c/o Magic International, P.O. Box 801839
Santa Clarita, CA 91380–1839

CHAPTER 1
CARD MAGIC

Tricks with cards form their own branch of magic. From the moment you start doing card tricks, you naturally acquire a manipulative ability. The acts of cutting, shuffling, and dealing a pack of cards demand skill. Next, you may find fancy cuts and flourishes to your liking.

There are many tricks involving the discovery of cards selected by members of the audience. These depend upon a variety of methods that enable you to keep a jump ahead of keen-eyed and keen-witted spectators. Basically, there are three ways of discovering a chosen card. One is to "force" it on the spectator, so that you know the card beforehand and therefore can predict it, name it, or produce a duplicate from some unexpected place. Another is to "locate" the card by its position in the pack, so you can find it by simply looking through the pack or studying the cards as you deal them. The third way is to "control" the chosen card by shuffles, cuts, and other manipulations that enable you to reveal it at any time.

CARD-HANDLING TECHNIQUES

Throughout all card magic, you will find that there are certain basic card-handling techniques which are essential to your ability to perform tricks. These include shuffling and dealing. These techniques will not necessarily appear in each card trick, but there are very few tricks that do not require at least a shuffle.

You probably already know one, but you will find that there are several kinds of shuffles. Most of them serve some special purpose, such as controlling the position of a card. Together, they give you the opportunity to introduce variety into your card handling.

Similarly, there are different techniques for dealing. The success of a trick frequently depends on your skillful accomplishment of this manipulation. Therefore, you are urged to practice all of the following manipulations until you can do each one smoothly, confidently, and without hesitation.

Remember, the mere appearance of skill and confidence in your handling of cards will add much to your audience's respect for your ability as a magician.

RIFFLE SHUFFLE

The riffle shuffle is probably the most widely used method of shuffling cards. For that reason alone, you should be familiar with it. This shuffle is not difficult, but it will require some practice to perform it smoothly.

METHOD

1 Hold the pack in your right hand with your thumb at one end and your second, third, and fourth fingers at the other. The tip of your first finger (bent at the knuckle) should rest against the back of the top card of the pack. The pack should be held so that your right thumb is toward the ceiling with the face of the pack pointing to your left.

2 Place the palm of your left hand on the bottom of the pack, as shown. With your right hand, bend the pack outward and riffle about half of the pack with your right thumb, allowing the cards to fall forward onto the left fingers.

3 Place the tip of your left thumb on the back of this new packet (B) and raise the lower end of Packet B upward until it clears Packet A in the right hand. As the end of Packet B comes clear, shift your left thumb to the right-hand end of Packet B.

4 The two packets should be facing each other, held with the same grip in each hand. Your thumbs should be at one end of the packets with your first fingers resting against the backs of the packs and the remaining fingers at the opposite ends.

5 Turn both packets face down and move the "thumb end" of each packet together. The backs of the second, third, and little fingers of both hands should rest on the top of the table.

6 Slowly begin releasing (riffling) cards from both thumbs, causing the cards to fall to the table and become interlaced at the inner ends. The ends of the cards should overlap about 1/2" as they are shuffled together.

7 When all the cards have been shuffled from both packets, push the two packets completely together and square the deck. This completes the riffle shuffle.

8 Repeat Steps 1 through 7 in quick succession, executing the shuffle as many times as you wish to thoroughly mix the cards.

TABLE SHUFFLE

This basic exercise is intended to show you how to shuffle a deck of cards properly. This is similar to, but considerably more "professional," than the standard riffle shuffle.

When working with cards, it is to your advantage to be able to mix the cards in a quick, graceful fashion. Since some of the best card tricks are performed while seated at a table, you should be familiar with the table shuffle. It gives your work an expert look, convincing your audience that even your simplest tricks are the result of great skill.

MARK WILSON'S CYCLOPEDIA OF MAGIC

EFFECT

You divide the pack into two packets that rest face down on the table. Lifting the rear edges of both packets, you begin to release the cards in succession, causing their corners to interweave as they fall. You push the two packets together and square the deck, thoroughly mixing the pack.

METHOD

1 Place the pack face down on the table in front of you and grasp the sides of the pack from above, as shown. Using your thumbs, lift about half the pack from the top of the deck, near the middle.

2 Separate the halves and place the packets on the table, as shown. The outer ends of both packets should be angled toward you to bring the innermost corners of the packets very close together. Hold both packets with your thumbs along the inner edge. The first finger of each hand rests on the top of the packs, and the remaining fingers rest along the outer edges.

3 Lift the inner edge of both packets with your thumbs and move the packets together so that the innermost corners will overlap slightly. Begin releasing the cards from your thumbs, allowing them to riffle downward onto the table so the inner corners of the cards weave together.

4 The cards are released from your thumbs, interlacing at the corners only, as shown in this close-up view.

5 Release the remaining cards in the same fashion.

6 Move your fingers to the extreme ends of both packets and push them together to form one pack.

7 Repeat the shuffling process as many times as you like until all the cards in the pack have been completely mixed.

COMMENTS AND SUGGESTIONS

This type of shuffle, sometimes known as the "Dovetail Shuffle," is often used by gamblers or professional dealers. Therefore, it is particularly effective when doing card tricks that have a gambling theme. Many gamblers, after completing the shuffle, will cut the pack by drawing out the lower half of the pack and placing it on top of the upper half of the pack. As a magician, you can follow the same procedure, adding a natural and professional touch to your card work.

DEALING THE CARDS

Few actions are simpler than dealing cards from the top of the pack, but to do it smoothly, neatly, and sometimes rapidly, the hands should work together, as described here.

METHOD

1 Hold the deck in the dealing position in your left hand, as shown in the illustration.

2 With your left thumb, push the top card forward and to the right about an inch. At the same time, move the right hand toward the pack in readiness to receive the card.

3 Grasp the top card between the thumb and fingers of the right hand, as shown.

4 At the same time, relax the pressure of the left thumb on the top card, allowing the right hand to carry the card from the deck to the table.

5 The right hand releases its grip on the card and leaves it on the table. The action can be repeated as often as necessary to deal the appropriate number of cards.

COMMENTS AND SUGGESTIONS

With some tricks, you may deal the cards in a single pile; with others, you may deal them in a row or in some special formation. When dealing cards in a pile, one on top of the other, you will reverse the order of the cards as you deal them. This is known as the "Reverse Deal," an important element in certain tricks.

CHAPTER 2
SELF-WORKING CARD TRICKS

There are many excellent card tricks that practically work themselves and are nearly foolproof from the magician's point of view, yet really baffle the spectators.

In this section, you'll find some of the best of these self-working mysteries that are both deceptive and easy to perform. You can concentrate almost entirely on the presentation without worrying about any special moves or sleights.

Often, when smart spectators are watching for special moves, you can really flabbergast them with a self-working effect. Make it your policy to include a few self-workers when the occasion demands. You may discover that such effects will be regarded as highlights of your program.

Most importantly, never neglect practice with a self-working trick, even though it seems unnecessary. If you fumble or hesitate, the effect will lose its impact. Always remember that a trick is only as good as you make it look!

AUTOMATIC CARD DISCOVERY

EFFECT

Perhaps one of the most puzzling of all card effects is when a magician causes a selected card to reverse itself and appear face up among the face-down cards in the deck. Here is one of the most basic and yet most effective means of accomplishing this feat.

SECRET AND PREPARATION

Simplicity is the answer here. The trick depends upon having the bottom card of the deck reversed from the start.

A This can be set up beforehand with the deck in its box, or it can be executed easily and quickly at the moment when the spectators' eyes leave your hands.

B With the deck resting face up across the fingers of your left hand, your right thumb and fingers grip the ends of the pack from below, as shown. Slide the pack toward the tips of the left fingers, at the same time tilting or rotating the deck up on its left edge. This leaves the lone card—in this case the eight of spades—still resting on the left fingers.

C Continue the rotary motion until the right hand has turned the pack face down on the eight of spades, which thus, without the spectators knowing it, has become a face-up card at the bottom of the pack. You are now ready to present the trick.

METHOD

1 Spread the cards in your hands face down so that a spectator has an opportunity to freely select any card from the deck. Care must be taken here not to spread the cards too near the bottom of the deck, to avoid accidentally flashing the face-up bottom card.

2 As soon as the card is selected by the spectator, square up the deck in your left hand and ask the spectator to look at the card.

3 At the moment when the spectator's eyes are focusing on the card, the left hand turns completely over and sets the deck of cards on the table. This action turns all of the cards in the deck face up, except for the "bottom" card which is now face down. Because of this single reversed card, it appears that the deck is still face down.

4 Leave the deck sitting on the table, as you tell the spectator to show the card to the other spectators.

5 When the spectator has shown the card, pick up the deck, in its secretly reversed position, with your left hand. Particular care must be taken here to keep the deck squared up so as not to flash the face-up pack below the top, single reversed card.

MARK WILSON'S CYCLOPEDIA OF MAGIC

6 Holding the deck firmly, ask the spectator to push the card face down anywhere in the deck. Unknown to the spectator, the card is really being put into a face-up deck. (Except for the top card.)

7 When the spectator has inserted the card into the deck, place the deck behind your back and explain that since the spectator touched only one card in the deck, that card will be a bit warmer than the other cards. State that, due to your highly trained sense of touch, you will be able to find the card and reveal it in a startling way.

8 When you place the deck behind your back, simply turn over the single reversed card and replace it face up on the deck. Now, every card in the deck is facing in the same direction, *except* the spectator's card. It is the only reversed card in the deck.

SUPER AUTOMATIC
CARD DISCOVERY

In performing the AUTOMATIC CARD DISCOVERY, here is another very easy and clever method for reversing the bottom card and secretly turning over the pack.

METHOD

1 It is not necessary to have the bottom card reversed before the start of the trick.

2 After the spectator has selected a card from the deck, tell the spectator to remember the card. Announce that after the card is replaced in the deck, you are going to place the deck behind your back and locate the card in a very startling fashion.

3 Place the deck behind your back. Turn the bottom card face up. Turn the whole pack over so that it is all face up, except for the one face-down card on top.

4 Bring the deck out from behind your back. You are now ready for the spectator to replace the card in the pack.

COMMENTS AND SUGGESTIONS

With this method, you can perform the trick at any time with no preparation. The spectator may even shuffle the deck before freely selecting a card. It only takes a moment to set up the pack behind your back as you "demonstrate" the first part of the startling way in which you are going to find the spectator's card. However, when you do this "demonstration," do not tell the spectator that the card will later be discovered face up in a face-down pack, or you may alert the spectators to your secret.

This method not only allows you to reverse the bottom card, but also to turn the pack over for the replacement of the selected card without any tricky moves whatsoever. When you first place the deck behind your back, just do it naturally, as if you were illustrating what is going to happen next. You can now present a very puzzling, self-working card trick that appears to require great skill yet is practically automatic in every respect.

FANTASTIC FIVE

EFFECT

This is a clever, self-working card discovery utilizing a prepared deck in its simplest form. The trick finishes with a double twist that will leave the onlookers completely baffled. Adding one surprise onto another is always a good policy, especially with card tricks.

A card is freely selected by a spectator and returned to the top of the deck. The pack is then given a cut. You spread the pack on the table, revealing that one card is face up. It is a five. You explain that the face-up card, the five, is your magical indicator card. Then you count down five cards in the deck below where the face-up card was located. Turning up the fifth card, it proves to be the card chosen by the spectator! If that were not enough, you now turn the four cards that were between the face-up card and the spectator's card. All four are aces!

SECRET AND PREPARATION

To prepare, run through the pack and remove the four aces and any five-card. Square up the pack and place the five face up on the bottom of the face-down pack. Place the four aces face down below the five.

A The first illustration shows the proper preparation with the pack held face up.

B This shows the pack held in its normal face-down position. Square up the pack and you're ready to begin.

METHOD

1 Spread the pack and invite a spectator to select a card. Be sure not to spread the pack too near the bottom, thereby accidentally exposing the face-up five.

2 Tell the spectator to be sure to remember the card. Square up the deck and place it on the table.

3 Ask the spectator to place the card on top of the deck.

4 Have the spectator cut the deck.

5 Let the spectator complete the cut.

NOTE: Unknown to the spectator, when the deck is cut, the four aces and the face-up five are placed directly above the selected card.

6 Explain to the spectator that something magical is going to happen. At the same time, spread the deck, face down, on the table. Call attention to the one face-up card in the deck.

7 Separate all the cards to the right of the face-up five.

8 Explain that the face-up card is your magical indicator card and that it will help to locate the card the spectator selected. Since the card is a five, that must be a clue. Count down five cards in the deck.

9 Push the five, the four face-down aces below it, and the next card (the spectator's card) all forward from the pack.

10 Turn over the fifth card and show it to be the card that the spectator selected.

11 The spectator will assume that the trick is over. Not content with this, you turn over the four remaining cards to reveal the four aces. This second, added surprise, the appearance of the aces, adds greatly to the effect. This is also a good lead-in to any four-ace trick.

COMMENTS AND SUGGESTIONS

Here is another presentation idea. After the spectator has returned the selected card to the pack and completed the cut, pick up the deck and give it a snap before you spread it along the table. Say that this will cause a card to turn over somewhere in the deck. When the spread reveals the face-up five, count down to the chosen card. Turn it over, revealing it to be the spectator's selected card. Now for the added touch. Gather up the upper and lower portions of the pack, placing the "aces" half of the deck on top. Say, "Wherever I snap the pack a second time, something good always turns up,". . . SNAP! . . . "like the four aces!" Then, deal the four aces from the top of the deck, turning each ace face up as you place it on the table.

TURNOVER CARD

This surprising effect is performed with a pack of ordinary playing cards. It can be done with a borrowed deck and requires no skill or practice. The trick depends on the use of a key card, which is one of the most basic and simple methods used in card magic to locate a selected card in a pack of cards.

EFFECT

You have a spectator shuffle a pack of cards and cut the cards anywhere the spectator wishes. Tell the spectator to look at the card that was cut to and then complete the cut, thus burying the card in the deck. At this point, you take the cards in your hands for the first time and proceed to find the selected card.

SECRET AND PREPARATION

The secret of the trick depends entirely upon the performer secretly learning the bottom card of the pack before it is placed on the table to begin the trick. This card is called a key card because it will be your key to the location of the selected card. In the following description, we will assume that your key card (the card on the bottom of the deck) is the two of clubs.

METHOD

1 If you use a pack of cards that is already in its case at the start, you can glimpse the bottom card as you remove the cards from the case. Just lay the pack face down and go right into the trick without a shuffle.

2 Even better, if people want to shuffle the pack, let them. Often when a spectator is squaring up the pack after shuffling, he will flash the bottom card in your direction, not realizing it has anything to do with the trick.

3 If you don't get a glimpse of the card during the shuffle, pick up the pack in your hands, turn it face up, and begin running the cards from hand to hand, as shown.

Comment that the cards appear to be well-shuffled, and it would be impossible for you to know their order. Of course, here you see and remember your key card. Lay the pack face down on the table and you're ready to begin.

4 With the pack lying face down on the table and the audience satisfied that the cards are well mixed, ask a spectator to divide the pack into two parts.

5 Tell the spectator to cut anywhere in the deck and to place the upper portion on the table.

NOTE: The card that the spectator has cut to, which will be the selected card, is marked with an X in the illustrations to make it easier for you to follow. Of course, when you perform the trick, there will be no X on the card.

Spectator Looks At Card

6 After the cards have been cut, tell the spectator to remove the top card of the lower half, look at it, remember it, and place it on top of the other half of the pack. Let's assume that the card is the five of diamonds.

7 Point to the lower half and ask the spectator to put those cards on top of the selected card so that it will be buried somewhere in the pack.

NOTE: In placing the lower half on top of the upper half, the spectator is also placing your key card directly above the chosen card. Ask the spectator to give the pack another complete cut and then to let someone else cut it also.

8 When this is done, take the pack and begin dealing cards one by one on the table, turning each card face up. Announce that you are trying to get an impression of the selected card, but that the spectator is not to say anything, even if the selected card appears, or you will have to begin all over.

Key Card

9 As you deal cards one at a time from the pack, turning each face up, watch for your key card, the two of clubs. When it shows up, deal it on the table along with the others. You now know that the next card will be the spectator's card (the five of diamonds).

Selected Card

10 Deal the next card, the five of diamonds, but instead of stopping, just continue dealing as if you haven't reached the chosen card.

11 After you have dealt several more cards, tell the spectator you have received an impression. Say, "The next card I turn over will be your card." The spectator will probably say you are wrong.

12 But instead of dealing the next card off the pack, reach among the face-up cards on the table and draw out the five of diamonds.

13 Turn over the five and lay it face down on the table, saying, "I said the next card I turned over would be yours—and it is!"

NOTE: This trick is very effective because of its surprise ending! When you deal past the selected card, the spectator is sure that the trick has gone wrong. But when you actually do turn the selected card face down, you really prove your magical powers.

DOUBLE TURNOVER

In this card effect, the spectator plays such an active part that trickery seems impossible, yet the magical result is attained while the pack is practically in the spectator's hands. The secret is so simple that once you know it, you can fool an audience the first time you try.

EFFECT

You place a deck of cards on the table and invite a spectator to remove the upper half of the pack, while you take the remaining, lower half. Each of you puts your half behind your back and removes a card at random. Each lays a half pack on the table and looks at the card selected. Then you and the spectator exchange selected cards without looking at each other's cards. You insert the cards face down into the respective half packs—your card in the spectator's half pack and the spectator's card in your half. The full pack is immediately reassembled and both call out the names of the cards each has selected. The pack is spread face down on the table, and both cards have magically turned face up in the deck!

METHOD

Glimpse Bottom Card

1 Before the trick, give the pack a few cuts or a shuffle. In the process, casually spot the bottom card of the deck, in this case, the five of hearts, and remember it.

2 Lay the pack on the table and tell the spectator to cut the pack halfway and hold it behind the back. You do the same with the remaining lower half.

Spectator Takes Top Half

Cards Behind Magician's Back

3 Instruct the spectator to remove any card from the top half of the deck, while you supposedly do the same from the bottom half. Actually, you turn your half face up. Then turn the card you glimpsed, the five of hearts, face down on top of the face-up packet.

Magician

Cards Held Behind Back

4 Also remove any other card from your half. Turn this card face down and bring it out from behind your back. To the spectators, this is the card you selected.

NOTE: The spectators do not suspect that your actions are different from the spectator's. In the illustration, your card, the five of hearts, is marked with an M; the spectator's card, in this case, the two of diamonds, is marked with an X. The random card that you place on the table is marked with a D because it is a decoy that plays a special part, as you will see.

5 Tell the spectator, "Look at the card you drew and remember it, while I do the same with my card." The spectator looks at the card and notes that it is the two of diamonds. You look at your card, but it is not necessary to remember it—just don't forget your special card, the five of hearts.

6 You continue, "Hold your card so I cannot see what it is, and lay your half of the pack face down on the table, just as I am doing. Do not tell me what card you selected. I will also keep my card a secret for just a moment."

7 You bring out your half of the pack from behind your back and set it on the table. Your half appears to be the same as the spectator's half. Actually, all of the cards in your half are face up except for the five of hearts, which is face down at the top.

NOTE: Care must be taken to place the cards on the table squarely so as not to flash any of the face-up cards beneath the five-card.

8 You add, "Give me your card, and you take mine, but I won't look at the face of your card, and you don't look at mine. That way, only we will know which cards we took."

9 With your half of the pack resting on the table, insert the spectator's card into your half near the center, keeping your half well squared with your left hand. Tell the spectator to push your card face down into the other half of the pack.

NOTE: At this point, your half of the pack has all its cards face up except for the five of hearts which is face down on top and the spectator's card, the two of diamonds, which is face down near the middle.

10 Place your left hand over the top of your half in readiness to pick it up from the table. At the same time, with your right hand, reach for the spectator's half, stating that you will add it to your own.

"Turn Over"

11 At the exact moment your right hand picks up the spectator's packet, lift your packet from the table with your left hand and, in the same motion, turn your half over. Your half now really is face down except for the face-up five of hearts on the bottom. This is the only tricky part of this effect. It does not require skill, merely the correct timing. It should be practiced before you present the trick.

12 Move your hands together and place the spectator's half on top of your half, squaring the halves together.

13 The entire pack is face down, except for your five of hearts, which is on the bottom, and the spectator's two of diamonds, about a dozen cards above.

Remove Top Third of Deck and Place on Table

14 Cut the pack about 1/3 of the way down in the deck and place these cards on the table.

15 Complete the cut by placing the remainder of the deck on top.

Complete Cut on Table

1/3 2/3

16 As you complete the cut, say to the spectator, "My card was the five of hearts, what was yours?" Of course, the reply will be, "The two of diamonds." Square the pack and riffle the ends twice with your finger. Say, "Good! Now I'll make both cards magically reveal themselves."

17 Ribbon spread the pack (see page 189) along the table, face down, separating the cards rather widely. As you do, the two cards, the five of hearts and the two of diamonds, are seen to be face up in the spread, providing a startling climax.

COMMENTS AND SUGGESTIONS

When only a few spectators are present, it is not necessary to put the packs behind your back. Instead, you and the spectator can simply turn away so that neither sees what card the other takes. This gives you an easy opportunity to note a card and place it face up on the bottom, while drawing out another card to serve as a decoy.

In either case, always use a pack with backs that have a white margin around the edges and be sure to keep the cards well squared when handling your half of the pack. Otherwise, a sharp-eyed spectator may notice the face-up cards in your supposedly face-down packet. In turning your left hand over to bring your inverted half of the deck to normal, as shown in Figs. 10 and 11, you can cover the turnover by moving your left hand, with its packet, to the right. This way, you must reach across your left hand with your right in order to pick up the spectator's packet. That brings your right arm directly over your left hand, allowing you to do the dirty work under cover.

DOUBLE X MYSTERY

EFFECT

Two spectators are invited to assist you. You give the spectator on your left a pack of cards and a pen and ask that spectator to place the pack behind their back and mark an X across the FACE of any card with the pen. You give the same deck and pen to the spectator on your right and ask that spectator to mark the BACK of any card, with the pack behind the spectator. You return the deck to the spectator on your left and ask that spectator to run through the deck and find the card with the X on the FACE, remove it, and hold it between both hands so that it is out of sight. This done, the spectator on the right is again given the deck and asked to find their card, the one with the X on the BACK. Upon searching through the deck, the spectator on the right finds that the card is missing. When the spectator on the left turns the card over, it is found to have an X on the BACK. It appears as if both spectators have chosen and marked the same card!

SECRET AND PREPARATION

The secret to this "coincidence" is so simple it's surprising. It all depends upon the fact that the pen that you give to the spectators just doesn't work. For best results, use a pen with a felt tip. All that is required is to let it sit without the cap on until the tip is dried out. If a pencil is used, it is necessary to dip the top of the pencil in clear varnish and allow it to dry overnight. This will prevent the pencil from making a mark on the cards, although it appears to have a perfectly good point.

To prepare, remove any card from the pack and mark an X on both sides with a pen or pencil that really works and matches the special one you will use in the trick. The lines that form the X should appear irregular, as if the mark were made behind the back. Place the card back in the deck, and you're ready.

METHOD

1 With two spectators to assist you, give the deck, face up, to the spectator on your left. Ask this spectator to place the deck behind their back, to run through the cards, and without looking at it, to bring any card to the top of the deck.

2 When this has been done, give the spectator the prepared pen and instruct the spectator to mark an X across the face of the card and then return the pen to you. Ask the spectator to mix the cards behind their back so the marked card is lost somewhere in the deck. Have the spectator hand you the deck.

3 Turn the deck face down and hand it to the spectator on your right. Instruct the second spectator just as you did the first spectator. But tell this spectator to mark an X on the back of any card and mix the cards.

4 Take back the deck and put the pen away. Give the deck again to the spectator on your left, and ask this spectator to look through the cards face up and remove the card the spectator marked from the deck. Have the spectator hold this card between the palms of the hands so no one else can see the card. Actually, the reason for doing this is so that no one sees the X on the back of this card.

NOTE: Because of the prepared pen, neither spectator has made a mark on any card, and both are unaware of the prepared X card in the deck.

5 Give the deck to the spectator on your right and ask this spectator to do the same: "Please run through the deck and remove your card, the one with the X on the back." Of course, the spectator will be unable to find the card.

6 After several attempts, call attention to the fact that the only card missing from the deck is the one that the other spectator is holding. Tell the spectator on your left to look at the back of the card. It appears that the two spectators were somehow able to freely select and mark the very same card in the deck!

COMMENTS AND SUGGESTIONS

It is a good idea at the start of the trick to run through the cards face up and show them to be an ordinary deck. In order to do this, it is necessary to have the secret X card close to the bottom of the deck. Then, run through the cards face up, supposedly to show that they are all different. Just be careful not to spread the cards near the position in the deck where the X card is located. The spectator will believe everything is on the up-and-up. You will be amazed at the effect that this trick has, as there appears to be no reasonable explanation for the astonishing results. Properly performed, no one will ever suspect the special pen is the secret to the mystery.

SUPER DOUBLE X MYSTERY

One very subtle convincer, which can make this trick a complete baffler, is to introduce a duplicate pen (the one that really made the X on the card), after the prepared pen has done the dirty work. Simply have the duplicate in your pocket and, after the second spectator has made a "mark," casually place the pen in the pocket with the duplicate. As the second spectator is looking for the card with the X, remove the unprepared pen and help the spectator search by pointing to various parts of the deck with the real pen. Then just lay the pen somewhere in plain sight. Now everything can be examined.

SUPER ANYTIME DOUBLE X MYSTERY

With this method, you can perform the DOUBLE X MYSTERY at any time during your card routine, even though the deck has been used for a number of other tricks and even examined by the spectators!

SECRET AND PREPARATION

Before you begin, place the X-marked card either (A) under your belt behind your back or (B) in a gimmick card holder made from a safety pin and a paper clip. The special card is placed in the paper clip and the holder pinned inside the back of your coat (C) so that the card is just hidden by the bottom edge of your coat.

METHOD

1 Have one of the spectators shuffle the deck. Then place the deck behind your back to illustrate to the spectators what they are to do. At this time, you secretly remove the X card from beneath your coat and add it to the deck!

2 You are ready to proceed with the SUPER DOUBLE X MYSTERY, as previously described.

YOU DO AS I DO

As a "two person" trick, this is a real baffler. All you need are two ordinary decks of playing cards. It is a good idea to use packs with different colors on their backs, so that the spectators can keep track of them as the trick proceeds.

EFFECT

Two packs of cards are thoroughly shuffled. One is shuffled by a spectator, and you shuffle the other pack. You and the spectator then exchange packs, and each selects a card, taking care that the other person does not see it. The cards are both replaced in their decks. You and the spectator exchange decks again, and each finds the duplicate of the card selected in the other pack. You and the spectator then place the selected cards face down on the table. When the two cards are turned up, they prove to be identical!

SECRET AND PREPARATION

This is one of the finest self-working tricks in card magic. You need only two ordinary decks of cards. The trick can be performed anytime, anywhere, with no previous preparation. Let's assume that one deck has red backs and the other blue.

METHOD

1 Place both decks on the table and ask the spectator to select either one. This is a free choice. Let's assume that the spectator takes the deck with the red backs. This leaves you with the blue-backed deck.

2 Tell the spectator to "do as I do." Shuffle your blue deck, and the spectator should do the same with the red deck.

Key Card

3 As you complete the last shuffle, square up your deck, as shown in the picture. As you do, turn the deck on its edge, glimpse the bottom card, and remember it. Do not call attention to this, just remember the bottom card, as it will serve as your key card for the rest of the trick.

NOTE: In the illustration, the eight of diamonds is your key card.

4 Stress to the spectator that, to make sure that all is fair, you will trade decks, so you will be using a deck that the spectator personally has shuffled. Exchange decks with the spectator. Unknown to the spectator, you know the bottom card of the blue deck the spectator now holds.

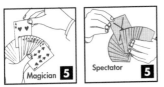

5 Instruct the spectator to fan open the blue deck, holding the deck up, so that you cannot see the faces, just as you are doing with the red deck. The spectator is to freely select any card from the deck, and you will do likewise. Tell the spectator it's best if the spectator selects a favorite card, and that you will do the same and select your favorite card.

NOTE: To make the illustrations easy to follow, we have marked the spectator's card with an X.

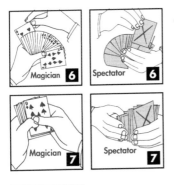

6 Ask the spectator to place the selected card on the top of the deck, as shown, as you do the same with your card. It is not necessary for you to remember the card that you have selected at this point. Just remember your key card, the one that is on the bottom of the deck now held by the spectator—the eight of diamonds.

7 Have the spectator square up the cards, as you do the same. Each of you places your deck on the table.

8 Tell the spectator to cut the deck, as you cut your deck, thus burying the selected cards somewhere in the middle of each pack. Unknown to the spectator, this cut places the bottom card, which is your key card (the eight of diamonds), directly above the spectator's selected card.

9 Have the spectator complete the cut and ask the spectator to cut two more times, as you do the same. Be sure that each cut is a single cut and that the cut is completed each time. No matter how many times you cut the deck, as long as each cut is completed before the next cut is started, the key card will stay next to the selected card.

10 Stress the fact that there's no possible way that you could know where the spectator's favorite card is now located in the deck, and, likewise, the spectator could not know where your card is.

11 Trade decks with the spectator once more. You now hold the one you originally shuffled, the blue deck with your key card.

12 Have the spectator look through the red deck and remove the card which matches the spectator's favorite card, and you will do the same with the blue deck.

13 While the spectator does this, you spread your deck until you locate your key card, the eight of diamonds. The card immediately to the right of the key card will be the card the spectator selected.

14 Tell the spectator to remove the selected card without showing its face, and you will do the same. Actually, you remove the card which you now know to be the one the spectator selected, the two of clubs.

15 Have the spectator place the card on the table, and you place yours beside it.

16 Say, "It would be quite a coincidence if we both had the same favorite card, wouldn't it?" Again, stress the fact that you each have been doing the same thing: YOU DO AS I DO. You and the spectator turn your cards face up at the same time. The spectator will be amazed to see that the cards match!

CHAPTER 3
HINDU SHUFFLE TRICKS

The Hindu shuffle is ideally suited to the needs of present-day magicians, and therefore, is a manipulation that all card workers should acquire. Various factors stand out strongly in its favor. It is easy to learn, it is a legitimate shuffle in its own right, and it is especially suited to card tricks.

As you become familiar with the Hindu shuffle, you will also find that it can be readily adapted to important magical purposes, such as forcing, locating, and controlling desired cards—and all without suspicion on the part of the spectators.

Because of its speed and precision, the Hindu shuffle will give your audience the impression that you are an accomplished performer. That is an important aim when presenting card magic. Some of the simplest tricks can become utterly baffling when the spectators suppose that skilled manipulation is involved.

HINDU SHUFFLE

This type of shuffle supposedly gained its name from the fact that it was occasionally used by Hindu magicians who were unfamiliar with the usual shuffling methods. Whatever its origin, other magicians found that it gave them a great advantage when performing close-up card tricks, as the pack can be handled under the very eyes of the spectators in a deceptive manner without fear of detection. Hence, it is recommended as the first and most important step toward acquiring skill as a card manipulator.

EFFECT

The magician holds a pack of cards in one hand. With the other hand, the magician proceeds to shuffle by repeatedly drawing cards off of the top—from the end of the pack—instead of drawing them sideways as with the overhand shuffle.

METHOD

1 Hold the pack face down near one end, with your right thumb and fingers at opposite sides of the pack.

2 Move the pack toward the left hand and grip the top portion of the deck between the tips of the left thumb and fingers.

NOTE: The first finger of the left hand is placed at the end of the pack, as shown. This finger helps to keep the pack squared as you make the following movements.

3 With your right thumb and fingers, draw the bulk of the pack (B) out from beneath as you retain a small block of cards (A) with the fingers of your left hand.

4 As your right hand draws the bulk of the pack (B) clear, release the stack (A) in your left fingers, so that it drops onto the palm of the left hand.

5 Again, move the hands together and grip another small portion of cards from the top of the pack (B) between your left thumb and fingers.

6 Draw the bulk of the pack (C) from beneath the top stack (B).

7 As soon as the pack is clear, let the second stack (B) fall on the first stack (A) already lying in the left hand.

8 Continue drawing off packets into the left hand until the right hand has only a small stack of its own (C), which you simply drop on the pack in the left hand.

COMMENTS AND SUGGESTIONS

The shuffle should be executed at a moderately rapid pace, keeping the hands in continuous motion as you draw off the packets. This gives a polished and professional look. Because it is adaptable to various uses, the Hindu shuffle is the basis for a whole series of clever but easy manipulations that will be described as we proceed. You will run into frequent mentions of the basic Hindu shuffle and its more advanced forms throughout this series of lessons.

HOW TO USE
THE HINDU SHUFFLE

Although the Hindu shuffle actually mixes the pack, it has many magical uses as well. Once you have practiced and learned the regular Hindu shuffle just described, you can use it to accomplish any of the three following purposes. These are indispensable in the presentation of good card magic.

1 LOCATING A SELECTED CARD: A card, freely selected from the pack, is replaced wherever the chooser wishes. Yet, you can find the card in the shuffled deck. This uses a combination of a key card and the Hindu shuffle. (HINDU KEY-CARD LOCATION and SHORT CARD LOCATION.)

2 FORCING A SPECIFIC CARD: A spectator has apparently free choice of any card in the pack, but you force the spectator to pick the one you want (HINDU FLASH FORCE).

3 CONTROLLING THE LOCATION OF A CHOSEN CARD (OR CARDS): After a card has been replaced in the pack, you can control it to the top or bottom of the deck while giving the deck an honest Hindu shuffle (HINDU SHUFFLE CONTROL).

HINDU GLIMPSE

The HINDU GLIMPSE is a very useful and valuable move used with the Hindu shuffle. It enables you to see the bottom card of the deck secretly, in a natural manner that even the keenest observer will overlook.

EFFECT

The magician mixes the pack thoroughly, using the regular Hindu shuffle. To keep the pack well squared during this procedure, the magician taps the inner end of the left-hand packet with the right-hand pack, pushing any protruding cards into place. This very action would seem to the spectators to eliminate the possibility the magician might have of seeing any cards in the pack. Actually, it works to the magician's advantage, enabling the performer to secretly note the bottom card of the right-hand packet.

METHOD

1 Begin with the regular Hindu shuffle, drawing off small blocks of cards from the top of the deck into the left hand.

2 At some point during the shuffle, when you hold about the same number of cards in each hand, turn the right-hand packet at a slant, toward you, and tap the inner end of the left-hand packet in the pretense of squaring up the cards in that hand. This gives you the opportunity to sight the bottom card of the right-hand packet, the two of diamonds.

3 Continue the shuffle, pulling off small packets from the top of the right-hand cards.

COMMENTS AND SUGGESTIONS

You only need a brief moment to glimpse the bottom card. Just make the move as a natural part of the shuffle. The HINDU GLIMPSE has many magical uses, as you will see.

HINDU KEY-CARD LOCATION

 Here is an example of a clever use of the HINDU GLIMPSE.

EFFECT

A spectator freely shuffles the deck as many times as desired and then has a free selection of any card. While the magician gives the deck a Hindu shuffle, the spectator returns the card to the pack at any time. The magician then shuffles the cards and gives them several cuts, yet the magician is still able to find and announce the spectator's selected card.

METHOD

1 Let the spectator freely shuffle the deck as many times as desired so that you cannot know the location of any card.

2 Ribbon spread (see page 189) the cards on the table, or just spread them face down in your hands, so the spectator may have a completely free selection. Ask the spectator to pick any card.

3 Gather up the cards and begin the Hindu shuffle. As you do the shuffle, glimpse and remember the bottom card of the packet in your right hand (HINDU GLIMPSE, see page 51), in this case, the two of diamonds. This will be your key card in locating the spectator's card.

4 Tell the spectator to look at the selected card (X) and remember it. Continue to shuffle and tell the spectator to stop you when ready to replace the card.

5 When the spectator says, "Stop," have the spectator return the card (X) to the top of the packet of cards in your left hand.

6 You immediately drop the cards in your right hand on top of the left-hand packet, burying the spectator's chosen card in the pack. This places the two of diamonds (your key card) directly above the spectator's chosen card (X).

7 Give the deck a few single cuts or let the spectator make the cuts. Turn the deck face up and spread it between your hands. Act as if you are concentrating on the spectator's face. When you sight your key card, the two of diamonds, the selected card (X) will be immediately to its right. After a suitable period of time, announce the name of the card.

IMPORTANT NOTE: In using the HINDU KEY-CARD LOCATION system just described, you may sometimes encounter a hesitant spectator who does not wish to replace the chosen card until you are about to drop your last few cards on top. That means that you may have to complete the shuffle and begin all over, which is perfectly natural. However, if that happens, your key card becomes lost. Just start the shuffle again and glimpse and remember the new bottom key card.

COMMENTS AND SUGGESTIONS

This is an example of using the HINDU GLIMPSE to get your key card next to the spectator's selected card in a very clever way, even though the spectator has first shuffled the deck.

HINDU FLASH FORCE

There are many ways of forcing a spectator to select a certain card without having the spectator realize it, but to do this naturally and repeatedly was formerly somewhat difficult. It took the Hindu shuffle to produce a surefire way of forcing a card at a moment's notice. Try the method that follows and you will see why.

EFFECT

During the course of a Hindu shuffle, at any time the spectator requests, the magician pauses long enough to give the spectator a "flash" of a card in the pack. Though the magician keeps his own head turned so that he cannot possibly see the card, the magician has actually forced the spectator to select the very card that the magician wanted.

METHOD

1 Suppose you want to force the five of diamonds. Place the five on the bottom of the pack. Start the usual Hindu shuffle, telling the spectator to call, "Stop," at any time.

2 Continue the shuffle at the usual speed, pulling packets from the top of the cards in the right hand. This leaves the five of diamonds at the bottom of the right-hand cards.

3 When the spectator says, "Stop," slant the right-hand packet toward the spectator, showing the spectator the face of the card on the bottom. This is the original bottom card of the pack, the five of diamonds!

4 Tell the spectator to remember the selected card. (Here is a view as the spectator sees it. Notice that the right hand is well forward toward the spectator to ensure that you cannot see the card on the bottom.)

5 Drop the right-hand cards on the cards lying in your left hand to

bury the card the spectator thinks was freely chosen from the deck. Actually, you already know the card. You have forced him to select the five of diamonds, just as you had planned!

COMMENTS AND SUGGESTIONS

This is called a "flash force" because you simply flash the card before the spectator's eyes. However, it is more than that. You can hold up the packet as long as you want. Just assure the spectator that you cannot see the card. When the spectator is looking at the card, you should turn your head away to emphasize that you are the one person who cannot possibly see that card. This is important because it diverts the audience from the fact that you don't need to see it, because you already know what it is. This is one important use of misdirection.

HINDU
COLOR CHANGE

Here is a quick, baffling trick that makes a good opening number for a card routine. It depends on the Hindu shuffle, so the skill that you have acquired in learning that important move can also be put to good use with this trick.

EFFECT

You take a red-backed pack of cards from its case and spread them face up so the spectators can see that they are all different. Then, running through the face-up pack with a series of short cuts, you show the backs of the cards at frequent intervals. The spectators can see that all the cards have red backs. Giving the face-up pack a "magic tap," you turn it face down and spread the cards along the table, and to everyone's astonishment, all the backs have turned from red to blue!

SECRET AND PREPARATION

All you need is a regular blue-backed pack and a single red-backed card, which you place on top of the pack before putting the deck in its box. You should use a red case, as the pack is supposed to have red backs at the start.

METHOD

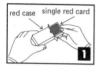

red case   single red card

1 Open the box and bring out the pack face down, with the one red-backed card showing. Keep the cards well squared so you don't accidentally flash any of the blue cards beneath the top red card. As you bring out the pack, say, "Here is a pack of red-backed cards."

2 With that, lay the box aside and turn the pack face up in your hands.

3 Spread the pack face up in your hands showing the faces of the cards and say, "As you can see, the cards are all different, as they should be."

4 Now square the pack face up in the left hand and begin a regular Hindu shuffle, but with the deck face up.

5 At various intervals throughout the shuffle, swing the right-hand packet away from you. Tilt the back of the packet toward the spectators, showing them the single red-backed card, and say, ". . . and the backs are the same, red, as they should be." NOTE: Here you are simply combining the Hindu shuffle with a repeated FLASH FORCE while the pack is upside down. The audience thinks that you are cutting the pack at various places, showing a different red-backed card each time. Actually, you are always showing the same red-backed card. Because of the face-up Hindu Shuffle, the red card remains on the bottom of the face-up right-hand packet. Do this deliberately and cleanly, keeping the pack well squared with each flash to prevent anyone from glimpsing a portion of a blue back during the process.

red backed card

6 As you complete the series of flashes, drop the last few cards face up on the pack. Or, the shuffle can even be carried to the very last card, thus placing the single red card at the top of the face-up deck.

Single red back   All blue backs

7 Square the face up pack and give it a sharp snap or riffle, saying you will change the backs from red to blue. With that, turn the pack face down (the single red-backed card is now face down at the bottom, or close to it) and spread or fan the pack except for the last few bottom cards. Apparently all the backs have magically changed from red to blue!

COMMENTS AND SUGGESTIONS

The success of this effect depends upon keeping the upper packet well squared throughout the entire shuffle, so that the red-backed card can be shown repeatedly without exposing any blue card. To keep the packet square while shuffling you can tap it against the inner end of the pack, as described in the HINDU GLIMPSE (see page 51). When showing the blue backs at the finish, fan the cards from hand to hand, or spread them face down along the table. Be careful not to spread the cards too close to the "secret" red-backed card. The simplest follow-up is to gather the pack and replace it in the case, which then goes in your pocket.

NOTE: By using a short red-backed card (see Chapter 8: Short-Card Tricks), after the color change, you can gather the out-spread pack, turn it face up and give it a Hindu shuffle, this time flashing a blue-backed card with each pause. Then turn the back of the pack toward to spectators and slowly riffle the cards, showing all blue, as the short card will ride along unseen. Finally turn the pack face up in your left hand. With your right hand, riffle to the short card, and cut it to the face of the pack. Pick up the card case and dispose of the short red-backed card as described.

COLOR-CHANGING DECKS
TWO-DECK VERSION

In this modified version of the HINDU COLOR CHANGE, you take the mystery one step further by adding a second pack of cards—of a different color—and converting the effect from a color change to a magical transposition of the two packs.

EFFECT

The magician removes a red-backed pack of cards from its case and spreads them face up so that everyone can see that they are all different. Then, running through the face-up pack with a series of short cuts, the magician shows the red backs of the cards at frequent intervals, finally placing the pack face up on the table next to its red box. The performer then follows the exact same procedure with a blue-backed pack of cards, and places it face up on the table next to its blue box. The mystery begins when the magician removes one card from each pack. The one red card is placed on the face of the blue-backed pack, and the one blue card is placed on the red-backed pack. Explaining that this will cause the rest of the cards in both packs to "follow the leader," the magician turns over each pack and spreads it face down next to its correct colored box. The audience is amazed to discover that all the blue-backed cards have magically changed places with all of the red-backed cards!

SECRET AND PREPARATION

The only items required for this mystery are a red-backed pack of cards and its red box and a blue-backed deck and its blue box with a matching design. To prepare, remove a single blue card from the blue pack and place it face down on top of the red deck. Place a single red card on top of the blue deck. Now, place the red deck (with the one blue card on top) into the blue box and place the blue deck (with the one red card on top) into the red box. You are now ready to perform COLOR-CHANGING DECKS.

METHOD

1 To begin, place both packs (in their boxes) on the table. Say, "I have two packs of cards, one red and one blue."

2 Pick up the blue box and remove the pack of cards, face down, so the single blue card, which matches

the color of the box, is seen by the spectators. They will assume it to be an all blue pack.

NOTE: As you remove the pack from the box, keep the cards squared so you do not accidentally shift the top blue card exposing the red cards below it.

3 Place the empty blue box on the table and turn the pack over (face up). Run through the pack, showing the faces of the cards. Say, "As you can see, all the cards in the pack are different, as they should be."

4 Square the pack face up in your left hand and begin a regular Hindu shuffle, with the deck face up. At various intervals throughout the shuffle, execute a repeated flash force. The audience believes you are cutting the pack at various places showing a different card each time. Remark, "And the backs are all blue, as they should be."

NOTE: In this trick, the Hindu shuffle must be carried out to the very last card.

5 As you complete the Hindu shuffle, the left fingers draw off all the remaining red cards, leaving the single blue card in your right hand. Finish the shuffle by dropping the blue card on top of the face-up deck.

6 Next, square up the pack and place it face up on the table next to the empty blue box from which you removed it.

7 Pick up the red box and remove the "red" pack (actually the blue pack with the single red card on top).

8 Follow the same face-up Hindu shuffle procedure using the repeated flash force, showing the red card. Finish by shuffling the single red card to the top of the face-up pack. Square up this pack and place it face up on the table next to the empty red box.

9 The packs are now resting face up next to their "own" colored boxes.

10 Lift the two top cards (the single red card and the single blue card) from the face of each pack and transpose them.

11 Place the red-backed card on the real red pack and the blue-backed card on the real blue pack. As you do this, say, "If I move just one card from each pack and place it on the pack of the opposite color, the rest of the cards in each pack will 'follow the leader.'"

12 Pick up both packs, one in each hand, and spread them face down on the table next to the box you first removed them from. The audience will be amazed to see that the blue cards have magically changed places with the red cards—right before their eyes!

HINDU SHUFFLE
BOTTOM STOCK CONTROL

In certain card tricks, it is important that during a shuffle the bottom card (or a group of cards already on the bottom) is retained there for some future purpose. Here is a way of accomplishing that with the aid of the Hindu shuffle. This is an important utility sleight that every card worker should learn.

MARK WILSON'S CYCLOPEDIA OF MAGIC

EFFECT

To all appearances, the magician gives a pack a regular Hindu shuffle. Yet, in this modified version, the bottom stock of cards remains undisturbed or unshuffled. Despite that important difference, the magician can switch from this form of the Hindu shuffle to another without any chance of detection.

METHOD

1 Hold the pack in the tips of the fingers of the left hand, ready for the Hindu shuffle.

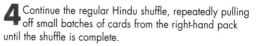

2 Unlike a regular Hindu shuffle, where the right hand begins by drawing off a group of cards from the bottom of the pack, this time the right hand pulls out a section of cards from the center, leaving the bottom group intact. The left hand retains the bottom stock and a small batch of cards from the top as in the usual shuffle.

3 Once the right hand has drawn the center packet of cards clear of the bottom and top packets, the left hand allows the top packet to fall onto the bottom packet.

4 Continue the regular Hindu shuffle, repeatedly pulling off small batches of cards from the right-hand pack until the shuffle is complete.

5 The pack has now been fairly shuffled except for the small batch of cards that remains undisturbed. You are also now set to repeat the HINDU SHUFFLE—BOTTOM STOCK CONTROL as often as you like.

FALSE CUT

EFFECT

Many very good card tricks depend on your knowing the bottom card of the pack or bringing a chosen card to the top. At that point, a suspicious spectator may want to cut the pack. So, to prove that all is fair, your best policy is to beat them to it by cutting the pack yourself. You can do that with the following FALSE CUT that looks like the real thing but actually leaves the pack just as it was.

METHOD

1 Hold the deck in the left hand between the tips of the left fingers and thumb.

2 With the thumb and fingers of your right hand, start to draw out about half the pack (B) from the lower part of the deck.

3 As this lower stack (B) comes clear, sweep your right hand toward your body.

4 Continue this sweep, carrying the cards (B) in your right hand up and over the top stack (A) in your left hand.

5 Place the packet in your right hand (B) on the table and leave it.

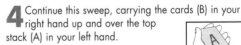

6 With your right hand, take all of the cards (A) from your left hand.

7 Place these cards directly on top of the stack (B) on the table.

8 It will appear as if the cards are fairly cut. Actually, the order of the cards has not changed at all.

COMMENTS AND SUGGESTIONS

FALSE CUT should be performed at a moderate speed, not too slowly and not too rapidly. Do not call special attention to it, just do it as if you were cutting the cards in a normal manner. If it is done correctly, no one will question it.

HINDU SHUFFLE
PICK-UP CONTROL

♠ This is one of the most deceptive and useful controls in all of card magic. If this sleight were the only one you used with the Hindu shuffle, it would be worth learning it. HINDU SHUFFLE—PICK-UP CONTROL is not difficult to learn. Once you have mastered it, you will be using it in many of your best card effects.

EFFECT

A spectator returns a selected card to the pack while the magician is giving the deck a Hindu shuffle. This apparently loses the card somewhere deep in the pack, yet the magician has secretly controlled the card to the top of the pack.

METHOD

1 Ask a spectator to select a card freely from the pack as you spread the pack between your hands. You can also let the spectator take a card by telling you to "stop" during the course of a Hindu shuffle.

2 While the spectator is looking at the selected card, you square the pack and begin a new Hindu shuffle, inviting the spectator to replace the card at any time. You do the shuffle quite slowly, apparently to aid the replacement, but actually to prepare for a simple but special move.

3 After the spectator has replaced the card (X) on the left-hand section of the pack, move the bulk of the pack held in your right hand above the cards in your left hand as if to merely continue the shuffle.

4 This is the important move. As the left fingers slide off another packet from the top of the bulk of the pack, the tips of your right thumb and second finger squeeze inward, grip the sides, and pick up a small packet of cards from the lower left-hand heap. Carry this small packet away on the bottom of the right-hand bulk of cards. Keep a break or gap between that small batch and the upper bulk of the pack in the right hand.

Pick up small packet with right fingers

Selected card on top of small packet

5 The selected card (X) is the top card of this small packet.

6 Continue the shuffle, drawing off cards from the top of the right-hand packet, still holding the small packet on the bottom of the right-hand bulk of cards, always maintaining the gap between the two portions.

Selected card

7 As you finish the shuffle, the left hand takes all the remaining cards above the gap.

8 At the same time, the right hand draws the little batch out from beneath.

9 The right hand drops the little batch on the left-hand pack to complete the shuffle.

10 Since the chosen card is the top card of the batch, it now becomes the top card of the pack. This means that you have controlled the chosen card to the top of the pack.

HINDU SHUFFLE TRICKS

67

COMMENTS AND SUGGESTIONS

The HINDU SHUFFLE—PICK-UP CONTROL is one of the easiest and best ways to bring a selected card to the top of the pack. It also has many other uses and is one of the most valuable sleights you will learn in this book. Study the pictures carefully.

The most important move, and the key to this entire sleight, is in Step 4. This is when you pick up the small batch of cards, with the selected card on top, with your right thumb and fingers from the top of the left-hand packet. At the same time that you do this, you pull off a small batch of cards from the top of the right-hand packet, just as if you were continuing the regular Hindu shuffle. This completely covers your secret pick-up. You then continue the Hindu shuffle in the normal fashion until you get to the last small batch of cards with the selected card on top. Just place that packet as the last shuffle on the top of the deck in the left hand. Thus, you have secretly brought the selected card to the top.

The description of this sleight has been repeated here because of its importance. Once you have mastered the Hindu shuffle and the HINDU SHUFFLE—PICK-UP CONTROL, you have opened the door to hundreds of wonderful, baffling mysteries with cards. If you are interested in performing card tricks, practice and learn this important sleight.

CHAPTER 4
OVERHAND SHUFFLE TRICKS

The overhand shuffle is the most common of all shuffles. The very simplicity of the shuffle makes it easy to locate and control certain cards, bringing them to the top or bottom of the pack and retaining them there.

For that very reason, it should be practiced until it becomes second nature, so that the various subterfuges can be introduced without arousing suspicion. By using the overhand shuffle constantly in card tricks, as well as in card games, you will have a simple opportunity to practice.

Hundreds of excellent tricks can be developed directly from the overhand shuffle, many of which have been included in this book.

OVERHAND SHUFFLE

The overhand shuffle is an honest shuffle. However, it can be adapted to many special uses, such as controlling certain cards without the audience knowing it.

METHOD

1 Hold the deck with the thumb and fingers of your right hand.

2 Bring both your hands together. With your left thumb, from the top of the deck, pull off a block of several cards (A) into your left hand, leaving the remainder of the deck (B) in the right hand.

3 Separate your hands completely. Hold the block of cards now in your left hand (A) firmly between the left thumb and fingers.

4 Lift your left thumb enough to allow the packet in the right hand to be reinserted into the "pull-off" position. With the left thumb, pull another block of several cards (B) into the left hand on top of the cards (A) already in the hand, leaving the remainder of the deck (C) in your right hand.

5 Separate your hands, allowing the cards just removed (Block B) to fall on the cards already in the left hand (Block A).

6 Continue pulling off blocks of cards until all of the cards in the right hand have been shuffled into the left hand.

COMMENTS AND SUGGESTIONS

This is a natural way of shuffling a pack of cards and mixing it quite thoroughly, but it can also easily be diverted to magical uses, particularly in controlling cards on either the top or bottom of the pack or to a particular position in the deck. Therefore, easy as this shuffle is, you should practice it repeatedly until it can be executed without hesitation. This will enable you to perform the special variations as required.

OVERHAND REVERSE SHUFFLE

The overhand shuffle can also be done as a reverse shuffle. The movements are exactly the same as described in the overhand shuffle, except that the right hand holds the deck so that the faces of the cards are outward (with the backs of the cards toward the right palm) instead of inward (with the faces of the cards toward the right palm). The operation of the shuffle is the same. However, the reverse has an important bearing on the control shuffles that follow.

OVERHAND IN-JOG CONTROL

METHOD

1 After a spectator has drawn a card from the pack and is looking at it, you start an overhand shuffle, drawing cards from the top of the pack with your left thumb. Tell the spectator to replace the card in the pack as you near the center.

2 The spectator's card goes on the left-hand packet. As you resume the shuffle, bring your right hand slightly inward toward your body, a matter of 1/2" or so. This is a simple action that might occur during any shuffle.

3 With your left thumb, draw off a single card from the right-hand packet. Let this meaningless card fall on the selected card, which is on top of the left-hand packet. The inward movement that you made in Step 2 will make this one card protrude slightly inward, toward your body, from the rest of the left-hand cards.

4 This single, off-center card is called an "in-jog." You can prevent anyone from noticing it by simply moving your right hand forward to its normal position and continuing your overhand shuffle. The remainder of the cards go into their regular position, "evened up" with the first cards shuffled.

MARK WILSON'S CYCLOPEDIA OF MAGIC

5 As more cards cover the jogged card, they help to hide it from view, particularly if they are shuffled in a somewhat irregular manner.

6 As you continue shuffling off blocks of cards, be sure that the in-jogged card is not pushed back into the deck.

7 Continue shuffling until all the cards from the right hand are held in the left hand.

8 After you have completed the shuffle, the deck should look like this with the jogged card protruding toward you. Of course, since this is a secret maneuver, you do not call the spectator's attention to it.

9 You can now easily find the jogged card by pressing upward with your right thumb at the inner end of the pack.

10 This upward pressure causes the deck to divide at the jogged card. By gripping the ends of the lower packet between your right thumb and fingers, you can lift the lower portion entirely clear of the rest of the deck. The selected card (X) will be on top of this lower portion.

11 With the right hand, carry the lower section completely over the upper section in the left hand.

12 Drop the packet in the right hand (with the select card on top) down in front of the cards held in the left hand. This is called a "throw," and to all appearances, it adds a final and convincing touch to the shuffle.

13 Actually, the throw brings the selected card to the top of the pack.

COMMENTS AND SUGGESTIONS

Treat the jogged card much as you would any other key card. Never appear to pay any attention to its position, which should be easy, since you are depending on your sense of touch alone. Make the shuffle look natural, even sloppy, if you wish. If your shuffle is too neat, you may lose track of the jogged card. Don't worry if you pull down an extra card or two when making the jog. A little group of jogged cards will function just as effectively as a single card, for when you press the lowest card of the group upward, the others will go along with it, and you will still be able to cut to the selected card and throw the packet to the top of the deck.

CARD CASE ESCAPE

Variety is an important factor in card tricks that end with the discovery of a card selected by a spectator. Many card discoveries, though clever, are too much alike to be presented in the same program. It is a good idea to inject something distinctly different. This effect will vary your program.

EFFECT

After a card has been selected by a spectator and shuffled back into the pack, the magician puts the entire pack into its box and closes the flap. Showing the box from all angles, the magician openly places it in a shirt pocket. Then, showing that both hands are empty, the magician reaches into the pocket and instantly removes the chosen card. Immediately, the magician brings the card box from the pocket and gives it to the spectator, allowing that person to open it and examine both box and pack. Apparently, the selected card managed to penetrate the card box under its own power!

METHOD

1 Remove a regular pack of cards from its box, shuffle it, and have a spectator select a card. Tell the spectator to remember the card and return it to the pack. As the card is returned to the pack, use your favorite method to control it to the top (see pages 72, 79 and 80).

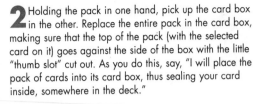

2 Holding the pack in one hand, pick up the card box in the other. Replace the entire pack in the card box, making sure that the top of the pack (with the selected card on it) goes against the side of the box with the little "thumb slot" cut out. As you do this, say, "I will place the pack of cards into its card box, thus sealing your card inside, somewhere in the deck."

3 Begin to close the lid of the box. As you do, squeeze the sides of the box containing the cards, as shown. This squeezing action will cause the top few cards of the pack to "bow" outward against the top of the box, making a small gap between each of the top few cards.

4 As you tuck the flap in, slide it beneath the top card of the pack (the spectator's card), as shown.

5 Close the flap completely and transfer the box to your right hand.

6 As you hold the case, make sure the fingers of your right hand cover the thumb slot, thus concealing the visible portion of the spectator's card from view. With the pack held in this manner, you can display it casually on both sides before you proceed to the next step.

7 After briefly showing the box, place it in your shirt or coat breast pocket as you remark, "With the pack sealed in its box and hidden in my pocket, it would be very difficult for me to find your card."

8 Show that your hand is empty and reach into your pocket. Use your fingers to work the end of the spectator's card out of the box by pulling it from the thumb slot. As soon as you have a good grip on the card, immediately withdraw it from your pocket.

9 The back of the card will be toward the spectator; therefore, the spectator will not know what card you have in your hand. Ask the spectator to name the selected card. When the spectator replies, turn the card in your hand face up and show it to be the selected card. Immediately remove the pack from your pocket and toss it on the table for all to examine.

COMMENTS AND SUGGESTIONS

The proper type of card case for this trick is one with a flap that slides in easily and rather deeply. Some short flaps will not stay in place while you are extracting the chosen card. As you draw the card from its box, be careful that the flap remains closed. As soon as one hand removes the chosen card from the pocket, the other hand can bring out the case and offer it for examination.

SHUFFLE CONTROL
WITH KEY CARD

Whenever you are using a key card to locate a chosen card, you must be careful not to let anyone shuffle the pack, as that may separate the two cards. However, you can do an actual shuffle of your own.

METHOD

"Selected" Card
"Key" Card

1 In Step 6 of the HINDU KEY-CARD LOCATION (see page 52), after you have dropped the upper half of the pack on the lower, placing the key card next to the selected card, begin an overhand shuffle, drawing off little packets of cards from the top of the deck with your left thumb.

Draw off a large packet

2 When you near the center, draw off a large block of cards together. This section contains your two cards, the key card and the selected card. You draw off the large packet of cards so that they will not be separated.

3 Complete the shuffle by drawing off the lower cards in small packets again. You may cut the pack as often as you want.

MARK WILSON'S CYCLOPEDIA OF MAGIC

OVERHAND SHUFFLE CONTROL
TOP CARD TO BOTTOM

With the overhand shuffle, you can control the top card of the pack and bring it to the bottom of the pack while apparently giving the deck an honest shuffle.

METHOD

1 Your control card is on the top of the deck. Hold the pack in your right hand.

2 Start by drawing off only the top card with the left thumb.

3 Let it fall alone into the left hand.

4 Continue the shuffle, pulling blocks of cards from the right hand with the left thumb on top of the control card, until all of the cards have been shuffled into the left hand. The control card will now be on the bottom of the deck.

OVERHAND SHUFFLE CONTROL
BOTTOM CARD TO TOP

In addition to controlling the top card to the bottom of the pack, the overhand shuffle (see page 70) can be worked in reverse to bring the bottom card to the top of the pack.

METHOD

1 Hold the deck face outward as described in the overhand reverse shuffle (see page 71). Your control card will be the three of diamonds, the bottom card.

2 Turn your body to the left so that the back of your right hand is toward the spectators. This keeps the bottom card out of their sight.

3 With your left thumb, draw off the front card (the three of diamonds) by itself.

4 Continue as already described, shuffling the rest of the deck on top of the three of diamonds. This will bring the bottom card to the top of the pack.

OVERHAND IN-JOG
TOP CARD CONTROL

With this control, you perform what appears to be an ordinary overhand shuffle. Yet, when you finish, the top card of the deck is the same card as when you started.

METHOD

1 The card you will control is on the top of the deck. Start the shuffle by removing a block of cards from the top of the pack with the left hand. The control card is now the top card of this packet.

2 Immediately in-jog the first card you shuffle off from the right-hand packet on top of the control card in the left-hand packet.

3 Shuffle off the remainder of the deck in the regular manner, making sure not to disturb the jogged card. After all of the cards have been shuffled into the left hand, cut to the in-jogged card as you did in Step 9 of the OVER-HAND IN-JOG CONTROL (see page 72) and throw the lower packet on top of the other cards in the left hand. The control card will now be back on the top of the pack.

MAGNETIZED CARD

There are many ways in which a magician can discover a card selected by a spectator, but those in which the card actually reveals itself are perhaps the most spectacular. One of the most impressive is the "Rising Card Trick," which has been shown in various forms over a period of many years. Usually, special preparation is needed, but here is a quick and simple impromptu version that can be performed as a close-up mystery with surprising effect!

EFFECT

A card is selected and returned to the pack which is shuffled by the magician in the usual fashion. Holding the pack upright in the left hand, with its face toward the audience, the magician rests the tip of the right first finger on the upper end of the pack. The performer states that the chosen card will be magically magnetized, causing it to rise from the pack of its own accord. As the magician lifts the finger, the card obeys, rising slowly and mysteriously until it is almost clear of the pack.

METHOD

1 From an ordinary pack of cards, invite a spectator to select any card, look at it, and remember it. Using the HINDU SHUFFLE—PICK-UP CONTROL (see page 65), or the OVERHAND IN-JOG TOP CARD CONTROL (see page 81), have the spectator return the card, which you then control to the top of the pack.

2 Hold the pack upright in your left hand with the thumb at one side and the fingers on the other side. The bottom card of the pack should face toward the palm of your left hand, and the back of your left hand should face the audience.

MARK WILSON'S CYCLOPEDIA OF MAGIC

3 With the pack held firmly in this position, extend the first finger of the right hand, pointing it toward the audience. The remaining fingers should be curled into the palm of the hand. Hold your right hand about 6" above the top edge of the pack.

4 Slowly lower your right hand until the tip of the first finger rests on top of the pack, as shown. Continue this up and down motion a few times as you say, "I will now attempt to magnetize the chosen card with my finger and cause it to rise from the pack on its own. Watch closely!"

5 With that, lower the right hand until the first finger touches the top of the pack. When it does, straighten out your little finger so it touches the back of the spectator's card, as shown. Because the spectator sees the pack from the front, the extended little finger will not be seen, as it is hidden by the pack.

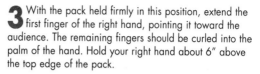

6 Without hesitation, slowly move the right hand upward as you apply a slight pressure on the back of the spectator's card with the tip of the little finger. This will cause the top card to slide upward and appear to be clinging to the tip of your right forefinger.

7 As the card slides upward, the tips of your left thumb and fingers serve as a guide or track for the card during its rise.

---

8 When the card has risen almost to the top of the pack, move your right hand away. Let the left thumb and fingers hold the card securely for a moment before removing it with your right hand and tossing it out for inspection.

COMMENTS AND SUGGESTIONS

The important factor in this trick is to guard against bad angles. If your audience is spread out, stand well back so that everyone will have a front view of the deck and be unable to see your little finger extended behind the pack. For close-up work, when performing for just one person, you can hold the pack right before the spectator's eyes, giving your viewer no chance at all to see past the edges.

OVERHAND IN-JOG CONTROL
PLACING A CARD AT A SPECIFIC LOCATION IN THE DECK

EFFECT

This control is very useful in placing a selected card any number of cards down in the pack that you wish. Let's assume that for a particular trick you need the card to be fourth from the top.

METHOD

1 With the selected card on top of the pack, begin a regular overhand shuffle, drawing about half of the top of the pack into your left hand.

2 One at a time, shuffle off three cards on top of the selected card. Do not jog these cards.

3 In-jog the fourth card and shuffle the rest of the cards on top of it into the left hand.

4 Cut the lower portion of the pack at the jogged card and throw the lower block of cards to the top of the deck. The selected card will now be fourth from the top.

SURPRISE APPEARANCE

This is a quick and clever card discovery using the control just described.

EFFECT

The magician has the spectator select a card from the deck and then return it while the magician is doing an overhand shuffle. The magician states that the selected card will be brought to the top of the deck. After the magician fails three times, the selected card makes a surprise appearance.

METHOD

1 Have a card selected and then use the OVERHAND IN-JOG CONTROL (see page 72) to bring the selected card to the top. Using the OVERHAND IN-JOG CONTROL—PLACING A CARD AT A SPECIFIC LOCATION IN THE DECK (see page 84), control the spectator's card so that it is fourth from the top of the deck.

2 Give the deck a FALSE CUT (see page 64) as previously described.

3 Hold the deck in your left hand and state, "I will now bring your card to the top of the deck." Slap the deck with your right hand and show the spectator the top card.

4 When you remove the top card to show it, just slide the card over to the right with your left thumb and then grasp the outer right corner of the card with your right thumb underneath and right first finger on top. Turn the card over, as shown, toward the spectator, so that it is face up.

5 Ask the spectator if this is the selected card. Of course, the reply will be, "No." Replace this card on the bottom of the deck.

6 Slap the deck again and show the next card. Again, you have failed to bring the selected card to the top. Replace this card on the bottom of the deck as well.

7 Each time you show a "wrong" card, hold it with your right thumb and first finger and have your hand close to the top of the deck, as shown.

8 As you show the third "wrong" card, push the top card of the pack, which is now the selected card (X), over slightly to the right.

9 As you display your third "mistake," grip the corner of the top card (X) between the tips of the third and little finger of your right hand.

10 Replace the third card on the top of the deck. At the same time, retain your hold on the selected card (X) with your right thumb and little fingers. The selected card (X) will pop up unexpectedly, facing the spectators, held between your two fingers for a SURPRISE APPEARANCE.

CHAPTER 5
FORCING A CARD

Maneuvering a spectator into selecting an object of your choice is called "forcing." Although the spectator believes there is a free choice, you are actually forcing them to choose the object you have prepared.

Forcing a card on an unsuspecting spectator is a sure way of bringing a trick to a successful conclusion. Since you already know what card will be chosen before you start, you can finish the trick almost any way you want—and the more surprising, the better. Try the methods given in this section, and you will realize how effective they can be.

It is a good policy to vary your forcing methods so that spectators will not become too familiar with your procedure. With most tricks, it is best to use a regular card location to reveal a chosen card, reserving the force for times when it is definitely needed. One such time is when a skeptical spectator wants to snatch the pack from your hands and shuffle it until you can't possibly find the chosen card. If you force a card on such a customer, you won't have to worry about this shuffle.

SLIP FORCE I

When you want a sure, deceptive force, using any pack of cards, this is one of the very best.

EFFECT

After shuffling a pack of cards, the magician holds the deck face down in the left hand. With the left thumb, the magician riffles the outer corner of the pack downwards. To a spectator, the magician says, "As I riffle the cards, please tell me when you want me to stop."

When the call comes, the magician grips the top portion of the pack in the right hand. Then, lifting that part of the pack upward, the magician extends the bottom portion in the left hand, so that the spectator can look at the top card of that packet—the place where the magician stopped. Apparently, this is a completely free selection, yet the card has actually been forced, thanks to the slip.

SECRET AND PREPARATION

The top card of the deck is the one that is forced. So, you must know the top card beforehand. To do this, glimpse the bottom card using the HINDU GLIMPSE (see page 51). Then, shuffle the bottom card to the top, using the OVERHAND SHUFFLE CONTROL—BOTTOM CARD TO TOP (see page 80). Begin once the top card is known. (Instead of forcing a particular card, position the card on top of the pack before the spectator makes the free selection.)

METHOD

1 Begin by holding the deck in your left hand using the mechanic's grip dealing position: your left thumb is at one side of the pack, your first finger is at the front edge, and the other three fingers are curled over the top of the pack at the right side. (In the illustrations, the force card is marked with an "X.")

2 With your left thumb, bend the outer left corner of the pack downward. Slowly begin releasing cards from the tip of the thumb, allowing them to spring upward, as shown. This is called riffling the cards. As you do this, ask the spectator to call "Stop" at any time during the riffle. Tell the spectator to take the card at the point where you are stopped.

3 Slowly begin riffling the cards. When the call comes, you stop. Without hesitation, move your right hand over the pack and grasp the upper packet of cards (above the point where you stopped) between your right thumb and fingers, as shown. Note that your left fingers are curled over the top card of the pack (X).

4 Begin drawing the top packet upward. The left fingers maintain a downward pressure on the top card (X).

5 Hold the top card (the force card) in place with your left fingers as your right hand slides the top packet from beneath it.

6 The right hand continues to slide out the top packet until it clears the edges of the slipped force card (X), which falls on top of the left-hand packet.

7 Offer the left-hand packet to the spectator. Have them remove the

top card, which is now the force card (X), and look at it. You have successfully forced the card on the spectator using the SLIP FORCE. Reveal the name of the card in any manner you choose.

COMMENTS AND SUGGESTIONS

The great feature of the SLIP FORCE is that it is absolutely undetectable when properly handled. As long as the back of your right hand is toward the spectators, the slip will be completely hidden. The same applies when the left hand tilts the pack upward, with the bottom turned toward the audience. (SLIP FORCE II, see below.) That is the very reason why you should get it exactly right. In your regular cuts, handle the pack as though you were about to do the slip, then there will be no suspicion when the time comes to actually execute the SLIP FORCE.

SLIP FORCE II

The SLIP FORCE is one of the most useful and deceptive methods of having a spectator select a forced card. After you have learned the basic method just described, try this variation which can make the trick even more effective.

METHOD

1 As in the initial description of the SLIP FORCE (see page 89), the top card (indicated by an "X") is the card that will be forced. Follow Steps 1 through 5, just as described in the SLIP FORCE.

2 When you get to Step 6, the right hand is sliding out the top packet as the fingers of the left hand hold the top card of that packet, which will fall on top of the left-hand packet. At the same time this action is being executed, both hands turn their packets face up. The hands rotate in opposite directions, as indicated by the arrows.

3 Turning the hands over as you make the slip hides the move completely from the spectator's view, even if you are completely surrounded.

4 At this point, the right-hand packet is face up and the left-hand packet is also face up with the "X" card on the bottom. Extend your left forefinger and point to the card on the face of the right-hand packet. Say, "I don't want you to take this card because I know what it is."

5 With that, turn both hands over, back to their original position. Extend your right forefinger, pointing to the top card of the left-hand packet. Say, "Instead, take this one where you said, 'Stop.' "

COMMENTS AND SUGGESTIONS

As stated above, this variation should be learned after you master the "regular" SLIP FORCE. When you can perform the first method with ease, you can then add this "extra" touch which makes the SLIP FORCE totally undetectable under all conditions.

10-20 COUNT FORCE

EFFECT

The performer asks a spectator to call out any number between 10 and 20, stating that the number that is called is the number of cards that will be counted out from the pack onto the table. This done, the magician then adds the two digits of the selected number together to arrive at a total. The magician counts that many cards from the top of the already dealt pile to arrive at a single card. The spectator is asked to look at that card and remember it. The performer automatically knows the name of this card which was really forced. The magician may now reveal the card in any manner desired.

SECRET AND PREPARATION

Because of a simple but clever mathematical principle, this force actually works itself. The only preparation necessary is that you know the tenth card from the top of the deck beforehand. (In the illustrations, this card is marked with an "X.")

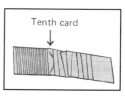

Tenth card

METHOD

1 Hold the deck face down in dealing position in your left hand. Ask the spectator to name any number between 10 and 20. Suppose the spectator says, "13." Count off 13 cards, one at a time, face down in a pile on the table, as shown. This dealing action reverses the order of the cards on the table. This places the force card fourth from the top in your new pile.

2 Lay the pack aside and pick up the new pile of 13 cards in dealing position. State that you will add the figures of the chosen number "13" (1 + 3 = 4) and count down that many in the pile.

3 You do this with the following result: When you counted the original 13 cards in a pile, you reversed their order as already stated. Now, by counting four cards, one at a time, from that pile, you reverse them again. This system, which works with any number between 10 and 20, causes the count to always end on the original tenth card, your force card!

4 Place the remaining cards with the rest of the deck and ask the spectator to look at the top card of the pile of four and remember it. You have now successfully forced a card using the 10–20 COUNT FORCE. You may reveal the selected card in whatever manner you choose.

COMMENTS AND SUGGESTIONS

The subtle mathematical principle that causes this effect to work can be easily understood by sitting down with the pack and trying out the various number combinations a few times. No matter what number the spectator selects (between 10 and 20), the result is always the same. The original tenth card from the top of the deck always ends up as the selected card.

ROLLOVER FORCE

Here is a surefire method of forcing a card where the actual handling of the pack seems so haphazard and disorderly that it appears impossible for the magician to have control over the position of any card in the pack. This makes for a very convincing force which is ideal for any card worker's program.

SECRET AND PREPARATION

For the ROLLOVER FORCE, all you need is an ordinary pack of cards with the force card on top. (In the illustrations, the force card is marked with an "X.")

METHOD

1 Hold the pack face down, in dealing position, in your left hand. State that you wish to have one card selected from the pack at random. To make sure that this choice is not influenced by you, the magician, you will let the pack itself determine which card will be selected.

2 With that, you lift off the upper 1/4 of the pack (about 10 to 15 cards).

3 Turn these cards over, face up.

4 Replace them on top of the face-down pack, as shown. As you turn the packet over, say, "To completely confuse the order of the pack, I will not only mix the cards, I'll turn some face up and some face down."

5 To make things more confusing, lift off nearly half the deck (20 to 25 cards).

6 Turn these over as before.

7 Replace these cards on top of the rest of the pack.

8 To add to all this, lift off another stack of cards, this time cutting closer to the bottom (about 3/4 of the deck).

9 Turn these cards over.

10 Replace them on top of the remaining cards.

11, 12, 13

You then state, "To confuse matters even further, I'll turn the whole pack over," which you do.

MARK WILSON'S CYCLOPEDIA OF MAGIC

14 After turning the pack over, say, "Now, we'll run through the pack and take the first face-down card that comes along." With that, you start to spread the pack, "running" the cards from your left hand to your right.

15 The first face-down card you reach will be the force card, the three of clubs. The audience thinks it is just a random card. Have a spectator remove that card from the pack and look at it. When that is done, you have successfully forced the card, using the ROLLOVER FORCE.

ROLL ANY NUMBER

The following force illustrates how you can cleverly manipulate a spectator, without anyone catching on.

METHOD

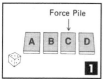

Force Pile

A B C D

1 This force uses a single die from any pair of dice. It will work with any four objects. To aid in the explanation, we will assume that the object to be forced is one of four piles in a single row. The pile to be forced should be in the third position from your left. The four piles are numbered A through D in the illustrations. The pile to be forced is the C pile. If you want to force a single card, that card should be on top of the "force" pile.

2 Explain that the spectator should roll the die and that you will count its number along the row in order to choose a pile.

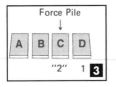

3 If the roll is two, begin counting from the right to the left. Your count will end on the desired pile.

4 If the roll is three, begin counting from left to right to reach the correct pile.

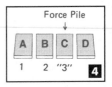

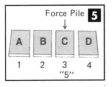

5 If the spectator rolls a five, count from left to right. When you reach the end of the row on four, continue the count, back from right to left, to land on the proper pile (C).

NOTE: Do not count pile D as five, just immediately start your count back from four on pile D to five on pile C, your force pile.

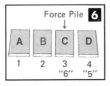

6 If the roll is six, count from right to left and then return to the right to finish the count.

NOTE: In this case, you do count pile D as four. Then just continue as if starting from the right, counting pile D as five and pile C as six.

7 The force will not work with rolls of one or four, but such rolls make it all the better, as they allow you to inject a clever twist that adds to the effect. If a one or a four turns up on the die, immediately say, "Good! We will use the 'hidden number,' the one that nobody knows!"

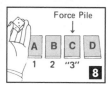

Force Pile
↓

A B C D
1 2 "3"

8

8 With that, pick up the die, turn it over, and point to the bottom number, referring to this as the hidden number. If one is rolled, the hidden number will be six. If four is rolled, the hidden number will be three. In either case, you end up with a number that enables you to count to the required pile. Tell the spectator to look at the top card of the pile, and you're done!

MAGICIAN'S CHOICE FORCE

Cards are not the only objects that can be forced. With the MAGICIAN'S CHOICE FORCE, you control which piece of paper the spectator will choose. You can force the spectator to pick any of the three pieces of paper, but in this case you will force the piece of paper with the circle.

EFFECT

You will be able to correctly predict which of three drawings a spectator will select from the table.

SECRET AND PREPARATION

You will need three pieces of paper on your table. On one piece, you will have drawn a square; on the second, a circle; and on the third, a triangle. You will also need a spectator to assist you.

METHOD

1 Point out to the spectator that you have drawn a different figure on each of three papers you have placed on the table. Ask the spectator to point to any one of the three slips. One of two situations will arise:

2 First Situation: If the spectator points to the circle, say: "Would you pick up the paper that you have selected and hold it in your hand."

3 When the spectator does this, you pick up the other two papers and tear them up, saying: "We will not need these, so I'll tear them up."

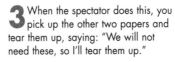

4 Second Situation: If the spectator points to the square or the triangle, you pick up the one they point to.

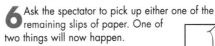

5 After picking up the spectator's choice, you say, "Fine, I'll tear this one up and that leaves only two."

6 Ask the spectator to pick up either one of the remaining slips of paper. One of two things will now happen.

7 The spectator may pick up the paper with the circle on it.

8 If that happens, then you pick up the one remaining slip on the table and tear it up saying, "OK, the circle is the one you selected, so we won't need this one either."

9 The spectator may pick up the paper without the circle on it.

10 If that happens, you say, "OK, you tear up that slip, which leaves just the one on the table." Of course, the one that is left is the circle!

COMMENTS AND SUGGESTIONS

This is a very crucial trick for setting up other tricks. There is no sleight of hand or special skill needed. However, it is a trick that must be studied thoroughly and practiced until you can easily deal with each possible situation. After you have mastered it, you will be able to baffle your friends with one of the finest forces in the entire Art of Magic.

CHAPTER 6
DOUBLE LIFT TRICKS

Holding two cards together and exhibiting them as one is perhaps the oldest artifice in card magic. It has attained new value in the comparatively modern sleight known as the DOUBLE LIFT. This maneuver is utterly deceptive in the hands of experts (many of whom have their own pet twist), but the basic principle is the same in all versions.

The DOUBLE LIFT is an effective and useful sleight, providing it is not used too often or too boldly. Originally intended simply to cause one card to "change" into another, newer and more subtle uses for the DOUBLE LIFT were soon devised. You will find a nice variety in this section. The DOUBLE LIFT is most effective when worked in conjunction with other moves. Results can be achieved that seem impossible—and all with an ordinary pack of cards.

LITTLE-FINGER BREAK

This secret move is very important. The LITTLE-FINGER BREAK has many uses. One of the most useful is to prepare for the DOUBLE LIFT (see page 105).

METHOD

1 Hold the deck in your left hand in dealing position. However, unlike the regular dealing position (A), where the second and third fingers curl over the top of the deck, hold the deck so that just the tips of these three fingers extend above the right edge of the deck (B).

2 Bring your right hand over the deck, right thumb at the inner end, your right first finger resting on top of the deck, and your remaining fingers at the far end of the pack, as shown.

3 With the ball of your right thumb, slightly raise the inner end of the top card off the top of the deck.

4 In the same motion, bend your right thumb inward just enough to catch the edge of the second card (the one just below the top card) and raise it also just slightly off the top of the deck.

NOTE: The right first finger should apply a slight downward pressure on the top of the deck nearest the audience to assure that only the inner ends of the cards are raised. From the audience's view, it should appear that you are just holding the deck with both hands.

5 When both cards are raised off the inner end of the deck, press lightly against the right side of the deck with your left little finger. This will cause the skin on the ball of the little finger to overlap the top edge of the deck just enough to hold a small break between the two raised cards and the rest of the cards in the deck.

6 Relax your right thumb, allowing the two lifted cards to come to rest together on the fleshy tip of your left little finger. You have now secured a LITTLE-FINGER BREAK beneath the top two cards.

7 Move the right hand away and, at the same time, move the left thumb so that it rests on top of the pack with your left first finger curled around the front of the pack. Keep the "audience end" of the top two cards flush with the deck. The pack, from the audience's view, should look completely natural.

COMMENTS AND SUGGESTIONS

The entire procedure of securing the LITTLE-FINGER BREAK should be done deliberately in the pretense of squaring up the deck as it is held in the left hand.

NOTE: It is also important, after you learn the sleight, not to look at the pack as you make the break. This is an example of misdirection, because the audience will look where you look. Make some comment and look at the spectators when you make the secret move.

MARK WILSON'S CYCLOPEDIA OF MAGIC

DOUBLE LIFT

Once you have mastered the LITTLE-FINGER BREAK (see page 103) to the point where you can execute the move quickly and without arousing suspicion, you are ready to learn the DOUBLE LIFT. This multi-purpose sleight is one of the most deceptive and practical moves in card magic. It has many uses.

Learn it well, as it will soon become the basis for many of your most baffling card mysteries.

METHOD

1 As mentioned earlier, you must first learn the LITTLE-FINGER BREAK before you learn the DOUBLE LIFT. To execute the DOUBLE LIFT, first secure a LITTLE-FINGER BREAK beneath the top two cards of the pack. (These two cards have been marked "A" and "B" in the illustrations.)

2 Bring your right hand over the pack with your thumb at the inner end, your first finger resting lightly on top, and your other fingers at the outer end of the pack, as shown. This is the same position your right hand was in after securing the LITTLE-FINGER BREAK.

3 With the ball of your right thumb, raise the inner end of the two cards (A and B) you hold above the break. With your right hand, lift both cards together (as one) completely off the top of the pack. Your right first finger should press lightly against the back of the cards. This keeps them from "bowing" apart and holds their edges squared so the two cards appear to be one card.

Two cards,
A & B

4 Turn your right hand over, showing the face of the card.

NOTE: The audience believes you have simply picked up the top card of the pack and shown them the face of that card. Actually, the face of the card they see is that of the second card, thanks to the DOUBLE LIFT.

Two cards,
A & B

5 Replace the cards back on top of the pack. Be sure that the two cards are squared with the rest of the cards in the pack.

6 With the left thumb, deal the real top card (A) off the pack where it is taken by your right fingers.

7 Set the pack on the table and turn this card face up, to show that the top card of the pack has magically changed to a different card!

COMMENTS AND SUGGESTIONS

Magically changing the top card into another card is only one of the countless uses of the DOUBLE LIFT. In fact, one of the dangers of the DOUBLE LIFT is that it is so effective, you may be tempted to use it too much. Don't worry about that right now. Just practice and learn this sleight well. As you will see, it will be of tremendous value to you.

RIFFLE REVELATION

This basic application of the DOUBLE LIFT (see page 105) provides a very surprising discovery of a selected card. It can be presented at any time during your regular card routine.

EFFECT

A card is selected and shuffled back into the pack. The magician then shows that the selected card is not the bottom card or the top card, so it must be buried somewhere in the middle. The magician hands the chooser the top card, telling this person to push the card into the pack face down, while the pack is being riffled. Presumably, this card will find the chosen card, but it doesn't. The magician tries again and fails once more. In desperation, the magician looks through the faces of the cards, wondering what could possibly have gone wrong. The magician asks the spectator what card was chosen. When the spectator replies, the magician says, "Well, that explains why we couldn't find your card in the deck. It's the one you had in your hand all the time." To everyone's surprise, the card the spectator holds has magically changed into the selected card!

METHOD

1 From an ordinary pack of cards, have one card selected and returned to the deck. Using any of the methods you have learned (HINDU SHUFFLE PICK-UP CONTROL [see page 65], OVERHAND IN-JOG CONTROL [see page 72], etc.) bring the selected card (X) to the top of the deck.

2 With the chosen card (X) on the top, grip the deck between the right fingers and thumb and turn the entire pack face up, calling the spectator's attention to the card at the bottom of the deck. Say, "There's only a small chance that your card would be the bottom card of the pack. Is this it?" The spectator will answer, "No."

Getting
Little
Finger
Break

3 Turn the pack over and hold it in your left hand in position to execute a DOUBLE LIFT (see page 105). However, before letting go of the cards with the right hand, secure a LITTLE-FINGER BREAK (see page 103) beneath the top two cards of the deck.

4 Double-lift the top two cards as one card with the right hand. Turn the cards face up, calling attention to what the spectator believes to be the top card of the deck. Ask, "And is this your card at the top of the deck?" Again, the spectator will answer, "No."

5 Replace the two cards on top of the pack. With your right hand, take the top card (X) and hand it, face down, to the spectator. Say, "With the aid of the top card, we will find the exact location of your card in the deck."

6 Riffle the outer end of the pack with your right fingers. Explain that as you riffle the deck, the spectator is to insert the end of the card into the pack anywhere desired. Tell the spectator that when this is done, the exact spot in the deck where the selected card lies will be found.

MARK WILSON'S CYCLOPEDIA OF MAGIC

7 Here is a side view as the spectator inserts the supposedly meaningless card (really the selected card) into the deck as you riffle. Be careful not to let the spectator see the face of the card and be sure the card is not released. Say, "Just hold onto it firmly."

8 After you have riffled the end of the pack, and the card has been inserted into the deck by the spectator, lift all the cards above the inserted card and turn this packet face up in your right hand to show the card at that point. Inform the spectator that the card on the face of the right-hand packet should be the selected card. But it isn't.

9 Remind the spectator to maintain a hold at all times on what is believed to be a meaningless card (actually, the card the spectator holds is the chosen card).

10 Reassemble the deck and riffle the cards again, explaining that you will give the spectator a second try at finding the card. When you are wrong again, act as if the trick has failed and you don't know why. Turn the cards face up and run through them, as if trying to find the spectator's card.

11 Again, still puzzled at your failure, and without looking up from the cards, ask the spectator, "What card did you take?" When the spectator replies, say, "Well, that explains it. You were holding the card all the time." Of course, when the spectator looks, everyone will be surprised that the card has changed in the spectator's hand, while the spectator had control of it all along!

COMMENTS AND SUGGESTIONS

This is a good trick to use when a chosen card is actually found by inserting another in the pack. When people want to see it again, you can use another card instead.

SNAP-IT!

This quick way of magically changing one card into an entirely different card will create a real surprise when injected into a regular card routine. It is guaranteed to keep people wondering what will happen next. This is a classic utilization of the DOUBLE LIFT (see page 105).

EFFECT

The magician removes the top card of the pack and shows it to be the eight of hearts. Turning the card face down, the magician gives it a "snap" with a finger. When the card is turned over, it is seen to have magically changed to an entirely different card!

METHOD

1 Hold the deck face down in dealing position in the left hand and with the help of the right hand, secure a LITTLE-FINGER BREAK (see page 103) beneath the top two cards of the pack.

2 With the right hand, execute the DOUBLE LIFT by picking up the top two cards (as one).

3 Turn the cards over, showing the face of what the spectators believe to be the top card of the pack (the eight of hearts). As you display the cards, say, "You will notice a peculiar characteristic of these playing cards."

4 Replace the two cards on top of the packet.

5 Deal the real top card off the deck into the right fingers.

6 Place the rest of the deck aside. Continue by saying, "If I take the top card of the pack, in this case the eight of hearts, and give it a snap..."

7 Holding the card firmly in the right hand, give the back of the face-down card a sharp snap by hitting it with your left fingers.

8 Say, "...it causes the card to change, like this!" Turn the card face up.

9 The card has changed from the eight of hearts to the four of clubs!

10 Toss the card on the table, just in case a suspicious spectator should want to examine it—and chances are someone will!

COMMENTS AND SUGGESTIONS

Instead of the change as just described, you can add a clever twist by secretly placing two cards of the same suit on the pack with the lesser-value card on top. For example, you might use the four of diamonds on top of the pack with the five of diamonds just below it. Execute the DOUBLE LIFT, replace the cards on the deck, remove the single top card, and hold it in your right hand. Pretend to "knock" one of the spots off the card by snapping it. This can also be done with any two cards of the same suit, just remember to "knock off" enough spots to correspond to the difference in the values of the two cards. If you're working standing up, and have no place to lay the deck aside, simply strike the single card against the pack to "knock off" the spots.

COLOR-CHANGING ACES I

This is a novel and baffling trick that can be presented in a quick, effective form, ending with a real surprise. In many Four-Aces routines, extra cards are used; but here, only the four aces are involved, making the entire trick clean, simple, and most startling. The only sleight necessary for this trick is the DOUBLE LIFT (see page 105).

EFFECT

The magician displays the four aces. Holding them in the left hand, the magician deals the two red aces, one at a time, face down on the table. To avoid any confusion, the magician openly shows the face of each red ace before dealing it. This automatically leaves the magician holding the two black aces. At the magician's command, the aces instantly change places. The spectators can even turn over the cards themselves, to find that the black aces are now the two cards on the table and that the magician holds the pair of red aces!

METHOD

1 From an ordinary pack of cards, remove the four aces and place the rest of the pack aside. Display the four aces to the spectators.

2 Arrange the aces in the following order: one black ace on top of the packet (ace of clubs), the two red aces in the middle (ace of hearts and ace of diamonds), and the other black ace (ace of spades) at the bottom of the pile. This should be done casually without calling attention to the fact that the cards

are in any specific order. (In the illustrations, the aces have been numbered 1 through 4 to make them easier to follow.)

3 With your right hand, place the fanned packet of cards (in their proper sequence) into your left hand, and as you close the fan, secure a LITTLE-FINGER BREAK (see page 103) beneath the top two aces (the ace of clubs and the ace of hearts).

4 You are now ready for the DOUBLE LIFT.

5 Lift the two cards together (DOUBLE LIFT) off the packet and show the face of what the spectators believe to be the top card, the ace of hearts, as you say, "Here is the ace of hearts, a red card, on top."

6 Replace the two cards on the packet and then deal the real top card, the ace of clubs, from the top of the packet to the table as you state, "I will place the first red ace on the table."

7 This next step is very important. Reverse count the remaining three aces, one at a time, from the left hand into the right hand, as you say, "That leaves one, two, three remaining aces."

8 The reverse count moves the two red aces to the bottom of the packet and the remaining black ace, the ace of spades, to the top.

9 Place the packet face down in your left hand as before and, as you square the cards, secure a LITTLE-FINGER BREAK beneath the top two cards, the ace of spades and the ace of diamonds.

10 Lift these two cards as one (DOUBLE LIFT) off the packet and show the face of what the spectators believe to be the top card, the ace of diamonds, as you say, "Here is the ace of diamonds, the other red card."

11 Replace the two cards on the packet and deal the real top card, the ace of spades, from the top of the packet next to the ace of clubs already on the table as you say, "The second red ace goes on the table with the first."

12 The rest of the trick is just presentation. After a little byplay, turn over the red aces in your hand and invite a spectator to turn over the black aces on the table to prove that the aces have actually changed places!

COMMENTS AND SUGGESTIONS

By handling the cards in an apparently casual manner, this trick can be built into an extremely deceptive mystery. Here is another clever procedure you can use when you do make the "setup." After you have opened and removed the aces from the pack and displayed them to the audience, hold them so that only you can see the faces as you arrange the aces in their proper order. Say, "I'll put the black aces in the middle and the reds on the top and bottom." Actually, the reds go in the middle. After showing the first red ace and placing it (really the black ace) on the table, when you reverse-count the three aces, one at a time, from the left hand to the right hand, you can call each card by its supposed color, i.e., "Black, black, red."

SPECIAL NOTE: In many cases, you can place the two "red" (really black) aces directly onto the spectator's outstretched palm. After you deal each card into the spectator's palm, have the spectator put the other hand flat on top of the cards. Apparently, this is so that you cannot do anything "tricky." In reality, this keeps the spectator from looking at the faces of the cards. With this form of presentation, the aces apparently change places while held tightly in the spectator's own hands!

SANDWICHED ACES

Here is a baffling four-ace routine that people will talk about and want to see again. Once you have mastered it, you will probably keep it as a highlight in your program. Best of all, only a few special moves are required, and they fit into the routine so neatly that there is little chance that anyone will begin to suspect them.

EFFECT

The magician openly deals the two black aces face down on the table. The spectator freely selects any card from the pack, say the five of diamonds. The five is turned face up and "sandwiched" between the two face-down black aces. The three cards are then turned over as a group and placed on top of the pack.

Without hesitation, the magician spreads the top two cards, showing that the five of diamonds has vanished from between the black aces. The magician deals the black aces onto the table and immediately spreads the pack face down along the table, revealing the two red aces face up in the center, with a single face-down card between them. "I knew your card was sandwiched between two aces," the magician declares. When a spectator turns over the face-down card, it proves to be the missing five of diamonds!

SECRET AND PREPARATION

The success of this trick depends on the proper setup of the four aces in the deck before the trick begins. From a regular pack of cards, remove the aces and arrange them in the following positions:

A♠ A♥ A♣

A Place the two black aces (ace of clubs and ace of spades) face down together and one of the red aces (ace of hearts in the illustrations) face down between them.

B Place this group of three cards on top of the face-down pack.

C Place the remaining red ace (ace of diamonds) face up on the bottom of the pack, and you're ready. (In

the illustrations, the aces have been numbered 1 through 4 to make them easier to follow. 1 is the ace of clubs, 2 is the ace of hearts, 3 is the ace of spades, and 4 is the ace of diamonds. The selected card is indicated by an "X.")

METHOD

1 With the pack held in dealing position in the left hand, grasp the top card of the pack (1—the ace of clubs) between the thumb and fingers of your right hand in the same grip as if you were executing the DOUBLE LIFT.

2 Do not do the DOUBLE LIFT! Just pick up the ace of clubs and turn it face up, showing it to the audience. Say, "The top card of the pack is the ace of clubs."

3 Replace the ace on top of the pack.

4 Without hesitation, take the ace of clubs with your right fingers and place it face down on the table. Say, "I will place it here on the table."

5 Secure a LITTLE-FINGER BREAK between the next two cards on top of the pack (2—the ace of hearts and 3—the ace of spades).

6 Execute a DOUBLE LIFT, lifting both cards (as one) from the top of the pack. Turn them over, showing the face of what the spectators believe to be the top card (3—the ace of spades). As you display the ace, remark, "Here is the next card, the ace of spades..."

7 Replace the two cards back on the top of the pack.

8 Immediately take the real top card (2—the ace of hearts) from the top of the pack and place it face down next to the ace of clubs (1) on the table. Say, "... which I will place here, next to the ace of clubs."

NOTE: As it stands, you have one red ace and one black ace face down on the table. The spectators believe the two cards are the two black aces. The other black ace is really on top of the pack, and the last red ace is face up on the bottom of the deck.

9 Run through the pack face down and invite the spectator to select any card. When the card has been chosen, square the pack and hold it in dealing position in your left hand.

10 Instruct the spectator to turn the card face up and slide it between the two "black aces" on the table, thus sandwiching the card between them.

11 Secure a LITTLE-FINGER BREAK under only the top card of the pack (3—the ace of spades). Because the attention of the audience is focused on what the spectator is doing, obtaining the LITTLE-FINGER BREAK will go completely unnoticed.

12 Next, pick up the three cards on the table.

13 Place them on top of the pack, adding them to the ace of spades, and square all four cards together above the break.

14 Without hesitation, turn over all four cards (as three) face up on the pack, as shown.

15 The two black aces will now be face up on top of the pack; the spectator's card will be face down below the aces, and below that will be the face-up ace of hearts.

16 As soon as the four cards have been turned over, carefully take the two black aces (1 and 3) with your right hand and place them face up on the table. Remark, "Your card seems to have disappeared from between the two black aces." Be sure when you deal the two black aces off the pack that you do not shift the face-down card below them, accidentally exposing the face-up ace of hearts.

17 Holding the pack in your hands, give the deck a single cut. This places the face-up ace of diamonds, the bottom card, directly on top of the selected card and the face-up ace of hearts below it. You have automatically sandwiched the selected card between the two face-up red aces.

18 All that remains is to spread the pack face down on the table, revealing the two red aces and the face-down card between them. When the spectator turns over the sandwiched card, everyone will be amazed to see that the chosen card has mysteriously appeared between the two red aces, the ace of hearts and the ace of diamonds!

COMMENTS AND SUGGESTIONS

Precision, more than skill, is the main factor in this mystery, so practice can make it perfect. In showing the first black ace, display it just as if you were doing a DOUBLE LIFT, replacing it on the pack and dealing it face down as a single card. When you show and deal the ace of spades, your action is identical, so the DOUBLE LIFT will never be suspected.

DOUBLE THOUGHT PROJECTION

This is an exceptionally fine mental effect, using only two ordinary packs of cards with contrasting backs, such as one red-backed deck and one blue-backed deck. It requires only one sleight, and you have already learned it!

EFFECT

The magician runs through a deck of cards face up and asks a spectator to freely name any card in the pack. Assume that the spectator selects the seven of diamonds. The magician removes this card from the pack and turns it face down, showing that it has a blue back. With that, the magician spreads the rest of the pack face down on the table, revealing that every card in the deck except the seven of diamonds has a red back! Then, to take the mystery one step further, the magician spreads the blue-backed deck face down on the table to reveal a single red-backed card right in the middle of the pack. When this card is turned face up, it is found to be the seven of diamonds from the red-backed deck!

SECRET AND PREPARATION

The only sleight used in this amazing mystery is the DOUBLE LIFT (see page 105).

You will need two matching decks of cards with different-colored backs, say one red and one blue. Beforehand, remove a card from the blue-backed deck and place it on the bottom of the red-backed deck. (In the illustrations, this card is shown as the four of clubs; however, any card may be used.) Replace the red pack with the one blue card in its case and have the blue-backed pack lying openly on the table. In fact, you can use the blue pack for a few preliminary tricks if you wish, as the absence of a single card (the blue-backed four of clubs) will not be noticed.

METHOD

Blue backed card

1 Bring out the case containing the red-backed pack and announce that you will mentally project the name of one card to the spectator. Fan or spread the cards face up in your hands and ask the spectator to name any card desired. Stress the fact that the spectator has absolutely free selection of any card.

2 When the spectator names a card, in this case, the seven of diamonds, divide the pack into two sections at the place in the deck where the card is located. Keep the selected card at the top of the packet in your left hand.

NOTE: The four of clubs, the secret blue-backed card, is at the face of the right-hand packet.

3 As you comment about the fact that the spectator made a completely free selection, deal the seven of diamonds from the top of the left-hand packet directly on top of the blue-backed four of clubs in the right-hand packet.

4 Reassemble the halves of the pack, placing the right-hand packet on top of the left-hand packet. This leaves the spectator's card on the face of the deck with the blue-backed four just below it.

5 At this point, get ready for the DOUBLE LIFT by securing a LITTLE-FINGER BREAK (see page 103) beneath the seven of diamonds and the blue-backed four of clubs under it.

6 As you remark that the spectator could have selected any card in the pack, execute the DOUBLE LIFT and turn the two cards over (as one), displaying the blue back of what the spectator believes to be the chosen card, the seven of diamonds. Actually, the blue back the spectator sees belongs to the four of clubs.

7 To prove that you knew which card the spectator would choose all along, turn over the pack you are holding in your left hand and spread the deck face down on the table, showing them all to be red-backed cards. Be sure to keep the two cards in your right hand held firmly, as shown. (Remember, the audience thinks you are holding a single card.)

8 Immediately pick up the blue-backed pack (which has been sitting on the table all along) in your left hand and turn it face up.

9 Place the two cards (which the audience thinks is only one) face up on the face of the blue-backed pack as you remark that the blue-backed seven of diamonds really belongs in the blue deck.

NOTE: What the spectator does not know is that the seven of diamonds you have just placed on the blue-backed deck is really a red-backed card, thanks to your secret four of clubs! You are now perfectly set up to add a double-barreled impact to this mystery.

10 Cut the deck, burying the seven of diamonds somewhere near the center.

11 The final proof of your miraculous powers comes when you spread the blue-backed deck face down to reveal one red-backed card in the center of the deck.

12 Remove the card and turn it face up to reveal it is the seven of diamonds, the only red-backed card in the blue deck.

CHAPTER 7
GLIDE TRICKS

When you add this sleight to your routine, you can practically duplicate the work of some of the greatest card experts. Once you have mastered the glide, you have taken a major step along the road to card magic. There are some excellent routines for it described in this section.

GLIDE I

For directness, efficiency, and complete concealment, the glide rates high among card sleights. Simple though it is, it does require practice to be done properly and convincingly. The glide is an effective sleight, especially suited to beginners. It is equally valuable to all card workers, because it enables the magician to show a card and undetectably switch it for another.

EFFECT

You hold a pack of cards face up in your left hand. Call attention to the bottom card, say the two of clubs. Turning the pack face down, you draw out the bottom card with the tips of your right fingers and place it, still face down, on the table. When the card is turned over by a spectator, the two of clubs has changed into a totally different card!

METHOD

1 Hold the pack face up in your left hand with the thumb at one side and the fingers at the other side. The tips of the second, third, and little fingers should curl over the top of the pack and rest gently, as shown, against the face of the bottom card (the two of clubs).

NOTE: Your first finger remains on the side of the deck and does not touch the face of the bottom card.

2 Turn the left hand over, toward yourself, rotating your hand at the wrist.

3 As soon as the pack is face down, with the tips of your left second, third, and little fingers, slide the bottom card back, so that it extends beyond the inner end of the pack about 1/2". From underneath, the deck now looks like this.

4 From above, the pack should appear to be completely natural, with the back of your hand hiding the protruding bottom card.

Bottom view

5 With your right hand, reach beneath the pack and press the tips of your right first and second fingers against the face of the now exposed second card from the bottom (the eight of spades).

Audience view

6 Begin to slide this card (the eight of spades) out from beneath the pack with the tips of your right fingers. When it is far enough out, place your right thumb on top of the card and draw it clear of the pack.

7 This is the view of the pack from the bottom.

8 Place the card on the table.

NOTE: The audience believes you have just pulled the bottom card (the two of clubs) from the deck. Really, you have removed the second card (the eight of spades).

9 As the right hand places its card on the table, use the left fingers to return the "glided" bottom card back to its original position, flush with the rest of the pack. (See optional move described in the following note.)

10 The card on the table can now be turned over to show that it has magically changed to a different card.

NOTE: If you find it difficult to return the glided card to its original position using only the second, third, and little fingers of the left hand, you may wish to use this optional move in Step 9. After the card has been removed by the right hand and is clear of the deck, extend your left first finger over the front of the deck. By a combination of pushing back with the left first finger and forward with the second, third, and little fingers, you will find that you can quite easily return the bottom card to its squared-up position on the bottom of the deck.

COMMENTS AND SUGGESTIONS

The glide may be performed with only a few cards, rather than the entire pack, and still be equally deceptive. As you practice, you will find that only a very light pressure from your left fingers is required to glide the bottom card back. Practice so that you can draw back only the bottom

MARK WILSON'S CYCLOPEDIA OF MAGIC

card, neatly and secretly, without having other cards tag along. Sometimes, you need a little more pressure, but always be careful not to apply too much. Also, many beginners, when learning the glide, hold the deck too tightly in the left hand. The pack should be held so that the back of the pack does not touch the palm of the left hand. Hold the deck so that just enough of your second, third, and little fingers extend around the bottom of the pack to touch the face of the card to be glided. When working with a new or borrowed pack, test the glide before using it, to get the "feel" of the cards. If necessary, the right fingers can actually take over the whole operation, by simply pushing back the bottom card and pulling out the next. However, this slows the action and should only be used in an emergency.

GLIDE II

After you have learned the basic glide, you may wish to add this extra touch. When you begin turning your hand over (Step 3 of GLIDE I), begin at the same time to draw back the bottom card with the tips of your second and third fingers. If both the turning of the pack face down

 and the glide are executed simultaneously, the movement of your left fingers becomes even less detectable.

COLOR-CHANGING ACES II
DOUBLE LIFT AND GLIDE

One good trick deserves another, and that rule applies to the second version of the COLOR-CHANGING ACES. This method is very similar to the method already given (see page 112). However, this version depends on GLIDE I (see page 126) as its second move instead of a second DOUBLE LIFT.

EFFECT

From the audience's view, the effect is identical to COLOR-CHANGING ACES I (see page 112). The magician displays the four aces. Holding them face down in a packet, the magician shows the face of both red aces while dealing them onto the table. Holding the two black aces, the magician commands the aces to change places. When the cards are turned over, the black aces are on the table, and the magician is holding the red aces!

METHOD

For this trick, you must do GLIDE I (see page 126) and the DOUBLE LIFT (see page 105).

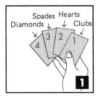

1 From a regular pack of cards, remove the four aces and place the rest of the deck aside. (In the illustrations, the aces have been numbered 1 through 4 to make them easier to follow.) As you display the aces, gather them into a packet and casually arrange them so that the aces alternate in color—starting with a black ace at the top of the face-down packet.

2 Place the packet face down in dealing position in the left hand.

3 Obtain a LITTLE-FINGER BREAK (see page 103) beneath the top two cards of the packet (ace of clubs and ace of hearts).

4 Using a DOUBLE LIFT, lift these two cards (as one) off the top of the packet and show the face of what the spectators believe to be the top card, the ace of hearts. At the same time, say, "Here is the ace of hearts, the top card of the pack."

5 With that, replace the two cards on top of the packet.

6 Deal the real top card, the ace of clubs, from the top of the packet to the table as you say, "I'll place the first red ace here on the table."

NOTE: So far, this follows exactly the COLOR-CHANGING ACES I routine, except for the color setup. Next comes the special added twist.

7 Instead of doing a reverse count and another DOUBLE LIFT, turn the packet face up in the left hand, in position to execute the glide. As you do this, point to the bottom card of the packet (the ace of diamonds) saying, "And here is the ace of diamonds, the other red ace."

8 With that, turn the packet face down and execute the glide, drawing out the card second from the bottom (the ace of spades) instead of the real bottom card, the ace of diamonds.

9 Place the card on the table as you say, "I'll put the ace of diamonds on the table along with the ace of hearts."

10 At this point, the trick is really over; all that's left is presentation. After a little byplay, turn over the two red aces in your hand to show that they have changed from black to red and invite a spectator to do the same with the black aces on the table!

COMMENTS AND SUGGESTIONS

As you arrange the aces in order (clubs, hearts, spades, and diamonds), you can miscall their position by remarking, "Blacks in the middle, reds on top and bottom." Then, using the DOUBLE LIFT, you apparently deal one red ace from the top. Immediately turning the packet face up, you supposedly deal the other red ace from the bottom.

One good presentation is to hold one pair face down in each hand and slap their free ends together, with an up-and-down action. Then, deliberately turn both pairs face up to show that they have magically changed places.

OIL AND WATER

"Dealing" tricks form a definite departure from other forms of card magic because they usually require only a small group of cards rather than a full pack. In addition, they generally get away from the usual procedure of having a spectator select a card from the pack. As a result, "dealing" tricks help to produce a varied program.

EFFECT

Six cards, three red and three black, numbering from ace through six, are arranged in alternating colors and number values. After displaying the cards in that manner, the magician turns them face down in the left hand and draws them, one at a time, from the bottom. The magician transfers them to the top, calling out their colors, "Red, black..." and so on. At intervals, individual cards are shown face up to prove that they are still in their alternating color order. The climax comes when the entire packet is turned face up and fanned. Amazingly, the cards have rearranged themselves into two separate groups. One is composed of three black cards; the other, of three red cards, all in perfect number order from ace to six!

SECRET AND PREPARATION

The only sleight used in this trick is GLIDE I (see page 126).

From a regular pack of cards, remove the ace, deuce, and three of diamonds, and the four, five, six of spades. Arrange the six cards so they appear in the exact order shown. This accomplished, you are ready to begin.

METHOD

1 Fan the six cards face up and call attention to the fact that their number values are mixed and the cards alternate in color. Square up the packet of cards. Hold them face up in your left hand in position for THE GLIDE. Explain that, "Like oil and water, red cards and black cards just don't mix."

NOTE: Make sure that the spectators understand that the cards in your hand alternate in color.

2 As you display the red ace at the face of the pack, call out, "Red." Then, turn the left hand over so that the cards are face down. Remove the card from the bottom, the ace of diamonds, with your right fingers.

3 Place it on top of the packet. Do not do the glide; simply remove the ace from the bottom and move it to the top.

4 With the left hand still face down, remove the next card, the five of spades, from the bottom in your right fingers. To assure the audience that this card is, in fact, a black card, turn the five over to show its face. As you do this, say, "Black." Turn the card back over and place it face down on top of the packet.

5 Again, turn the left hand over to show the face of the bottom card (the three of diamonds) to the spectators. Call out, "Red." Immediately, turn the packet face down, and this time, execute the glide, actually drawing out the card second from the bottom, the four of spades. Once the card has been removed from the bottom, place it face down on top of the pack of cards.

6 Still holding the cards face down in the left hand, draw out the bottom card of the pack, the three of diamonds, and hold it face down in your right hand. Pause for a moment as you call out, "Black." Do not turn this card face up. Instead, place the card face down on top of the packet.

7 With the packet still face down, remove the bottom card of the pack, the two of diamonds, and turn it face up in the right hand. Pause for a moment, and call out, "Red." Then, place this card face down on top of the packet.

8 Finally, turn the packet face up, in position for the glide, and display the face of the six of spades as you say, "Black." Turn the pack face down and once again execute the glide, actually removing the second from the bottom card, the ace of diamonds. Place this card on top of the rest of the cards in the packet.

NOTE: Apparently, you have just shown each card in the packet, one at a time, without disturbing their alternate color or number order. Of course, you know that isn't the case!

9 All that remains is to fan the packet face up, displaying that the cards have arranged themselves in numerical order, and that, like oil and water, red and black playing cards just don't mix.

COMMENTS AND SUGGESTIONS

Practice with the six cards until you memorize the routine, and this trick becomes virtually self-working. Its only move, THE GLIDE, should be done smoothly and at exactly the same pace as when you are really removing the bottom card. The total routine has been carefully designed so that each time you display a red card or black card, either on the bottom of the packet or in your right hand, you are psychologically convincing the spectators of the honesty of moving each card from the bottom to the top, diverting them from the real secret.

BIRDS OF A FEATHER

This is a modernized version of a card classic known as FOLLOW THE LEADER. Here, all difficult sleights have been eliminated, reducing the routine to a single, simple sleight, GLIDE I (see page 126), with everything else working almost automatically.

EFFECT

From an ordinary pack, the magician removes five red cards, the ace through the five of diamonds, and five black cards, the ace through the five of clubs. Placing the ace of diamonds and the ace of clubs face up on the table to serve as "leaders," the magician deals the four remaining red cards face down on the red ace and the four remaining black cards face down on the black ace. The magician openly "transposes" the face-up aces, and at his command, the two deuces invisibly jump to the pile of the opposite color, each next to the ace of its own suit. Next, the face-down piles are transposed, and yet another pair of cards, this time the threes, follows in the same mysterious fashion, magically moving to their matching aces. This continues, transposing the piles in every possible combination. Yet, each time two cards are turned up, they prove to be a matching pair, having magically changed places to appear next to the aces of their own suits!

SECRET AND PREPARATION

From an ordinary pack, remove two groups of five cards—one group of red cards numbering ace through five, and one group of black cards with the same values. (In the illustrations, all clubs and diamonds have been used.) Place the two aces face up on the table and casually arrange the remaining eight cards in a fan from left to right in the following sequence: five of clubs, four of clubs, three of clubs, two of clubs, three of diamonds, four of diamonds, five of diamonds, and two of diamonds. (See illustration for Step 1.) With the cards arranged in this order, you are ready to begin.

METHOD

1 Display the eight cards in a face-up fan, pointing out that the cards are separated into two groups, red and black. Do not call attention to the numerical sequence of the cards. Shown casually, they will not appear to be in any special order.

Glide

2 Close the fan and turn all the cards face down. Hold the packet in your left hand in position for the glide. Now, execute the glide, apparently dealing the bottom red card (really the second from the bottom) onto the table next to the ace of diamonds. Say, "I will deal the red cards here on the table next to their leader, the red ace of diamonds."

Deal from bottom

3 After dealing the second card from the bottom, do not return the bottom, glided card back to its former position. Instead, hold the card in its glided position and deal three more cards, one at a time, apparently from the bottom of the pack, onto the first card.

4 Stop dealing after you have the four cards face down in a pile next to the red ace. Because of the glide, the last card dealt on the red pile is really a black card.

5 Square up the packet in your left hand (secretly bringing the glided card even with the rest of the packet) and deal the remaining cards, one at a time, from the top of the packet onto the table next to the black ace. As you deal these cards, say, "All the black cards go next to their leader, the black ace."

Deal from top

6 As shown in the illustration, unknown to the audience, you now have one red card on top of the black pile and one black card on top of the red pile. If you have executed the glide and the deal correctly, the rest of the trick will work automatically.

7 Exchange the positions of the two "leader" aces. Say, "No matter how I change the aces, the rest of the cards will `Follow the Leader' and turn up in matching pairs."

8 With that, turn over the top cards of both face-down packets. These two cards will be the deuces that match in suit and color their new, leader aces. Place the deuces face up on top of their correct color aces and continue.

9 Next, exchange the positions of the two face-down piles. Say, "Even if I switch the piles, it always works out the same."

10 Turn over the top card of each pile, revealing the threes, as they, too, follow their leaders.

11 Exchange either pile of face-up cards with the face-down pile of cards diagonally across from it, as shown.

12 Turn over the top two cards from the face-down piles to show the matching fours. Place them on their respective leader packets.

13 Exchange the other pile of face-up cards with the single face-down card diagonally across from it, as shown.

14 Turn over the remaining two face-down cards. These will be the fives that also match the color of their leader packets!

COMMENTS AND SUGGESTIONS

After practicing this trick until you can present it smoothly and without hesitation, you can add the following touch: Instead of starting with the cards in a prearranged sequence, begin by openly shuffling the four red cards and place them face down on the table. Shuffle the four black

MARK WILSON'S CYCLOPEDIA OF MAGIC

cards and place them face down on the red cards. Since no one knows the bottom card, you can glide it back and show the faces of the first three red cards, as you deal them to the table. The fourth card (really a black card) you deal on top of the red cards without showing it. Next, deal the first three black cards in the same manner, showing their faces and dealing the last card (really a red card) face down without showing it. Those two final cards are the first to follow the leader. The rest of the cards travel automatically as already described.

The one disadvantage to this method is that when you turn over each set of cards to show that they have changed piles, the cards will not be matching pairs. In the first method, however, if you were to show the faces of the cards before you dealt them, someone might notice that the first red card you deal from "the bottom of the packet" is not the card they saw on the bottom when you showed the fan at the start.

CHAPTER 8
SHORT-CARD TRICKS

The short card is one of the most useful devices ever designed for card magic. It can be used for locating, forcing, or even vanishing a card. It will pass totally unsuspected by even the keenest observers. As its name implies, it is a card that is "shorter" than those in the rest of the pack and can be simply and easily prepared with any deck.

HOW TO MAKE A
SHORT CARD

1 To make a short card, first draw a ruled line 1/32" from both ends of a standard playing card.

2 With a pair of sharp scissors, carefully trim off the ends using the ruled line as a guide.

3 Next, "round" all four of the cut corners so they will match the corner of the regular cards in the pack.

NOTE: For rounding corners, a pair of curved manicure scissors is helpful, but ordinary scissors will also work. Just cut the corners very carefully.

4 This illustration compares a short card with a regular card from the same pack. As you can see, it would be difficult for anyone to detect the short card when it is mixed with the regular cards in the pack.

5 Some magicians carry a pair of small "fold-away" scissors with them, to use with a borrowed deck. All you have to do is to secretly pocket a card from the borrowed deck. Then, work some trick, such as a "mental" effect, in which you leave the room. While outside, you cut the end from the card and round the corners. You can then return the card to the pack later. The pack can still by used by its owner in regular card games, without the players ever realizing that one of the cards has been shortened.

COMMENTS AND SUGGESTIONS

For purposes of practice, you can make your first short card from the joker (or the extra joker, if the pack has one). In this way, you can then either add the joker when you wish to do a short-card trick, or you can later shorten any other regular card after you have learned how to use your practice short card.

SHORT CARD
TO THE TOP

No matter where the short card may be in the pack, you can find it almost instantly by sense of touch alone in a number of ways. (In all of the following illustrations, the short card is indicated by an S.)

METHOD

1 Squeeze the shuffled pack and hold it in dealing position in your left hand. Cut the pack a few times by riffling the inner end of the deck with your right thumb.

2 Stop your riffle about halfway through the pack and transfer the remaining upper half to the bottom of the pack to complete the cut.

3 On your last cut, when you riffle the inner end of the pack upward with your thumb, if you listen and feel with your thumb, you will notice a slight "snap" when you reach the short card. When this happens, stop your riffle. Make your cut, lifting off all of the cards above the short card.

4 Complete the cut by placing this upper packet beneath the lower, as shown. This puts the short card on top of the pack.

SHORT CARD
TO BOTTOM

 In some tricks, it may be necessary to control the short card to the bottom of the pack instead of the top. This can be done in several ways.

FIRST METHOD

Bring the short card to the top of the pack as just described in SHORT CARD TO TOP (see page 144). Then, using the OVERHAND SHUFFLE CONTROL—TOP CARD TO BOTTOM (see page 79), shuffle the top card (the short card) to the bottom of the deck. You have not only placed the short card where you want it, on the bottom of the pack, at the same time you have convinced the spectators that all the cards in the pack are well mixed.

SECOND METHOD

A second method of bringing the short card to the bottom of the pack is simplicity itself. After your riffle which places the short card on top, simply turn the pack face up in your left hand. Proceed with the instructions for SHORT CARD TO TOP, as described. This brings the short card to the top of the face-up pack; if you turn the pack over, the short card will be at the bottom!

THIRD METHOD

Of the three methods described, this is the cleanest and quickest method of getting the short card to the bottom of the deck, although it will require a bit more practice. In the first method, you have to riffle the card to the top and then shuffle it to the bottom. In the second method, the deck must be held face up and the short card may be noticed, particularly if you are doing a number of tricks in which the same short card is used. This third method avoids both of the "shortcomings" (pardon the pun) of the previous two methods.

1 Hold the deck in your left hand as if you were starting to perform an overhand shuffle. Your right hand grasps the deck with the first finger on the face of the pack, your other three fingers cover the outside end, and your thumb is at the end nearest you, as shown.

2 Riffle the deck downward with your right thumb, starting with the top card. When you get to the short card and hear and/or feel the "snap," stop your riffle.

Short Card on bottom

3 Either cut the bottom portion to the top of the pack or overhand shuffle the bottom portion to the top of the pack, leaving the short card on the bottom.

SHORT CARD AS LOCATOR

Once you have controlled the short card to the top of the pack, you can use it effectively as a "locator" for finding other cards as well. This is highly baffling to those spectators who think they have followed a trick up to a certain point, only to find that it goes completely beyond their idea of how it's done. This is a combination, consisting of the short card and the Hindu shuffle, that is always effective, as each helps the other to gain results that neither could gain alone.

EFFECT

A card is freely chosen from the pack. The spectator is allowed to replace it wherever desired. The magician gives the pack a thorough, genuine shuffle. Then the magician causes the card to appear on top of the pack or finds it in some other unaccountable way. In brief, this method can be used as a very baffling card control in many standard tricks.

METHOD

1 A short card is already in the pack and is brought to the bottom by the SHORT CARD TO TOP (see page 144) method. From then on, the trick is handled in conjunction with the Hindu shuffle and standard riffle shuffle (see page 17).

2 With the short card on the bottom of the pack, spread the cards and let a spectator take any one desired. Tell the spectator to show the card to the audience before returning it to the pack.

3 This gives you ample time to square the pack in readiness for the Hindu shuffle. Don't actually begin shuffling until the spectator is about ready to return the card to the pack; otherwise, you may have to go through the shuffle more than once, and this is apt to slow the action.

Short Card

4 Proceed with the regular Hindu shuffle, drawing back the lower portion of the pack with your right hand. Keep the short card on the bottom of the packet in your right hand as you draw off small batches of cards with the fingers of your left hand. Tell the spectator to say, "Stop," at any time during the shuffle.

5 Let the spectator return the chosen card (X) on the portion of the pack resting in your left hand. Drop the right-hand packet on the left-hand cards, as with the HINDU KEY-CARD LOCATION (see page 52). In this case, the short card becomes the key card, as it is placed directly on the selected card (X).

6 Square the pack, cut it, and give it a regular riffle shuffle, riffling the ends of the two halves of the pack together. This can be repeated, and it will not separate the two cards, because the short card (S) will ride along with the longer selected card (X). (Try this shuffle a few times to see how well it works.)

7 Tap the end of the pack on the table to make sure that the short card is down in the pack.

8 Continue shuffling, and after each shuffle, square and tap the pack. Finally, riffle the inner end upward with your right thumb. You will note the click when you come to the short card. Cut the pack at that point. The short card (S) will stay on top of the lower packet.

9 In cutting, place the right-hand packet beneath the left-hand packet. This will automatically bring the short card (S) to the top, with the selected card (X) just beneath it. Thus, you have used your key card to bring a chosen card to the top without looking through the pack; and you have legitimately shuffled the pack as well!

10 Since you now know the position of the selected card in the pack, you may proceed with any "discovery" that you wish.

COMMENTS AND SUGGESTIONS

The SHORT CARD AS LOCATOR can be used in any trick where you must first bring a chosen card to the top of the pack. In Step 10, the selected card (X) is actually second from the top, but you can handle that quite easily. One way is to turn up the top card, asking if it was the card the spectator took. The answer, of course, will be, "No." Push the short card face down into the middle of the pack, saying that you will find the card in a most mysterious way, which you are now prepared to do.

SURPRISE DISCOVERY
SHORT CARD AS LOCATOR

METHOD

1 For an immediate and effective discovery of the chosen card, you can proceed as follows: Take the short card (S) from the pack, removing it face down with your right hand. Tap the short card on top of the pack and tell the spectator that this will cause the selected card to rise to the top of the pack.

2 Since the selected card (X) is already there, the trick is really done. For added effect, you should thumb the top card (X) onto the table, then casually replace the short card (S) on top of the pack, as though it had played no real part in the trick.

MARK WILSON'S CYCLOPEDIA OF MAGIC

3 Have the spectator turn up the card on the table (X). To everyone's surprise, it will be the very card the spectator selected! If you prefer, you can have the spectator name the card and let someone else turn it up. This will dumbfound the spectators, particularly those who did not see the spectator's card when it was removed from the pack by the spectator.

A WEIGHTY PROBLEM
SHORT CARD AS LOCATOR

Here is another good effect using the short card as a locator. When the selected card is second from the top, directly under the short card, cut a dozen or more cards from the bottom of the pack to the top. Then start dealing the cards face up from the top of the pack, one at a time, stating that, "Since our volunteer is concentrating on the particular card selected, that concentration will add an infinitesimal amount of weight to the card. Through long study and practice, I can tell which card our volunteer took just by this small bit of increased weight." Deal the cards one at a time, pretending to weigh each card on the fingertips of your right hand before you turn it face up. You don't actually know the chosen card, but when you turn up the short card, you know that the spectator's card will be next, so you will have no trouble weighing it, and then announcing, "This is the card you selected." Only then do you turn the card over to show the sensitivity of your magical fingers, as you comment that the spectator certainly is a "heavy thinker."

QUICK RIFFLE LOCATION

This form of the SHORT CARD AS LOCATOR (see page 147) is very effective when done briskly and convincingly. It forms a nice variation from the usual "location."

METHOD

Have the short card either on the bottom or on the top to start. While the spectator is looking at the chosen card, cut the short card to the center of the pack. Then, riffle the pack for the card's return, but stop at the short card. The spectator's card is replaced in the pack where you stopped, on top of the short card. You can then locate the card by riffling the short card to the top of the pack. This automatically brings the spectator's card to the bottom where you can reveal it in any manner you wish.

SHORT-CARD FORCE

As stated before, the forcing of a card on an unsuspecting spectator is essential in many tricks. Not only must you have several methods at your disposal, you should also take advantage of any special device that can render forcing more effective. The short card meets both of these qualifications, because you can force it on a volunteer almost automatically, leaving the audience totally unaware that the force took place.

EFFECT

Give a pack of cards a thorough shuffle and hand it to a spectator to do the same. Then, gripping the pack firmly in your left hand, riffle the other end of the pack with your right fingers, telling a volunteer to call, "Stop!"

while the riffle is in progress. Cut the pack at that point and extend the lower portion to the volunteer, telling the volunteer to look at the card. When this is done, the volunteer will be looking at a card that was just forced without anyone even realizing it!

SECRET AND PREPARATION

The only requirements for this force are an ordinary pack of cards and one short card that matches the rest of the cards in the pack.

METHOD

1 To prepare, place the short card somewhere near the center of the pack. (In the illustrations, the short card is indicated by an "S.") Square up the deck and you are ready to begin.

2 Hold the pack face down firmly in your left hand with the outer end of the pack extending halfway out of your hand.

3 Move your right hand over the pack and grip it between the inner end of your thumb and your first and second fingers at the outer end, toward the volunteer.

4 Explain that as you riffle the end of the pack, the volunteer is to call, "Stop" at any time during the riffle. Demonstrate this by riffling the end of the pack a few times.

5 When the volunteer understands what to do, slowly start to riffle the end of the pack. Try to time the riffle so that you nearly reach the short card just when the volunteer is about to call, "Stop."

6 When the call comes, allow the short card and any remaining cards below it to quickly riffle onto the lower packet of cards. This should be done deliberately, as if a few extra cards just happened to riffle after the volunteer said, "Stop."

7 Divide the pack at this point and extend the lower packet toward the volunteer. Instruct the volunteer to remove the top card and look at it. You have now successfully executed the SHORT-CARD FORCE. The forced card can now be shuffled back into the pack and revealed in any manner that you wish.

COMMENTS AND SUGGESTIONS

Since you already know what card the volunteer will take, you can use the force for a prediction effect. Simply write the name of the short card on a slip of paper, fold it, and give it to another volunteer beforehand. Tell that volunteer that it is not to be opened until after the force. You can also reveal the card by pretending to read the volunteer's mind or by producing a duplicate of the forced card from some unexpected place.

Another way is to "discover" the card by bringing it to the top of the deck after the cards have been thoroughly shuffled by the volunteer. Simply riffle the short card to the top of the deck and turn it over, showing it to be the volunteer's card. Or, since you have the chosen card on top, you can reveal it in a variety of ways described in other areas of the course.

CUTTING THE
ACES

People are always impressed by card tricks involving the four aces, particularly when a magician shows the ability to find an ace in a pack that has been shuffled and cut. This ranks with the fabled feats of famous gamblers, yet you can accomplish the same effect with very little skill.

EFFECT

Without looking at the faces of the cards, shuffle the pack and cut it repeatedly. In the course of the shuffling and cutting, you turn up an ace and place it on the table. As you continue to shuffle and cut the cards, you find the three remaining aces in the same baffling fashion.

SECRET AND
PREPARATION

This is a perfect example of a trick demonstrating your ability to control the location of cards in a deck while it is being shuffled. The success of this trick depends on the use of a short card.

To prepare, place the four aces on top of the pack with the short card just above them, making the short card the top card of the pack. Place the pack back in the box, and you're ready to begin. (In the illustrations, the aces have been marked 1, 2, 3, and 4; and the short card is indicated by an S.)

METHOD

1 Remove the pack from the box and start by giving it a regular overhand shuffle. Be sure that the first batch of cards you shuffle from the deck consists of a dozen cards or more to retain your five card setup in its original order. Once this first batch of cards has been shuffled off, continue shuffling the rest of the cards in the pack on it.

2 After the pack has been shuffled, cut about one-third of the pack from the top of the deck to the bottom. You have now fairly shuffled and cut the pack leaving your setup, the four aces and the short card, somewhere near the center of the pack in their original order.

3 Square up the pack in your left hand. With your right thumb at the rear end of the pack, riffle the end of the pack from bottom to top until you feel the short card.

4 Cut all the cards above the short card to the bottom of the pack, bringing your setup to the top.

5 Take the short card from the top of the deck with your right hand. With your left thumb, push the first ace (1) a little to the right so that it protrudes about an inch off the right side of the pack.

MARK WILSON'S CYCLOPEDIA OF MAGIC

6 Using the short card as a lever, raise the right side of the first ace, causing the ace to hinge on its left edge. Continue rotating the ace on edge with the short card until the first ace is turned completely over (face up) on top of the deck.

7 With your left thumb, push the first ace from the top of the pack face up on the table and replace the short card face down on top of the deck. (This places the short card back on top of the three remaining aces.)

8 Square the pack and do the overhand shuffle, making sure that the first batch you pull off contains the short card and the three aces. Cut and riffle as you did before, bringing the short card to the top and use it again to turn up the second ace.

9 After dealing the second ace face up on the table, replace the short card on the pack and repeat the same shuffle, cut, and riffle routine, bringing up the third ace.

10 As the suspense increases, repeat the procedure with the fourth ace, dealing it on the table alongside the other aces, and the effect is complete. You have cut all the aces to the top of the pack!

CHAPTER 9
GIANT-CARD TRICKS

Giant cards, available in most toy and novelty stores, are four times as large as ordinary playing cards. Their added thickness makes them harder to handle. However, they can be dealt face down or face up and shown in a fan in the same way as smaller cards, making them adaptable to some tricks. Giant cards can also be identified by suit and value, so that the discovery of chosen cards in giant sizes can be worked in conjunction with cards from ordinary packs.

Most important is the use of giant cards when performing for large audiences, where smaller card effects would be less effective and those of the "table" type would be lost entirely. "The bigger the audience, the bigger the cards" is the rule in this case, just as with any other magical appliances.

When working before smaller audiences, you can reserve a giant card trick for a "smash" ending to a regular card routine. People are always impressed by a climax that tells them that the show is over, and a giant-card finish will fill that purpose perfectly.

BIGGER-CARD TRICK

A bit of comedy usually adds spice to a mystery, and this trick stands as a good example. By having it ready, you can inject it at a timely moment, depending on the mood of your audience. It can also serve as a prelude to a more ambitious effect.

EFFECT

A card is selected and returned to the pack. The magician shuffles and places the pack in a paper bag. Showing that the right hand is empty, the magician thrusts it into the bag, announcing that the chosen card will be found with a "magic touch." The magician brings out a card, such as the three of clubs, and shows it triumphantly, only to have the spectator who selected the card say it is the wrong card. The magician asks the spectator if the card was a "bigger card." The spectator replies, "Yes." The magician tries and fails again. The card is still not big enough. This third time, the magician is successful and brings out the chosen card, the nine of hearts, which is not only bigger in value, but proves to be four times bigger in size, for it emerges in the form of a giant card!

SECRET AND PREPARATION

A All that is required for this effect is a regular pack of cards, an ordinary paper bag, and one giant card. The giant card should be a seven or higher in value.

B Place the giant card (in the illustration, the nine of hearts) inside the paper bag.

B

C Fold the bag flat and place it aside. Find the nine of hearts in the regular pack and place it in position in the pack, ready for one of the card forces you have learned.

METHOD

1 Begin by forcing the nine of hearts by any method you have learned. After the audience has seen the card, have it returned to the pack and have the pack thoroughly shuffled by a spectator. When the deck is returned to you, thumb through the deck and say something like, "Well, you have mixed so thoroughly that I certainly couldn't find your card just by looking. So, I'll find it without looking at all!" As you run through the deck, pick any two "smaller" value cards and place them on top of the deck.

2 Pick up the folded bag and shake it open. Be careful to keep the giant card inside the bag as you do this. Place the deck into the bag. Do not disturb the cards as you put them in so that you will be able to find the two small cards on top of the deck.

3 Once the cards are in the bag, announce that you will attempt to find the selected card by your magic touch alone. With that, reach into the bag and pretend to grope around, as if searching for the spectator's card.

4 Actually, grasp the top card of the deck (the three of clubs in the illustration). After a few seconds, remove the three and show it to the audience triumphantly, as you remark, "Here is your card!" The answer will be that it is not the right card. Act puzzled for a moment and then ask, "Was yours a bigger card?" Naturally, the spectator will reply, "Yes."

MARK WILSON'S CYCLOPEDIA OF MAGIC

5 Place the three aside and repeat the procedure, removing the second small card from the top of the pack.

6 Now, even more puzzled, reach into the bag as you say, "Even bigger?" Remove the giant nine of hearts and ask, "Well, is this big enough?" The audience will not only be surprised that you have found the correct card, they will be amazed that it has grown to four times its normal size!

COMMENTS AND SUGGESTIONS

Handle the paper bag casually, as though it had nothing really important to do with the trick. If you present the effect in a serious vein, as if you were honestly attempting to find the spectator's card through your sense of touch, it will turn the climax into a real comedy surprise when you produce the much bigger card.

SYMPATHETIC CARDS

Here is a really magical effect performed with any standard pack of cards and a giant card. No special skill is required; proper timing is the important factor. Therefore, the trick should be carefully rehearsed until you are familiar with the entire procedure. After that, the presentation will become almost automatic. You may be amazed by the way it will mystify your audiences, even at the closest range, because the trick depends on a subtle principle that truly deceives the eye.

EFFECT

The magician displays an ordinary deck and asks a spectator to shuffle it until the cards are well mixed. Holding the pack face down in one hand and a giant card face down in the other hand, the magician begins dealing cards, one at a time, onto the back of the giant card. The performer tosses the cards, again, one at a time, into a pile on the table.

This continues, card by card, as the magician tells the spectator to give the order to "Stop!" at any card desired. When the spectator does this, the magician remarks what a magical coincidence it would be if both the giant card and the card from the pack which the spectator selected were identical. The magician then turns both cards face up, revealing them to be exactly the same!

SECRET AND PREPARATION

The only items you need for this effect are a giant card and an ordinary pack of cards from which the duplicate of the giant card is removed in advance. To prepare, place the giant card face down on top of the regular-size duplicate card. Hold both cards in your right hand, with your fingers beneath, keeping the duplicate small card and your thumb on top of the giant card. (In the illustrations, the giant card and its duplicate are the ace of hearts. The duplicate, regular-size ace of hearts is indicated with an "X.")

METHOD

1 Hand the pack to a spectator to shuffle. Pick up the giant card and (secretly) the duplicate regular card in your right hand. Hold the two cards face down above the table, as shown. Be careful not to show the face(s) of the card(s).

NOTE: For a clever method of presetting the giant card and its duplicate which makes the "pickup" of the two cards quite easy, please see Comments and Suggestions at the end of this trick.

2 After the spectator is satisfied that the cards are well mixed, and you have the giant card and its secret duplicate held firmly in your right hand, pick up the shuffled deck in your left hand. Hold the pack in dealing position, as shown in Step 1.

NOTE: You may find it easier to position the shuffled pack in your left hand first, and then pick up the giant card and its duplicate. In that case, just reverse Steps 1 and 2.

3 Tell the audience that you are not going to show the face of the giant card. Explain that you are doing this for a special reason, since the object of the mystery is for the spectator to magically determine the suit and value of the giant card without knowing it.

4 Deal the top card from the pack in your left hand, face down, onto the back of the giant card, as shown. (Just push the card from the top of the pack onto the back of the giant card with your left thumb.)

5 Pause a moment and then tilt the giant card, allowing the smaller card to slide off the giant card and drop, face down, on the table.

6 With your left hand, deal the next (top) card from the pack onto the back of the giant card in exactly the same way. After a brief pause, your right hand tilts the giant card, letting the smaller card slide off, landing on top of the first card already on the table. Continue thumbing off cards, one by one, onto the back of the giant card, then letting them slide onto the pile of cards on the table.

7 Ask the spectator to say, "Stop!" at any time as you deal through the deck.

NOTE: Be careful that none of the regular cards turns face up as you slide them from the giant card onto the pile of cards on the table.

8 Stop when the call comes. If you are in the middle of a deal, or if you are sliding one of the regular cards onto the pile on the table, ask the spectator which card is being selected. This proves that you are giving the spectator every opportunity to make a free choice. Whatever the final decision, see that the selected card is positioned on the back of the giant card as shown in Step 6.

NOTE: Here is the situation at this point: The giant card is held in your right hand. It acts as a tray for the spectator's freely selected card which rests on the back of the giant card. Unknown to the audience, with your right fingers, you are holding the secret duplicate of the giant card underneath the giant card.

9 Spread the remainder of the cards that you are holding in your left hand face up on the table with your left hand. As you spread the left-hand packet face up, remind the audience that the spectator could have chosen any of those cards.

10 Pick up the pile of cards already dealt, and turn them all face up. Casually spread them on the table, as shown. State, "If the spectator had stopped me sooner, one of these would have been chosen."

11 As you make the statement about the already dealt cards in Step 10, your left hand moves its fingers beneath the giant card. With your left fingers, hold the regular duplicate card against the bottom of the giant card. Your left thumb holds the spectator's selected card above. This allows your right hand to release its grip on the giant card and the secret duplicate card.

12 With the first finger of your right hand, point to the selected card lying on top of the giant card. Say, "Out of all the different cards in the pack, this is the card you chose."

NOTE: In transferring the giant card from your right hand to your left hand, you have subtly convinced the audience that all is fair, as both hands are obviously quite empty.

13 The following three steps (13, 14, and 15) are the most important in the routine. Study them carefully. Your right hand now returns to its former position so that the fingers of your right hand also hold the duplicate card under the giant card. Your left fingers release their hold on the duplicate card, but your left thumb continues to press against the spectator's selected card on top of the giant card, as shown in Step 11.

14 You begin three actions that take place simultaneously. First, both hands begin tilting the audience end of the giant card upward. Second, at the same time, your right fingers begin to draw the secret duplicate card to the right, off the face of the giant card. Third, with your left thumb, retain the spectator's selected card on top of the giant card.

15 Continue rotating the giant card so that the face of the giant card is toward the audience. You secretly retain the spectator's selected card on top of the giant card with your left thumb. With your right fingers, draw the hidden duplicate card, face up, fully into view. You have now undetectably switched the selected card for the secret duplicate card. To the spectator, it will appear that you are merely turning the selected card and the giant card face up at the same time. This is a totally convincing move.

NOTE: At this point, the spectator's card is hidden under the face-up giant card. The duplicate regular card, which matches the giant card, is face up in your right hand. To your audience, it will appear as though the duplicate card came off the back of the giant card, instead of from below.

16 Casually place the giant card face up on the face-up pile of cards on the table. The hidden selected card falls unnoticed beneath the giant card and becomes another of the miscellaneous face-up cards in the pile of cards on the table.

17 Drop the duplicate regular card face up on the giant card, proving that the spectator has miraculously picked the exact duplicate of the giant card from the pack!

18 The trick is now over. However, at this point, you can add a subtle touch by picking up the giant card and its duplicate from the table and handing them to the spectator. As you hand them over, turn both cards over, showing the backs to be unprepared. The original selected card lies forgotten in the mass of cards on the table.

IMPORTANT NOTE: This entire, very clever effect hinges on the secret move (Steps 13, 14, 15). This is when you secretly switch the spectator's selected card for the duplicate card under the giant card. Here is the sequence as seen by the spectators.

19 As described in Step 13, your right hand moves to the giant card and your right fingers grasp the secret duplicate card and press it against the bottom of the giant card. Then, both hands start to rotate the giant card, face up, toward the spectator.

20 Your right fingers begin to slide the duplicate card off the face of the giant card. Your left thumb maintains its pressure on the selected card on top of the giant card.

21 The selected card is now hidden by the giant card, as your right hand continues sliding the duplicate card to your right.

22 Your left hand drops the giant card and the selected card face up on the pile of face-up cards already on the table. Your right hand displays the duplicate small card as if it were the freely selected card.

COMMENTS AND SUGGESTIONS

If you wish to perform this effect during your card routine, rather than at the start, you can use the following setup:

A Place the giant card and its regular duplicate on the edge of the table so that they both overlap the edge. You may then present any card effects which do not involve the duplicate card.

B When you are ready to perform the SYMPATHETIC CARDS, reach over with your right hand and pick up the giant card and the secret duplicate card, as shown. You are now all set to present this extremely clever close-up mystery.

If more convenient, you may also place the giant card and the secret duplicate card on a book, ashtray, or some other handy object that is already on the table, rather than placing the two cards on the edge of the table. Just be sure that both the giant card and the secret duplicate can be easily picked up at the same time.

NOTE: In the switch of the duplicate for the spectator's card, timing is the key factor. For best results, you should practice in front of a mirror. The draw-off should begin as the edge of the giant card is level with the eyes of the spectators. That is the time when the ends of all three cards are toward the spectators. At that instant, the spectators lose sight of the backs before they see the faces. When your right hand draws the card to the right, as it comes into view, look at it. The audience will follow your eyes, never suspecting that the card they are watching came from the front and not the back of the giant card. This is another excellent example of misdirection.

APPLAUSE CARD

The APPLAUSE CARD provides a surprise ending for a card routine in which a clever trick is followed by a comedy gag. Audiences appreciate such touches and, even if you have patterned your program along serious lines, it is often good to conclude your show with a magical comedy closing effect such as this one.

EFFECT

A spectator selects a card and returns it to the pack, which is then thoroughly shuffled. The audience is told that the magician will produce the chosen card by using the sense of touch alone. The magician places the pack in an inside coat pocket. After several wrong cards are removed, the magician reaches into the pocket and brings out the spectator's card, but it is now a giant-size card! When the audience applauds, a banner that says, "Thank You," drops from beneath the giant card.

SECRET AND PREPARATION

The props needed for this effect are a deck of cards, a jumbo or giant card, and a piece of light colored paper approximately 2' long and 3" wide. With a heavy marking pen, print the words, "Thank You," or some other appropriate phrase such as "Good-bye" or "Applause" down the length of the paper, allowing enough blank space (about half the length of the large card) at the top of the piece of paper before beginning the lettering. Then, pleat the strip of paper, accordion fashion, as shown.

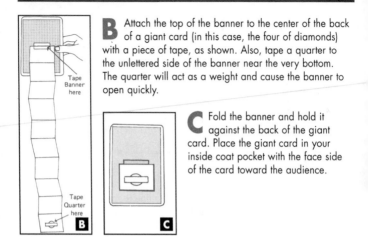

B Attach the top of the banner to the center of the back of a giant card (in this case, the four of diamonds) with a piece of tape, as shown. Also, tape a quarter to the unlettered side of the banner near the very bottom. The quarter will act as a weight and cause the banner to open quickly.

C Fold the banner and hold it against the back of the giant card. Place the giant card in your inside coat pocket with the face side of the card toward the audience.

METHOD

1 From a regular-size pack of cards, force the four of diamonds on the spectator using any of the forcing methods previously explained (see pages 22, 38, and 41). After the card is noted by the spectator and shown to the rest of the audience (but, of course, not to you), let the spectator replace the card anywhere in the deck and have any member of the audience thoroughly shuffle the pack.

2 Be sure that the spectator is satisfied that the card is lost in the shuffled deck and that you could not possibly know where it is. If the spectator wishes, the deck may be shuffled again. When the spectator is completely satisfied, state that your supersensitive fingers will now find the card, while the deck is hidden from view in your pocket. Place the deck in the same inside coat pocket that contains the giant card.

NOTE: When you take the shuffled deck back from the spectator, casually look at the first two cards on the face of the deck to make sure that neither is the four of diamonds. If either one of them is the four, just remove the cards from the bottom of the deck, instead of from the top of the deck, in Step 3.

3 Reach into your pocket and remove one of the regular cards that you know is not the four of diamonds. Display the card triumphantly and ask the spectator if you are correct. The spectator will reply, "No." Say that this is an extremely difficult trick, and you will try again. Remove the second card, and, with a bit less confidence, ask the spectator if this is the one. Again, the response is, "No."

4 You become even more embarrassed. You might say something like, "I hope none of you has any place you were planning to be soon, as we have fifty cards left to go." Then, ask the spectator to help by concentrating on the card. Say, "Just make a big mental picture of it." Reach into your coat pocket and get ready to remove the giant card. Be sure to hold the pleated banner with your thumb so that it does not unfold.

5 Ask the spectator to name the card, and at the same time, remove the giant card.

6 As you show the huge four of diamonds, and the spectator acknowledges that you have at last found the right card, say something like, "Well, I see you really did make a big mental picture!"

7 The unexpected appearance of the giant card will always get a laugh and applause. As the spectators react to this first surprise, draw back your right thumb and allow the banner to unfold to reveal your "Thank You" message. This is sure to get an even greater response from your audience.

COMMENTS AND SUGGESTIONS

This particular card trick can be seen by a large group of a hundred or more people, particularly if you leave the stage and go into the audience to have the card selected. While your back is turned, have the spectator show the card to the rest of the audience. Have the spectator replace the card in the deck and return to the stage. If more convenient, you may also have the spectator join you on the stage for the selection of the card and the follow-up comedy discovery. This is a very clever comedy effect as well as good magic. It makes an excellent closing number for your show.

DOUBLE APPLAUSE CARD

It is possible to tape two or more pleated banners on the same giant card for a repeated comedy effect. For instance, the first banner can say, "Thank You," and the second can read, "Both of You." For a birthday party, try, "Thank You" and then, "Happy Birthday, Mary," etc.

After the first banner falls, simply tear it off and set it aside, still keeping the second banner in place with your thumb. Move your thumb, allowing the second banner to fall for the double-barreled impact. When using more than one banner, tape them directly above one another so you are able to hold them both in position with your thumb and release them one at a time. You can also print the second message on the back of the banner. In this case, just turn the card around after the audience reads the front side of the banner. You'll need to make the banner "double" to hide the quarter you are using as a weight.

GIANT MISTAKE I

Comedy effects add a light touch to a card routine, so it is always wise to have a few ready for the right occasion. Here is one that should bring a big laugh to match the big card you use.

EFFECT

This is similar to the APPLAUSE CARD except that it has a different comedy ending. A volunteer selects a card, remembers it, and returns it to the pack. You announce that you will find the selected card using only your sense of touch. Place the deck in your inside coat pocket. Reach into your pocket and draw out several wrong cards (just as in the APPLAUSE CARD). In desperation, ask the volunteer to form a mental picture of the card. Reach into your pocket and start to draw out a giant seven of spades! Pausing with just the top half of the large card in view, ask, "Was this your card?" The volunteer replies, "No," stating that the card was the five of spades. You respond, "Then this is your card," and draw the seven completely out of your pocket, showing it to be only a part of the jumbo seven of spades, bearing only five spots!

SECRET AND PREPARATION

The only requirements for this effect are a regular pack of cards and one giant card.

To prepare, cut off a portion of the giant card, reducing its value from that shown on the card to the spot value of the card you will later force on the volunteer. (In the illustrations, the seven of spades has been cut to show five spots instead of seven. Other combinations that make an effective change are a six changed to a four, a nine changed to a seven, a ten changed to a five, a three changed to a two, etc.) No matter what combination you choose, remove the card that matches the lowered value of your prepared giant card from the deck. Place this card in the position in the deck for your favorite force. Put the cut giant card in your inside coat pocket, and you're ready.

METHOD

This trick works exactly the same as the APPLAUSE CARD, except that you use the comedy cut card instead of the APPLAUSE CARD.

COMMENTS AND SUGGESTIONS

When you first start to show the top part of the giant card coming from your pocket, hold the cards as shown in Illustration A. Then when you remove the card completely from your coat, cover the index number of the card with the tops of your fingers, as shown in Illustration B, so that only the spots on the face of the card are visible. Then, point to the spots on the card and count them out loud, proving that you have humorously discovered the volunteer's card!

GIANT MISTAKE II

Here is another clever method of presenting this effect.

METHOD

From the regular pack of cards, force the card that matches the prepared jumbo card using your favorite method. Ask the volunteer to show the card to all the members of the audience and then to return the card to the pack. Then have the volunteer thoroughly shuffle the cards so that there is no chance for you to know the location of the card in the pack. Now, instead of placing the deck in your pocket, explain that you will attempt to find the volunteer's card by extrasensory perception, as the volunteer concentrates on it. As you say this, start running through the pack, face up, as if looking for the volunteer's selection. Then, after several wrong guesses, confess that you seem to be having some trouble reading the volunteer's mind. Explain that whenever this happens, you always have "The Magician's Special What-To-Do-If-A-Trick-Goes-Wrong Trick." With that, reach into your inside coat pocket and triumphantly start to remove the giant seven from your coat, but withdraw the card so that only half of the card is visible. Ask, "Is this the card you are concentrating on?" Of course, the answer will be, "No." Ask the spectator what the selected card was and, when the answer comes, remove the jumbo card completely from your coat pocket as you say, "This is your card."

COMMENTS AND SUGGESTIONS

You can also do a clever impromptu version of this comedy effect on a small scale by simply carrying the cut portion of a normal-size card taken from an old pack. In this version, the half card can be brought from your shirt pocket, the outside pocket of your coat, or even your wallet.

GIANT MYSTERY

Here is a mystery that goes well beyond the scope of many card effects; therefore, you may wish to use it as a special feature, possibly the finale of your routine. You could also use it as an encore, on the theory that when people are eager for you to show them one more trick, it should not only be something different, but also something big. This striking effect meets both of those qualifications.

EFFECT

Starting in a conventional manner, ask a volunteer to select a card from the pack, remember it, and return it. After you shuffle the pack thoroughly, announce that you will make the card reveal itself in a very unusual way. For this purpose, use two large pieces of stiff cardboard. Show the boards on both sides, finally placing them together and resting them on the table. Explain that you will make the chosen card appear between the panels. After some byplay, separate the two panels only to find that the card has failed to materialize. Again show the two boards and place them together for another try. This time, you succeed in a big way—for when the boards are separated, a giant card, a duplicate of the very card the volunteer selected, is found between them!

SECRET AND PREPARATION

You will need a regular deck of cards, two pieces of stiff cardboard or artist's construction board, approximately 8" x 10", and a giant card.

A On one of the cardboard pieces, attach a giant card with glue, double-stick tape, or a magic loop. For clarity, the prepared board is a darker color than the unprepared board in the illustrations. (We will call the side of the prepared board that has the giant card attached to it, the "face" of the prepared board.)

B To set up, place the regular board on top of the prepared board with the giant card side of the prepared board face up. The regular board should be angled slightly to the right so that the four corners of the prepared board show beneath it. Place the two boards on your table in this position.

C From a regular pack of cards, remove the card that matches the giant card (in this case the ten of hearts) and place it in the deck in position for your favorite force. Put the deck in its box, and you are ready to begin.

METHOD

1 Remove the pack of cards from the box and force the ten of hearts on a volunteer using any of the methods you have learned. Tell the volunteer to remember the card, return it to the pack, and shuffle the deck until the cards are thoroughly mixed.

2 Place the pack aside and pick up the two cardboard panels in your left hand, thumb on top, fingers beneath, saying, "I have here two pieces of cardboard."

3 As you say this, grasp the two boards in your right hand, fingers on top, thumb beneath, and turn both cards over, toward the audience.

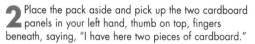

4 The prepared board is now on top, face down.

5 Without hesitation, pull the two boards apart, keeping the top prepared board in your right hand and the regular board in your left hand.

6 As soon as the two boards are apart, place the regular board on top of the prepared board and slide it to the right, completely across the top of the prepared board onto the tips of your right fingers.

7 Your left fingers grip the prepared board, as both hands begin to pull the boards apart, as shown.

8 Continue to pull until the two boards are completely apart.

9 Turn the regular board (in your right hand) over, toward yourself, to show the other side of the board, saying, "As you can see, they are the same on both sides."

10 With that, turn the right hand "regular" board back to its original position. Slide the two boards together, placing the prepared board on top of the regular board.

11 Put the boards on the table.

12 As you execute this series of movements, the audience will believe they have seen all sides of both panels of cardboard and will be convinced that everything is on the level.

13 Pick up the pack of cards and state that you will attempt to make the chosen card appear between the two boards. Toss the pack face down on top of the boards as if to force the selected card to penetrate between them.

14 Place the deck aside and pick up both boards. Separate them so that the regular board is in your left hand and the prepared board is in your right. Obviously, you don't find a card between the boards. Tell your audience that you must have made a minor error, and you will attempt the feat once more.

15 As you make this remark, turn the left-hand panel over toward yourself, showing the other side of the regular board, as if hoping to find the selected card there.

16 Turn the left-hand panel back over to its original position.

17 Now, slide the two boards together. Place the prepared board on top of the regular board.

18 This time, however, instead of immediately placing them on the table, grasp the boards in your right hand, fingers on top and thumb below, and turn both boards over. This places the prepared board on the bottom with the regular board on top, hiding the now face-up ten of hearts.

19 Place both boards on the table and pick up the deck. Explain that you expect the trick to work this time. Toss the cards onto the boards.

20 Place the pack aside and pick up the boards. Separate them to reveal the giant ten of hearts, as you say something like, "When this trick works, it works in a big way!"

COMMENTS AND SUGGESTIONS

The beauty of this effect lies in its certainty. This is another reason why it is a good effect to use as a finish or an encore. It cannot fail if you rehearse it to the point where every move is second nature. The smoother the routine, the more deceptive it becomes. Simply follow the steps as described, and the big climax will take care of itself automatically.

CHAPTER 10
FLOURISHES

Fancy flourishes with cards date far back to the self-styled "Kard Kings" of the vaudeville era. Houdini himself had lithographs showing him performing a myriad of masterful card flourishes.

One thing is certain, card flourishes are sure to impress your audience. Whatever practice you give to such manipulations is time well spent. Your audience will recognize your skill and respect it.

The more you practice them, the more your card work will improve in general, making your entire performance more effective.

ONE-HAND CUT I

To many people, the sign of a real card expert is the ability to "cut" a pack of cards using only one hand. It appears to be a difficult maneuver, but it's really much easier than it looks.

METHOD

All of the illustrations are from the audience's point of view. The deck is held in the left hand.

1 Hold the pack between the tips of your thumb and fingers, as shown. Your first finger and little finger are at the opposite ends of the pack. Your other fingers and thumb are at the sides, as shown. Be sure your thumb and fingers point almost straight up. Hold the deck at the tips of your fingers to form a deep "well" between the deck and the palm of your hand.

2 To begin, bend your thumb just enough to let the lower half of the deck drop into the palm of your cupped hand. (We will refer to this lower half as Packet A.) The upper half (Packet B) remains held between the tips of your thumb and your two middle fingers. Your little finger will help to keep the cards from sliding out of your hand.

3 Bring your first finger below the lower half (Packet A) and push the packet upward, sliding it along the bottom card of the upper half (Packet B).

4 Continue pushing the edge of the lower half (Packet A) all the way up to your thumb, as shown.

5 Gently extend your fingers just enough to allow the edges of the two halves to clear, so that your thumb releases Packet B, which drops on top of your curled first finger.

6 By curling your first finger lower into your hand, Packet B will come down with it. Packet B now becomes the lower half.

7 Slowly begin closing up your hand, bringing both halves together, with Packet A on top of Packet B.

8 Extend your first finger around the end of the pack, squaring the halves into place. You have just done ONE-HAND CUT I.

COMMENTS AND SUGGESTIONS

Although this flourish appears to be quite difficult, once you take the deck in your hand and follow the steps as shown in the pictures, you will find ONE-HAND CUT I quite easy to do. It is best, particularly when first learning, to use the narrow, bridge-size cards rather than the wider poker-size cards. After you have mastered the sleight, you may wish to try it with the larger cards. You can also begin to practice the variations that follow.

ONE-HAND CUT II

This is the first of two variations of ONE-HAND CUT I, enabling you to display your dexterity while also serving as a step toward other card manipulations involving the same basic sleight.

EFFECT

Holding a pack of cards in one hand, the magician starts a simple one-hand cut (see page 182), but pauses during the early stage to turn it into a three-way cut. The magician transposes the bottom, center, and top portions of the pack. This makes an impressive ornamental flourish when the three sections drop neatly into place.

METHOD

NOTE: In all one-hand cuts, you may hold the deck in either your right or your left hand, whichever is easier for you. All of the illustrations are from the spectator's view with the deck held in the left hand.

1 Begin by holding the pack in the same position as you did for ONE-HAND CUT I. Your first finger and little finger are at opposite ends of the pack; your two middle fingers and thumb are at the sides. Be sure that your fingers and thumb point up, or slightly to the right, if this is easier for you. Be certain, as before, that you have formed a deep well between the deck and the palm of your hand.

MARK WILSON'S CYCLOPEDIA OF MAGIC

2 Unlike ONE-HAND CUT I, where the pack is cut into two equal sections, in this modified version, begin by bending your thumb just enough to let the lower third (Packet A) of the deck drop into your cupped hand. Your little finger will help to keep the cards from sliding out of your hand.

3 Bring your first finger below Packet A and begin pushing its edge upward toward your thumb, as shown.

4 Continue pushing Packet A all the way up to your left thumb. The top edge of Packet A will contact your thumb near the bend of the first joint of the thumb.

5 Your hand now holds the bulk of the deck between the tip of the thumb and your fingers, while the bottom third of the deck (Packet A) is held between the bend of your thumb and the palm of your hand, as shown in Step 4.

6 With the cards held firmly in this position, relax the tip of your left thumb, allowing the middle third of the deck (Packet B) to drop from the bulk of the pack into your cupped hand.

7 Once again, bring your first finger below Packet B and push it upward toward your thumb until it is all the way up against the bottom of Packet A. The remaining third of the deck, Packet C, is still being held by the tips of your thumb and fingers, as shown.

8 Release your thumb tip from Packet C and allow its top to clear the top edge of Packets A and B. You can help the packets to clear by pushing the bottom of Packet B with your first finger. Packet C will come down with it into your palm. Packet C now becomes the lower third of the packet.

9 Slowly begin closing up your hand, bringing all three sections together to complete the cut.

10 Finally, extend your first finger around the end of the pack and square the deck as the sections settle into place. You have just executed ONE-HAND CUT II.

COMMENTS AND SUGGESTIONS

Practice this flourish with a narrow, bridge-size pack. It is much easier to handle than the wider poker-size deck. Later, you can switch to the wider size, if your fingers are long enough to handle it easily. The dropping of the center section, Packet B, is the vital point, because your thumb must hold both Packets A and C in place until your first finger releases Packet B. If Packet A should accidentally drop during that maneuver, that's OK, just let it fall on top of Packet B and complete what would then be a slightly different cut than you had originally planned.

ONE-HAND CUT III

This is another variation of ONE-HAND CUT I (see page 182) that can be used interchangeably with the one already described. The two cuts can also be worked in combination, starting with one, and ending with the other, all in the same sequence.

EFFECT

In this triple cut, the magician divides the lower section into two packets and lets the upper third drop in between. This can be repeated several times, either in slow motion, or at a rapid speed once the knack is acquired. Either way, it increases the audience's admiration of the magician's skill.

METHOD

1 In the usual one-hand cut style, hold the pack between the tips of the thumb and fingers of either hand. The first finger and little finger are at opposite ends of the pack, the other fingers and thumb are at the sides. Be sure the fingers point straight up (or nearly straight up, if this is easier for you). Just be sure to form a deep well between the deck and the palm of your hand.

2 To begin, bend the thumb just enough to let the lower 2/3 of the pack drop into the cupped hand. The little finger will help to keep the cards from sliding out of your hand.

3 Bring your first finger below the bulk of the pack and push its edge upward, sliding it along the bottom of the upper third of the pack. Continue pushing the lower section all the way up to the ball of the thumb, as shown.

4 Your left thumb retains hold of half of the bulk of the pack, as you begin to open your first finger, allowing the other half to drop back into your hand.

5 As the packet falls into your hand, relax the grip of the tip of your thumb on the top third of the pack and allow this packet to fall into the hand between the two packets already formed.

6 Slowly begin closing up your hand, bringing all three packets together to complete the cut. Finally, extend your first finger around the end of the pack and square the pack as the three packets settle into place. You have just executed ONE-HAND CUT III.

COMMENTS AND SUGGESTIONS

Along with serving as an ornamental flourish, this variation of ONE-HAND CUT I fulfills a useful purpose. With it, you can "bury" the top card of the pack somewhere in the middle of the deck. As you call attention to that fact, the audience doesn't realize that the bottom card remains the same and can, therefore, be used as a key card in a trick that follows.

MARK WILSON'S CYCLOPEDIA OF MAGIC

RIBBON SPREAD

EFFECT

In performing card tricks, it is often necessary to spread the entire pack of cards across the table so that all of their backs or faces are visible to the spectators. The following describes the method for executing a RIBBON SPREAD which looks very nice and demonstrates your ability to handle cards skillfully.

METHOD

NOTE: The RIBBON SPREAD is difficult to do on a slick or hard surface. However, it is quite easy on a soft, textured surface such as a felt-top table, a rug, a heavy table cloth, or a magician's "close-up mat."

1 Place the deck on the table, face down, slightly bevelled or slanted at the side of the deck, as shown.

2 Lay all four fingers of your right hand across the top of the pack, with the tips of the fingers extending over the bevelled edge.

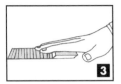

3 With a slight downward pressure of the hand, move your arm and hand to the right. The cards will begin to spread apart evenly from the bottom of the pack as you slide the bulk of the pack along the table.

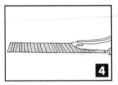

4 Continue this sliding motion, releasing cards from the bottom of the pack until all of the cards are evenly spread in a ribbon pattern along the table.

COMMENTS AND SUGGESTIONS

In practicing the ribbon spread, be sure you have a soft surface and remember that the sliding motion of the hand must be smooth and unbroken in order to achieve even spacing between the individual cards. The motion should not be done too slowly. A moderately fast movement produces the best results. As always, practice is the key to success.

RIBBON-SPREAD TURNOVER

This is an ideal flourish to use when doing card tricks at a table. Though easily learned, it gives the impression that you are displaying great skill. Always take advantage of such opportunities, because they create a lasting impression on the audience regarding your work. It's all part of the game called magic.

EFFECT

The magician takes an ordinary pack of cards and spreads them in an even row face down along the table. Then, by tilting up one end of the spread, the magician causes the entire row of cards to turn face up!

METHOD

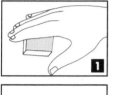

1 Set the pack face down on the table in preparation for the RIBBON SPREAD (see page 189).

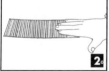

2 Ribbon-spread the pack from left to right, as described earlier. The cards in the spread must be evenly spaced. Any gaps or breaks in the spread will disrupt the turnover.

3 The completed spread should look like this.

4 With your left fingers, raise the outer edge of the card on the left end of the spread, tilting it up on its edge, as shown.

5 Rotate the card on its edge until it turns over (face up), causing all of the cards above it to turn over in sequence.

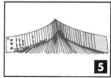

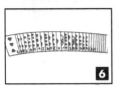

6 The turnover will progress throughout the spread until all of the cards are face up, as shown.

COMMENTS AND SUGGESTIONS

This is the basic turnover, a rather easy and most impressive flourish. To add even more to your display of skill, you can incorporate the two following variations.

REVERSE RIBBON-SPREAD TURNOVER

After completing the above, you may immediately reverse the procedure.

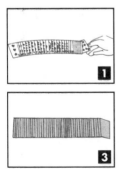

1 With your right hand, lift the card at the far right end of the now face-up spread. Using this card as the "pusher" card, pivot it on its edge.

2 This causes the cards to repeat the turnover.

3 This time, they return to their original face-down position.

COMMENTS AND SUGGESTIONS

By placing your left hand at the left end of the spread and your right hand at the right end of the spread, you can "flip-flop" the cards back and forth as they turn over in rotation—first, face up, then face down—making not only a remarkable display of skill, but also a very pretty picture.

TURNOVER CONTROL

This is another even more intriguing use of the turnover. It is particularly effective when used between effects in your card routine. This is also a most spectacular way of showing that the deck is ordinary and composed of "all different" cards.

METHOD

1 First, remove any card from the deck and place it on the table. Perform Steps 1 through 5 in the RIBBON-SPREAD TURNOVER (see page 190). When the cards have turned to approximately the middle of the spread, pick up the card you removed and hold it, as shown, in your right hand. This card will be used to control the sequence of the turnover.

2 You will find that, as you carefully touch the edge of the single card in your right hand to the "peak" of the turnover, you can very easily control the sequence and direction of the turnover. For instance, you can now reverse the turnover by moving the single card back to the left, as shown. As you move the card to the left, keep the edge of the card touching the new, constantly changing peak. This can be done back and forth as often as you wish, as long as the cards remain evenly spread on the table.

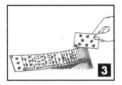

3 The single card is then used to control the turnover all the way over to the right end of the spread, where the cards will fall face up as they did at the conclusion of the regular RIBBON-SPREAD TURNOVER.

PRESSURE FAN

Giving your performance a professional look should be a primary aim when taking up card magic. Shuffles and cuts should all be done smoothly and neatly, as a prelude to fancier moves. This applies specifically to the PRESSURE FAN.

EFFECT

Holding the squared pack in one hand, the magician deftly spreads it in a circular fashion across the fingers of the other hand, finally displaying it in a broad fan with the index corners of the cards showing evenly throughout its colorful span.

METHOD

1 Hold the pack by the ends between the tips of the right thumb and fingers. Your thumb is at the center of the lower end and your first, second, and third fingers are across the upper end. Your little finger rests lightly on the side of the deck.

2 With the cards held firmly in the right hand, place the pack against the fingers of the left hand in the position shown. The ball of the left thumb rests at the middle of the lower end of the pack. (The right hand is not shown in the illustration in order to show more clearly the exact position in which the pack is held against the left hand by the right hand.)

3 To begin the fan, squeeze the fingers of your right hand downward, bending the cards over the left forefinger.

4 This is the audience's view as you begin the fan.

5 In one continuous motion, allow the cards to start "springing" from the right fingertips, as the right hand begins to rotate the pack to the right. The left thumb acts as a pivot point, holding the lower left corner of the pack.

6 Continue the circular motion of the right hand around the tips of the left fingers and down the side of the left hand.

7 Continue to "spring release" cards in succession until the fan is complete.

(This action is shown from the audience's point of view.)

COMMENTS AND SUGGESTIONS

The amount of pressure necessary to make the fan depends on the pack you are using. A brand new, high-quality pack can be fanned with a light touch, but it will need more bending pressure from the right thumb and fingers. With a new, "clean" deck, the cards are smooth enough to spread evenly and stiff enough to resist pressure. The more a pack is shuffled and used, the more flexible it becomes. The pressure must be decreased proportionately. As the deck becomes soiled, it becomes more and more difficult to get the cards evenly spaced.

CLOSING THE FAN—TWO-HAND METHOD

METHOD

All of the illustrations are from the spectators' viewpoint.

1 To close the fan, curl the tips of your right fingers around the extreme left edge of the fan, as shown.

2 Then, in one continuous motion, sweep your right hand in an arc around the left fingers, causing the cards to start to collect against the fingers of your right hand.

3 Continue to sweep the fan closed until all the cards have gathered together into a single packet, thus completing the procedure.

CLOSING THE FAN— ONE-HAND METHOD

The simple action of closing the PRESSURE FAN can be as impressive as the fan itself, particularly when it is executed without the aid of the other hand!

METHOD

1 Begin by forming a PRESSURE FAN, as described previously. Four fingers should be flat against the face of the pack with the thumb pressing inward at the pivot point on the back of the fan.

2 To close the fan, shift your left first finger so that its fingertip rests on the face of the first card as close to the outer edge of the fan as possible.

3 With a slight amount of pressure from your left first finger on the face card of the deck, begin to push your finger in a circular motion, upward and to the right, as you slowly begin to close the fan.

4 Continue pushing the fan closed. Open the remaining fingers of the left hand when necessary, allowing the first finger to sweep the cards downward as they collect in succession against the heel of the hand, until the fan is closed.

ONE-HAND FAN

Though basically a card flourish, this is also a useful move in connection with various tricks. That makes two good reasons why you should practice it.

EFFECT

Holding a pack of cards face front between the thumb and fingers of the right hand, the magician, with one deft move, instantly spreads the pack in a broad fan, showing the index corners of the cards in a colorful fashion. Closing the fan and turning the pack over, the magician fans them again, showing the backs spread evenly, allowing a spectator to select a card. This is an excellent opening move for many card effects.

METHOD

1 Hold the pack in your right hand with your thumb on the face of the pack and your fingers flat against the back. Position your thumb at the lower right-hand corner of the pack, as shown.

2 Here is a view of the pack from the other side. Notice that your fingers only cover half the length of the pack.

3 In one smooth, continuous motion, start to slide your thumb upward. At the same time, curl your fingers inward and downward, as the pack begins to spread out in the form of a fan.

4 Continue sliding your thumb upward as the fingers continue pushing the cards in a sort of "smearing" motion down the heel of the hand, until they curl into the palm, almost forming a fist with the cards held tightly between. When your thumb and fingers have reached this position, the fan should be fully formed, as shown.

5 Your fingers are responsible for forming the lower half of the fan, and the thumb is responsible for forming the upper half.

6 Here is a view of the completed fan from the other side. Notice the right fingers have curled into the palm of the hand to form a fist.

COMMENTS AND SUGGESTIONS

In tricks where you are using half a pack or less, fanning is just as effective as with a full pack. All the cards in the half packet can be spread out evenly and more of each card will show. Even when doing a trick with only a few cards, using a ONE-HAND FAN to show their faces has a striking effect and adds to your style as a performer. You may also wish to learn the fan with both hands. Then, by splitting the deck and holding half in each hand, the two fans will form a truly spectacular display.

Do not be disappointed if you cannot master the ONE-HAND FAN immediately. Careful practice will teach you exactly how much pressure to exert with the thumb and fingers in order for the cards to distribute properly from the top and bottom of the pack, forming an evenly spaced fan.

SPRINGING THE CARDS

This fancy flourish is the basis for many other flourishes with a pack of cards. It is one that should be practiced first on a limited scale (springing the cards only a short distance) with a pack that can be handled easily and comfortably. Then you can gradually increase the scope of this manipulation.

EFFECT

You hold a pack of cards lengthwise between your thumb and fingers. By applying steady pressure on the pack, you cause all the cards in the pack to spring in succession from one hand to the other—in midair! This has a very impressive effect on the spectators, as the cards form a colorful cascade that can cover a surprising distance.

METHOD

1 Hold the pack lengthwise in your right hand, with your thumb at the lower end and your first, second, and third fingers at the upper end. The pack should be held close to the tips of the fingers, as shown.

2 Your left hand is held palm up with the fingers spread wide, pointing upward. This forms a sort of trap to catch the cards as they cascade from the right hand into the left.

3 With the pack held firmly in your right hand, squeeze your thumb and fingers together, bending the cards inward toward the palm of your hand, and move the right hand about 3" above the cupped left hand.

4 Continue to squeeze the pack inward as you begin to release the cards from the tips of your right fingers, sending them springing, one by one, from the right hand into the left hand.

NOTE: The left hand should be positioned so that, as the cards arrive in the hand, the outer ends of the cards hit the left first fingers, preventing them from shooting out of the hand onto the floor.

5 As the cards start to spring from one hand to the other, gradually begin drawing your right hand farther away, a few inches at first, then more and more. No matter what distance you will eventually achieve, always begin with your hands close together. Then draw the right hand away, as the cards spring into your left hand.

6 When the bulk of the pack has arrived in your left hand, and only a few cards remain in the right, move your right hand toward your left hand, gathering all the cards in between to conclude the flourish.

COMMENTS AND SUGGESTIONS

In practicing the spring, place your left hand just below your right hand and spring the pack for a distance of only a few inches. Your purpose is to gain the knack of springing the cards smoothly and evenly without losing any of them. Once you learn to release the cards in an even stream, with practice you can then spread your hands a foot or so apart. When you first practice, it is best to use soft, flexible cards; an old, used deck works well.

It is also a good idea to practice over a bed, as a certain amount of failure is inevitable at first. One final suggestion: If you swing your body from left to right during the spring, the distance effect between your hands is further exaggerated, creating the illusion that the cards cover a distance of 18" to 2'.

One of the most spectacular of card flourishes, this also appears to be one of the most difficult. Proper technique, attention to detail, and a reasonable amount of practice combine to produce impressive results in this special branch of magic that blends juggling with wizardry.

EFFECT

You spread a pack of cards lengthwise along your left arm from the base of your fingers to your elbow. With the cards neatly set in place, you give your arm an upward toss and at the same time make a long, inward sweep with your right hand, scooping up the entire pack of cards in midair without dropping a single card.

METHOD

1 Hold the pack in your right hand, with your thumb at one end and your fingers at the other. Extend your left arm, palm up, and hold the pack slightly above the fingers of your left hand. Bend the entire pack inward toward the right palm (the same type of bending by the right hand as used in SPRINGING THE CARDS).

2 Slowly begin to release the cards from the tips of the right fingers onto the left hand. At the same time, move your right hand down the length of your left arm. The cards should begin forming an even spread along your left arm.

3 Continue releasing the cards from your fingertips along the left arm until all the cards have been spread. With practice, you can attain a spread that extends from the tips of your left fingers to your elbow.

NOTE: After the cards are spread along the arm, it is necessary to keep the arm very still in order to prevent the cards from falling.

4 With the cards neatly set in place, position your cupped right hand near your left fingertips, at the beginning of the spread, in readiness to catch the cards.

5 With an upward lifting and tossing motion of your left arm, gently throw the entire spread of cards into the air, as shown.

6 Without hesitation, and in one continuous movement, swing your entire body to the left and, with a long sweeping motion of the right hand, begin gathering or scooping up the cards in midair, from one end of the spread to the other.

7 With practice you should be able to catch the entire pack without any cards falling to the floor. At first, practice the ARM-SPREAD CATCH using half of a pack and a shorter arm spread. Gradually add more cards until you can perform the flourish with a full pack that is spread from the tips of the fingers to the elbow.

COMMENTS AND SUGGESTIONS

In early trials, as you practice springing the cards along the arm, the spread may prove too irregular for an effective catch. In that case, simply lower your left arm rapidly and let the pack slide down into your cupped left hand. This is a neat manipulation in itself, so you can use it as a preliminary warm-up before the catch.

WATERFALL

EFFECT

You grasp the entire pack in your right hand with your left hand cupped beneath it. Skillfully you begin to release the cards in rapid succession, causing them to cascade downward, one at a time, like a waterfall into your waiting left hand. The flourish reaches its conclusion after the entire pack has made its impressive journey through the air into your left hand.

METHOD

1 Grasp and hold the deck lengthwise in your right hand with your thumb at one end of the pack and your four fingers at the other end. Your right fingers and thumb should be straight with only the edges of the top card touching your right hand.

2 Keeping your fingers and thumb straight, slowly squeeze them together so that the cards bend inward toward your right palm. This action is very similar to SPRINGING THE CARDS, except here the object is to get a small amount of space between each and every card, as you hold the pack.

3 The special grip described here allows the ends of the cards to spread along the length of your thumb and fingers. Performed correctly, the cards should fill up all the open space between your thumb and fingers. Careful practice will teach you just how to bend the pack to secure this small gap between the individual cards.

4 With the cards held in this manner, you are ready to begin the WATERFALL. Position your cupped left hand directly below your right hand, in readiness to receive the cards as they fall. The illustration shows the proper position of both hands at the beginning of the flourish. This and all of the following steps are shown from the spectators' point of view.

5 Slowly begin to spread open your right thumb and fingers, releasing the cards in succession from the face of the pack. This action causes the cards to fall into the left hand in an even flow.

6 At the same time, move your left hand downward as the cards continue to fall from your right hand. If you release the cards in an even flow, they will resemble a waterfall as they cascade from one hand to the other.

MARK WILSON'S CYCLOPEDIA OF MAGIC

7 To achieve maximum distance between your hands, move your right hand up a few inches at the same time you move your left hand down. With practice, you can attain a "waterfall" of 8" to 12", or even longer.

8 When nearly all the cards have been released from your right hand, quickly move your hands back together, squaring up the cards, to complete the flourish. You are now prepared to repeat the WATERFALL as many times as you wish. The spectators will be more than convinced that you possess great skill as a card manipulator.

COMMENTS AND SUGGESTIONS

The real secret of the WATERFALL is your initial grip on the pack, as shown in Steps 1 and 2. The cards must be spread evenly along your thumb and fingers. At the start, practice the flourish with your hands very close together. Then as you begin to acquire the knack necessary to release the cards in an even stream, move your hands farther apart. When selecting cards to use for this flourish, it is a good idea to experiment with different decks. Choose cards that bend easily enough for you to space them evenly in your hand. If you practice this flourish with a deck that suits you well, you will be pleased at the progress you will make in achieving a perfect waterfall effect.

THROWING A CARD

Many famous magicians have intrigued spectators throughout the world with their ability to sail cards to the highest balconies of the largest theaters. How far you can go toward achieving a similar result will depend on how much practice you are willing to devote to this very impressive flourish.

EFFECT

Upon concluding your card routine, you offer several cards for examination by sailing them across the room to different spectators. This is done in a smooth, graceful manner, sending the cards skimming into the air while the spectators watch in amazement as the cards whiz by.

METHOD

1 Holding the card in the proper throwing position is essential in attaining effective results. There are two correct positions, and you should try them both to see which works best for you. (The other holding position will be described in the next effect, the BOOMERANG CARD.)

2 To place the card in the first position, clip the very end of the card between the first and second fingers of your right hand, as shown. Do not allow the card to droop. Hold it firmly so that it is level with the fingers at all times.

3 Here is the card held in proper throwing position, as seen from the spectators' point of view.

4 Start by bending all four fingers inward, until the lower right edge of the card touches the heel of your hand. (This is shown from above.)

5 In the same movement, bend your wrist inward, toward yourself, as far as it will go.

6 To make the actual throw, snap your wrist open, as hard as you can. At the same time, straighten out your fingers and release the card to send it spinning out of your hand.

COMMENTS AND SUGGESTIONS

Keeping the card level with your fingers and maintaining a consistent wrist action are essential factors in developing the throw, which can cover a long range once the knack is acquired. When aiming for higher levels, the hand must be kept on target, and the force of throw increased. Along with accuracy, the practiced magician can propel the cards an impressive distance by combining a throwing motion of the arm with the action of the wrist, as a means of gaining still greater distance.

BOOMERANG CARD

After demonstrating your skill by throwing playing cards great distances to the spectators, you begin throwing cards toward the ceiling—only to have them sail out into the air and return to your hand, much like a boomerang.

METHOD

1 In order to achieve the boomerang effect, the card should be held either in the position described in THROWING A CARD or in this new position as follows: Hold the card at one end between the tips of the right thumb and fingers, as shown. Grip the card near the outer right corner between your right thumb and second finger. Your first finger rests against the left corner of the card, to serve as a pivot point to start the spinning action of the card as it leaves the hand.

2 With the card held in this position, it can be sent spinning out of the hand using the same arm and wrist action as described in THROWING A CARD.

3 To achieve the boomerang effect, hold the card in either throwing position. Instead of throwing the card out of the hand on a level plane, throw it at an upward angle of 45° or more, with just enough force to send it only a few yards away from you. In throwing the card, concentrate on obtaining as much spin as possible. This is done by snapping your hand back toward your body just before you release the card. Your first finger on the outer right corner acts as the pivot point, to aid in starting the card in its spin as it leaves your right hand.

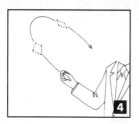

4 Once the card has reached its maximum distance in the air and begins its downward fall, it will return to you instead of falling straight down to the floor. This is due to the 45° angle of the card in the air. With practice, you will be able to cause the card to return directly to your hand, where you can catch it between your thumb and fingers.

COMMENTS AND SUGGESTIONS

Practice the BOOMERANG CARD until it can be done with neatness and precision. Performed properly, it creates an impression of great skill and dexterity. A certain amount of failure is inevitable at first; but once you develop the knack of throwing a card, this effect should come quickly and easily.

CHAPTER 11
GENIE CARDS

In contrast to tricks with regulation playing cards, Genie tricks require a special type of card.

While several tricks may be performed with the Genie cards, all depend upon the same simple but deceptive move. Although this move is excellent, you should not perform more than one Genie trick at any performance. It is better to keep a few Genie tricks in reserve, so that for your next show you can switch to another. This keeps people wondering just what to expect, which is an important factor in magic.

If you wish, you can use the Genie cards for an introductory trick, or as an interlude during a program of effects with playing cards, and you will always be on the safe side.

The Genie cards and their routines were specially devised for use with this magic course, which means that they will be entirely new to many people who see them. This gives you a real advantage over the spectators from the start—so make the most of it!

GENIE CARDS

PREPARATION

To perform the tricks in this section, you will need to create your own set of Genie cards by copying or tracing these patterns onto business-card stock and cutting the cards out. You will need fifty full-size Genie cards and twenty half-cards.

GENIE OF THE LAMP

In this very basic form of the Genie, the only props needed are the cards themselves. The effect is that a Genie mysteriously appears, thanks to the magic of Aladdin's lamp.

EFFECT

A You show a stack of cards with a rubber band around it. The top card shows a magic lamp giving off a cloud of smoke, but no Genie.

B Remarking that this represents Aladdin's wonderful lamp, you invite a spectator to write their initials in the lamp. You then remove the card and state that whenever Aladdin rubbed the lamp, the Genie appeared.

C Holding the card face down in one hand, you rub the lamp with the fingers of your other hand.

D After a few rubs you turn the card over, showing that the Genie has magically appeared in the cloud of smoke and the spectator's initials are still in the lamp!

SECRET AND PREPARATION

This basic trick and all the other tricks with the Genie cards depend on a simple, natural movement that secretly switches one card for another. We call this the MASTER MOVE. Here is the explanation of the trick and how the MASTER MOVE makes this a real mystery.

E A special half-card showing only an empty cloud is used, shown here next to the packet of regular full-size cards. Approximately ten full-size cards should be used to make up the packet.

F Before the trick, one half-card is placed on the packet so that it covers the cloud portion of the top card with the Genie in it.

G You put the rubber band around the cards so that the half-card is held firmly in place, and its bottom edge is completely hidden by the rubber band. Once the half-card is in position and held there by the rubber band, the top card of the packet looks like a full-size card showing a lamp, a cloud, and nothing else. Use only one half-card when you set up the packet for the trick. Save the others for spares.

1 You show the packet to a spectator, and ask the spectator to write their initials in the lamp of the top card.

2 Now for the MASTER MOVE. Holding the packet in your left hand, as shown, you lift up the lamp end of the initialed card with your right finger.

3 Your left hand starts to turn the packet over as you begin to pull out the Genie card with your right fingers.

4 Here is the action as seen from below. The spectators see the back of the packet instead of the face. Everyone is sure you are drawing out the initialed card.

5 As the card comes clear, both the packet and the card have been turned all the way over so that no one can see their faces. Although you have actually drawn out the initialed card, the secret half-card remains on the packet. Place the packet face down somewhere out of reach, or drop it in your pocket, so that no one will learn about the half-card.

6 Hold the initialed card face down in your left hand. Place your right fingers under the card and rub the lamp a few times.

7 When you turn the card over, the Genie is found to have magically appeared in the cloud of smoke!

COMMENTS AND SUGGESTIONS

Using the MASTER MOVE, you have secretly switched what the spectators thought was the original Genie card for another; yet the change seems impossible because the person who wrote the initials on the card will find that they are still there. This is something of a miracle in its own right; and when used in association with other effects, it becomes even more sensational. These added details will be covered in the Genie tricks that follow, all using the MASTER MOVE just described.

GENIE'S NUMBER

In this trick, the Genie does magical mathematics and predicts a chosen number. The Genie does it very well, as you will see.

SECRET AND PREPARATION

A Before the trick, write the number 1089 in the cloud at the top of the Genie card.

B Cover it with the empty half-card and place a rubber band around the packet.

1 Have a spectator write their initials in the lamp, as you did in GENIE OF THE LAMP.

2 Remove the initialed card using the MASTER MOVE (actually removing the card with 1089 written on it) and place it face down on the table.

3 Lay a pad and pencil beside it.

4 Tell the spectator, "I want you to write a number that uses three different figures, any number between 100 and 1,000, without letting me see it." Let's say that the spectator writes 318.

5 You continue, "Reverse that number and subtract the smaller number from the larger."

NOTE: Here you tell the spectator that if the answer is less than 100 to leave a zero in front of it so the number will still have three figures.

6 As soon as the spectator has done the subtraction, you state, "Reverse your answer and write it just below." When the spectator does this, say, "I want you to add those two numbers so you will get a grand total."

7 Tell the spectator to circle the grand total and lay the pad down beside the Genie card.

8 Explain that you will call on your invisible Genie to check the spectator's arithmetic. Pick up the Genie card and place it face down on top of the pad. Pretend to catch the Genie out of the air and slip the Genie between the pad and Genie card.

9 After a few moments, ask the spectator to turn over the card. To the amazement of the spectator, the Genie has appeared showing the same number as the spectator's slip, 1089.

COMMENTS AND SUGGESTIONS

Whatever the original three-figure number, the grand total will always be 1089, unless the original figures are all alike, as 333 or 555. That is why you tell the spectator to write a number with three different figures. When subtracted, they will always produce numbers that, when reversed and added, will total 1089. In some cases, such as 463 minus 364, the subtraction yields 99. That is why you tell the spectator to put a zero in front of anything under 100, so if the spectator makes it 099 and reverses it to form 990, the two numbers will add up to the usual 1089. If the spectator should get some other total, simply check the figures and the spectator will find that the Genie was right all along!

GENIE PREDICTS

 In this Genie trick, you need the pack of Genie cards and an ordinary pack of playing cards, which may be borrowed.

EFFECT

You show the Genie packet with the rubber band around it. The top card shows a magic lamp giving off a cloud of smoke, but no Genie. A spectator writes their initials in the lamp of the top card of the Genie packet. This card is then removed from the packet and placed face down on the table. A card is chosen by the spectator from the pack and placed on the table beside the Genie card. You pick up the Genie card. Keeping the Genie card face down, you reach beneath and, with your finger, rub the lamp a few times. When the card is turned over, both the Genie and the words, "three of clubs," have mysteriously appeared in the cloud. When the chosen card is turned over, it is the three of clubs, proving the Genie's prediction to be correct!

SECRET AND PREPARATION

Before the performance, write the name of any card, say the three of clubs, in the cloud section of the top card of the Genie packet. Cover this top card with the half-card and place the rubber band around the packet. Go through the pack of playing cards, find the three of clubs, and move it to the position in the pack ready for your favorite force. (In the illustrations, the three of clubs has been marked with an X to make it easy to follow.) Place the pack in its box or simply have it lying handy on the table, and you're ready to begin.

METHOD

1 Lay the Genie packet face up on the table and place the pack of playing cards face down beside it.

2 Pick up the Genie packet and point out the empty cloud on the top card, stating, "The Genie, who usually lives in the lamp, apparently isn't home today." Ask a spectator to write their initials in the lamp.

3 Remove the initialed card from the packet (actually the prediction card) using the MASTER MOVE, and place it face down on the table.

4 Put away the rest of the Genie packet and pick up the pack of playing cards. State that you wish to have one card selected at random from the pack. With that, use the ROLLOVER FORCE to force the three of clubs on the spectator. Have the spectator place the chosen card face down on the table next to the Genie card.

5 Tell the spectator to turn over the Genie card and see if the Genie has anything to say. The spectator will see that the Genie has appeared and has written "three of clubs" in the cloud.

6 When the spectator turns over the playing card, the Genie's prediction proves correct!

COMMENTS AND SUGGESTIONS

In this Genie routine, after you have drawn out the Genie card and placed it on the table, you can let the spectators see the packet of Genie cards face up. Since the half-card is still in place and has no writing in the cloud, it will be mistaken for the second Genie card. Just make sure that the rubber band is still in the proper position, hiding the edge of the half-card. If the half-card has slipped from place, put the packet away without turning it face up. A quick glance will tell you what to do.

Also, if you use a pencil to write the Genie's prediction, you can later erase it and use the Genie card over again.

SANDWICHED GENIE

EFFECT

This is similar to GENIE PREDICTS. In this trick, after the spectator has initialed the lamp, the spectator places the Genie card in the center of a deck of playing cards. When the deck is spread, the spectator finds that the Genie has not only mysteriously appeared, but the Genie has also magically written the names of two playing cards in the cloud of smoke. Upon inspection, the spectator finds that these are the two playing cards that are next to the Genie card in the deck!

SECRET AND PREPARATION

In addition to the Genie cards, you will need a regular deck of playing cards.

A Before you perform the trick, use a pencil to write the names of any two playing cards in the cloud of smoke on the top card of the Genie card packet. Let's suppose that you write the six of clubs and the two of spades. This is now your Genie prediction card.

B Cover your prediction card with one of the empty-cloud half-cards and put the rubber band around the packet. From the deck of playing cards, remove the two of spades and the six of clubs.

C Put the six of clubs on the top of the deck of playing cards.

D Put the two of spades on the bottom of the deck of playing cards and place the deck back in the box. You are ready to perform the trick.

NOTE: In the illustrations, we have marked the six of clubs with the letter A and the two of spades with the letter B to make them easier to follow.

METHOD

1 To begin the presentation, lay the Genie packet face up on the table with a pencil and the box of playing cards. Remark that the Genie who usually lives in the lamp must not be home. Ask a spectator to write their initials in the lamp of the top card.

2 Remove the initialed card using the MASTER MOVE (actually removing the prediction card) and lay it face down on the table. Put the rest of the Genie cards in your pocket or just lay them aside.

3 Tell the spectator to write their name on the back of the Genie card. While the spectator is writing, pick up the deck of playing cards, remove it from the box and set it on the table next to the Genie card.

4 Ask the spectator to divide the deck into two parts. Tell the spectator to cut anywhere in the deck and to place the upper portion on the table on the other side of the Genie card.

5 Stress the fact that the spectator is the one who is deciding where to cut the pack.

6 Tell the spectator to place the Genie card face down on top of this new pile (which places it on top of the six of clubs).

7 Tell the spectator to place the lower half of the deck on top of the Genie card, thus burying it in the deck. (This now places the two of spades, which was on the bottom of the deck, directly above the Genie card.)

NOTE: At this point, the Genie card has been "sandwiched" between the six of clubs and the two of spades, while the spectators think the Genie card was placed in the deck at a freely chosen spot.

8 State that you will have to call on the Genie to help with this trick. Explaining that the Genie is always invisible when not at home, pretend to spot the Genie in the air. Reach out and "catch" the Genie in your hand. Pretend to slip the Genie into the pack of cards on the table.

9 Pick up the pencil, lay it on the end of the pack, and say, "This Genie is very intelligent. With a pencil, this Genie can even write." Move the pencil forward, sliding it completely across the top of the pack. Lay the pencil aside.

10 Say, "That gave the Genie time to write a message. Let's see if that happened." With that, you spread the pack along the table.

11 Push the Genie card out of the deck along with the card just below it (A) and the card just above it (B), as shown.

12 Say, "I'll just turn over the Genie card, and we'll see what the Genie knows." When the signed Genie card is turned over, the names of the two playing cards are seen in the cloud with the spectator's initials still in the lamp.

13 Turn over cards A and B, showing the six of clubs and the two of spades, amazing the spectators.

COMMENTS AND SUGGESTIONS

As in the previous trick, once you have drawn out the previously prepared Genie prediction card, you may allow the spectators to see the face of the packet of Genie cards. As long as the half-card is still in place and securely bound by the rubber band, they will think they are seeing the second Genie card in the packet. Be sure to glance at the face of the packet, though, to be sure that the rubber band is still hiding the edge of the half-card.

GENIE
SAVES THE DAY

EFFECT

In this Genie card effect, you make a prediction, writing it in the Genie's cloud. When the prediction goes wrong, the Genie magically fixes it, producing a double surprise. Again, the MASTER MOVE is used along with the ROLLOVER FORCE of a card from a regular pack of playing cards.

SECRET AND PREPARATION

To prepare, write the name of a playing card, say the three of clubs, in the cloud section of the top Genie card. Cover this with one of the blank half-cards and place the rubber band around the packet. From an ordinary pack of cards, remove the three of clubs and place it at the correct position in the pack, ready for the ROLLOVER FORCE.

METHOD

1 State that you are going to make a prediction—you will predict the very same card that a spectator will later select from an ordinary deck of playing cards! Openly write the name of some other card, say the five of hearts, in the Genie's cloud, stating that this is your prediction.

2 Actually, your prediction is written on the half-card that no one knows about. You have the spectator put their initials in the lamp to identify the prediction card.

3 Go through the MASTER MOVE, laying the Genie card (actually the three of clubs prediction card) face down on the table and place a coin or other small object on top of it. The half-card with your five-of-hearts prediction remains on the Genie packet.

NOTE: Placing a coin or other small object on the Genie card is important, as it discourages anyone from turning the card over until you're ready.

4 Drop the Genie packet in your pocket and bring out the pack of playing cards. Remove the pack from its box and force the three of clubs on the spectator using the ROLLOVER FORCE.

5 Ask the spectator to look at the selected card and see if your prediction is correct. The spectator sees that you are wrong, since the spectator saw you write "five of hearts" on the Genie card, and the card the spectator selected is the three of clubs.

6 That's when you call on the invisible Genie for help. Remove the coin and ask the spectator to turn over the prediction card. The spectator will find that the Genie has magically appeared and has changed your prediction to the three of clubs, the same card the spectator selected. Hooray for the Genie!

COMMENTS AND SUGGESTIONS

This effect is super for three reasons. One, it fulfills a prediction; two, it mysteriously changes one prediction into another; and three, it proves you are right when the spectator thinks that you are wrong. The combination will have your spectators trying to figure out three things at once, which is sure to leave them totally baffled.

One word of caution. You must keep the packet of Genie cards face down after the MASTER MOVE, so that no one will see the false prediction on the half-card. Just drop the packet in your pocket and you will find that by the end of the trick, the spectators will have forgotten about the packet completely.

GENIE'S LIBRARY

EFFECT

You have a spectator write their initials in the lamp on the face card of a packet of Genie cards. The picture on the card shows a magic lamp giving off a cloud of smoke, but no Genie. You remove the initialed Genie card from the stack and place it face down on the table.

You display an ordinary paperback book and riffle through its pages, inviting the spectator to call, "Stop," at any time during the riffle. When the call comes, you insert an envelope in the book to mark the exact page selected by the spectator. The spectator is then asked to note the word in the text located in the upper right corner of the selected page.

In an attempt to locate the Genie and learn the selected word, the Genie card is partially inserted into the book for only a brief moment. When the card is removed and turned face up, it shows that both the Genie and the exact word that was selected from the text have magically appeared—with the word written in the Genie's cloud of smoke!

SECRET AND PREPARATION

A Carefully cut one page from the center of the paperback book you plan to use and place it on your table, with the front of the page (that is, the odd-numbered side of the page that was originally facing the front of the book) facing up. Apply a very thin strip of rubber cement along the binding edge of the page and on the top edge of the envelope, as shown.

B Allow the cement to dry on both surfaces and attach the glued edge of the page to the glued edge of the envelope. Be sure that the edges of the page are exactly even with the left side and the lower edges of the envelope. Although this is difficult to describe in written form, it is really quite simple to make. Just study the pictures and you will see exactly how to make this special envelope-prop that is the key to the entire trick.

NOTE: The envelope should be longer and wider than the book page, so that when it is turned over, the page will be completely hidden from view beneath the envelope.

C After the glue has set, insert the prepared envelope into the book so that the secret page is lined up with the rest of the pages in the book. If this is done correctly, everything should appear natural from all angles. It will look like a book with an envelope stuck in its pages.

D Write the prediction word from the force page (the page you have glued to the envelope) in the cloud of the top card of the Genie packet. Cover this with the half-card and place the rubber band around the entire stack.

METHOD

1 Place the packet of Genie cards on the table and bring the book into view, casually showing it on both sides. Turn the book face up and remove the envelope with your right hand. Make sure not to flash the attached page as you do this.

2 Pick up and display the packet of Genie cards. Have a spectator write their initials in the lamp of the top Genie card as usual. Remove the initialed card using the MASTER MOVE (actually removing the prediction card). Place the card face down on the table.

3 Pick up the book in your left hand and riffle through the pages with your left thumb. Ask the spectator to call, "Stop," at any time during the riffle.

MARK WILSON'S CYCLOPEDIA OF MAGIC

4 When the call comes, stop riffling.

5 Insert the envelope into the book at that point. Be sure the bottom of the envelope is lined up evenly with the bottom edge of the book. Also, insert the envelope all the way into the book so that the glued edge of the envelope and the secret prediction page are wedged securely into the binding of the book.

6 Without hesitation, gently tap the bottom edge of the book on the table. This squares up the envelope (and the hidden page) with the rest of the pages of the book.

7 Immediately lay the book on the table and pick up the initialed Genie card.

NOTE: Picking up the Genie card at this time is actually a clever ruse to let you set down the book with the special envelope inserted into it. If you did not use the Genie card here, there would be no reason for you not to show the spectator the page that was selected.

8 Slide the Genie card face down through the pages of the book. Say, "I will now attempt to locate the magic Genie within the pages of this book, where the Genie frequently visits on vacation. If we're lucky, perhaps the Genie will also reveal to us the word that you selected." After this bit of banter, replace the prediction card face down on the table.

9 Here is the most important move in the trick. Pick up the book and open it.

Force Page

10 The book should hinge open between the envelope and the secretly attached page. The envelope should cover the left-hand portion of the book, exposing the front side of the attached force page. Point out to the spectator the last word in the top line of this page (actually the force word). Ask the spectator to remember that word.

NOTE: Do not look at the page or the word as you do this. Hold the book away from you so that it faces the spectator and you obviously cannot see the freely selected page. Unknown to the spectator, you have now forced the spectator to choose a word that appears to be the result of random selection.

11 Close the book and remove the envelope, bringing along the secret page. Immediately place the envelope aside, or better yet, into your coat pocket, making sure not to expose the secret page as you do.

12 To bring the mystery to its close, ask the spectator to call out the selected word. When the spectator does, turn over the Genie card, revealing both the Genie and the word written in the cloud that exactly matches the word selected from the text of the book!

COMMENTS AND SUGGESTIONS

Be sure to use a book that does not open out flat for this trick. A paper-back book is best. If the book opens wide, the audience might notice that the page the spectator freely selected is actually glued to the envelope.

Do not call any unnecessary attention to the envelope during the presentation. Handle it as if its only purpose is to mark the selected page in the book. After it has done its work, place it in your pocket and continue. By the end of the trick, the spectators will most likely forget that you ever used any additional prop other than the book.

SPECIAL NOTE: Since all of the Genie tricks use the same magical principles, the half-card and the MASTER MOVE, you should present only one of the Genie tricks at any one performance. Never repeat a trick for the same spectators.

CHAPTER 12
MONEY MAGIC

Tricks with coins and dollar bills are not only baffling but also quite impressive. When you show both hands empty, and then reach out into the air and pluck a number of tens or twenties from nowhere, respect for your magical powers will increase greatly.

Money magic can be performed almost anywhere and under almost any conditions—if you do the right thing. Magically producing money from the air is just as effective in Moscow or Singapore as it is at your local McDonald's. You don't even need to speak the audience's language for them to be impressed. As the old saying goes, money talks.

Whether performing feats of surprising wizardry or impromptu work, stress the fact that you are using ordinary items. Whenever possible, borrow money from spectators, thus proving that skill, not trickery, is the great factor in your work. The more you have your audience believing that, the more fascinating your money magic will appear.

COIN FOLD

EFFECT

You borrow a coin from a spectator, who marks it for later identification. A small sheet of paper is then folded around the coin so it is completely enclosed within the paper. This little package can even be tapped on the table so the spectators can hear that the coin is actually inside. At all times, the folded paper remains in view of the spectators; but you cause the coin to vanish from within the paper, which you tear into pieces. You then produce the coin from your pocket, the spectator's lapel, or anywhere you wish.

SECRET AND PREPARATION

No special items are required for this effect. The coin, however, should be large enough for an effective vanish. A half-dollar or dollar-size coin works well and is easily visible even at some distance. The piece of paper used should measure approximately 4" x 6".

METHOD

1 Borrow a coin from a spectator and have the spectator mark the coin with a permanent-ink marking pen for later identification. Hold the paper in your left hand and display the coin openly in your right fingertips. You remark, "I will seal the borrowed coin with the folds of this piece of paper."

2 Place the coin in the center of the paper and hold it there with your left thumb and fingers, as shown.

3 With the right fingers, fold the upper half of the paper toward you, as shown—completely over the coin—so that no part of the coin is visible to you or to the spectators.

4 Fold the left side of the paper away from you, against the back of the coin. This seals the coin in the paper at the left side. Do not fold the paper tightly against the edge of the coin. Instead, leave about 1/4" of "play" between the fold and the left edge of the coin.

5 Fold the right side of the paper away from you, against the back of the coin so it overlaps the left-hand fold. This seals the coin in the paper from the right side. Again, leave 1/4" of "play" between the crease of the right fold and the right edge of the coin.

6 At this point, the coin is sealed in on all sides except for the bottom edge of the paper, which remains open. In making the folds, be sure to maintain enough pressure on the coin through the paper to keep it inside, so that it doesn't slide out the open bottom edge.

7 The last fold is the most important. If you folded the bottom edge upward—toward you—it would seal the coin inside. Instead, the last fold is made upward—but toward the spectators. This leaves the bottom edge of the package open, providing a means of escape for the coin.

8 When the last fold been made, press the paper firmly around the edge of the coin, leaving a distinct impression of the coin outlined on the surface of the paper. This impression is important. It will later convince the spectators that the coin is still wrapped securely within the folded package.

9 Hold the small package with the tips of your right fingers. Tap the edge of the folded paper on the table, allowing the spectators to "hear" the coin inside. Say, "The coin is now securely sealed within the folded paper. If you listen, you can even hear it."

10 To make the coin vanish, you hold the folded paper with the "opening" pointing downward, toward the base of your fingers. Relax the pressure of your right thumb and fingers, and the coin will slide out of the bottom of the paper into your right hand, where it remains hidden in your curled fingers.

11 After the coin drops into your hand, take the package with your left fingers. Your right hand falls casually to your side with the coin secretly held in the finger-palm position (see page 47), as shown.

12 With your left hand, casually display the folded package to the spectators, who believe that the coin is still wrapped inside. This is where the outlined impression of the coin becomes so valuable. As you display the paper, casually show both sides, allowing the spectators to see the impression made by the coin, thus proving the presence of the coin.

13 Another way to get rid of the coin is to place your hand casually in your right pants or coat pocket as the folded package is transferred from the right to the left hand, instead of leaving the coin in your right hand. This way, your right hand will be empty as you move on to the next step.

14 Bring both hands together in front of you and tear the paper in half. (The illustration shows how to hold the coin in the finger-palm position as you tear the paper.) Toss the pieces onto the table. You can even tear the paper into many pieces to prove, without a doubt, that the coin has truly vanished. The coin can then be reproduced from your pocket; or if you still hold the coin in your hand, you can produce it from the spectator's coat lapel, tie, or anywhere you desire.

COMMENTS AND SUGGESTIONS

The COIN FOLD is a standard method for vanishing a coin and can be used in conjunction with many coin routines where the vanish of a coin is necessary.

COIN THROUGH HANDKERCHIEF I

 Here is a clever effect using a pocket handkerchief and a coin (a half-dollar is a good size to use).

EFFECT

You display the coin at the tips of your right thumb and fingers. You drape the handkerchief over the coin so that the coin seems to penetrate the fabric of the handkerchief, without leaving a trace of a tear or a hole. You can then hand a spectator both the coin and the handkerchief for examination.

METHOD

1 For this effect you may use your own handkerchief, but the trick is stronger if you utilize a borrowed one. In either case, first display the coin by holding it at the tips of your right thumb and first two fingers. Your fingers and thumb are pointing up, with one side of the coin facing the spectators.

2 With your left hand, drape the handkerchief over the coin and over your right hand. The coin should be under the center of the handkerchief.

3 With your left hand, adjust the handkerchief around the coin. At the same time, underneath the handkerchief, secretly lift a small bit of cloth behind the coin with your right thumb and fold it around your left thumb, as shown.

4 Remove your left hand, leaving the small bit of handkerchief nipped between your right thumb and the back of the coin. This places two layers of fabric between the right thumb and the coin.

5 Grasp the front edge of the handkerchief with your left hand, lifting it up, back, and completely over the coin. This action will expose the coin to the spectators, supposedly to assure them that the coin is still in its original position.

6 The following move is the real secret of the trick. With your left hand, grasp both edges of the handkerchief and lift them both up and over the coin, as shown.

7 The effect on the spectators will be that you simply exposed the coin for them to show that it was still there and then recovered it with the handkerchief as before.

8 In actuality, you are now holding the coin outside the back of the handkerchief.

9 With your left hand, grasp the coin through the now doubled-over fabric and remove your right hand, as shown. It will appear to the spectators as if the handkerchief is draped completely around the coin.

10 With your right hand, twist the lower part of the handkerchief around the coin.

11 As you twist the handkerchief, the shape of the coin will become visible under the fabric.

12 You may also adjust the cloth over the exposed "back" of the coin and show the handkerchief on all sides, if you wish.

13 Slowly push the coin upward in the handkerchief, as your left hand comes over to take the edge of the coin, as it "penetrates" the handkerchief.

14 You may hand both the handkerchief and the coin to a spectator for examination.

COIN THROUGH HANDKERCHIEF II

This effect will appear exactly the same to the spectators as the first COIN THROUGH HANDKERCHIEF, yet the method is entirely different. But because it is so direct and bold, it will fool anyone who might know the first method described. This is another example of an ingenious mystery devised by "Gen" Grant.

EFFECT

You display a half-dollar between the tips of the fingers of your right hand. Your left hand holds a handkerchief that you drape over both the coin and your right hand. With your left hand, you grip the coin through the cloth from the outside, holding it there while your right hand is withdrawn from beneath. Your right hand again grasps the coin—this time through the material. Now you move your left hand down and grasp the hanging corners of the handkerchief, while your right hand continues to hold the coin. You give a sharp downward jerk to the handkerchief, and the coin "penetrates" completely through the cloth, leaving no trace of a hole.

METHOD

All of the following illustrations are as seen from your point of view.

1 Hold the coin by the tips of your right finger and thumb, as shown. Pick up the handkerchief with your left hand.

2 As you display the coin, begin to cover it with the handkerchief. Notice that your left hand holds the edge of the handkerchief by the side, not by the corner.

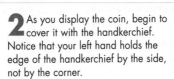

3 When the coin is completely covered, the front edge of the cloth (the edge toward the spectators) drapes a little lower than the back edge. This leaves the handkerchief a bit shorter in back than in front.

4 Your left hand grips the coin through the cloth, from the outside, between the thumb and fingers, as shown.

5 As you withdraw your right hand from beneath the handkerchief, you really keep the coin in your right hand and secretly bring it down below the rear edge of the handkerchief. Your left hand holds the handkerchief at the center, as if it were still holding the coin through the cloth.

MARK WILSON'S CYCLOPEDIA OF MAGIC

6 With your right hand, bring the coin up behind the handkerchief and slide it under your left thumb, clipping the coin behind the cloth, out of the spectators' view.

7 With your right fingers, pretend to adjust the folds of the right side of the handkerchief by sliding your fingers down along the cloth.

8 Bring your right hand back up to the center (top) of the handkerchief and transfer both the coin and the handkerchief from your left fingers to your right fingers, still keeping the coin hidden behind the cloth.

9 With your left fingers, pretend to adjust the left side of the handkerchief, sliding the fingers down the cloth as before.

10 Gather all four corners of the handkerchief into your left hand. Your right hand still holds the coin behind the cloth.

11 Hold the corners tightly in your left hand. Jerk the handkerchief sharply downward, out of your right hand. Pull the handkerchief away from the coin, which remains held by your right fingertips. The coin has apparently penetrated the center of the handkerchief! The handkerchief and the coin can then be tossed to the spectators for examination.

COMMENTS AND SUGGESTIONS

As bold as this may seem, when it is performed correctly, every movement is natural and will be accepted by even the sharpest observers, who are looking for quick or suspicious movements. Rehearse it first by actually leaving the coin under the handkerchief and going through the rest of the steps. Then repeat the same actions, following the magical penetration routine given here. When both look the same, you will be ready to present this second version of the COIN THROUGH HANDKERCHIEF.

MAGICALLY MULTIPLY YOUR MONEY

For a neat, close-up effect, this is ideal. It can be set up in a moment and performed almost anywhere, provided the spectators are close enough to fully appreciate it. It makes an excellent close-up trick, but it also can be worked while you are standing.

EFFECT

You display a nickel between the tips of your right thumb and first finger. The other fingers of your right hand are open wide. Everyone can see your hand is empty, except for the nickel.

After showing that your left hand is just as empty, you slowly grasp the nickel with your left thumb and first finger. For a brief moment, both hands hold the coin at the fingertips, then the hands draw apart in a slow, outward motion. The spectators are amazed to see two half-dollars emerging instead of the nickel. When both hands are separated, each unmistakably holds a real half-dollar, proving that your money has multiplied twenty times over. That's magic!

SECRET AND PREPARATION

Top view

The entire effect depends upon an artful form of concealment, which is simplicity itself yet so deceptive that no one will suspect it. Skill is reduced to a minimum.

To prepare, hold the two half-dollars edgewise (horizontally) near the tips of your right thumb and forefinger, keeping the two coins together. Place the nickel upright (vertically) between the tips of the same thumb and forefinger, as illustrated. Center the nickel against the outer edge of the half-dollars. With the coins held firmly in this position, you are ready to begin.

METHOD

1 As you face the spectators, position your right hand straight at them, showing the nickel at their eye level. The spectators will not see the halves hiding edgewise behind the nickel if, and only if, your hand is held so that the halves are parallel to their line of vision—hidden behind the much smaller nickel. Illustration A shows the starting position as it would be seen from slightly above.

Notice how the nickel masks the half-dollars since the edges of the halves are at the exact center of the nickel.

2 From the spectators' view, your right hand is so obviously empty (except for the nickel) that any suspicion would be directed toward your left hand, which you show as empty—front and back.

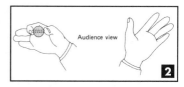

Audience view

3 Slowly and deliberately, bring your hands together, with the thumbs and forefingers of both hands pointing toward each other. The remaining fingers of both hands should be slightly opened to give the spectator a clear view of your "empty" hands.

NOTE: Keep your hand level with the spectators' eyes so that they do not see the concealed halves as you turn your hand.

4 As your hands move closer together, your left thumb comes beneath the coins, pushing the lower edge of the nickel inward, rotating the nickel up against the bottom half-dollar. All three coins are now horizontal. This is the one moment when the coins are out of the direct view of the spectators.

5 All in the same action, tip the three coins upright toward the spectators with your left thumb and first finger. The coins are all held together in a stack, with the nickel hidden in back.

6 Without stopping, grip the stack between your thumbs and fingers and begin drawing the two halves apart. Your left hand draws the front half-dollar to the left, while your right hand draws the rear half-dollar and the nickel to the right.

7 Your right thumb keeps the nickel hidden behind the rear half-dollar, retaining it there as you separate the two halves. To the spectators, the nickel will appear to have magically enlarged and doubled before their eyes—in an instant!

8 The coins are then drawn completely apart and shown as two half-dollars at the fingertips of each hand. Be careful not to accidentally flash the hidden nickel when displaying the two halves to the spectators.

COMMENTS AND SUGGESTIONS

This is a brief but baffling effect. The only question left concerns the disposal of the nickel, which, if seen, would spoil the mystery. When seated at a table, after displaying the half-dollars bring both hands near the edge of the table and dip your right hand a little behind your left hand. This hides your right hand momentarily. At that moment, your right thumb releases the nickel, letting it fall into your lap.

NOTE: This is one method of "lapping." Both hands then come forward and toss their coins on the table. The hands can be shown to be completely empty, proving that the nickel is no longer there. If you are standing, just place the "right-hand" in your pocket (along with the secret nickel) and proceed with any effect using the "left-hand" half-dollar.

FOUR-COIN ASSEMBLY

This highly effective table trick is performed with the simplest of objects. You will only need four coins (either half-dollars or quarters), two pieces of 3" x 5" cardboard (index cards work nicely), and a napkin or fairly thick handkerchief.

EFFECT

A handkerchief is spread on the table and four coins are placed near the corners, with the two cards lying along with them. Picking up the cards, you show various ways in which they can be used to cover any two of the coins. After deciding on diagonal corners, you take the uncovered coins, one at a time, under the handkerchief and cause each coin to mysteriously penetrate the cloth under the card at Corner A. At the end of the trick, all four coins appear under the card—including the coin at Corner D—which you apparently never touched during the entire performance.

METHOD

The presentation depends upon a well-designed routine that directs the spectators' attention away from the few simple moves required.
By following it with the actual items, all the details can be easily learned and mastered.

1 Begin by laying out four coins, one on each corner of the cloth, as shown. The cards are tossed on the handkerchief as you say, "Here are four coins, two cards, and one handkerchief."

2 Pick up a card in each hand, thumb on top, fingers below, and cover the two coins at Corners C and D. Say, "I can use these cards to cover the two coins in this row."

3 Lift the cards and move them to cover the coins at Corners A and B. Say, "Or I can cover the coins in this row."

4 Your right hand moves again to cover the coin at D, while your left hand moves its card from A across to B. State, "Also, I can cover two coins at the sides."

5 As you cover the coin at D, your right thumb presses down on the left edge of the coin so that the fingers of your right hand can slide under the coin and secretly pick it up and hold it against the card.

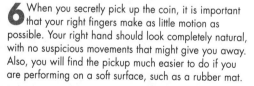

6 When you secretly pick up the coin, it is important that your right fingers make as little motion as possible. Your right hand should look completely natural, with no suspicious movements that might give you away. Also, you will find the pickup much easier to do if you are performing on a soft surface, such as a rubber mat.

7 Your left hand draws its card toward you, sliding it over the right-hand card, as if to cover the coin at Corner D.

8 Your right hand draws its card toward you, holding the coin under it, as shown in this view from below. Your left hand leaves its card at D over the exact spot where the "stolen" coin was located.

9 Your right hand then places its card over the coin at Corner A, leaving with it the coin that it secretly brought from D. Leave the cards at A and D as you comment, "Or I can cover two coins, 'crisscross,' like this."

10 The buildup and timing are important. By covering C-D, then A-B, then B-D, you condition the spectators to expect another simple placement of cards. The fact that the left hand is moved first, showing the coin at B, will cause people to think they also saw the coin at D before the left-hand card covered it.

11 Remark that you have now covered coins at the diagonal corners (A and D). Pick up the coin from C with your right hand and lift that corner of the cloth with your left hand, as shown. State that you will now magically push the coin up through the cloth, causing it to join the coin under the card at Corner A.

12 Here you make another secret move. As you remove your right hand under the cloth, secretly clip the coin between the tips of the fingers of your left hand. Your right hand should continue its forward motion under the cloth as you secretly transfer the coin from your right to your left hand.

MARK WILSON'S CYCLOPEDIA OF MAGIC

13 The secret transfer of the coin is shown from a different view here.

14 When the now-empty right hand is under the coins at Corner A, make a slight upward flicking movement with the right fingers, causing the coins under the card to clink together. Explain that the coin has just penetrated the cloth and joined the coin under the card.

15 The right hand is now removed from under the cloth and casually shown to be empty, as it reaches to turn over the card at Corner A. The left fingers still hold the clipped coin, but they keep it hidden beneath the handkerchief.

16 The right hand turns over the card at Corner A, and in the same motion moves the card toward your left hand, bringing it directly over Corner C.

17 In one continuous motion, your right hand slides the card under your left thumb, as the left hand draws the clipped coin from under the cloth, pressing it up against the card.

18 The left hand places the card over the two coins at Corner A, secretly adding the coin it holds under the card.

19 Your left hand returns to Corner C and lifts the cloth, while your right hand picks up the coin at Corner B. Announce that you will push another coin up through the cloth.

20 Place your right hand under the cloth the same as before, with your left fingers clipping the coin and stealing it away as your right hand goes beneath the cloth.

21 The right hand then pretends to push the coin up through the cloth under the card at Corner A (also with a clink).

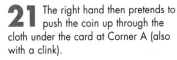

22 Remove your right hand from beneath the cloth and lift the card at Corner A.

23 As you reveal the three coins, turn the card over toward your left hand, which has the clipped coin ready. Remark, "And another coin has come up through!"

24 As before, the right hand transfers the card to the left hand, which secretly carries the coin away beneath the card. Place the card over the three coins at Corner A, just as before, secretly adding the fourth coin.

NOTE: Be careful not to let the secret coin clink against the other coins as you lay the card down.

25 With no more coins in view, you remind the spectators that one coin is still under the other card at Corner D. Command it to join the other three. When you lift the card at Corner D, the spectators see, to their amazement, that the coin has really gone!

26 Use your left hand to lift the card at Corner A, showing all four coins there, making the mystery complete!

COMMENTS AND SUGGESTIONS

The entire routine should be practiced until it can be done smoothly and without hesitation, especially where the secret moves are concerned. You may experiment with other patterns of covering the coins that work well in directing attention away from the right hand when it secretly picks up the coin at Corner D. For example, cover the coins at A and B, then bring the right-hand card down to D, so that A and D are covered. Now the left hand moves its card from A to B, while your right fingers secretly pick up the coin at D. All attention is naturally centered on the left-hand card. From there, simply proceed with the usual routine. Watch the reactions of the spectators whenever you present this excellent close-up mystery, and other ideas will suggest themselves.

SLEIGHTS WITH COINS

The following four effects are "pure" sleight-of-hand and are all done with an ordinary object that you almost always have with you—a coin. After you have mastered them, you will not only have acquired several great effects that can be presented anywhere and anytime, but also you will have opened the door to a multitude of additional, truly sensational magical mysteries. Most important of all, you are beginning to learn two of the basic prerequisites to becoming an expert magician—dexterity and misdirection.

FRENCH DROP

This important coin sleight must be mastered before performing many coin tricks, including COPPER-SILVER PENETRATION (see page 284).

METHOD

The illustrations on the left are the magician's view and on the right the spectators' view.

1 Hold a coin so that it is level between the tips of your left thumb and fingers. All four fingers and the thumb of your left hand should point upward. Your fingers should be held closely together so the spectators cannot see between them.

2 Your right hand approaches from behind to apparently take the coin by sliding your right thumb beneath it and your right fingers above the coin. Your left hand should be held so the coin can still be seen.

3 The fingers of your right hand close over the coin, covering it, as shown.

4 As your right hand pauses momentarily, your left thumb releases the coin, so that it secretly drops into the bend of your left fingers.

5 Without hesitation, your right hand closes into a fist as if taking the coin from your left fingers.

6 In one continuous motion, turn both hands over (see arrows) as you turn your body to the right. Just twist your left hand inward, toward your body, so the coin stays hidden from view; at the same time, turn your right hand so that its closed fingers face the spectators. As you rotate your hands, your left first finger casually points toward your right hand. Follow your right hand with your eyes, as it is supposed to contain the coin.

7 As your right hand moves away, casually let your left hand fall to your side with the coin held secretly in its curled fingers. Your eyes should remain fixed on your right hand at all times. This is misdirection.

8 Slowly begin to make a rubbing motion with your right fingers, as if to rub the coin away. Then, open your hand to show the coin has vanished.

FINGER-PALM VANISH

EFFECT

The FINGER-PALM VANISH is an important sleight to master. In this vanish, a coin is retained in the same spot in your left hand from start to finish. This allows you to perform the sleight either swiftly or slowly, as you prefer. You will need to learn this trick in order to perform many MONEY MAGIC tricks.

METHOD

The illustrations on the left are the magician's view and on the right the spectators' view.

1 Display a coin lying on the fingers of your right hand, as shown.

2 Your left hand is held palm up, about waist high, with your left fingers pointing just to the right of the center of the spectators. The little finger of your right hand rests across the tips of your left fingers.

3 The right hand starts to turn over toward you. At the same time, curl your right fingers inward just enough to hold the coin securely in the right fingers, as shown. The coin is now in the finger-palm position.

4 Tip your right hand over even more. This is the moment when the coin should be falling into your left hand. Actually, the right hand secretly retains the coin in the finger-palm position.

5 Your left fingers close, as if they contained the coin. Your right hand begins to move away from your left hand with the coin secretly finger-palmed.

6 As your left hand closes into a loose fist, your right hand pauses briefly, pointing the first finger toward the closed left hand, which carries attention away to the left.

7 Lower your right hand casually to your side as your eyes follow your left hand. This is misdirection.

8 The left hand is now on its own. It apparently squeezes the coin into nothing and opens to show that the coin has vanished.

PINCH-OR-DROP VANISH

METHOD

The illustrations on the left are the magician's view and on the right the spectators' view.

1 Hold a coin at the tips of your left thumb and first three fingers so it projects straight upward. Keep your fingers close together so that the viewers cannot see between them. The palm of your hand faces you.

2 Your right hand approaches your left hand as if to grasp the coin.

3 The right hand continues to move until it completely covers the coin, as if to remove it from your left thumb and fingers.

4 As soon as the coin is concealed by the right fingers, your left thumb releases its pinching grip, allowing the coin to slide secretly down to the base of the left fingers.

5 The coin remains concealed in your left hand, held in the finger-palm position. Your right hand moves away, apparently taking the coin with it. As you move your right hand away, keep your eyes fixed on your right hand, as if it really contained the coin. The audience will follow your right hand, while you casually drop your left hand to your side with the coin secretly held in your fingers.

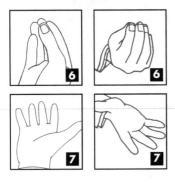

6 With the back of your right hand still toward the audience, rub your thumb and fingers together, as if to dissolve the coin in your fingertips.

7 Finally, to complete the vanish, open your hand and show it is empty.

NOTE: In Steps 6 and 7 of this vanish, your right hand does not close into a fist. It appears to take the coin from your left hand and then pretends to display it before grinding it into nothing.

COMMENTS AND SUGGESTIONS

In Steps 5, 6, and 7 and in all other sleight-of-hand vanishes where the coin is apparently transferred from one hand to the other, it is essential that your eyes follow the hand which apparently contains the coin. This is one of the most basic and important examples of misdirection. In fact, in this case, where you look is as important as the sleight itself. The audience will look where you look. Therefore, when you practice this or any other similar sleight, you should first practice really taking the coin away in your right hand. This will accomplish two things. First, you want the audience to believe that you are taking the coin in your right hand when you are really concealing it in your left. The more natural this move looks, the more your audience will believe. By really taking the coin, you will discover for yourself exactly how the move should look when you perform the sleight. Second, and of equal importance, you will see that if you really take the coin in your right hand, that is where you will look. You would not take the coin in your right hand and look at your left.

MARK WILSON'S CYCLOPEDIA OF MAGIC

Stand in front of a mirror, hold the coin at the tips of your left fingers, and then, really take the coin in your right hand. Do this a number of times. Make your actions correspond to the pictures on the right-hand side of the page. Just make the "pickup" motion in an easy and natural way. Then, still standing in front of the mirror, try the sleight. As you pretend to take the coin, let it slide down into your left hand, as shown on the left side of the page. By using the mirror and the two sets of illustrations, you can see exactly how this sleight will appear to you and to your audience.

Remember your misdirection; always look at the hand that supposedly contains the coin!

CLASSIC PALM

This is probably the oldest and most basic of all coin sleights. It is used to conceal a coin in the hand in a natural manner. It is also one of the most difficult to master. However, once learned, it will be of great value to you, not only with coins but with other objects as well. You will need to master the CLASSIC PALM in order to perform COINS ACROSS (see page 294).

METHOD

1 Place a coin on the tips of your two middle fingers and hold it there with the tip of your thumb.

2 Move the thumb and bend your fingertips inward, sliding the coin along the underside of your thumb until it reaches your palm. As you slide the coin into the palm, stretch your hand open so the muscles at the base of your thumb and little finger are fully expanded.

3 Press the coin firmly into the palm and contract the muscles of your hand inward, thus gaining a grip on the edges of the coin. Draw your thumb inward only as far as needed to retain the coin comfortably. Too much grip will make your hand appear cramped and tense.

4 Seen from the back, the hand should look relaxed and natural, with the fingers close together.

5 Avoid the common fault of holding the coin too tightly and spreading the thumb and fingers wide, as shown here. This will give away the fact

that you are hiding something. Only when the hand looks natural will you be above suspicion and thus have mastered the CLASSIC PALM.

COMMENTS AND SUGGESTIONS

The term "palm" comes from this method of concealment, as the coin is actually gripped in the palm of the hand. Keep practicing until you can place the coin in just the right position. It will then become second nature and will prove extremely useful. Once the knack is acquired, coins of various sizes can be retained. It is a good idea to use the hand containing the palmed coin for various gestures such as snapping the fingers, pulling back the sleeve, or picking up articles from the table. These natural

MARK WILSON'S CYCLOPEDIA OF MAGIC

actions will direct attention away from the hand, because people will automatically assume that it is empty.

NOTE: The object being palmed must be placed in the classic-palm position with the aid of only the finger and thumb of the hand doing the palming. There should be no help from your other hand. You should also practice this important sleight so that you can palm objects in either hand with equal ease.

MASTER COIN MYSTERIES

Now that you have learned four basic coin sleights—French Drop, Finger-Palm Vanish, Pinch-or-Drop Vanish, and Classic Palm—you are ready to move ahead to the outstanding Master Coin Mysteries that follow.

COIN-VANISHING HANDKERCHIEF I

EFFECT

You borrow a coin from a spectator and have it marked for future identification. You place the coin under a pocket handkerchief and give it to another spectator to hold. Under these conditions, even though the spectator can feel the coin through the fabric of the handkerchief and the audience can plainly see its shape, you cause the marked coin to vanish right from under the spectator's fingertips!

SECRET AND PREPARATION

The following method for the vanish of a coin or any other small object has many uses.

A You will need an inexpensive pocket handkerchief. Place the handkerchief flat on a table. Place a coin of the same size as the one which you will later borrow from the spectator on the lower right-hand corner of the handkerchief.

B Cover the coin with a small, square piece of matching fabric (a piece cut from a duplicate handkerchief is perfect). Sew the four edges of the small square of cloth to the handkerchief. The coin is now hidden inside a secret pocket you have made in the corner of the handkerchief.

METHOD

1 Put the prepared handkerchief into your pocket or lay it on your table. If you can do so, it's a nice touch to wear it as a part of your wardrobe. If worn in your topcoat pocket, as an example, it subtly influences the spectators into assuming that the handkerchief is not a magical prop.

2 Borrow a coin from a spectator that duplicates the coin hidden in your handkerchief. Bring the spectator up on the platform with you and have the spectator mark the coin for identification. Stand the spectator to your left and remove your pocket handkerchief.

3 Hold the borrowed coin between your left thumb and first fingers, with your fingers and thumb pointing up and one side of the coin pointing toward the spectators. With your right hand, cover the coin and your left hand with the prepared handkerchief. The corner with the secret pocket should be on the side of the handkerchief that is toward you, as shown.

4 Grasp the hidden coin with the right thumb and fingers and, with your right hand, lift the corner with the concealed duplicate coin up under the handkerchief. Position it next to the borrowed coin.

5 At this point, you substitute the hidden coin for the marked coin by palming the marked coin in your left hand. Withdraw your left hand, holding the borrowed coin, as shown.

NOTE: Either your right or your left hand can be used for palming and removing the borrowed coin. Use whichever hand is easier for you and whichever works best for producing the coin at the end. In the illustrations, your left hand is shown palming the spectator's coin, while your right hand holds the handkerchief and the secret, duplicate coin.

6 Grasp the secret coin through the fabric of the handkerchief with your left hand. Remove your right hand from beneath the handkerchief as you hold the coin with your left thumb and fingers. With your right hand, twist the cloth around below the coin. Make sure that the audience doesn't get a flash of the marked coin that is palmed in your left hand.

7 Grasp the handkerchief beneath the coin with your right hand and offer the cloth-covered coin to a spectator to hold. Act naturally, and remember that the audience's attention is on the duplicate coin which is now under the handkerchief. Ask the spectator to hold the coin through the fabric of the handkerchief as you either casually drop the marked coin into your pocket or place it in position for its mysterious reappearance.

8 When you are ready for the vanish, ask the spectator if the coin can still be felt under the handkerchief. Of course, the spectator will reply, "Yes."

9 Grasp one corner of the handkerchief and jerk the handkerchief and the coin away from the spectator's grasp. It will appear as if the coin has vanished from the spectator's fingertips.

10 Casually show the handkerchief on both sides and replace it in your pocket. You may now reproduce the borrowed coin in any manner you wish.

COIN-VANISHING HANDKERCHIEF II

EFFECT

The effect is the same as COIN-VANISHING HANDKERCHIEF I except that in this case the borrowed coin is further secured in the handkerchief by a rubber band before the vanish.

MARK WILSON'S CYCLOPEDIA OF MAGIC

SECRET AND PREPARATION

In addition to the specially prepared handkerchief, you will need a small rubber band, which you place in your left coat pocket.

METHOD

1 Proceed with COIN-VANISHING HANDKERCHIEF I through Step 7.

2 As the left hand leaves with the palmed marked coin, reach into your coat pocket and remove the rubber band, leaving the coin in your pocket.

3 Place the rubber band around the handkerchief below the coin, as shown.

NOTE: The reason for the rubber band is twofold. First, it permits a natural way in which to dispose of the marked coin in your pocket temporarily. Second, it prevents the spectator from visually inspecting the contents of the hand-kerchief while the spectator is holding the coin.

4 When you are ready for the vanish, ask the spectator to be sure the coin is still there. After the spectator says that it is, remove the rubber band. Quickly snap the handkerchief out of the spectator's hand as usual.

COMMENTS AND SUGGESTIONS

The addition of the rubber band can come in handy to cover what might otherwise be a suspicious move when you pocket the borrowed coin. The rubber band could also be placed in the location from which the marked coin will reappear.

GRANT'S SUPER COIN-VANISHING HANDKERCHIEF

"GEN" GRANT

Here is a clever variation of the COIN-VANISHING HANDKERCHIEF. The construction of this handkerchief is different in that the secret coin, which is concealed in the corner of the handkerchief, is removable. Therefore, the handkerchief can be adapted to many different tricks requiring the vanish of various-size coins or other small objects.

METHOD

1 Purchase two identical pocket handkerchiefs. Open up one of them on your table, as shown.

2 Cut a 2" square from the corner of the second handkerchief and place it over the matching corner of the first handkerchief.

3 Sew three of the edges of the small square of cloth (indicated by dotted lines in the illustration) to the first handkerchief. Leave the outside seam, A to D, open.

NOTE: The unhemmed edges of the corner patch, A to B and B to C, should be turned under before sewing to prevent the cut edges from fraying.

MARK WILSON'S CYCLOPEDIA OF MAGIC

4 Sew two small dress snaps on the inside hem of the open seam (A to D), as indicated. You now have a secret pocket in the corner of the handkerchief that will safely conceal a coin or other small object inside.

NOTE: The most important value of this specially prepared handkerchief is that you can insert any coin or small object into the secret pocket. A ring, coin, or folded-up dollar bill are just a few examples of small items that can be vanished with this versatile and inexpensive piece of magical apparatus.

SUPER-DOOPER VERSATILE VANISHER

SECRET AND PREPARATION

A Purchase two identical pocket handkerchiefs that are made with a colorful pattern or design. (A common bandanna works well.) Place one on top of the other as shown.

B Sew the two handkerchiefs together along the four sides and leave the top hem open at one corner. This opening is between Points B and C in the illustration. The opening should be about 2" wide or slightly larger than the object you intend to vanish.

C Also sew the handkerchiefs together as indicated by the dotted line in Illustration C. The stitching from A to X to C forms a V-shaped pocket inside the handkerchief. Point X should be slightly below the exact center of the handkerchief.

D Sew two small dress snaps inside the open hem between B and C as shown. Any size coin (or any other small object) may then be inserted into the opening and sealed inside with the snaps. In the following description, you will be vanishing a coin, so place a coin that matches the one that you wish to vanish inside the secret pocket, and you are ready to begin.

METHOD

1 To vanish the coin, grasp the handkerchief in both hands at Corners A and C. The "hidden" coin will automatically position itself in the center of the double handkerchief.

2 Drape the handkerchief over your left hand so the hidden coin rests on your open left palm. Place the borrowed coin directly on top of the hidden coin, as shown.

3 With the fingers of the right hand, hold the borrowed coin and the secret duplicate in place.

MARK WILSON'S CYCLOPEDIA OF MAGIC

4 Turn the entire affair upside down so that the handkerchief falls over your right hand and the coins.

5 With your left hand, grasp the duplicate coin through the fabric. At the same time, your right hand allows the spectator's coin to fall into the finger-palm (see page 256) position as shown.

6 Casually withdraw your right hand (and the spectator's coin) from beneath the handkerchief and ask the spectator to grasp their coin (really the duplicate) through the fabric of the handkerchief. At this point, your right hand, which secretly holds the borrowed coin concealed in the curled fingers, can be nonchalantly placed in your right pocket where it leaves the coin to be reproduced later.

7 When you are ready to vanish the coin, grasp the bottom corner of the handkerchief and give it a sharp downward tug, pulling it from the spectator's grip. The duplicate coin is retained within the double handkerchief, giving the impression that the borrowed coin vanished between the fingertips of the spectator.

COMMENTS AND SUGGESTIONS

There are three advantages to this type of vanishing handkerchief. First, you may insert any small object into the secret pocket to be vanished. Second, because the duplicate is located in the center, the placement of the object under the handkerchief as described in Steps 3 and 4 is very natural. Third, the V-type pocket is so constructed that a somewhat bulkier object may be used and will still not show after the vanish because of the size of the secret pocket and the location in the center of the handkerchief.

COIN THROUGH LEG

EFFECT

You apparently cause a half-dollar to magically pass completely through your right leg.

METHOD

All that is required are an unprepared half-dollar and mastery of the finger-palm position.

1 Display a half-dollar to the spectators. The coin is held between the thumb and fingers of your right hand. Lower the coin to your right side, next to your right pants leg, slightly above your right knee.

2 Place the coin on your leg, as shown. Your right thumb holds the coin against your pants leg just above the knee.

3 Bring your left hand over beside the coin. With the fingers of both the right and left hands, lift a portion of the pants fabric up and under the coin.

4 Fold the cloth, which you pulled under the coin, up and over the coin. Your left thumb holds the fold of cloth in place.

5 This is how the coin and folded cloth should look to you.

6 As soon as the coin is covered by the fold in the pants leg, the thumb of your right hand secretly pulls the coin up behind your right fingers.

7 Finger-palm the coin in your right hand. Move your right hand away and, slowly and deliberately, place it behind your right leg.

NOTE: Your right hand will appear to be empty, while your left hand is apparently still holding the coin behind the fold of cloth in your pants leg.

8 Now for the vanish. The left hand releases the fold of cloth in the pants leg. The fabric will drop, revealing the vanish of the coin. Turn your left hand over to show the spectators that it is empty.

9 With your right hand, slowly withdraw the coin from behind your right knee. Magically, the coin has gone right through your leg!

COMMENTS AND SUGGESTIONS

This is a very clever and easily learned sleight that can be used as a trick in itself as just described; or it can be used for the vanish of a coin, as explained in the next effect, which can be useful in other coin routines.

CHALLENGE COIN VANISH

EFFECT

You display a coin and place it in a fold of cloth on the leg of your pants. A spectator is allowed to feel the coin to see if it is still there. Yet, under these seemingly impossible circumstances, the coin vanishes completely.

SECRET AND PREPARATION

Place a duplicate of the coin you intend to vanish in your right pants pocket.

METHOD

Proceed exactly as in COIN THROUGH LEG, through Step 5.

1 However, when you place the coin that will vanish on your leg in Step 1 this time, position it directly above the secret duplicate coin in your right pants pocket.

NOTE: Because of the location of the duplicate coin in your pocket, it will be necessary to place the vanishing coin slightly higher on your pants leg than in the COIN THROUGH LEG.

2 When you fold the cloth up around the coin, make sure that the duplicate coin is in the fold of cloth on top of the coin that will vanish.

3 You now have the real coin, the one that the spectators know about, under the duplicate coin, which is really in your right pants pocket.

4 Proceed to "steal" the coin away in the finger-palm position as explained in Step 7 in COIN THROUGH LEG.

5 Ask a spectator to feel and see if the coin is still there. The spectator will feel the duplicate coin, which is in your pocket. This gives you ideal misdirection to secretly drop the finger-palmed coin into your right coat pocket.

6 After the spectator is satisfied that the coin is still there, merely let the fold of cloth drop, as before. You may then show both hands to be completely empty. The coin has vanished.

COIN À GO-GO

EFFECT

You borrow a half-dollar from a spectator. The spectator is handed a pencil with which to mark the coin. Working at very close range, you cause the coin to vanish right before the spectator's eyes, utilizing the pencil and an impromptu wand. You show both hands to be unmistakably empty, and you even hand the pencil to the spectator to examine. Then, to bring the mystery to a happy conclusion, you simply tap the back of the spectator's left hand with the pencil and magically reproduce the marked coin.

SECRET AND PREPARATION

This is a very good impromptu trick. Carry a marking pen, ballpoint pen, or just a regular lead pencil in your left inside coat pocket, and you are always ready to perform. To insure the proper working of the effect, do not use a coin smaller than a quarter. Only one sleight is used, the FINGER-PALM VANISH (see page 256). After you have mastered this move, this routine will become an excellent addition to your impromptu program.

METHOD

1 Borrow a half-dollar from a spectator and have the spectator mark it with the pen or pencil. Let's suppose you are using a pencil. After the spectator is satisfied that the coin can be identified later, replace the pencil in your left-hand inside coat pocket.

2 Place the coin in the palm of your right hand.

3 Toss the coin from hand . . .

4 . . . to hand . . .

5 . . . finally ending up with the half-dollar enclosed in your left hand.

6 Reach into your inside coat pocket with your right hand and retrieve the pencil.

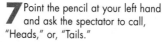

7 Point the pencil at your left hand and ask the spectator to call, "Heads," or, "Tails."

8 After the spectator makes a choice, open your left hand and allow the spectator to verify whether the choice was correct.

NOTE: All of the preceding has nothing to do with the actual working of the trick, but it has added greatly to the misdirection, as you will see.

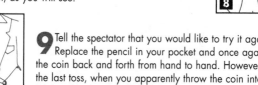

9 Tell the spectator that you would like to try it again. Replace the pencil in your pocket and once again toss the coin back and forth from hand to hand. However, on the last toss, when you apparently throw the coin into your left hand, execute the FINGER-PALM VANISH with your right hand. Secretly retain the coin in your right hand as your left hand apparently closes over the coin.

10 As far as the spectators are concerned, the effect should be exactly the same as before. With the coin concealed in your right hand, reach into your coat for the pencil. This time, however, drop the coin down the top of your left sleeve at the inside armhole of your coat. The coin will fall down your sleeve to your left elbow and will remain there as long as you keep your left arm bent, as shown. This move should be accomplished smoothly.

11 As you remove your right hand from your jacket, bring the pencil into view, and once again use it to point to your left hand. Ask the spectator to call, "Heads," or, "Tails." Since every move you have just made duplicates the first run-through, the spectator will have absolutely no reason for doubting the presence of the coin in your left hand.

12 After the spectator has made the choice, slowly open the hand and reveal the startling vanish of the coin. Hand the pencil to the spectator and show that both of your hands are completely empty.

13 Lower your left arm to your side, as you ask the spectator to return the pencil.

14 The spectator's eyes will be diverted by the pencil, as the marked coin falls silently into your left palm. Take the pencil back from the spectator, as you close your left hand around the coin.

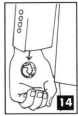

MARK WILSON'S CYCLOPEDIA OF MAGIC

15 Raise your left hand to waist level and tap it with the pencil.

16 Slowly open your hand, revealing the magical reappearance of the coin. Have the spectator identify the half-dollar as being the original borrowed coin and thank the spectator for assisting you.

CONTINUOUS COINS

Catching coins from the air and dropping them in a high hat was long a classic among old-time magicians. Coins are still with us, and to produce them magically in endless fashion is even more wonderful when done at close range. In this modern version, you either borrow a handkerchief or use one of your own and begin to extract countless coins from its folds to the amazement of your audience.

EFFECT

Your hands are unmistakably empty as you remove a handkerchief from your pocket. This handkerchief is draped over your right hand and then your left hand. The audience is surprised to see a large silver coin has magically appeared in the folds of the handkerchief! Removing the coin, you place it into the right-hand pocket of your pants. Now, you transfer the handkerchief back to your right hand. Another coin is seen to materialize from the center of the handkerchief. After pocketing this second coin, you increase your pace, producing coin after coin in an apparently unlimited supply. Finally, you set the handkerchief aside and remove the coins from your pockets. The spectators see them shower from both of your hands into a container on the table.

SECRET AND PREPARATION

The only sleight needed for this clever bit of skullduggery is the FINGER-PALM VANISH (see page 256) and some practice so that you present the routine smoothly. It will be necessary for you to perform the FINGER-PALM VANISH with both your left hand and your right hand, which you should find quite easy to learn as you practice. The items needed to present this effective mystery are an ordinary pocket handkerchief, twelve coins (half-dollars are recommended for visibility —even silver dollars if you have large hands), and a glass or metal bowl which you place on your table. Put the handkerchief in your coat pocket or simply have it ready on the table. Place six of the coins in your left pants pocket and the other six in your right pants pocket. Now, you are ready.

METHOD

1 Remove the handkerchief and display it on both sides. Show clearly that you are not concealing anything in either hand or in the handkerchief.

2 Position your right hand as shown. Your fingers and thumb should touch at the tips, and they should all point upward.

3 With your left hand, drape the handkerchief over your right hand. Make sure that your fingertips are near the center of the handkerchief.

4 Show that your left hand is empty, then grasp the center of the handkerchief with your left fingertips as shown.

5 The object of the next move is to reverse the positions of your hands. That is, to cover your left hand with the handkerchief and to free your right hand. With the left fingers grasping the center of the handkerchief as shown in Step 4, the right hand throws the handkerchief over the left hand. The left hand turns over, assuming the same position previously held by the right. The left hand is now covered by the handkerchief.

6 You then pretend to see something protruding from the center of the handkerchief. Your right fingers grasp the phantom object. By keeping the back of your hand to the audience, they will assume that you are holding some item they cannot see.

7 Without hesitation, place the imaginary object into your right- hand pants pocket. You now secretly finger-palm one of the six coins in your pocket in your right hand.

NOTE: The total action here must be timed so that you give the impression of putting something into your pocket, not removing something.

8 Bring your hand out of your pocket, keeping the back of your hand toward the audience. This will effectively conceal the finger-palmed coin. Grasp the center of the handkerchief with the right fingertips as shown.

9 Once again, you are going to reverse hand positions. This time, you will be covering your right hand, which contains the hidden coin, with the handkerchief. The left hand throws the handkerchief over the right hand as the right hand turns over, assuming its original position.

10 Again, you pretend to see something protruding from the center of the handkerchief. However, this time, the left fingers grasp the phantom object.

11 You promptly thrust this newly found item into your left pants pocket as in Step 7. While your hand is in your left pocket, finger-palm one of the six coins located there in your left hand and remove your hand. Then, with the coin secretly held in the finger-palm position, reach for the center of the handkerchief with your left fingertips.

12 This move is important! With your left fingers and thumb, grasp the handkerchief in the center and also grasp the hidden coin through the cloth. This is the coin that is under the handkerchief in your right hand.

NOTE: Make sure not to "flash" the finger-palmed coin in your left hand during this action. It must look as if you are only grasping the handkerchief, when in reality you are also lifting the hidden coin in your right hand.

13 Repeat the moves described in Step 5. However, this time the result will be the sudden appearance of a half-dollar in the center of the handkerchief! The "appearing" coin is held through the cloth by your left fingers.

14 Grasp the coin and display it between the right thumb and fingers as shown. Place the coin into your right-hand pocket. Actually, as soon as your right hand is inside your pocket, finger-palm the coin. Then, withdraw your hand with the secretly finger-palmed coin. The effect is that you left the coin in your pocket since your hand will appear to be empty when you bring it out.

15 With your right fingers and thumb, grasp the center of the handkerchief and the coin hidden underneath it in your left hand. Repeat Step 12 for the left-handed production of the next coin.

16 These moves are repeated between the right and left hands until you have apparently produced a dozen coins.

17 Finally, discard the handkerchief, reach into both pants pockets, and grasp all of the coins. Remove your hands and allow the coins to shower from your palms into the receptacle on your table. At this point, your audience will be completely convinced that you actually produced all of the coins from your empty hands and the equally empty handkerchief, when in reality, you accomplished the effect using only two coins.

COMMENTS AND SUGGESTIONS

The usual way to conclude this effect is simply to spread the handkerchief and give it back to its owner, telling the owner that you hope that the handkerchief will produce the same results later on. If it is your own handkerchief, put it in your pocket and go on with your next trick, letting the audience wonder where the coins could have come from.

A clever effect is to have coins of different values and sizes in each pocket. Then, after producing and pocketing several half-dollars, you can switch to a dollar-size coin in your right pocket and begin producing those. Your left hand could then switch to a large copper coin, such as an old English penny. You can finish by switching to a dime or a nickel, that gives you an excuse for ending the production since the coins are dwindling in size, indicating that the magic must be running out.

COPPER-SILVER PENETRATION

EFFECT

You request the assistance of a spectator and ask that the spectator stand to your left. You remove two coins from your pants pocket. One of the coins is an English penny; the other is an American half-dollar. Both of these coins are the same size, but the copper penny contrasts with the silver half-dollar. The coins are handed to a spectator for examination. You then display an empty pocket handkerchief and wrap the silver half-dollar in it. The half-dollar, wrapped in the handkerchief, is given to the spectator to hold. You call the spectator's attention to the English penny. You then invisibly throw the penny toward the handkerchief. To everyone's surprise, the vanished penny is heard magically penetrating the handkerchief and falling alongside the half-dollar! The spectator is asked to open out the handkerchief to verify the coin's arrival.

SECRET AND PREPARATION

In order to present this effect, it will be necessary for you to have mastered the FINGER-PALM VANISH (see page 256) and the FRENCH DROP (see page 254) or any other sleight-of-hand vanish of a coin. You will also need two English pennies, one half-dollar, and a pocket handkerchief. (If you do not have two English pennies, see the Comments and Suggestions section at the end of this trick.) Fold the pocket handkerchief and place it in your inside coat pocket. Place one of the English pennies next to the handkerchief, so that you will be able to grasp it easily. Then, put the half-dollar and the duplicate English penny into your right pants pocket.

METHOD

1 Ask for the assistance of a spectator and have this person stand to your left. (This will give you the most protection from accidental exposure during the presentation.)

2 Remove the penny and the half-dollar from your right pants pocket and give them to the spectator for examination.

3 While the spectator is busy examining the coins, reach into your inside coat pocket with your left hand and secretly finger-palm the duplicate penny. As soon as the coin is securely palmed, grasp the handkerchief and bring it into view. Make sure the spectators do not catch a glimpse of the hidden coin as you display the handkerchief.

4 After showing the handkerchief, hold it in your left hand. This disguises the fact that you are also concealing a coin in that hand.

5 Ask the spectator for the half-dollar. Hold the coin by your right fingertips and display it to the spectators. Transfer the half-dollar, so that it is held by your left finger-tips. Your left hand is now holding the half-dollar in plain view, the duplicate copper penny in a finger-palm, and a corner of the handkerchief. The illustration shows the positions of the three objects.

6 Your right hand grasps the bottom corner of the handkerchief and snaps it free of your left hand. Cover your left hand and the coin(s) with the handkerchief.

NOTE: Position the handkerchief so that the half-dollar is near the center of the handkerchief.

7 With your right fingers, grasp the half-dollar through the fabric and lift the coin out of your left fingers.

8 Under cover of the handkerchief, with your left hand, secretly place the finger-palmed penny into the palm of your right hand. The English penny stays under the handkerchief as your right fingers curl around the handkerchief and the penny and hold the penny through the fabric under the handkerchief, as shown.

9 Have the spectator grasp the half-dollar through the fabric of the handkerchief. As the spectator does this, slide the penny down, inside the handkerchief, as you continue to hold the penny with your right fingers.

10 Turn the handkerchief parallel to the floor. Slide your right hand to the right end of the handkerchief (where the corners are). As you slide your hand, leave the penny in the middle area, as shown. The penny is now in the handkerchief between your right hand and the spectator's hand holding the half-dollar.

11 Immediately reach up with your left hand and hold the penny in place by grasping the handkerchief in the middle, as shown.

12 Ask the spectator to hold the handkerchief with a free hand somewhere between your right and left hands, as shown.

NOTE: Since the duplicate penny is being held by your left hand, the spectator cannot accidentally feel the penny.

13 You can now remove your hands from the handkerchief. As long as the spectator's hands are held apart and the handkerchief is kept level with the floor, the hidden penny will stay in place. Pick up the visible penny and display it in your left hand.

14 Reach over with your right hand and execute the FRENCH DROP. As you know, the move will lead the spectators to believe that the penny is in your closed right hand, when actually it is secretly being held in your left hand. (If you prefer, any other vanishing sleight may be used here.)

15 Move your right hand, supposedly containing the penny, above the handkerchief being held by the spectator. You are about to slap the handkerchief free of the spectator's right hand. To accomplish this correctly, be sure to strike the handkerchief as close to the half-dollar as possible. Make a sharp downward motion with your right hand. Open your hand just before it hits the handkerchief.

16 The handkerchief will fall free of the spectator's right hand, causing the hidden copper coin to fall into the center of the handkerchief and strike the half-dollar. It appears that the penny penetrated the handkerchief and joined the half-dollar.

17 The spectator is told to unfold the handkerchief. Both coins will be discovered in its center. While the spectator is examining the coins, secretly drop the duplicate penny into your pocket.

COMMENTS AND SUGGESTIONS

This is an excellent sleight-of-hand trick. Although it requires a bit of practice to get all of the moves and the timing correct, it is well worth the effort. If you do not have two English pennies, you may substitute any two heavy coins. Foreign coins are best since you can get more contrast between the coins. However, two American coins may be used as well: for instance, one half-dollar and two quarters, or one silver dollar and two half-dollars. In this case, it is better to use the smaller as the duplicate coin, as these are the two that are involved in all of the palming. The different sizes will not matter since the spectator feels only one coin (the larger coin) when they hold the coin under the handkerchief. Thus the difference in size will not be noticed. Just be sure that the duplicate coin is heavy enough to fall within the handkerchief when it makes its mysterious appearance with the other coin.

SHRINKING COIN

EFFECT

You borrow a finger ring from one spectator and a half-dollar from another. You also request that these two spectators assist you on stage as you present your next mystery. You have the spectators stand beside you, one spectator on your left side and the other on your right. You remove a handkerchief from your pocket. The borrowed half-dollar is wrapped secretly in the center of the handkerchief, and one of the spectators threads the four corners of the handkerchief through the ring, imprisoning the coin in the handkerchief. Each of the spectators is asked to hold two corners of the handkerchief (one in each hand) and to stretch the handkerchief out between them so that it is parallel to the floor. You reach underneath the handkerchief and grasp the ring and the imprisoned coin. You then ask the spectators to gently pull on the corners of the handkerchief. To the amazement of all, the coin slowly penetrates up through the ring. The ring is now free. You remove it from under the handkerchief, and the coin lies on the handkerchief held between the two spectators. All of the items can be examined. The ring and coin are returned to the spectators, along with your thanks for their assistance.

SECRET AND PREPARATION

All that is required for this effect is a pocket handkerchief, a half-dollar, and a finger ring, all of which are quite ordinary. You must also be able to perform the COIN THROUGH HANDKERCHIEF I trick. No preparation is necessary because this is a completely impromptu mystery.

METHOD

1 Borrow a half-dollar and a finger ring from spectators. You will also need the assistance of two spectators. If they are the same ones who lent you the borrowed articles, so much the better.

2 Remove your pocket handkerchief and display the borrowed half-dollar. Wrap the coin in the center of the handkerchief as described in COIN THROUGH HANDKERCHIEF I (see page 238). As you know, the special way in which you wrap the coin leaves the coin on the outside of the handkerchief. To the spectators, it appears as though the coin is actually held inside the handkerchief. Follow the COIN THROUGH HANDKERCHIEF I routine only through Step 10. Do not perform the penetration of the coin through the handkerchief.

3 Hold the handkerchief and coin with both hands, as shown. Be sure the side of the handkerchief that was toward you in Steps 8 and 9 of the COIN THROUGH HANDKERCHIEF I, where a portion of the coin might be visible, is resting next to your left fingers, so the spectators cannot see that the coin is not really inside the handkerchief.

4 Have the spectator thread the four corners of the handkerchief through the ring, as shown. As the spectator does this, retain your grip on the coin with your left hand. Also hold the handkerchief above the coin with your right hand, as shown, so the handkerchief does not untwist, revealing the coin.

MARK WILSON'S CYCLOPEDIA OF MAGIC

5 After the spectator has threaded the ends through the ring, tell the spectator to slide the ring down the handkerchief until it rests tightly against the wrapped coin. This will lock the coin into position and keep the handkerchief from unwrapping.

6 Ask the spectators to hold the four corners of the handkerchief, as shown. The handkerchief should be level with the floor. The coin and ring are hanging underneath the handkerchief.

NOTE: To the spectators, it appears that you have placed the borrowed coin underneath the handkerchief. Then a spectator has threaded the ring over the corners of the handkerchief, imprisoning the coin in the center. Since the coin is much larger than the inside of the ring, there is apparently no way for the coin to escape.

7 Using both hands, reach underneath the outstretched handkerchief. Grasp the ring with the thumb and first finger of your left hand. Work the ring slightly upward so that you gain a bit of slack in the handkerchief. With the right hand, you can now slip the coin free of the handkerchief, as shown.

8 It is important to remember that from now until the coin penetrates the ring in Step 13, you have to hold the center of the handkerchief with your left hand, so that the spectators are not aware that you have removed the coin.

9 Under the handkerchief, secretly finger-palm the coin in your right hand. As your right second and third fingers hold the coin finger-palmed, your right first finger and thumb pull the ring off the handkerchief and place it in your left hand, so that the ring may be held by your left third and fourth fingers, as shown.

NOTE: As pointed out in Step 8, be sure to maintain your grip on the fabric with your left thumb and first finger, so that the spectators are unaware that either the coin or the ring has been removed.

10 Bring your right hand with the secretly finger-palmed coin out from beneath the handkerchief. Move your right hand directly over the center of the handkerchief, as shown.

11 The following step is most important. Your right hand secretly drops the coin into the well in the center of the handkerchief (which the spectators think is made by the ring and coin). Under the handkerchief, your left fingers open momentarily to let the coin into the well.

NOTE: The drawing in Step 11 shows the right hand held high above the handkerchief. This is only to illustrate the move. When you are actually performing the trick, your hand should be resting directly on top of the fabric when the drop is made.

12 When the coin is dropped into the well, the left fingers open to receive it and then close around the coin and the fabric. To the spectators, the handkerchief appears just as it did before. Your right hand continues to move over the handkerchief, apparently smoothing out its folds. This smoothing move is used before and after the drop as misdirection of what you are really doing, which is secretly bringing the coin from beneath the handkerchief and dropping it into the well.

MARK WILSON'S CYCLOPEDIA OF MAGIC

NOTE: At this point, the spectator's borrowed ring is held by your left third and fourth fingers under the handkerchief. The coin is now on top of the handkerchief in the well. Your left thumb and first finger hold the handkerchief closed over the coin, so that all appears as it did at the start.

13 As your left hand continues to hold the ring and coin, have the spectators gently pull on the four corners of the handkerchief. With your left fingers, let the coin slowly appear from the well, as it works its way up through your left fingers. To the spectators, it will appear that the coin is passing through the ring, which is much smaller than the coin.

14 When the coin is completely on top of the handkerchief, and the handkerchief is stretched flat between the two spectators, with your left hand slowly and dramatically bring the ring from under the handkerchief. Drop it next to the coin on the outstretched cloth. The effect is twofold. The coin has passed through the much smaller ring, which also releases the ring from the handkerchief.

You may now pass the ring, the coin, and the handkerchief for examination, as you thank the spectators for their assistance.

COMMENTS AND SUGGESTIONS

This is a very clever adaptation of the coin through handkerchief move. It is particularly misleading for the spectators since the effect is that the coin does not penetrate the handkerchief but passes through the ring instead. The outstretched handkerchief forms a perfect cover when you secretly palm the coin and slip the ring off the handkerchief. This makes an ideal close-up effect since it may be performed at any time and uses small borrowed articles, all of which may be examined. The effect works particularly well if performed so that the handkerchief is held over a low table (such as a coffee table) at which you and the other participants are seated. If performing for a larger group, have the spectators who are holding the handkerchief tilt the side nearest the audience slightly downward so that the handkerchief is angled toward the audience. This will allow you all of the cover necessary and also keep anyone from seeing under the handkerchief as you perform this miniature miraculous mystery.

COINS ACROSS

EFFECT

You are seated at a table. From your pocket you remove six coins and place them on the table, arranging them in two rows of three coins each. You gather three coins into each hand and magically cause the three coins from your right hand to travel, one at a time, to your left hand.

SECRET AND PREPARATION

In order to present this classic sleight-of-hand effect, you must first have learned the CLASSIC PALM. Since this mystery is presented as a close-up trick, you should practice until you can perform the CLASSIC PALM easily. You also will need seven identical coins. Be sure to pick coins that are easy for you to palm. Use quarters, half-dollars, or silver dollars, depending on the size of your hands. Place the seven coins in your right pocket.

METHOD

1 Reach into your pocket and remove the coins. As you do, secretly palm one of the coins. Arrange the six remaining coins on the table in two rows of three, as shown. In the illustrations, we have lettered the six coins on the table A, B, C, D, E, and F, and the seventh palmed coin, as G.

2 With your right hand concealing the seventh coin, G, reach across the table and pick up the first coin, A, from the left row.

3 If the angles permit (that is, if the spectators are located in front of you), you may now display Coin A at the tips of your thumb and fingers of the right hand while still concealing the palmed coin, G, as shown here. The fingers and thumb of the right hand point up, and the palmed coin is concealed from the spectators. If, on the other hand, you are surrounded by the spectators, just keep your right hand with your palm toward the table, as you place the coins into your left hand.

4 Throw this first coin, A, into your open left hand.

5 With your right hand still concealing Coin G, reach across the table and pick up the second coin, B, from the left-hand row.

6 Throw Coin B into your open left hand alongside Coin A.

7 The right hand picks up the third and last coin, C, in the left-hand row. Coin G is still hidden in your right palm.

NOTE: Watch your angles to be sure that you do not flash the palmed coin, G, during Steps 1 through 7.

8 This time, when you throw the third coin into your left hand, simultaneously release the palmed coin, G, so that both the third coin, C, and the palmed coin, G, go into your open left hand together.

9 Close your left hand immediately around the four coins and turn your hand over. At this point, the spectators believe that you simply counted three coins into your left hand.

NOTE: Although the illustration in Step 8 shows Coin C on top of Coin G, this is not necessarily the way the coins will land. Just drop both coins as one and immediately close your hand.

10 With your left hand apparently holding the three coins from the left row (really four coins), your right hand starts picking up the three coins (D, E, and F) still on the table.

11 Pick up the first coin, D, and display it in your right hand. As you do, position the coin in your hand in readiness for the CLASSIC PALM.

12 Close your right hand and turn it over. Use your fingers to push Coin D into the classic-palm position. Pick up the two remaining coins (E and F) with your thumb and fingers. Close your right fingers around all of the coins.

13 Make sure to keep the palmed coin, D, separated from the last two coins (E and F).

NOTE: At this point, the spectators will believe that each hand contains three coins.

14 Make a slight throwing motion with your right hand in the direction of your left hand. Loosen your left fingers so that the coins in your left hand will clink together. Tell the spectators that one of the coins has magically traveled to your left hand.

15 The right hand retains Coin D in the classic-palm position.

16 At the same time, the right hand places the other two coins (E and F) on the table.

17 The left hand immediately spreads the four coins on the table.

18 The effect is that one coin magically traveled from your right hand to your left hand.

19 Casually show that your left hand is empty, but be sure the spectators are not aware of Coin D hidden in your right hand.

20 You have just learned the basic sequences in creating this effect. From this point on, the basic moves are repeated, from Step 2 through Step 9.

21 The right hand picks up the four coins from the left row one at a time and throws them into your open left hand. As you throw the last coin, G, the palmed coin, D, is added to the other four coins in the left hand.

22 The right hand picks up the two remaining coins on the table. The first coin, E, is placed in the classic-palm position. Be sure to keep the second coin, F, separated from the first coin, E, as in Steps 12 and 13.

23 Make the throwing motion with your right hand. Clink the coins in your left hand to signal the mysterious arrival of the fifth coin.

24 The right hand places only one coin, E, on the table, keeping the other coin, F, in the classic-palm position. The left hand then spreads the five coins on the table.

25 Repeat Steps 2 through 9 as you place the five coins into your left hand. Secretly add the palmed coin, E, from your right hand on the fifth throw.

26 At this point, you will be left with one coin on the table. For this you use a special method of LAPPING called the PULL-OFF METHOD, which is described next.

LAPPING—PULL-OFF METHOD

EFFECT

You pick up a coin from the table and it vanishes completely from your hand!

SECRET AND PREPARATION

The following vanish describes how this useful sleight is used for the magical transposition of the last coin in COINS ACROSS.

METHOD

1 Cover the last coin with your right-hand fingers and slide it toward yourself, as if you were going to scoop it up into your hand.

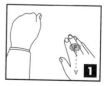

2 Instead of actually picking up the coin . . .

3 . . . allow the coin to fall unseen off the back edge of the table onto your lap, as your right hand continues the scooping motion with the fingers apparently closing around the coin.

4 Hold both hands closed on the table in front of you.

5 Lift your right hand above your left and apparently rub the coin through the back of your left hand. Show that your right hand is empty.

6 Dramatically spread the six coins on the table.

7 While the spectators are examining the six coins, casually retrieve the extra coin from your lap. Add this coin to the six on the table as you gather them up to put them away, or secretly drop it in your coat pocket as you continue your routine.

MARK WILSON'S CYCLOPEDIA OF MAGIC

COIN IN A BALL OF WOOL

The following effect is one of those classic tricks that deserves your very best effort.

EFFECT

You borrow a quarter from a spectator in the audience and ask the person to mark the coin so that it can be identified at a later time. (A black grease pencil carried in your pocket is good for this purpose.) You remove your pocket handkerchief and wrap the coin in its folds. The spectator is given the folded package to hold. This person can and does confirm the presence of the coin by feeling it through the fabric.

A ball of wool is shown to the audience and dropped into a clear glass. (In the illustrations and the written instructions, we will use a brandy snifter; however, any glass of the correct size will do.) A second spectator is asked to hold the glass containing the ball of yarn. It is held high enough so that all can see. Returning to the first spectator, you cause the borrowed coin to vanish from the handkerchief. You explain that, since the first spectator apparently lost the borrowed coin, you must give that person a chance to recover it. You grasp the loose end of the ball of yarn and pass it to the first spectator. As the spectator pulls on the yarn, the ball unwinds, spinning merrily in the brandy snifter held by the second spectator. A matchbox bound with rubber bands is found in the center of the wool ball. The second spectator is asked to remove the box from the snifter and open it. The spectator's marked quarter is found inside the box!

SECRET AND PREPARATION

Hidden Coin

A In order to present this effect, you will need the following items: a ball of wool (heavy knitting or rug yarn is good for this), a common "penny" matchbox or some other small box, a brandy snifter or other transparent container large enough to contain the ball of yarn, a vanishing handkerchief of the type described in SUPER-DOOPER VERSATILE VANISHER (see page 269)—in this case a quarter is placed in the secret corner—four small rubber bands, and a special coin "slide" which may be constructed with the following instructions.

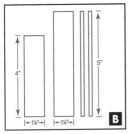

4"

5"

|←1¼"→| |←1¼"→|

B To construct the slide, cut four pieces of heavy cardboard (1/16" thick is about right), as shown. The two narrow strips and one of the wide strips should measure approximately 5" in length. The shorter pieces should be cut about 1" shorter.

C Glue the four pieces together to form a tube. When finished, the slide must be large enough to allow a quarter to pass completely through it without binding.

D The short side of the tube makes it a simple matter to insert the coin into the tube.

E Open the drawer of the empty matchbox.

F Insert the blunt end of the slide into the open drawer.

G Wrap the four rubber bands around the box, as shown.

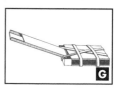

NOTE: The rubber bands serve two purposes. The first is to hold the slide in position in the matchbox. The second is to close the box after the slide has been removed.

H Wrap the matchbox with the yarn until you have formed a ball with the matchbox hidden in the center. This must be done loosely so that you don't create a bind in the tube or prevent its easy removal.

I Attach the ball of yarn and tube to the rear edge of your table or on the back of a chair. The important thing to look out for here is that the ball must not be visible to the spectators. If necessary, throw an attractive drape over the tabletop prior to attaching the prepared ball to its rear edge. In the event a chair is used, be sure the back is solid. Regardless of which method you are using, no one should get a glimpse of the coin slide.

J Put the brandy snifter on top of your table or on the seat of the chair, depending on the method you have chosen, and pocket the special vanishing handkerchief. You are now ready to present a very startling mystery.

METHOD

1 Borrow a quarter from a spectator and have them mark the coin for future identification. While this is being done, remove the special handkerchief from your pocket and spread it over your left hand. The coin previously concealed in the handkerchief should now be in the rear right-hand corner of the special handkerchief, as previously explained.

2 Take the marked coin from the spectator and pretend to place it in the handkerchief. Actually, you will retain the marked coin secretly in your right hand and bring up the duplicate quarter to take its place.

3 Allow the spectator to hold the handkerchief containing the duplicate coin. The spectator's marked quarter is finger-palmed (see page 256) in your right hand.

4 Ask for the assistance of a second member of the audience. At this point, the spectator holding the wrapped coin should be standing to your left. Have the second spectator stand to your right.

5 With your left hand, reach for the brandy snifter. During this move, your right hand grasps the rear edge of the table as if to steady it. When your left hand lifts the snifter into the air, your right hand secretly drops the marked coin into the tube at the rear of the table. Immediately hand the snifter to the spectator standing to your right.

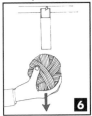

6 Go back to your table, reach behind it, and grasp the ball of wool. Pull it down and off the slide.

7 Display the ball to the audience before you drop it into the empty brandy snifter. Hand the glass to the second spectator.

8 Turn and ask the first spectator if the coin is still in the handkerchief. After the spectator answers in the affirmative, jerk the handkerchief away and show that the coin has vanished. Display both sides of the handkerchief.

9 As the second spectator holds the brandy glass, grasp the loose end of the ball of yarn and hand it to the first spectator. Instruct the spectator to unravel the ball. As the spectator pulls on the ball of yarn, it will spin in a very attractive manner.

10 When the wool has been exhausted, the matchbox will be left inside the brandy snifter. Take the brandy snifter from the second spectator and "pour" the box into this spectator's hand.

11 Instruct this spectator to remove the rubber bands and open the box. The spectator discovers the marked coin inside. Have the spectator return the coin to the first spectator for positive identification.

COMMENTS AND SUGGESTIONS

Properly presented, this is one of the finest tricks in magic. Here are some additional important points:

A The audience is never aware of the coin slide.

B The slide can be made from cardboard as described or, if you are handy with tools, from a thin sheet of metal which can be cut with tin snips and bent into the correct shape. The slide, matchbox, and the ball of yarn can also be purchased if you do not wish to make them yourself.

C The small box can either be a matchbox or a small box with a hinged top. Either will be automatically closed by the rubber bands when the slide is removed.

D In Steps 5 and 6, if you are working surrounded, or if it is more convenient, you may have the ball of yarn with the slide in place inside a box or even in a paper bag which is sitting on your table. In this case, after the first spectator is apparently holding the coin under the handkerchief, just put both of your hands, one of which contains the palmed quarter, into the box or bag. Drop the coin down the slide and remove the slide from the ball of yarn. Then, bring out the ball cupped in both hands.

E If you use a grease pencil to have the spectator mark the quarter, be sure that you do not rub off the mark while carrying the palmed coin in your hand or inserting it into the slide. If you do, no one will ever believe that the coin inside the ball of yarn, inside the sealed matchbox, is the same quarter that you borrowed from the spectator. You may wish to have the coin marked by having the spectator scratch it with some sharp object like a knife.

F While the first spectator is pulling on the end of the yarn and the second spectator is holding the brandy snifter, have them move several feet apart as the yarn unravels. This presents a very interesting and dramatic picture to the audience.

G After the ball of yarn is in the brandy snifter and before the coin has vanished from beneath the handkerchief, emphasize that the spectator is holding the marked coin and that you will not touch or go near the brandy snifter or the ball of wool until the conclusion of the trick. Be sure that you do just that!

H Allow the spectator to remove the rubber bands from the matchbox. Do not touch the box at any time until after the marked coin has been removed and identified.

Follow the above rules and you will have not just another magic trick, but one of the classic miracles of our art.

COIN ROLL

Though this is strictly an ornamental flourish and not a magical effect, it belongs in every coin manipulator's program. When you are doing coin tricks, it is always wise to impress the spectators with your skill, causing them to believe that the simplest of your routines must depend upon your remarkable dexterity.

EFFECT

You demonstrate your dexterity as a magician by causing a half-dollar to roll from finger to finger across the back of your hand. When it has finished this surprising run, it drops from sight beneath your little finger and pops up again between the thumb and first finger, only to repeat its remarkable roll. You do this repeatedly, so that the coin really seems to come alive, rolling of its own accord. When you perform the COIN ROLL deftly, it will dress up your coin routine, giving the appearance of great professional dexterity.

METHOD

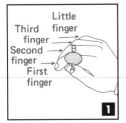

NOTE: So that you can follow the coin as it rolls over the fingers, we have added the letters A and B to the opposite edges of the coin.

1 Hold the coin by Edge A in your right hand between your thumb and first finger, as shown.

2 Push the coin up and release the thumb, allowing the coin to roll over the back of the first finger near the knuckles.

3 Lift the second finger and allow it to clip the right-hand Edge B of the coin. The coin will assume a temporary position clipped between the first and second fingers.

4 Without stopping, raise the first finger, which pushes the coin onto the back of the second finger.

5 Lift the third finger and grip Edge A, which allows the coin to roll over the second finger. The coin will again assume a temporary clipped position between the second and third fingers.

6 Without stopping, and by tilting your hand, the coin is allowed to fall onto the back of the third finger.

7 Lift the fourth finger and clip Edge B of the coin. The coin will now be temporarily held between the third and fourth fingers.

8 Move your little finger up and allow the coin to drop or be pulled down by the little finger through the opening between the third and little fingers. The majority of the coin is now protruding from the palm side of the hand, clipped between the third and little fingers.

9 Move your right thumb to a position beneath the coin.

10 Release the coin and balance it on the ball of your right thumb.

11 Move your thumb under your fingers and transfer the coin back to the original starting point at the base of the first finger.

12 You can push the coin up over the knuckle of the first finger and begin the entire sequence again. You may repeat the same set of moves as many times as you wish.

COMMENTS AND SUGGESTIONS

Along with its value as a flourish, the COIN ROLL is very helpful in developing skill in sleight-of-hand, as it loosens up your fingers so they can execute difficult moves with speed and precision.

It will require considerable practice on your part in order to master the COIN ROLL. Depending on the size of your hand, you may wish to use either a quarter or a silver dollar instead of a half-dollar. Also, although all of the moves are described in detail above, you may develop a slightly different technique that is better for your hand. Some performers, through a great deal of practice, are able to roll more than one coin on the same hand, or to roll one coin on the left hand and another on the right hand at the same time. But don't expect to master either of these variations quickly. One great advantage of this type of flourish, however, is that although it requires a great deal of practice, you may practice it while you are doing something else, such as watching television, listening to the radio, or even traveling. You can practice it at any time when your hands are free, and when you will not disturb anyone if you drop the coin, which you surely will as you learn this flourish. Once learned, it is a great attention-getter as you idly sit rolling a coin back, up, and around your fingers!

ROLL DOWN

EFFECT

You display a stack of four coins. Suddenly, the coins ROLL DOWN your fingers, until each coin is held separately between the fingers of your hand.

The ROLL DOWN might be classified as a master flourish. Once learned, it can truly demonstrate your skill as a manipulator. We recommend the use of half-dollars (or silver dollars if you can manage them) for two reasons: The flourish with larger coins appears to be more difficult (in truth it is easier), and a larger group of spectators can see the effect.

METHOD

1 Begin by placing four stacked coins in your right hand, holding them between your thumb and first finger. The palm of your right hand should be up, as shown.

2 Bend your second finger into your palm and tilt your hand slightly to the left.

3 The object at this point is to allow the top two coins (A and B) of the stack to slide or be rotated by the little finger to the left and to wedge themselves between the third and little fingers.

NOTE: It is important that you master Steps 1, 2, and 3, before moving on to Step 4. The security with which Coins A and B are held between the third and fourth fingers will determine the success or failure of the next steps.

4 With Coins A and B held between your third and fourth fingers, lift your second finger and grip the edges of Coin B and Coin C. Your thumb applies pressure to Coin D.

5 Slowly straighten out your fingers. Your thumb pivots Coin D to the right, as your little finger pivots Coin A to the left. The second finger rolls in between Coins B and C, holding their edges.

6 The coins are now in position, dramatically displayed between your fingers.

COMMENTS AND SUGGESTIONS

If you have followed each of the above steps with the four coins in your hand, you will have discovered that this is not an easy flourish to learn. But, with practice, it can be mastered. The obvious display of skill will be instantly recognized and appreciated.

DOLLAR BILL MAGIC

ROLL THE BILLS

For a close-up mystery, this is a real puzzler. It's a good one to perform when someone asks you to do a trick and you're not really prepared.

EFFECT

You lay two bills on the table, say a one-dollar bill and a five-dollar bill, so that they form a V shape. With the one on top, you call attention to the fact that the one-dollar bill is on top of the five. You then begin rolling the two bills together, starting at the point of the V. While you are rolling the bills, you ask a spectator to place a finger on the corner of the one-dollar bill and another finger on the corner of the five. The spectator now has both bills pinned to the table. So far, so good—with no chance for deception. But now, when you unroll the bills, the five is on top of the one, yet the spectator still has a finger on each bill.

MARK WILSON'S CYCLOPEDIA OF MAGIC

METHOD

1 Lay the two bills on the table with the one-dollar bill on top of the five, as shown. Notice that the one is a bit further forward (toward the spectators) than the five. (This illustration is from your viewpoint.)

2 With the first fingers of both hands, start rolling the bills together, beginning at the point of the V.

NOTE: The illustrations for Steps 2 through 9 are from the spectators' viewpoint.

3 Continue rolling the two bills until just a small part of the corner of the five-dollar bill remains in view, then stop. As shown, more of the corner of the one shows, because it was placed further forward in the initial layout (Step 1).

4 The secret move occurs in Steps 4 and 5. As you continue to roll the bills forward, open the fingers of your left hand over the corner of the five. Apparently you are merely holding the bills as you roll them, but actually you are hiding the corner of the five from the spectators' view, as shown. At the same time, point to the corner of the one with your right hand. Ask a spectator to place a finger on that corner to hold it in place.

5 As the spectator does this, place your right finger on the center of the roll of bills and roll them slightly forward. The corner of the five, which is hidden by your left fingers, flops over. In other words, this corner goes beneath the rolled bills and does a forward flip-over back to its original position on the table. This is unknown to the spectators, as it is hidden by your left hand.

6 This is a view of the action as shown from the side. Notice how your left fingers cover the secret flip-over of the corner of the five.

7 Still holding the roll of bills with your right finger, lift your left hand and point to the corner of the five.

8 Ask the spectator to place a finger on the corner of the five. Emphasize that the spectator is pinning the corners of both bills to the table.

9 All that is left is for you to unroll the bills, as shown. As a result of the secret flip-over of the corner of the five, the position of the bills will be reversed—with the five-dollar bill now on top of the one-dollar bill!

COMMENTS AND SUGGESTIONS

It is not necessary to use bills of different values in order to perform ROLL THE BILLS. If the two bills are the same, simply turn one of them over and you have bills of different colors (one black and one green). So that the trick will be easily followed by the spectators, be sure to point out which color is on top before you start rolling them. For that matter, it is not even necessary to use bills at all; different-colored slips of paper will work just as well.

BILLS FROM NOWHERE I

EFFECT

You show your hands to be unmistakably empty. Then, holding your hands together, a quantity of one-dollar bills magically appears from out of your empty palms!

SECRET AND PREPARATION

You must be wearing a suit or sport coat in order to present this effect properly.

A Make a stack of five or six one-dollar bills.

B Roll them into as tight a roll as you can.

C Place the roll of bills in the crook of your left elbow.

D Pull the fabric of your coat sleeve up and over the bills. Keep your arm slightly bent in order to hold the roll of bills in place.

METHOD

1 With the bills "loaded" as described, face the spectators. Reach over with your left hand and grasp your right coat sleeve at the crook of your elbow. Pull the sleeve back, clear of your right wrist, as you show your right hand is unmistakably empty.

2 Reach across with your right hand and grasp your left coat sleeve at the crook of the elbow and pull that sleeve back and clear of the left wrist, as you show your left hand is empty.

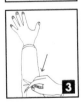

3 During this move, it is very natural for your right fingers to secretly steal the concealed bills from the fold in your jacket.

4 The roll is held in your right hand between your fingers and palm, as shown.

MARK WILSON'S CYCLOPEDIA OF MAGIC

5 Hold both of your hands in front of you at shoulder height, with your left hand in front of your right hand. This position will give you maximum coverage for the next move.

6 Using the thumb and fingers of both hands, unroll the bills so that they begin to appear at the top of your fingers.

7 After unrolling the bills halfway, suddenly pull the left hand down, so that the thumb of your left hand unrolls the bills the rest of the way from the bottom, leaving the open bills in your right hand. Fan the bills and display them to the spectators.

BILLS FROM NOWHERE II

EFFECT

You reach into your pocket and remove your wallet. Opening the wallet, you remove a single one-dollar bill. After replacing the wallet, you clearly demonstrate that, other than the one bill, your hands are absolutely empty. By suddenly slapping the bill against the palm of one hand, the single bill magically multiples into a quantity of new one-dollar bills!

SECRET AND PREPARATION

Place a single bill into a secretarial wallet or checkbook and put the wallet in your inside coat pocket. Prepare a stack of bills as described in Steps A, B, C, and D in BILLS FROM NOWHERE I.

METHOD

1 With the bills loaded into the crook of your left arm, reach into your coat pocket and remove your wallet. Take out the single bill and display it to the spectators. Clearly show your hands to be empty, except for the one bill.

Bills

2 With the bill in your left hand, reach over with your right hand and grasp your left coat sleeve at the crook in the elbow. Pull the sleeve back until your left wrist is bare. As you pull back your sleeve, secretly steal the hidden bills with your right hand (as in Step 3 of BILLS FROM NOWHERE I).

3 With the roll of bills hidden in your right hand, transfer the single bill from your left hand to your right fingers. Place the single bill in front of the roll. The secret roll of bills will be effectively hidden behind the single bill, as shown.

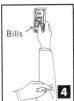

Bills

4 Without hesitation, grasp your right sleeve at the crook of the elbow and pull this sleeve back until you bare your right wrist.

NOTE: The spectators will have seen that both of your hands are empty except for the single bill, which has constantly been in view.

5 Behind the visible bill, unroll the hidden bills.

6 As you fan the new bills from behind the single bill, the effect will be the instant multiplication of a single bill into many, an effect sure to captivate any spectator's imagination.

TORN-AND-RESTORED
DOLLAR BILL

EFFECT

You display the front and back of a dollar bill and then tear the bill into two parts. Not satisfied with just the halves, you put the two parts together and tear through them both. Now, you have four separate pieces of what was a dollar bill. You fold the torn pieces neatly into a small package. Then, you make a magical gesture over the small green bundle. When you open it, the audience is amazed to see that all of the pieces have mysteriously joined together to restore themselves into a completely undamaged bill.

You will certainly want to practice this trick using play money. You can also cut some pieces of paper to the same size as a dollar bill and practice with them. When performing for an audience, you may prefer to use real bills. This certainly strengthens the effect.

SECRET AND PREPARATION

A Take one of the bills and place it flat on a table. "Accordion pleat" the bill into seven equal parts as shown.

NOTE: On a real dollar bill, the face of the bill is printed in black while the back is printed in green. To make the rest of the steps clear, they will be described as if you are using a real bill.

B With your bundle now folded into seven pleats, one of the outside surfaces of the packet will show part of the bill's face (dark side) while the other surface will show part of the back (green side). Place the folded bill with the back (green side) next to the table. The face (dark side) is on top. Now, fold over one-third of the left side of the bill to the center as shown.

C Fold the other end (right side) of the bill over as shown. This last fold should bring the corner of the back (green side) of the bill to the top of the folded package. The complete folded package should appear as shown.

Glue here

D If the preceding three steps have been done correctly, you should have a small, flat package approximately 3/4" square. Glue this packet to the back of the duplicate bill. (If you use rubber cement, the bills can be easily separated after the show.) Position the bills as shown here. The glue is applied to the third of the bill that was next to the table when you folded the bill in Step C.

METHOD

In order to make it easy to follow the two bills in the illustrations, the secret bundle has been colored darker than the open bill that you first display to the audience.

1 Display the dollar bill to your audience, holding the bill opened out between the thumbs and fingers of both hands. Your left thumb keeps the folded bill from opening and prevents spectators on the sides from seeing it.

MARK WILSON'S CYCLOPEDIA OF MAGIC

NOTE: You may wish to start the routine by holding the bill in your right hand with your right fingers on the side of the duplicate bill, completely hiding it from sight. In this way, you may show the bill on both sides. Then, turn the face of the bill to the audience and transfer your grip on the duplicate bill from the fingers of the right hand to the thumb of the left hand.

2 Tear the bill down the center line into two equal parts, as shown.

3 Place the right-hand half of the bill in front of the left-hand half.

4 Grip the two halves between the thumb and fingers of both hands and tear both halves, as shown.

5 Again, place the torn pieces in the right hand, in front of the pieces in the left hand and square the packet. To you, the torn pieces and the duplicate bill should appear as shown.

NOTE: A neat touch here can be added by first placing the torn pieces in the right hand to the rear of the packet held in the left hand. The four pieces can then be spread in a small fan and shown on both sides. The pieces at the rear will conceal the folded duplicate bill. Then, in squaring up the packet, you move the rear pieces back to the front and continue with the trick.

6 Fold the right-hand edges of the torn pieces forward so that they are even with the right side of the secret folded bill, as shown.

7 Fold the left-hand edges of the torn pieces forward, even with the left edge of the secret bill.

8 Fold down the top edges of the torn pieces, even with the top edge of the secret bill.

9 Finally, do the same with the bottom edges, folding them upwards, even with the bottom edge of the secret bill. You have now created a folded package of the torn pieces that matches exactly in size and shape the duplicate bill behind it.

10 Folded in this way, the total package gives the impression of being only the folded pieces of the original bill. This makes it easy to casually turn the package over showing both sides of the torn bill. When you finish showing both sides, be sure that you end with the duplicate bill in front and the folded torn pieces to the rear.

11 Make a magical gesture or say an appropriate magic word and begin unfolding the top and bottom thirds of the whole bill, as shown.

12 When these portions have been unfolded, grasp the right-hand edge of the bill with your thumb and first finger. Your left thumb holds the folded torn packet against the back of the bill, as shown.

13 By pulling your hands apart, the duplicate bill unfolds so quickly it will seem to the spectators as if the torn pieces have been restored.

14 Briefly, display the restored bill. Then, fold it in half back over the torn pieces, thus eliminating the possibility of accidentally exposing the torn packet as you return the restored bill to your pocket.

SIX-BILL REPEAT

The ability to throw away your money and still keep it would be real magic, like having your cake and eating it too. That is exactly what you do with the SIX-BILL REPEAT; at least, it is what you appear to do. The best part of this effect is that the surprise increases with each repeat, which is quite unusual. Most tricks lose their impact after they have been performed once. This makes the SIX-BILL REPEAT an outstanding number in any program, as you will find out for yourself when you perform it.

EFFECT

You remove your wallet and take out a number of dollar bills. The audience can see you counting six of them, one by one. Dealing three of the bills on the table, you call the spectators' attention to the fact that simple mathematics would dictate that you have just three bills left in your hand. After all, three from six leaves three, doesn't it? Well, not in this case, for when you recount the money, you find you still have six dollar bills. You keep discarding three bills, only to find that each time you are magically left with six. This continues until a sizable amount of money is displayed on the table.

SECRET AND PREPARATION

The secret lies in four specially constructed envelope-type bills. (We will assume that you will be using stage money for this effect, although real bills can be prepared in the same way.)

A The first step is to cut the upper-left corner off four face-up bills, as shown.

B Place the long edge of one of the cut bills next to an unprepared bill, as shown. Be sure that the unprepared bill is face down and the cut bill is face up.

C With a strip of cellophane tape, fasten the edges of the bills together.

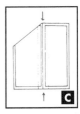

D Fold the cut bill down on top of the unprepared bill. By taping the narrow edges at the left end of the bills, you have created an envelope. To hide the tape on the narrow edges, fold the tape with the sticky side out and tape the narrow edges inside the bills.

E Insert three unprepared bills into the envelope bill. Be sure that the unprepared bills all face in the proper direction and are correctly aligned so they match the printing of the envelope bill.

F Make up three more envelope bills and insert three regular bills inside each.

MARK WILSON'S CYCLOPEDIA OF MAGIC

G Arrange the four loaded envelope bills and add two unprepared bills to the front of the final stack.

H Square up the stack so that the diagonal cuts of the prepared bills are at the top and facing in your direction. Place the bills in a secretarial-type wallet (or a business-letter size envelope), and you are ready to perform.

METHOD

1 Remove the bills from your wallet and hold the stack in your left hand. Slowly and deliberately count the bills into your right hand, making sure not to disturb the correct order.

2 At the completion of the count, all six bills should be in your right hand with the four prepared envelope bills still facing you.

3 Square up the stack and transfer all of the bills to your left hand.

4 Count off three unprepared bills, pulling them out of the top envelope bill one at a time. Count them aloud, "One, two, three," as you place them on the table.

5 You are now left with an empty envelope bill at the rear of the stack. Move this envelope to the front of the stack (audience side) and give the remaining three bills a deliberate snap with your fingers. As you do this, remark, "By placing the back bill in the front and giving the packet a magic tap, it magically doubles the amount of money left in my hand."

6 Slowly count the bills as before (Step 1), demonstrating the magical restoration to six bills.

7 It is important that during the counting you maintain the order of the two regular bills and the four envelope bills. In other words, from your point of view, you should now have in your right hand, starting from the side nearest you, three loaded envelope bills, two regular bills, and one empty envelope bill. In the illustration, the bills have been purposely fanned open to show more clearly their position at this point in the routine.

8 This process continues until all of the loaded envelopes have been emptied. All in all, twelve new dollar bills make their magical appearance. The effectiveness of this illusion is enhanced by repetition. The audience becomes more and more involved as the trick progresses.

COMMENTS AND SUGGESTIONS

This trick is quite effective. The props can be made inexpensively, and they can be seen by a large audience. The entertainment value of the trick lies in the "patter" story that you devise to accompany it. Here is an example:

MARK WILSON'S CYCLOPEDIA OF MAGIC

"I saw an ad in a magazine for the Mark Wilson Course in Magic. The ad said that one of the tricks I would learn is how to count, one-two-three-four-five-six dollar bills, remove one-two-three bills, and still have one-two-three-four-five-six dollar bills left. So, I ordered the course. While I was waiting for it, I wondered how you could possibly have one-two-three-four-five-six dollar bills, remove one-two-three, and have one-two-three-four-five-six dollar bills left. When I received the course, sure enough, I practiced and learned how to count one-two-three-four-five-six dollar bills, remove one-two-three, and still have one-two-three-four-five-six dollar bills left."

You have now emptied three of the envelope bills; you have one loaded envelope left. Your patter continues:

"And now I am going to tell you the secret. Instead of starting with one-two-three-four-five-six dollar bills, you really have one-two-three-four-five-six-SEVEN-EIGHT-NINE bills to start with. And that's how this trick works."

The last count of nine, with its comedy explanation, is performed by counting the three bills from the last envelope and then counting the envelope bills as well.

NOTE: When you use this nine count, be sure to place the envelope bills on the table so that the cut side of the bills is face down and cannot be seen by the audience.

BILL IN A LEMON

BILL IN A LEMON is one of the great classics of modern magic. Several famous magicians have featured it as the highlight of their programs. There are several different versions of this mystery. In the clever method described here, no special skill is required. Thus it is an ideal trick for new students of magic as well as advanced practitioners.

EFFECT

From a bowl containing three lemons, a spectator is given a free choice of the lemons. The selected lemon is then placed in an ordinary paper or plastic bag, and the spectator holds the lemon throughout the entire presentation. After the lemon has been selected and is securely held by the spectator, you borrow a dollar bill and write its serial number on the back of a small envelope. You then insert the bill into the envelope, seal it, and give it to a second spectator to hold. You recap exactly what has happened up to this point. Then the spectator holding the envelope is told to tear it open and remove the borrowed bill. When this is done, the spectator finds, instead of the bill, an IOU for one dollar, signed by you. The first spectator is given a knife and asked to cut open the selected lemon, which has remained in that person's custody at all times. Inside the lemon, a tightly rolled dollar bill is found. When the bill is opened, its serial number is found to be exactly the same as the number written on the envelope, proving that the borrowed bill has magically traveled from the envelope to the inside of the freely selected lemon.

SECRET AND PREPARATION

For this amazing effect, you will need the following items: a stack of a dozen or more envelopes (small "pay" envelopes are best, but any small, opaque envelope can be used), three lemons, a bowl, a dollar bill, your handwritten IOU on a piece of paper that is the same size as a dollar bill, a rubber band, a pocket knife, some glue, and a small paper or plastic bag. A transparent bag is best.

HOW TO PREPARE THE ENVELOPES

A To begin, write the serial number of your dollar bill on the back of one of the envelopes near the lower end, as shown. For future reference, this envelope has been marked with an O in the illustrations.

B Carefully cut off the gummed flap from another envelope. This envelope is identified with an X in the illustrations.

C This is how Envelopes X and O should look at this point.

D Fold the IOU and insert it into Envelope O.

I OWE YOU
$1.00
YOUR SIGNATURE

E Place Envelope O on top of the stack of regular envelopes so that the written serial number is facing up, as shown.

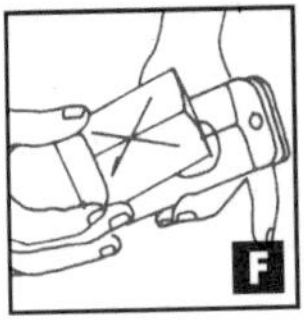

F Then place Envelope X (the one with the flap cut off) directly on top of Envelope O, concealing the serial number from view.

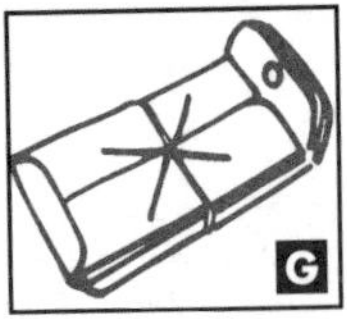

G Square up the envelopes and place the rubber band around the entire stack. Done properly, the gummed flap of Envelope O will appear to be the flap belonging to Envelope X.

HOW TO PREPARE THE SPECIAL LEMON

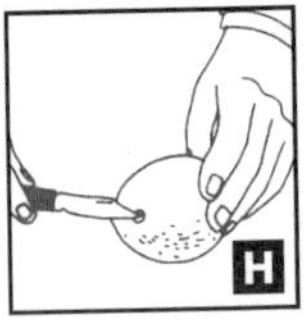

H Carefully remove the "pip" from one of the lemons with the point of a knife. Do not throw the pip away; you will need it later.

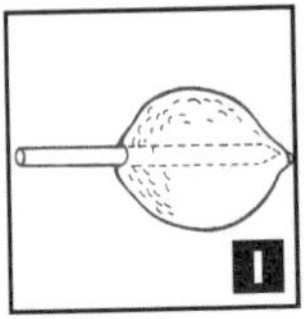

I Using a smooth, round stick (like the kind used for candied apples) or any similarly shaped slim, long object, carefully make a hole in the center of the lemon, as shown. This will expand the inner core area of the lemon and make the necessary space to accommodate a rolled bill. Be careful not to go too far and puncture the skin at the other end of the lemon with the stick.

NOTE: If a wooden stick of this type is not available, certain kinds of ballpoint pens and some pencils are thin enough to make the correct size of hole in the lemon. The important point here is that whatever object you are using be thin enough so that it does not puncture the inside, juicy portion of the lemon when it is inserted.

J Roll the dollar bill into a tight, compact cylinder.

K Push the rolled bill completely into the lemon. Be sure that you have written down the serial number of the bill before you insert it into the lemon. Use a small dab of glue (model-airplane glue works well) to fix the pip back on the lemon. When you glue the pip back in place, adjust it so that it hides the small hole in the end of the lemon.

L Finally, place the prepared lemon (marked X in the illustration) in a bowl with two ordinary lemons. Be certain that you are able to distinguish the prepared lemon from the other two at a glance.

NOTE: There may be a special blemish on the prepared lemon that you can remember, or you can make a small mark with a black pen or pencil on the lemon that will not be noticed by the spectators.

M Place the bowl of lemons, the stack of envelopes, the pencil, the knife, and the small bag on your table. You are now ready to present this classic mystery.

METHOD

1 The "free choice" of the special lemon is accomplished by forcing, using the MAGICIAN'S CHOICE FORCE, which is described in detail on page 99. In this force, the spectator believes there is a free choice of any of the three lemons. Actually, you cleverly maneuver the spectator to select the special lemon. After the "selection" is made, pick up the small bag from your table. Hold the bag open and have the spectator drop the lemon inside. Tell the spectator to hold the bag tightly so that the lemon cannot get away!

2 Borrow a dollar bill from one of the spectators. Explain that you will write its serial number on the top of the stack (Envelope X). As you pretend to copy the number from the borrowed bill, you actually write any number you wish on the envelope; it will automatically be switched for the correct serial number that is now hidden on the second envelope in the stack, Envelope O. (It is best if you remember the first letter of the serial number of your bill, as this is the most obvious thing that the spectators might see and remember.) Just casually copy the number (with your first letter) of the borrowed bill. Remember, the spectators do not know what trick you are going to perform, so they will not pay particular attention to the serial number if you do not call attention to it.

3 Fold the borrowed bill to about the same size as your IOU. Openly insert it into the flapless Envelope X. Be sure that everyone sees that the bill is definitely going into the top envelope of the stack. Be careful not to show that Envelope X does not have a flap.

NOTE: Inserting the bill into Envelope X requires some practice in the handling of the envelopes so that you can do it smoothly and not arouse suspicion. It may be helpful to remove the rubber band before attempting to insert the bill into the top envelope. This depends on how tightly the rubber band holds the packet of envelopes.

4 Once the bill has been inserted into Envelope X on the top of the stack, grip the uppermost flap (actually the flap of Envelope O) between your thumb and fingers and draw this envelope from the rest of the stack.

MARK WILSON'S CYCLOPEDIA OF MAGIC

5 What you are really doing is drawing out Envelope O instead of Envelope X, but you hide that move from the spectators by turning the stack completely over as you draw the envelope clear.

6 This makes a perfect switch of Envelope X, the one containing the borrowed bill, for Envelope O, the one that contains your IOU.

7 Make sure Envelope O is entirely clear of the rest of the stack.

8 Turn it flap-side up so that the serial number that you previously wrote on Envelope O is clearly visible to the spectators. The spectators will be convinced that it is the same envelope and that everything is legitimate.

9 Immediately place the rest of the envelopes in your pocket, eliminating the possibility of anyone discovering that a switch was made. Seal Envelope O and give it to a spectator to hold.

10 Ask the spectator holding the sealed envelope to raise it toward the light to see that the bill is really there. Of course, what they actually see is the outline of your IOU.

11 Ask the first spectator to make sure the lemon is still in the bag. After the affirmative reply, ask the spectator if anything could have gotten inside the bag with the lemon. After the reply, recap what has happened up to this point. Explain that first you had one of three lemons selected and that the chosen lemon has been securely held by a spectator at all times.

12 Emphasize that you borrowed a dollar bill from a spectator after the selected lemon was safely in the bag held by another spectator. The serial number of the bill was recorded on the outside of an envelope, and the bill was sealed inside. Emphasize again that the envelope, with the bill still sealed inside, is now held by the second spectator.

13 The trick is now already done, but the spectators don't know it! Ask the second spectator to tear open the envelope and remove the bill.

14 When the spectator opens the envelope, the IOU is discovered instead of the bill.

15 Give the knife to the person holding the bag with the lemon inside. Ask that spectator to remove the lemon from the bag. Once this is accomplished, take the bag from the spectator and hold it in your hand. With your other hand, give the spectator the knife and instruct that person to cut the lemon open. (It's even better if the spectator uses a pocket knife borrowed from another person!) Ask the spectator to rotate the lemon around the knife blade as if it had an inner core that should not be cut.

16 The spectator draws the halves of the lemon apart.

17 Inside, the spectator finds the bill embedded in the center. Emphasize that you have never touched the lemon since it was selected from the bowl.

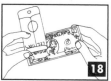

18 After the bill is removed from the lemon by the spectator, take the lemon halves and drop them into the bag. Put the bag on your table or casually toss it on the floor. (This subtly gets rid of the gimmicked half of the lemon so that it is not lying about where someone might pick it up and examine it later on.) Have the spectator compare the serial number on the bill that was in the lemon with that of the now-vanished, borrowed bill, which was written on the envelope. The spectator will find that the numbers are identical, proving that the borrowed bill has gone from the sealed envelope into the freely selected lemon—a magical miracle! Take back your IOU in exchange for the borrowed bill and thank the spectators for their assistance.

COMMENTS AND SUGGESTIONS

Be sure to write down the serial number of your bill before you load it into the lemon. Also, have the first letter of the serial number written somewhere handy for quick reference in case you forget it. You can strengthen the effect even more by writing the complete serial number of your loaded bill on Envelope X. To help you remember it, you may write the number very lightly (so that no one can notice it) on the back of Envelope X before the show. Another subterfuge for remembering the number is to have the number already written near the center of the envelope and then cover it with a wide rubber band. You can then shift or remove the rubber band toward you as you write. If you use this method, be sure to keep the stack of envelopes turned toward you as you write. When you have finished, you may display the stack freely to the spectators since the number matches identically the previously written number on Envelope O underneath. As for the rubber band, its main purpose is to keep the envelopes neatly in place during the early handling of the stack. Because it may prove helpful for the switch, the rubber band does not have to be removed from the stack during the performance unless it is too tight.

Another suggestion is to use an orange instead of a lemon. Because an orange is somewhat larger, it is easier to load, and you can easily withdraw the pip from the orange before inserting the bill.

It is a good plan to get several people to offer you a bill for the trick, so you can pick the one that most closely resembles the age and wear of the bill already in the lemon. Also, don't give the owner time to note the serial number, since you are going to give back your bill instead of the one you borrowed.

As you can see, this is one of the truly great tricks in magic. You can build your reputation on this one trick alone, so study it and practice it before you perform it. Add your own touches. Emphasize the impossible nature of what the spectators have seen. Remember, always protect the truly marvelous secret of the BILL IN A LEMON.

CHAPTER 13
ROPE MAGIC

Here is a highly popular branch of modern wizardry that has grown by leaps and bounds for a very good reason. Simple tricks with rope can be done in an impromptu fashion. One good rope trick invariably paves the way to another, gradually enabling you to build a reputation as well as a program.

Originally, rope magic was confined chiefly to trick knots that puzzled spectators but did not actually mystify them. A new era arrived with the CUT-AND-RESTORED ROPE. Variations of this trick led to improvements that were baffling even to magicians who depended on the old-time routines.

Now, instead of merely cutting a rope in half, a magician can cut it into several pieces before restoring it. Short ropes can be tied together with knots that disappear, leaving one long rope.

ROPE
PREPARATION

In performing Rope Magic, there are several tips you should know about the preparation of the rope to achieve the most effective results in practice and presentation.

CORING

In certain tricks, it is important that the rope be extremely flexible, even more so than it already is. In that case, you can do what is known as "coring" with many types of rope, especially the soft cotton rope used by magicians. If you look at the end of some types of rope, you will notice that the rope is constructed of a woven outer shell which contains an inner core. This core is made up of a number of individual cotton strands running the entire length of the rope. To remove the core, cut off a piece of rope and spread open the threads of the outer shell at one end. With your fingers, firmly grasp the strands of cord which make up the core. Now with your other hand, get a firm hold on the outer shell near the same end and start pulling the core from within the rope's outer shell. As you pull the core and slide the outer shell, you will find that the shell tends to bunch up and then bind, making it difficult to pull out the inner core. When this happens, grasp the rope just below the bunched-up shell and pull the shell down along the length of the remaining core until the shell is straight again, with the empty shell extending from the other end of the core. Then pull another length of core out from within the shell until it binds again. Continue this process of pulling and unbunching until the core has been completely removed from within the shell of the rope. This leaves you with the soft, flexible outer shell of the rope. To the audience, however, the rope will appear just the same as before you removed the core.

FIXING THE ENDS

Another suggestion which will aid in maintaining the appearance of your rope, particularly if it has been cored, is to permanently "fix" the ends of the rope so that they will not fray (come apart). This can be done in several ways.

1. A particularly good method is to dip the end of the rope into a small amount of white glue and allow it to dry overnight. This will permanently bond all the loose fibers together and prevent them from unraveling.

2. Another substance which works well for this purpose is wax or paraffin. After the wax is melted, the ends of the rope are dipped into the liquid wax and allowed to dry. This method has the advantage of a short drying period. Your ropes can be prepared only minutes before a performance.

3. Another method which works well is to tie off the ends of the rope with regular, white sewing thread after the rope has been cut to the desired length. Simply wrap the thread around the ends of the rope and tie the ends tightly to keep the rope from unwinding.

4. One final method is to wrap a small piece of white adhesive tape or transparent cellophane tape around the ends of the rope. Because tape is more easily visible, however, it may draw undue attention to the ends of the rope and distract from the effect being presented. However, the tape method is a good, fast way to get your rehearsal ropes ready.

CUT-AND-RESTORED ROPE I

This effect has become a magical classic in its own right and is one with which every magician should be familiar. Almost all versions of the CUT-AND-RESTORED ROPE are based upon the same simple method. Once you have learned it well, you can continue with other forms of the trick described later.

EFFECT

You display a 6' length of rope. Then, you form the center of the rope into a loop in your hand and cut it there, explaining that the rope must first be divided into two equal sections. However, it becomes immediately evident, first to the audience and then to you, that the two resulting lengths of rope are not the same length. Somewhat frustrated, you tie the cut ends together with a simple knot and wind the rope around your hand. After a little magic, you unwind the rope to show that the knot has dissolved, leaving the rope completely restored.

SECRET AND PREPARATION

The only items required for this effect are a length of rope, a coin (or some other small object), and a pair of sharp scissors. To prepare, place the coin in your right pants or jacket pocket. Have the scissors on a table nearby. This done, you are ready to begin.

METHOD

1 Display the rope to your audience, holding the ends between the thumb and fingers of your left hand, so that the center of the rope hangs down as shown.

NOTE: There are two key locations on the rope that will greatly

help in explaining the secret of the CUT-AND-RESTORED ROPE. The first is a point about 4" from the end of the rope. We will call this Point A. The second is the true center of the rope. This we will call Point B.

2 Insert your right thumb and first finger through the center loop, Point B, from the audience side of the rope as shown. Your right thumb and first finger are pointing upward and slightly back toward you as you insert them into the loop.

3 With your right hand, bring the rope up toward your left hand, keeping the loop, Point B, draped loosely over your right thumb and first finger.

4 As your hands come together, your right thumb and first finger grasp the rope at Point A as shown.

5 Here comes the secret move which makes the trick work. Pull Point A upward so that it forms a small loop of its own, which you hold between your right thumb and first finger. At the same time that you pick up Point A, tilt your right fingers downward so that Point B, the real center of the rope, slides off your right fingers into the cradle of rope formed when you lifted Point A into a loop. Study the illustration for Steps 4 and 5. These steps must be hidden from the spectators by your left hand.

6 As you raise Point A upward to form the new loop, your left thumb keeps the real center, Point B, down in your left hand, out of view of the spectators.

7 This new loop, Point A, takes the place of what the audience still believes is the real center of the rope, Point B, since your left hand concealed the secret switch.

8 With the scissors, cut the rope at Point A. Say, "I'll cut the rope at the center, which makes two ropes exactly equal in length."

9 After the cut, the audience will see four ends projecting above your left hand. Point A has now been cut into two parts, as shown.

10 With your right hand, draw the end at the far right away from your left hand.

11 Drop that end and say, "That is one rope ..."

12 Grasp the end of the rope at the far left.

13 Let it fall next to the first as you say, "... and here is the second rope." At this point, it will become obvious to the audience that the two ropes did not come out equal in length as you

MARK WILSON'S CYCLOPEDIA OF MAGIC

had intended. Pretend to be puzzled and somewhat frustrated at the results. Say, "Something seems to have gone wrong; the rope must be cut into two equal pieces."

NOTE: The two ends of the short piece of rope that project above your left hand look like the ends of two separate long ropes. The real center of the rope (Point B) is looped over the short piece of rope.

14 As an optional convincer, you can add the following move to prove that you actually have two separate pieces of rope. Cover the interlocking loops at Point B with your left thumb. Swing your left arm out to your left side so that the palm of your left hand is facing the audience. This lets you casually show both sides of the cut ropes, while your left thumb hides the fact that the upper ends are really the ends of a short loop, not the ends of two long ropes. Then, swing your arm back to its former position in front of your body and continue with the next step.

15 While your hands conceal the true condition of the ropes, tie the ends of the short rope around the center of the long piece of rope at Point B. Be careful not to reveal that you have one long rope and one short rope while tying the knot.

Short piece knotted around long rope

16 You can now openly display the rope to the audience, as you call attention to the knot which is tied slightly off center.

17 Starting at either end, begin to wind the rope around your left hand. What you really do, however, is slide the knot along the rope with your right hand as you continue the winding process. Keep the knot hidden in your right hand as you slide it along.

18 As you complete the winding, slide the knot off the end of the rope. Hold the knot secretly in your curled right fingers. Without pausing, dip your right hand into your pocket, remarking, "I will now need my magic coin," or whatever small object you are using. With that, leave the knot in your pocket and bring out the coin. Wave it over the rope as you make some remark about the magic coin.

19 Release the coin in your pocket and uncoil the rope, showing that the knot has vanished and the rope is completely restored! The rope can then be tossed to the audience for examination.

COMMENTS AND SUGGESTIONS

The length of the rope used in this trick can vary from 3' to 8' or so. It is a good plan to start with a long rope, as with each performance, the rope loses several inches. When it finally becomes too short to be effective, discard it and use another long rope or save it for some other trick in which a short rope is used.

CUT-AND-RESTORED ROPE II

EFFECT

You draw a long piece of rope through your hand and ask a member of the audience to call, "Stop," to select a point anywhere along the length of the rope. When the call comes, you cut the rope at the spot indicated by the spectator. After displaying the two pieces of rope, you decide that the rope served a more useful purpose as one long piece. As if by magic, you instantly restore the rope back to its original condition! The presentation can end at this point, or it can be used as a lead-in to a series of other rope effects.

SECRET AND PREPARATION

As in the CUT-AND-RESTORED ROPE I, the rope is unprepared. Again, the only items required are a sharp pair of scissors and a piece of soft rope about 5' or 6' in length.

METHOD

1 Display the length of rope, holding it by the ends as shown. We will call the ends of the rope A and B in the illustrations. End A is held in your left hand, and End B in your right.

2 With your right hand, place End B into your left hand between your first and second fingers. End B is positioned as shown, overlapping End A. Hold End B in place with your left thumb as shown.

3 Grasp End A with your right hand.

4 With End B held tightly by your left thumb, your right hand pulls End A down (toward yourself), as shown. As you pull the rope down, ask the spectator to tell you when to stop pulling.

5 As you pull End A, the loop in the rope will get smaller and smaller. The illusion created by this move is that the spectator is given a free choice as to where the rope will be cut. As you will see, it makes no difference where the spectator stops you.

6 When the spectator calls, "Stop," release End A and grasp the side of the loop closest to End B (Point X in the illustration). If you study the illustration, you will see that the spectator is actually cutting off only a small piece of rope close to End B, not near the center of the rope as the spectator thinks.

7 As soon as the spectator makes the cut, release your right hand. This allows the "new" end, which we will call X2, to fall next to End A. You now hold one short piece and one long piece of rope looped together in your left hand.

8 Adjust End X up next to End B and hold them with your left thumb and fingers. To the audience, it will appear that you hold two separate long lengths of rope.

9 At this point, comment to the audience that the two ropes have not come out equally and that you are a bit embarrassed by your mistake. With that, grasp End X2 in your right hand, as shown, keeping the end well within the hand.

10 Bring End X2 up to meet End X and grasp both ends together in your right hand, as shown in the illustration.

11 As soon as you have both ends held firmly together within your right fingers, release your left hand and shake the rope open, holding it with your right hand so that it appears to be one long rope restored into a single length. The effect is instant restoration.

12 Comment that, "It wasn't a very good trick anyway," as you tug on the now restored rope.

13 With the secret joint still concealed by your right hand, coil the rope and place it in your pocket.

COMMENTS AND SUGGESTIONS

In both methods of the CUT-AND-RESTORED ROPE, after you apparently cut the rope into two pieces (Step 13 in the first method, Step 8 in the second method), you are actually holding a long piece of rope which is secretly looped with a short piece. To the audience, it appears that you hold two separate long pieces of rope. At this point in the trick, because your left fingers conceal the interlocking loops, you may conclude the effect using either method of restoring the rope back to one long piece.

If you restore the rope as described in the second method, and you wish to continue with other rope tricks, you will need to dispose of the short end which extends from your right hand. A natural way to do this is to reach into your pocket to remove some object and simply carry the end of the restored rope and the short piece along. Then, when you remove your hand with the object, leave the short piece behind. The audience will not notice that the long rope has now become a bit shorter than before. If you used a pocketknife to cut the rope, this is a logical item to return to your pocket. You can leave the short piece behind with the pocketknife. You could also remove some small prop which you plan to use in your next trick, such as a ring, coin, or handkerchief. Another suggestion is to reach for some object on your table, carrying along the end of the rope and the short piece. When you pick up the object, you can leave the short piece on the table behind (or in) some prop that is already there.

Both methods of the CUT-AND-RESTORED ROPE are true classics of magic. Although quite simple, once learned they will become a permanent addition to your repertoire. Also, this is one of the few tricks that is just as effective when performed for a small, intimate crowd as it is for large audiences. This is a valuable and much used principle of magic. Practice it well before you present it, and, above all, do not reveal its secret.

TRIPLE ROPE TRICK

This differs from a cut-and-restore trick because no actual cutting is done. Instead, you start with three short lengths of rope and magically form them into a single, long rope. One particular advantage to this mystery is that no scissors are needed, so you can carry the ropes in your pocket and work the trick anytime, anywhere.

EFFECT

You show three pieces of rope that are about equal in length, pointing out that all three are knotted together at both ends. You untie one group of three knotted ends and then retie two of the ropes together again. Next you untie the other group of three knotted ends, and retie two of these ropes together. This leaves the three ropes tied end to end, forming one long rope—except for the knots! You coil the rope around one hand and remove a half-dollar from your pocket, which you wave over the rope. When the rope is uncoiled, the knots have vanished, and the three short ropes have amazingly turned into one single length that can be tossed to the spectators for examination.

SECRET AND PREPARATION

Actually, one long rope and two short pieces are used. The long rope is about 3' in length; the short pieces are each about 4" long. The preparation for this trick is as follows.

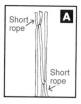

A Lay out the long rope in three sections. Loop a short piece of rope in the two bends of the long piece, as shown.

B Tie the three upper ends (one end of the long rope and two ends of the short rope) into one single knot, as shown. To the spectators, these appear to be the ends of three single ropes. Only you know that two of the ends are from the short rope and the third is one end of the long rope.

C This is how the knot looks when pulled tight.

D Tie the other three ends together in exactly the same way. This is all prepared ahead of time. To the spectators, it appears that you have three lengths of rope with their ends tied together.

METHOD

1 Display the "three ropes" to the spectators. With both hands, untie the large knot at one end. Make sure not to reveal that two of the ends are from the short piece of rope.

2 Hold the ropes in your left hand between your thumb and fingers, as shown. Your left thumb clips the short loop above where the long rope loops over the short rope, concealing it from view with your left fingers.

3 Let the end of the long rope drop, so that you are holding only the two ends of the short piece and the looped-over part of the long rope.

4 After you drop the long end, the rope should look like this.

5 Tie the short rope in a single knot around the long rope. Say, "I will tie two of the ropes together." Be sure to keep the small loop hidden by your fingers until the knot is tied. After that it can be freely shown.

6 Grasp the remaining large knot and repeat Steps 1 through 5. Say, "Now I will tie these two pieces of rope together as well."

7 Show what appears to be three short ropes knotted to form a single long one. Actually, it is one long rope with two short ropes tied to look like connecting knots.

8 Hold one end of the rope in your left hand and begin coiling the rope around your left hand with your right hand. As you wrap it around, the rope naturally slides through your right hand. When you come to the first knot, keep it in your right hand, secretly slipping it along the rope.

9 When you come to the second knot, slide it along in the same way with your right hand. The spectators will think that the knots are still on the rope coiled around your left hand.

10 As you complete the coiling, secretly slide both knots off the end of the rope.

11 Remark that you will now use your "magic coin." Your right hand goes into your right pocket—where you leave the knots and bring out the half-dollar.

12 Make a magical wave of the coin over the rope and replace the coin in your pocket. Unwind the rope from your hand, showing the knots completely gone!

13 The three short ropes have been magically transformed into one single, long rope—much to the amazement of the spectators!

COMMENTS AND SUGGESTIONS

The strong point of this clever mystery is that the trick is actually done before you begin. Therefore, you should stress that you have three single ropes at the start.

TRIPLE ROPE— MULTIPLE "DO AS I DO" KNOT

With receptive spectators, you can amplify this effect by giving out three sets of knotted ropes, letting two spectators follow along with you. Again, your ropes come out as one long piece and theirs do not. That is why it is called the "DO AS I DO" KNOT.

MARK WILSON'S CYCLOPEDIA OF MAGIC

METHOD

1 In using three sets (one special and two regular), the selection procedure is simple and neat. If both spectators (let's call them Joe and Anne) take an ordinary set, you keep the special one and proceed with your routine, having them copy your moves.

2 However, if Joe happens to take the special set, say, "You can see that your three ropes are knotted together at both ends." Then, take your set and give it to Joe, saying, "Take my ropes and give yours to Anne." As Joe gives the special set to Anne, take the ordinary set that Anne is holding. Continue, ". . . so Anne can give her ropes to me."

3 Briefly look at the set you took from Anne, then give it to Joe, saying, "Now take Anne's ropes and give her mine." As Joe does that, take the special set that Anne has, saying, "And Anne, give me yours." Then, speaking to both of them, you say, "Now that we have each checked all three sets of ropes to see that they are exactly alike, I want each of you to do exactly as I do."

COMMENTS AND SUGGESTIONS

In winding the coils around your left hand, be sure to tell your helpers to coil each knot inside the left hand, just as you do. Then go through the motion of bringing invisible "magic powder" from your pocket and tell them to do the same. The only difference is that your powder works, while theirs doesn't. This is proven when you each uncoil your rope and you have one long, single length, free of knots, while theirs haven't changed at all. You can also explain that your magic powder is truly invisible, whereas theirs is purely imaginary.

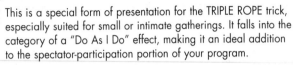

TRIPLE ROPE— "TIMES TWO"

This is a special form of presentation for the TRIPLE ROPE trick, especially suited for small or intimate gatherings. It falls into the category of a "Do As I Do" effect, making it an ideal addition to the spectator-participation portion of your program.

SECRET AND PREPARATION

This time start with two sets of knotted ropes. One is the special type already described: one long rope with two short loops, each looped to a portion of the long rope and knotted there to show three ends. The second set consists of three separate ropes, about the same length. These are actually knotted at both ends, so they look exactly the same as your fake set. You can identify the special set by making a small ink or pencil mark on one of the knots. The mark should be just large enough for you to notice.

METHOD

1 Bring out both sets of knotted ropes, remarking that each consists of three short ropes knotted at both ends. Explain that you intend to use one set in this mystery and the spectator is to use the other. Also explain that since both are exactly alike, the spectator may choose either set.

2 If the spectator takes the ordinary set, you keep the special set and say, "I want you to do exactly as I do. Untie your ropes like this." With that, you proceed step-by-step as already described in TRIPLE ROPE TRICK (see page 348).

3 If the spectator takes the special set, the one that you should have, you can handle the situation quite easily. Say, "Good, now I want you to do just as I do. Give me your three ropes, so I can untie their ends, while I give you my three ropes, so you can untie them." Thus the exchange of ropes becomes the first step in TRIPLE ROPE TRICK—MULTIPLE "DO AS I DO" (see page 352), and you simply carry on from there.

4 Proceed with the step-by-step process, moving slowly and deliberately so the spectator can copy your moves exactly. Since everyone sees that the spectator has three separate ropes, they will assume that yours are the same.

5 On the last step, you wrap the rope around your hand and then reach into your pocket to remove some invisible "magic dust." Tell the spectator, who has been duplicating your every move, to pretend to have a pocketful and to sprinkle it on the rope as you do the same. (It is at this point that you leave the two knots in your pocket.) Your rope now comes out all in one piece while the spectator's is still in three pieces—proving that there is no substitute for "real" invisible magic dust. Give the spectator a handful from your pocket along with the unrestored rope!

CUT-AND-RESTORED STRING

The following is one of those clever effects that can be presented anywhere and always leaves the spectators completely baffled. It might well be classified as a close-up version of the more familiar CUT-AND-RESTORED ROPE tricks. However, the method for this effect is quite different, which makes the mystery all the more puzzling.

EFFECT

You call attention to a single length of string that you proceed to cut into two equal parts. You give one end of each of the cut strings to a spectator to hold. With everything in full view, the spectator instantly restores the twine to its original condition. The stunned spectator is then given the piece of string as a souvenir.

SECRET AND PREPARATION

A The secret of this trick depends on a very clever principle. The properties of a certain type of common string are so obvious they go totally unnoticed by everyone. This type of string is composed of many individual strands of twine twisted together to form a multi-stranded string. It is sometimes referred to as "butcher's twine." It is usually thicker than ordinary string (like kite string) and is soft and white in color. To perform this mystery, all you need is a length of this type of string approximately 18" long. For the purpose of explanation, we will refer to the ends of the string as X and Y.

B Locate the center of the piece of string and spread the individual strands open, dividing the string into two equal sections of twine. We will refer to these sections as A and B.

C Pull Sections A and B about 5" apart, as shown. Slowly roll each section between your fingers so that they twist together to form two new false ends.

D Adjust the entire affair so that the two newly formed string ends (AX and BY) run so close together at the place where they connect (Point Z) that the secret connection between them is nearly impossible to detect.

E At this point, A and B form two fake ends of string, and X and Y (the real ones), the other ends. It appears that you have two separate strings.

F Apply a very small dab of rubber cement to Ends X and Y and allow them to become nearly dry. Then, attach the two ends (X and Y) together by rolling them between your fingers until they are joined.

G The resulting product should look like one continuous length of string, as shown. If this is done correctly, the string can be handled quite casually as you display it during the presentation.

METHOD

1 Display the prepared string, casually calling attention to the fact that you hold only one piece of string. As you prepare to cut the string, adjust your grip so that you hold it between the tops of your left fingers, as shown here. Your thumb and first finger should cover the secret connection (Z).

2 With scissors, cut the string (both pieces) near the bottom of the hanging loop just above Point XY. Let the glued joint (XY) drop to the floor, leaving you two new unglued X and Y ends. This automatically removes the only gimmicked part of the string for the astonishing conclusion of the trick.

3 Call attention to the absolute fairness of every move you make. The spectators will be convinced that you have merely cut a single length of twine into two equal parts.

4 Place the scissors aside and display the two separate pieces of string. Be sure to handle the string(s) in a casual manner so as not to give the impression that you are concealing something, but keep the strings together at the secret connection (Z).

5 Ask a spectator to grasp Ends X and Y. When this is done, you hold Ends A and B (and the secret connection Z) in your closed fist, as shown.

6 Tell the spectator to pull sharply on the ends in opposite directions. When the spectator does this, release your grip on the string. Allow the secret connection to untwist and thus restore itself to its original form—the center of the string! All of the spectators will be astonished to see the strings weld themselves together as the ends are pulled.

COMMENTS AND SUGGESTIONS

Stress the fact that the string actually restores itself while the spectator holds both ends. The beautiful thing here is that there are no secret gimmicks or extra pieces of string to get rid of. As you can see, this is another outstanding close-up mystery. Build it up properly and you will be credited with performing a small miracle.

THREADING THE NEEDLE

EFFECT

You call attention to an ordinary piece of soft rope that is approximately 3' in length. You explain that even under the most adverse circumstances it is easy to magically thread a needle, if you know the secret. To demonstrate, you form a small loop from one end of the rope to represent the eye of a needle; the other end will substitute for the thread. With the loop in your left hand and the thread end of the rope in your right hand, you make a quick thrust at the loop. In spite of your speed and the fact that you may not even come near the loop, the needle has been magically threaded!

METHOD

1 After displaying the rope to the spectators, lay the rope over your left thumb so that Length A will measure approximately 12" and Length B will measure about 24".

2 Grasp Length B with your right hand and wrap the rope around your left thumb twice. Be sure you wrap the rope around your thumb in the direction shown in the illustration.

3 With your right hand, grasp Length B and twist the rope to form a loop about 2" high, as shown. This loop is lifted and placed between your left thumb and forefinger.

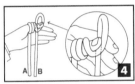

4 Grip the loop between your left thumb and forefinger so that it protrudes over the top of the thumb. This loop now represents the eye of the needle. End B of the rope must be the side of the loop closest to the palm of your left hand, as shown by the dotted lines in the illustration.

5 End A will now become the thread. Grasp A with your right thumb and fingers about 1" from the end. Lift A in front of B and hold, as shown.

6 Steps 6 and 7 are the actual threading. With End A in your right hand, move that hand forward, missing the loop with the end but allowing the lower part of A (marked with an X in the illustration) to pass between the left thumb and left fingers.

MARK WILSON'S CYCLOPEDIA OF MAGIC

7 As Length A passes between the left thumb and the left fingers, loosen your grip slightly by relaxing the left thumb as you pull Length A up sharply with the right hand.

8 The X part of Length A will now be through the loop, and it will appear as if you have threaded the eye without even coming close with the thread.

NOTE: There is now one less turn of rope around your left thumb. You lose one of these turns each time you thread the needle.

9 If you unthread the needle by really pulling End A back through the loop, you can immediately thread it again. (Notice again that there is one less turn around your left thumb.)

COMMENTS AND SUGGESTIONS

This effect is excellent when used in combination with other rope tricks to create an entertaining rope routine. On its own it also makes a good challenge at a party, for no matter how hard the spectators try to duplicate your movements, they will find it impossible to thread the eye of the needle.

When using the effect as a spectator challenge, be sure that the spectator attempts the threading using Length B as the thread. By substituting B for A, the trick becomes impossible to duplicate. You will also find, during practice, that you will be able to move your right hand as fast as you wish and still thread the needle, because the end of the thread never actually passes through the needle anyway.

ONE-HAND KNOT

EFFECT

You display a 3' length of soft rope. Casually tossing the rope into the air, a genuine knot appears magically in its center.

METHOD

1 Display a length of rope—a piece about 3' long is best. Drape it over your right hand, with End A hanging between the third and fourth fingers and End B between your thumb and first finger. Although End A may be any length, End B must not fall more than about 1' below your hand.

2 Turn your right hand over and grasp Length B between the first and second fingers at X, as shown.

3 Rotate your hand back up, as shown, holding B firmly between the first and second fingers.

4 Simply allow the loop that has been formed around your right hand to fall off your hand.

5 The end of B will be drawn through this loop, forming a knot in the rope. You may also snap the rope off your hand rather than letting it fall.

COMMENTS AND SUGGESTIONS

In order to disguise what is actually happening, practice the following movement: After grasping Length B firmly with the first and second fingers of the right hand (Step 2), throw the rope straight up into the air, letting go of Length B after it has passed through the loop. The effect will be that the knot was tied in the air.

NOTE: The softer the rope, the easier it is to do this trick. It will also work equally well with a soft handkerchief (silk is best) of the proper size.

MELTING KNOT

EFFECT

You slowly and deliberately tie a knot in the center of a 3' piece of rope. The spectators watch as you gradually tighten the knot by pulling on both ends of the rope. The knot becomes smaller until, just before cinching up tight, it melts away into nothingness!

SECRET AND PREPARATION

Once again, you will have use for that 3' length of soft rope. This mystery, combined with THREADING THE NEEDLE (see page 359) and other such effects, makes an entertaining routine with just this short length of rope.

METHOD

1 Display the rope to the spectators. (In the illustrations, we will call the end in your left hand End A and the one in your right End B.)

2 With your right hand, bring End B around behind your left hand and over the top of End A. Place End B between your left first and second fingers and release your right hand. You should now be hiding the rope, as shown.

3 Pass your right hand through the loop of rope and grasp End A between your right thumb and first finger.

4 Pull Ends A and B apart. Hold End B with your left thumb and fingers. As you do this, pull End A through the loop and slowly separate your hands.

5 You have now formed a false knot. In order to keep the knot from dissolving prematurely, you must roll or twist the rope with the thumb and first finger of each hand. Roll or twist the rope in the direction shown by the arrows (toward yourself).

6 You can clearly see the reasons for twisting the rope here. The rolling action of the ends forces the false knot to ride up and over itself, thus maintaining its knot shape.

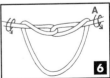

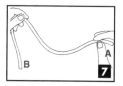

7 When the knot is just about to tighten up, blow on it as you pull the ends. The knot seems to dissolve into thin air. Properly preformed, the illusion is so perfect that you may immediately repeat the trick without fear of discovery.

SHOELACE ROPE TIE

EFFECT

You display a 3' length of soft rope to the spectators. Holding it between both hands, you skillfully tie a bow knot in the rope. You then thread the ends of the rope through the loops of the bows and pull the ends so that a hopeless knot is formed in the center of the rope. The spectators understand your problem, for they have probably had this happen with their shoelaces many times. However, as if to defy the laws of nature, you cause the cumbersome knot to dissolve before the eyes of the spectators!

METHOD

All you need for this clever effect is a soft rope approximately 3' in length.

1 Display the rope to the spectators and then lay it across the fingers of your right and left hands, as shown. Your left hand is above your right hand, your palms face you, and the backs of your hands are toward the spectators.

2 Hold the rope in position by pressing your thumbs against the rope.

3 Move your right hand next to your left hand, allowing the rope to hook underneath the left fingers and over the top of the right fingers.

4 Move your right hand behind your left hand, as shown.

5 Clip the rope at Point A between the tips of your right first and second fingers. At the same time, grasp the rope at Point B with your left first and second fingers. (Study the illustration carefully.)

6 Hold the two points (A and B) tightly between the fingers of each hand and begin to draw your hands apart.

7 As you continue to pull your hands apart, a bow knot will begin to form in the middle of the rope.

8 Gently pull the completed "bow knot" taut, as shown.

9 With your left thumb and first finger, reach through the left bow (B) and grasp the left end of the rope (C).

10 Pull the left end of the rope (C) back through the loop.

11 With your right thumb and first finger, reach through the right-hand bow (A) and grasp the right-hand end of the rope (D).

12 Pull that end of the rope (D) back through the loop (A).

13 Release the bows and gently pull on the ends of the rope, causing the bow to cinch up and form a large knot in the center of the rope. If you have followed the steps correctly, this knot will actually be a slipknot, or dissolving knot, as magicians often call it. Do not pull too hard on the ends or you will dissolve the knot too soon!

14 Instead, display the knot to the spectators as you comment about how bothersome a situation like this can be when it happens in everyday life. You might remark, "Being a magician comes in handy when this happens because all you have to do is to use the old 'knot-vanishing move' to get out of trouble." As you say this, pull on the ends of the rope, and the knot will magically vanish.

COMMENTS AND SUGGESTIONS

At first, when you start learning this clever effect, it may seem complicated and difficult to follow. Study the pictures carefully. The tying of the bow and the pulling of the ends through the loops will be perfectly natural and easy. These actions can be accompanied by clever patter, perhaps about how you became interested in magic as a child when you found that, in tying your shoes, the ends of the laces would slip through the bows and you always ended up with a knot. But when you began to study magic, you discovered that by merely pulling on the ends of the laces and blowing on the knot at the same time (or saying the magic words), the knot would dissolve itself.

RIGID ROPE

The legendary Hindu Rope Trick, in which the fakir would throw a coil of rope into the air and cause it to remain suspended, has long been a mystery. In fact, the exact method remains questionable to this day. The following trick might well be considered a smaller version of this great mystery. It can be performed anywhere, before small groups or larger audiences as well.

EFFECT

You display a length of rope about 3' to 4' long. The rope appears to be normal in every respect; and yet, upon your command, it becomes rigid and stands straight up from your fingertips. You pass your other hand around the rope on all sides, proving to the audience that the rope is unmistakably free from any threads or other hidden attachments. Then, with a mere wave of your hand, you cause the rope to gradually fall and return to its natural flexible state, right before the eyes of the spectators.

SECRET AND PREPARATION

A To present this trick, it is necessary to construct a special rope. First, remove the inner core from a piece of rope approximately 4' long (see page 338, Rope Preparation: Coring). This leaves just the woven outer shell, which now forms a small hollow tube 4' long.

B Cut a piece of solder wire (the kind of wire that is melted with a soldering iron to make electrical connections) so that it is slightly shorter than half the length of the rope. The solder should be about 1/16" to 1/8" in diameter and should be as straight as possible.

C Carefully insert the piece of solder into the hollow length of rope.

D Tie off both ends of the rope with white thread. This will prevent the solder from falling out of the rope during the presentation.

Ends tied with thread

Solder in rope

METHOD

1 Hold the prepared rope with one end in each hand as you display it to your audience. The end containing the solder is held in your left hand; the hollow end, in your right. Be sure to allow enough slack at the bottom of the rope so that it will curve naturally.

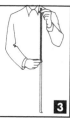

2 Release the hollow end of the rope from your right fingers and let it hang freely as shown in the illustration. This subtly conveys to the audience that the rope is flexible.

3 Grasp the rope with your right fingers slightly above the center of the rope. You will be able to feel the solder through the woven shell of the rope. At this point, your left hand still retains its grip on the top end of the rope.

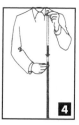

4 Relax the pressure on the solder with your right fingers and allow the wire to secretly slide down into the bottom half of the rope.

5 Release the upper end of the rope from your left fingers, and it falls limply over your right hand. At this point, the audience has seen that the entire length of rope is flexible.

6 Reach down and grasp the hollow end with your left hand and raise it upward.

7 Release the center of the rope from your right fingers and allow the rope to hang full length from your left hand.

8 Grip the center of the rope once again between your right thumb and forefinger; but this time, turn your right hand palm up so that your right thumb grips the rope from the audience side.

9 With your right hand still holding the center of the rope, release the hollow top end of the rope from your left hand and let it fall.

10 Grasp the bottom end with the solder in it with your left hand palm up.

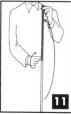

11 Here is the key move in the trick! As you keep the solder end of the rope pulled taut between your hands, with your left hand swing the solder end up to the top and, at the same time, rotate your right wrist, as shown. Using the pressure of the fingers of both hands, keep the solder in the top half.

12 Slowly and dramatically, remove your left hand from the top of the rope. Hold the bottom of the solder in the top half with your right hand. To the amazement of the viewers, the rope stays straight up, rigid! As the rope stands unsupported from your right hand, pass your left hand over the top and around all sides of the rope to prove that there are no outside connections responsible for this mystery.

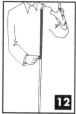

13 To restore the rope back to its flexible state, gradually relax your grip on the solder with your right fingers. Allow the solder to slowly slide into the bottom half of the rope. The effect will be that the rope gradually wilts. Gesture with your left hand as if the rope is always under your control as it loses its power to remain rigid.

14 When the rope falls completely limp, grasp the hollow end of the rope with your left hand. With your right hand still retaining its hold on the rope, begin to coil the hollow half of the rope around your left fist. When you reach the solder half of the rope, continue to wind the rope and the solder around your left fist. Due to the softness of the solder, the rope (with the solder inside) will coil around your hand. Place the coiled rope in your pocket or on your table and take your bows.

EQUAL-UNEQUAL ROPES

EFFECT

You display four lengths of rope by holding two ropes in each hand. Each pair is tied together in the center so that they form two sets of two ropes each. One of these sets consists of one long piece of rope and one short piece, while the other set contains two ropes exactly the same length. You ask for two spectators to come up on the stage. Each is then given one set of ropes. The spectator on the right, who holds the long and the short pair of ropes, is asked to turn around and face away from the audience. You pin one short and one long piece of ribbon on the back of this spectator to identify the sets of ropes. The spectator on the left, who holds the two equal ropes, is also asked to turn around and is marked by attaching two equal pieces of ribbon on their back. You point out that the ribbons enable the audience to easily identify the location of each set of ropes, even when the backs of the spectators are facing them. You then have both spectators face the audience as you explain that you will cause something magical to happen. With that, you ask them to again turn their backs to the audience and to untie their pairs of ropes. This done, they are asked to turn around and face the audience to show the ropes that they hold. To the surprise of the audience, as well as the two spectators, the two equal lengths of rope have magically exchanged positions with the two unequal pieces of rope!

SECRET AND PREPARATION

This clever mystery can be classified as a self-working trick, as the entire trick takes place in the hands of the spectators. The secret lies in the clever manner in which you have knotted the ropes before the show. For the trick, all you need are three pieces of soft rope about 5' in length, one piece of rope exactly half that long, and some ribbon.

MARK WILSON'S CYCLOPEDIA OF MAGIC

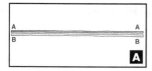

A To prepare, place two of the 5' lengths side by side, as shown. For the purpose of explanation, the ropes have been labeled A and B and, for clarity only, are shown in different colors. When performing the trick, all of the ropes must be the same color.

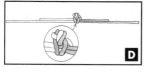

B Tie the two ropes together with a single overhand knot at a point approximately one-third of the distance from the end, as illustrated.

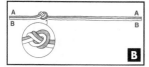

C Fold both ends of Rope B together, so that they run side by side in the same direction. Do the same with the ends of Rope A, as shown in this illustration.

D Tie another overhand knot on top of the first knot to further confuse the spectators. The result will appear to be one long and one short piece of rope tied together at the center.

E The next step is to tie the two unequal lengths of rope together so that they look as if they are equal in length. To do this, place the short piece (C) next to the long piece (D). The short rope (C) must be centered between the ends of the long rope (D).

F Tie the ropes together in the center using a single overhand knot, as shown.

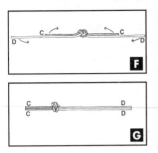

F

G Bring both ends of the short rope (C) together so they run side by side and do the same with the ends of the long rope (D). Secure the ends in place with another overhand knot. The result will appear to be two equal pieces of rope tied together at their centers.

G

H Finally, you will need three pieces of colorful ribbon about 2' long, and a fourth piece about 1' long. Attach a small pin to the end of each ribbon, and you are ready to present EQUAL-UNEQUAL ROPES.

METHOD

1

1 Display the two sets of ropes as you ask for the assistance of two spectators.

2 Give the spectator to your right the set of ropes that appears to be the unequal lengths (actually the equal ropes). To the spectator on your left, give the set that appears to be two equal lengths.

3

3 Have both spectators turn their backs to the audience and attach the corresponding lengths of ribbon to their backs. Have them turn to face the audience as you explain that the ribbons will serve to identify which spectator holds which set of ropes.

MARK WILSON'S CYCLOPEDIA OF MAGIC

4 Instruct the spectators to again turn their backs to the audience and then to untie their ropes. If you wish, you can now say something magical is going to happen. With that, instruct the spectators to turn and face the audience, holding one rope in each hand. Sure enough, when they turn around, the spectator on the left now has one short and one long rope instead of two of the same length, and the one on the right now has two ropes of the same length rather than two of unequal lengths. The two sets of ropes have magically exchanged positions while in the hands of the spectators!

COMMENTS AND SUGGESTIONS

This is a very clever novelty trick that always brings a laugh. Performed correctly, the two spectators themselves will not even get wise to the trick. Strange as it seems, when they untie these knots, the ropes seem to change length right in their hands, and they will not be able to understand how it happened! Of course, if you were to immediately repeat the trick, they would watch the ends and no doubt figure it out. However, the first time you work this, it will leave the spectators as mystified as the audience, enhancing the total effect.

GREAT COAT ESCAPE

Audience participation is the theme of this mystery, since you work directly with one spectator and call upon another for further assistance. The GREAT COAT ESCAPE is an excellent trick for a small group and also can be presented just as effectively before a large audience as part of your stage show.

EFFECT

You ask for the assistance of two spectators from the audience. Request that one of them bring a coat or jacket up on the stage. You then display two 8' lengths of rope which you proceed to thread through the sleeves of the borrowed coat. The spectator is asked to put the coat on while holding the ends of the ropes. This leaves the spectator with the two ropes running through the sleeves and the ends of the ropes protruding from both cuffs. Two of the ropes, one from each sleeve, are then tied together in a single overhand knot in front of the spectator. The knot is tightened. This draws the spectator's wrists together, thus imprisoning the spectator and the ropes securely within the coat or jacket. However, when the ends of the ropes are pulled sharply by you and the other spectator, the ropes seem to penetrate the spectator's body, leaving the spectator and the coat entirely free of the ropes!

SECRET AND PREPARATION

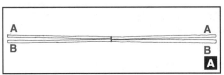

A The only items required to present this seemingly impossible mystery are two 8' lengths of soft rope and a small amount of ordinary white sewing thread. To prepare, lay the two lengths of rope side by side with their ends even. For the purpose of explanation, the two ropes have been labeled A and B in the illustrations. At the center of the ropes, tie a short piece of white thread around both ropes, forming a tight link that secretly holds them together.

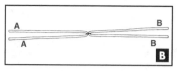

B Later, this secret link will enable you to double back the ends of the ropes as shown here, giving the appearance that the ropes are still running full length, side by side. You are now ready to proceed with the GREAT COAT ESCAPE.

METHOD

1 Pick up the two ropes and casually display them together with the secretly linked centers resting across your open fingers, as shown.

2 While the spectators are coming up on the stage, transfer the ropes to your left hand, swinging them carelessly back and forth while you reach for the spectator's coat with your right hand.

3 During that action, slide your left fingers between the ropes of both sides of the secret link, doubling back the centers of the ropes, as shown. This brings both ends of Rope A together at one side of the center link and both ends of Rope B together at the other side. The doubled centers remain concealed in the bend of your left fingers. To the spectators, everything seems normal, as you still hold the ropes at the center with the four ends dangling from your left hand.

4 (A and B) In Illustration 4A, the fingers are purposely lowered to show the secret link. Actually, the fingers should be closed around the centers of the ropes as shown in 4B so that the link is never seen.

5 With your right hand, take the spectator's coat and lift it so that your left hand can grip the coat by the collar, along with the doubled-back centers of the ropes, as shown. The back of your left hand is toward the audience during this action and in Step 6 which follows.

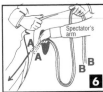

6 Have the spectator who lent you the coat grasp the ends of one set of ropes (A) with the right hand and insert it into the coat sleeve, carrying the ends of the rope (A) along. Note that your left hand still firmly holds and conceals the doubled centers of the ropes.

7 As the spectator's right hand emerges from the sleeve, tell the spectator to let go of the ends of the ropes so that they dangle from the sleeve. Then, bring your right hand up to your left and transfer the centers of the ropes, along with the coat collar, into your right hand. This frees your left hand, so it can open the left side of the coat as you ask the spectator to grasp the other ends (B) and carry them down the left sleeve. Then, have the spectator release those ends (B) as well.

8 As you adjust the spectator's jacket, push the doubled centers (and the secret link) inside the coat, down below the coat collar, and between the coat and the shirt, where they are hidden beneath the coat behind the spectator's back.

9 Take one end (A) that protrudes from the spectator's right sleeve and one end (B) from his left sleeve. Tie them together in a single overhand knot in front of the spectator's body. You must now have one End A and one End B paired up on each side of the spectator. By doing

MARK WILSON'S CYCLOPEDIA OF MAGIC

this, you have canceled out the secret link in the center of the ropes. As soon as you have tied the single ropes together (one from each sleeve), give the left-hand pair of ropes (one End A and one End B) to the assisting spectator and grasp the right-hand pair (the other End A and End B) in your own hands. This will position the bound spectator between you and the other spectator.

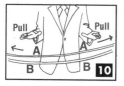

10 Upon your command, you and the spectator holding the other ends both pull your ropes sharply in opposite directions. This breaks the hidden thread, disposing of the secret link in the process. The two ropes will slide from the bound spectator's coat sleeves, completely releasing that person from the rope! Your spectators will be as mystified as your audience as to how you just accomplished an impossible penetration.

COMMENTS AND SUGGESTIONS

Be sure that the two pieces of rope you use are soft. If the rope is too stiff, the centers will not double properly. For that reason, it is a good idea to "core" the ropes as described earlier in this section. Each rope should be approximately 6' to 8' in length to allow for the crossing of the two ends that are tied. Extra length does not matter, because you and the other spectator can stand farther apart before you both pull the ropes.

Use a fairly strong thread (or wrap a lightweight thread around several times) to tie the centers. This will assure that it will not break before the ropes are pulled. Keep a firm grip on the centers when you are holding them along with the coat collar, particularly while the spectator is pulling the ropes down through the sleeves. Be sure to tell the spectator not to release the ends until the ropes are completely through, so there will be no extra strain on them.

This is an excellent effect that uses a proven, practical, basic, and very baffling magic principle. You can have great fun with the GREAT COAT ESCAPE.

ROPE-AND-COAT
RELEASE

EFFECT

You display a wooden coat hanger, pointing out to the audience that the hanger supports two lengths of rope and thus is a convenient way for you to store your props. However, this so-called "convenience" has its problems, one of which you demonstrate.

Two spectators are invited to join you on stage. After borrowing a jacket from one of them, you hang the jacket neatly on the coat hanger along with the two lengths of rope. The ends of both ropes are threaded through the sleeves of the borrowed coat. You take one rope from each sleeve and tie them together, imprisoning the jacket on the hanger. You hand a pair of rope ends to each spectator, supporting the coat and hanger with your other hand. Then, upon your command, the spectators pull the ropes in opposite directions. Magically, the ropes penetrate the hanger and the coat! The jacket is returned to the spectator unharmed. All of the equipment may be examined by the audience.

MARK WILSON'S CYCLOPEDIA OF MAGIC

SECRET AND PREPARATION

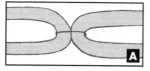

A Cut two pieces of soft rope approximately 6' in length. Now, fold each piece in the middle and tie them together with a lightweight piece of white thread as shown.

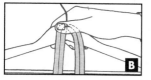

B It is best to use a wooden coat hanger with a wide shoulder support. You may already have one, but if not, most clothing stores use this type for displaying men's suits. (There are two important reasons for choosing this type of hanger. First, these hangers provide maximum protection for the spectator's jacket; second, they offer better concealment of the prepared ropes.) Place the ropes around the coat hanger. Cover the "join" in the ropes (where the ropes are held together by the thread) with the thumb and fingers of your right hand, as shown.

METHOD

1 Ask for the assistance of two spectators, one of whom must be wearing a suitable coat or jacket. Borrow this jacket and place it on the coat hanger. Keep the thread-connected loops to the rear of the hanger.

2 Have one of the spectators hold the hanger. Drop the pairs of rope ends down the corresponding sleeves of the jacket, as shown.

3 Turn the coat around and hand it back to the spectator to hold by the hook on the hanger. The secret thread "join" will now be concealed by the back of the jacket.

4 With the back of the jacket facing the audience, pick up any one of the two ends from each sleeve and tie them in a single overhand knot, as shown.

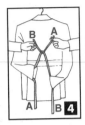

5 This is an important point in the trick. When you tie the ends, you automatically reverse their sides. This means that the single end that is tied from the left sleeve is handed to the spectator on the right, and the single end from the right sleeve is given to the spectator on the left. Be sure not to recross the tied pair and defeat your purpose.

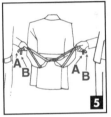

6 Stand behind the coat and hold the hanger, making sure that the spectators are standing one on each side holding their ends of the ropes. Now, instruct the spectators to pull on their ropes. This will cause the secret thread to break. The two lengths of rope will appear to penetrate the hanger and the jacket! You now return the jacket to your spectator and allow the audience to examine the ropes and the hanger.

MARK WILSON'S CYCLOPEDIA OF MAGIC

RING OFF ROPE

There are various tricks involving rings and ropes, and this is one of the best. RING OFF ROPE has the impact of an impromptu effect when done at close range, yet it can also be performed before a fairly large group with the assistance of two spectators, making it an equally good item for your stage show.

EFFECT

You borrow a finger ring from a spectator. You ask another spectator to thread it on a rope about 3' in length. Two spectators hold the rope, one at each end, yet you cause the ring to magically penetrate right through the rope! The ring is immediately returned to its owner. The ring can be thoroughly examined, along with the length of rope.

METHOD

1 Hand a spectator a piece of rope about 3' long for examination as you ask to borrow a finger ring from another. Retrieve the examined rope and invite a third spectator to thread the borrowed ring on the rope. Next, invite two spectators to help you with the trick. Ask one to stand to the left of you, and the other to the right.

2 Lay the threaded ring and rope across your upturned right hand. The ring should rest near the base of your first finger, and the ends of the rope should hang down from both sides of your hand, as shown.

3 As you display the rope in this manner, remark that it would be impossible to remove the ring from the rope without sliding it off one of the ends. With that, close your fingers over the ring and turn your hand completely over so that the back of your hand is up. The ring should be held loosely by your first finger near the very edge of your hand, as shown.

4 This illustration is a close-up view of how the ring should be held in your hand.

NOTE: To conceal the ring from the view of the spectator on your left, you can move your right thumb upward to fill in the open space where the ring might be seen in your hand.

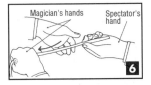

5 With the ring and rope held in this position, reach your left hand across your right forearm and grasp the dangling rope where it emerges from your right hand. Slide your left hand along the rope and give the right end of the rope to the spectator on that side. Ask the

spectator to hold that end. (The illustration is from the spectators ' viewpoint.)

Magician's hands   Spectator's hand

6 After the spectator grasps the right end of the rope, slide your half-cupped left hand along the rope, bringing it beneath your right fist.

7 At the very moment your left hand arrives below your fist, tilt your right hand slightly to the left and relax your right first finger. Allow the ring to secretly drop from your right fist into your left fingers.

NOTE: This drop should be done smoothly and without hesitation. If your left hand pauses for even the slightest moment, you will tip-off the audience that something suspicious is happening. This is the key move for this trick.

8 After your left hand catches the ring, raise your right hand upward. Look directly into the eyes of the spectator on your right and say, "Hold your end a little higher."

NOTE: This is a good example of the use of misdirection while the vital move of the trick takes place. By looking at and talking to the spectator, you take attention off the rope just long enough to make the secret steal. Also, by raising your right hand upward, the attention of the audience will be directed toward that hand, instead of your left hand, which secretly contains the ring.

9 As you raise your right hand upward, your left hand (and the ring) slides down along the rope and secretly carries the ring completely off the end of the rope. Without hesitation, as you secretly hold the ring in the finger-palm position (see FINGER-PALM VANISH, page 256), lift this end and give it to the spectator on your left. Tell the spectator to hold the end firmly.

10 Bring your left hand up beneath your right fist. Quickly open both hands, placing your palms together so that the rope and the now free ring are trapped between them. Start to roll your hands back and forth as if to cause the ring to dissolve through the center of the rope.

11 Lift your right hand to reveal the ring resting on your left hand next to the rope. Return the ring to its owner and pass the rope for examination.

COMMENTS AND SUGGESTIONS

Although using a borrowed ring is best, the routine is just as effective with your own finger ring, or even a small curtain ring or a metal washer. At the finish, everything can be examined, just as with the borrowed ring, so the effect on the audience is the same. The vital point is to make your presentation natural, so that no one will suspect the secret move. As you practice, working slowly and deliberately, you will find that the steal becomes easier and all the more deceptive. To condition the spectators to the naturalness of your actions, you can introduce the following before actually performing the trick: Hold the threaded ring in your open right palm as in Step 2. Say to the spectator on your right, "I am going to give you this end of the rope." With that, reach over with your left hand and start to give him the right end, but let it drop. Then say to the spectator on the left, "And I will give you this end," as you bring your left hand over and lift the left end of the rope and let it drop. Then say, "And all the while, I will keep the ring tightly in my right hand." With that, for the first time, turn your right fist downward. You are now all set to proceed, using almost the same moves with the ends of the rope, making the routine entirely natural throughout.

MARK WILSON'S CYCLOPEDIA OF MAGIC

IMPOSSIBLE ROPE ESCAPE
DON WAYNE

EFFECT

You call the audience's attention to two 5' lengths of unprepared rope. Then, you ask for the assistance of two spectators. Each spectator is handed one of the ropes for examination. While the spectators are busy with the ropes, you place a chair in the center of the stage. After they have confirmed the unprepared nature of the ropes, you sit in the chair and allow them to tie your knees and wrists together. When the spectators are satisfied that you are securely bound, they cover your wrists with a large cloth. Instantly, one of your hands is free; but before the spectators are able to remove the cloth, you plunge your hand back beneath the cloth. When the cloth is removed, the audience can see that you are still bound as tightly as before. The surprised spectators are asked to tie still another knot in the ropes above your wrist. They replace the cloth over your arms. Once more, you escape; but this time, upon lifting the cloth, you are completely free. The ropes have apparently penetrated your arms and legs as well!

SECRET AND PREPARATION

All you need for this excellent effect are two lengths of rope approximately 5' long, an opaque piece of cloth approximately 4' square, and a chair.

METHOD

1 Invite two members of your audience to join you on stage. Hand each of them one of the lengths of rope for their examination. While the two spectators examine the ropes, place the chair at stage center.

2 Take the rope back from the spectator on your right and drape it over the right hand as shown. We will call this Rope A. The middle of Rope A should rest on top of the first finger of the right hand near the thumb. Now, with the left hand, take the other rope from the spectator on your left. We will call this Rope B. Place the center of B between the first and second fingers of the right hand near the fingertips. Ropes A and B should now appear as shown.

3 The following series of moves will be made as you transfer the ropes from your right hand to your left. During this transfer, you will be inviting the spectator on your left to cross in front of you so that both spectators can examine the chair.

4 With your left hand, grasp Rope B at a point about 6" down from the loop of the rope (which is shown as Point X) and allow Rope A to slide off your right first finger onto the loop formed by B as shown.

5 With your right hand, pull Rope B up and over Rope A and down into the left hand to Point X.

6 Close the left fingers around the two hooked loops.

7 To the audience, the ropes will appear as if they both pass straight through your left hand.

8 The two spectators will have examined the chair by now, so position yourself in front of the chair. Have the spectators stand beside you, one on each side.

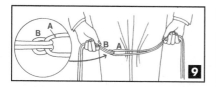

9 Reach behind your legs with your right hand and grasp both ends of Rope B. Be sure to hold the hooked loops securely in your left hand. Bring the ends of both A and B around your legs with the hooked loops behind your left knee as in the illustration. Now, sit down and, at the same time, place the loops in the bend behind your left knee.

10 The hooked loops must be positioned directly behind your left knee so that, as you sit down, the loops will be held firmly in place by the bend in your leg. Slide your left hand out along the ropes to your left.

NOTE: By holding the ropes as shown in Step 10, it appears to the audience that the two separate ropes pass directly under your legs.

11 Cross the two pairs of ends up and over your knees. Be sure that the left-hand Pair B crosses to the rear of the right-hand Pair A as shown. Pull the ropes tightly in opposite directions. This action apparently binds the knees together.

12 Position your wrists on top of the ropes. Still hold the loops firmly with the bend in your left knee.

13 Ask the spectator on your left to tie your wrists tightly, using as many knots as desired.

14 Ask the spectator on your right to cover your hands and knees with the cloth.

15 Under cover of the cloth, twist your wrists to the right. You will find that your left hand will easily come free of the rope. Bring your left hand into view and adjust the cloth. This action will bring a laugh from the audience. Quickly place your hand back under the cloth and into the ropes. Twist your hands to the left to retighten the ropes.

16 The spectator to your right is asked to remove the cloth. The audience will see that you are still securely tied. To make sure that you cannot escape, the spectator on your left is asked to tie another knot on top of those already there.

17 After the new knot is tied, have the spectator on your right cover your hand with the cloth again. As soon as you are covered, twist both hands to the right as in Step 16. This time, release both your hands from the loop and bring them both into view on top of the cloth. During the laughter, grasp the ropes through the cloth and lift sharply, as you relax your hold on the loops with your left knee. The ropes will come completely loose, apparently having penetrated both legs.

18 Stand up and drop the cloth containing the ropes on the chair seat. Thank your spectators and congratulate them on tying you so well as they leave the stage.

CHAPTER 14
SILK AND HANDKERCHIEF MAGIC

Tricks with handkerchiefs form a sizable category of magic. Besides playing a major role in certain tricks, a handkerchief often serves as an important adjunct in other effects where its purpose is totally unsuspected.

In certain tricks, the type of handkerchief used is important. With effects involving knots, larger handkerchiefs are better. In other effects, cotton handkerchiefs are excellent. A bandanna will aid concealment of small objects in the folds. You may borrow such handkerchiefs; then nobody will suspect trickery.

Some magicians go in for elaborate effects with colored silk handkerchiefs called "silks". Because they are compressible, they are excellent for production effects in which very large silks with colorful ornamental designs may be used. For less elaborate effects, such as bare-hand productions, vanishes, color changes, and the like, small silks are preferable.

HYPNOTIZED HANDKERCHIEF

EFFECT

You display a pocket handkerchief and twirl it between your hands in a rope-like fashion. Always under your control, the handkerchief stands erect, bows to the spectators, and moves back and forth in a very puzzling manner. You then attach an "invisible" thread to the upper corner of the handkerchief and cause the handkerchief to follow your lead by pulling on the magical leash. Even after crushing the handkerchief down with your other hand, you cannot seem to discourage the persistent performance of the HYPNOTIZED HANDKERCHIEF.

METHOD

1 Borrow a spectator's handkerchief (or use your own) and spread it open on the table. Hold the left-hand corner (A) between your left thumb and fingers and grasp the hem at the center of the right side (B) with your right hand, as shown.

2, 3 Pick up the handkerchief and hold it in front of you. Twirl the handkerchief between your hands.

4 Continue twirling until the entire handkerchief is rolled in a tightly twisted, rope-like configuration.

MARK WILSON'S CYCLOPEDIA OF MAGIC

5 As you continue to hold the twisted handkerchief, move your right hand above your left, so that the right end (B) is directly above the left end (A), as shown.

6 Move your left hand up, so that it can grasp the rolled handkerchief near the center. Do not allow the twists in the handkerchief to unroll as you change the position of your left hand. Your right hand maintains its grip on the top end (B).

7 Pull the handkerchief tight between your hands. Then, slowly release the handkerchief from your right fingers. It will stand erect, as if hypnotized. (In reality, the natural rigidity given to the material by the many twists is what causes the handkerchief to maintain its upright position.)

8 Pretend to pluck an imaginary strand of hair from your head and go through the motion of tying it to the upper end of the handkerchief (B). Holding the free end of this fictitious hair in your hand, slowly pull it toward your body. At the same time, draw your left thumb gently downward against your left fingers. The downward motion of your thumb will cause the handkerchief to obediently lean in your direction.

NOTE: Practice will teach you how to synchronize the handkerchief's leaning movement with the pulling motion of the "invisible" hair in your right hand.

9 Move your right hand and the "invisible" hair forward, toward the spectators. To make the handkerchief lean away from you and follow the "invisible" tug, simply slide your left thumb up and forward on the center of the handkerchief.

10 Here is a more detailed illustration of the move required for Step 8. This shows how the left thumb pulls down on the center of the handkerchief to make it lean toward you.

11 Here is the action, as your left thumb pushes up and forward on the center of the handkerchief, causing the handkerchief to lean away from you for Step 9.

12 After repeating this back and forth pulling movement with the "invisible" hair several times, bring the handkerchief back to its original upright position. Hold your right hand above the hypnotized handkerchief, as shown.

13 In one swift downward motion, bring your right hand down on top of the handkerchief, crushing it between your right palm and the top of your left fist.

14 Quickly raise your right hand back up. As you do, secretly use your right fingers and thumb to straighten the handkerchief.

15 Bring the handkerchief back to its original, hypnotized, upright position. With practice, you will learn to execute this upward movement so swiftly and smoothly that the handkerchief will appear to bounce back into shape of its own accord.

16 To conclude the effect, snap the handkerchief open and offer it to the spectators for examination.

FATIMA, THE DANCER

EFFECT

You tell the story of an exotic dancer named Fatima. Although she lived and danced many years ago, her exotic movements and high kicks have never been forgotten. To illustrate, you tie a knot in a pocket handkerchief. With a twist and a twirl, you turn it into a doll-like replica of the famous dancer. To the accompaniment of a short poem, you seem to make the cloth figure come alive, dancing about between your hands, finishing in grand style with a high, spinning kick!

SECRET AND PREPARATION

This clever bit of business never fails to create interest and laughter. Since the handkerchief is completely unprepared, you are able to present this effect anytime, with any handkerchief!

METHOD

1 Spread the handkerchief open.

2 Tie a knot in the center of one side of the hem, as shown. This knot represents the head of Fatima. Be sure that a small portion of the hem protrudes from the completed knot, forming a sort of tail, which you can use to hold the handkerchief later.

NOTE: Be sure you do not tie the knot in one of the corners of the handkerchief, or the effect will not work. Tie the knot in the center of one of the side edges of the handkerchief, as shown.

3 Grasp the two corners (A and B) on the side opposite the knot between the thumb and forefinger of both hands, as shown.

4 Twirl the handkerchief away from you, causing the knotted portion of the handkerchief to spin around Ends A and B that you are holding. Be sure to twirl the handkerchief as tightly as possible until it will no longer accept any additional twists in the material.

5 Bring Corners A and B together and grasp them both in your right hand, as shown. With your left hand, grasp the tail of the knot (Fatima's head) between your left thumb and first finger.

6 Turn the entire affair completely over. This brings Corners A and B to the bottom and the knot to the top. If you use your imagination, you can see the form of a dancer created by the handkerchief.

7 By moving your hands back and forth, Fatima will dance about and swing her hips as if to keep time with the music. You can recite the following poem, suiting the action to the words:

Fatima was a dancer gay.
For fifty cents she'd dance this way, (Shake the figure)
But if a dollar you would pay, (Release one leg)
She'd do "Ta-ra-ra boom de aye."

NOTE: The high kick could also be done at the word "aye."

MARK WILSON'S CYCLOPEDIA OF MAGIC

8 On the last line of the poem, bring the dance to its grand finale by pulling your left hand up and your right hand down. At the same time, release one of the bottom corners of the handkerchief (either A or B) from your right hand. The result will be a high kick and a dramatic spin, performed by Fatima at the peak of her career!

COMMENTS AND SUGGESTIONS

The clever poem was written by that excellent magician, showman, writer, and lawyer, William Larsen Sr.

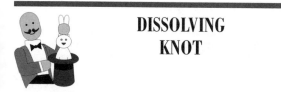

DISSOLVING KNOT

EFFECT

During a routine with a silk handkerchief, you casually tie a knot in the center of the scarf. Then, the knot simply "melts" away.

SECRET AND PREPARATION

You will require a handkerchief (silk is best) at least 18" square in order to present this trick effectively.

METHOD

1 Grasp the diagonal corners of the handkerchief between the first and second fingers of each hand.

2 Twirl the handkerchief into a loose, rope-like configuration. We will call the end pinched between the first and second fingers of your left hand End A and the end in your right hand End B.

3 Bring End B over toward your left and open the second and third fingers of your left hand, as shown.

4 Lay End B over End A, passing End B between the second and third fingers of your left hand.

5 Your right hand now reaches through the loop and grasps End A as shown. The third and fourth fingers of your left hand curl around the twisted silk below End A.

6 After the third and fourth fingers of the left hand are closed around the handkerchief, the second finger of your left hand hooks the silk just below where the two ends cross, below End B, as shown.

7 This is the key move. Pull End A through the loop with your right hand. End B is held firmly by the thumb and first finger of your left hand. The third and fourth fingers of your left hand release their grip around the silk as your left second finger hooks and pulls the lower portion of End B through the loop. Study the illustration carefully.

8 As you continue pulling on End A, a knot will form around the loop held by the second finger of your left hand, as shown. When this knot is tight enough to hold its shape, remove your finger from inside the loop.

9 You have apparently tied a real knot in the handkerchief. Really you have cleverly (and secretly) tied a "slip" knot. If you were to pull on the ends of the handkerchief now, the knot would disappear.

10 Allow the handkerchief to hang freely from the thumb and first finger of your left hand.

11 Grasp End A lightly with the thumb and first finger of your right hand. Hold the handkerchief horizontally in front of you and gently blow on the knot. At the same time, pull on the ends of the handkerchief, and the knot will "dissolve" away!

COMMENTS AND SUGGESTIONS

The DISSOLVING KNOT is one of the basic, classic effects in magic. It is important that you practice until you can tie the DISSOLVING KNOT as easily and quickly as you would a real knot. The ability to tie this trick knot will then become the basis for many other baffling effects. One of these stunners is the trick that follows.

KNOT THROUGH ARM

EFFECT

You display an ordinary handkerchief. Ask for a volunteer. This person should stand to your left. The spectator's left arm should be extended about waist high. Grasping the diagonal corners of the handkerchief, you spin the scarf into a loose, rope-like configuration. The handkerchief is now tied around the spectator's wrist. With a sudden jerk, the handkerchief seems to visibly penetrate the spectator's arm, leaving you with the undamaged handkerchief and the knot intact!

SECRET AND PREPARATION

This effect is one of those beautiful little gems that can be done anywhere at any time. All that is needed is a large pocket handkerchief, a silk scarf, or an 18" or 24" square "magician's" silk handkerchief.

This trick is based on the DISSOLVING KNOT (see page 397) which you must learn first.

METHOD

1 Grasp the diagonal corners of the handkerchief and spin it into a loose, rope-like configuration. In the illustration, we have marked the two ends A and B. Hold the handkerchief as shown.

2 Place the handkerchief around the spectator's left wrist and grasp both ends of the handkerchief in your left hand in preparation for the DISSOLVING KNOT.

3 With the spectator's wrist still in position, insert your right hand through the loop and grasp End A. Pull this end back through the loop and tie the DISSOLVING KNOT.

4 As you pull the ends in opposite directions (End B to your right), be sure to retain the small loop in End A with the second finger of your left hand as described in the DISSOLVING KNOT. This small loop will fall under End A between the handkerchief and the spectator's wrist. You can now pull on the ends to tie the handkerchief firmly around the spectator's wrist as long as you keep your left second finger in place holding the small loop. When the handkerchief is tightly around the spectator's wrist, remove your finger.

5 With your right hand, swing End A to the left, around the spectator's wrist. Continue to hold End A with your left hand. Be sure that End B goes in front of End A, as shown.

6 After you have wrapped End B around the spectator's wrist, the entire affair should look like this.

7 Tie a single legitimate knot on top of the DISSOLVING KNOT. This will put End A in your left hand and End B in your right.

8 Holding one end in each hand, pull up and out on both ends of the handkerchief. This dissolves the false knot around the wrist, creating a perfect illusion of the handkerchief penetrating the spectator's arm. The last (legitimate) knot is left in the handkerchief as a final convincer.

NOTE: After you have tied both knots, have the spectator clasp his hands together. In this way, you strengthen the mystery by making it impossible for the handkerchief to have been slipped over the end of the spectator's left hand when you perform the "penetration." Also, when tying the DISSOLVING KNOT in Step 3, try to make it a bit off center so that End A is longer than End B, as shown in Step 4. This way, you will have plenty of handkerchief left to wrap End A around the spectator's wrist the second time in Step 5.

COMMENTS AND SUGGESTIONS

This is an excellent impromptu trick which can be performed for one person or on stage for a large audience. I have used it for many years, and it is well worth the small amount of practice necessary to learn it.

HANDKERCHIEF
THROUGH HANDKERCHIEF

EFFECT

You display two silk handkerchiefs. You twist one into a rope-like configuration and give it to a spectator to hold outstretched between the spectator's hands. You then twist the second handkerchief in the same manner and tie it around the first handkerchief held by the spectator. The spectator is asked to tie a knot in the handkerchief so that both handkerchiefs are securely bonded together. Under these impossible conditions, you cause the handkerchiefs to melt apart, leaving their knots intact.

SECRET AND PREPARATION

In order to perform this trick, you must first have mastered the DISSOLVING KNOT. You will require two large silk handkerchiefs. They should be at least 18" square and preferably of contrasting colors. In the illustrations, one of the handkerchiefs is light in color, and the other is dark. This makes the description easier to follow.

METHOD

1 Grasp the light-colored handkerchief by two diagonal corners and twirl it between your hands into a loose rope. Hand it to a spectator and require that the spectator hold it outstretched by those same corners, as shown.

2 Twirl the dark-colored handkerchief in the same manner. Holding it by the ends, position it under the handkerchief being held by the spectator, as shown.

NOTE: In the illustration for Step 2, the spectator's hands have been omitted for clarity.

3 Utilizing the DISSOLVING KNOT, tie the dark handkerchief around the light handkerchief.

4 With the fake knot cinched up tightly against the light-colored handkerchief, loop the dark handkerchief around the light handkerchief a second time and tie one legitimate knot.

5 Ask the spectator to tie a knot in the other handkerchief. As the spectator does this, you may find it necessary to hold the dark-colored handkerchief by its knot. There are two reasons why this may be necessary. First, this will protect the fake knot from being pulled loose. Second, this prevents the spectator from tying the knot too tightly around your handkerchief. You can avoid this possibility by tying both knots yourself, but the effectiveness of the illusion is enhanced if the spectator ties the real knot in the light-colored handkerchief.

6 Have the spectator hold the corners of the light handkerchief, as you hold the corners of the dark handkerchief. With a gentle shaking motion, pull on the ends of your handkerchief and instruct the spectator to do the same. Your knot will dissolve, and the two handkerchiefs will magically separate from each other. Because of the second real knot that you tied and the real knot that the spectator tied, you are both left with knots in your handkerchiefs! Done correctly, this is a beautiful and baffling mystery.

MARK WILSON'S CYCLOPEDIA OF MAGIC

PENETRATING HANDKERCHIEF

Here is a simple but effective mystery involving objects easily found around the house. All you need is an ordinary drinking glass, two handkerchiefs, and a rubber band. This is another of those little gems from the inventive mind of "Gen" Grant.

EFFECT

You display a drinking glass, holding it mouth up with the tips of your fingers. You place a handkerchief in the glass and cover both the hand-kerchief and the glass with a second handkerchief. Next, you place a rubber band over the second handkerchief and the glass, thus sealing the first handkerchief inside the glass. Holding the glass from the outside, you reach under the handkerchief for a brief moment and instantly withdraw the first handkerchief—the one that was sealed inside the glass! The outside handkerchief is removed and all may now be examined An impossible penetration!

SECRET AND PREPARATION

This trick depends entirely upon a simple move that involves secretly turning the glass upside down while it is being covered by the second handkerchief. All of the illustrations are from your point of view.

METHOD

1 Begin by holding the drinking glass, mouth up, with the tips of the fingers and thumb of your right hand, as shown.

2 Display a handkerchief. With your left hand, push it into the glass. (This is the handkerchief that will later penetrate the glass.)

3 Pick up the second handkerchief with your left hand. Bring it up in front of the glass, momentarily hiding the glass from the spectators' view.

4 Here comes the secret move. As you begin to cover the glass with the handkerchief, your right hand slightly relaxes its grip on the bottom of the glass, allowing the glass to pivot between your thumb and fingers.

5 Let the glass pivot until it has turned completely upside down.

NOTE: The handkerchief inside the glass should be large enough so that it will not fall out when you turn the glass upside down.

6 As the glass turns over, your left hand finishes covering both your right hand and the glass.

7 After the glass is covered, grip the glass through the cloth with your left hand, as shown.

8 Remove your right hand, casually showing it empty, and pick up the rubber band from the table. Spread the rubber band with your right fingers and place it around the handkerchief and the top of the glass. (Unknown to the spectators, it is really the bottom!)

9 With your right hand, reach underneath the covering handkerchief and grasp the first handkerchief—the one that is inside the glass. Pull it straight down into view. To the spectators, it appears that the handkerchief has magically penetrated the bottom of the glass!

10 With your right hand, reach under the covering handkerchief and grip the glass in position to make the secret pivot once again, this time with the mouth of the glass (which is at the bottom because the glass is upside down) between the tips of your right thumb and fingers.

11 With your left hand, grip the outer (second) hand-kerchief between the tips of the fingers at the very "top" of the covered glass (actually the real bottom) and pull the cloth just enough to release the rubber band from around the glass, and then stop. Pause for a moment, just long enough to allow the glass to pivot in the fingers back to its original mouth-up position.

12 As soon as the glass is mouth up, draw the hand-kerchief away from the glass, and all can be examined.

MAGICAL PRODUCTION OF A HANDKERCHIEF

EFFECT

The following effects comprise an entire routine for the production and vanish of a silk handkerchief. You will first learn how to fold the handkerchief so that you can produce it from the air. Then, you will learn how to construct a "vanisher" to cause the handkerchief to disappear from your hands, leaving them completely empty.

SECRET AND PREPARATION

To perform the production, it is best to use a handkerchief made of pure silk. The type sold by magic supply houses, called "silks," works best. A silk handkerchief can be easily folded in the special manner described here, and it will spring open when it is produced. In addition, a magician's silk can be more easily compressed so that it makes a smaller package; thus, it can be more easily concealed for any production or vanish.

A Begin by placing the handkerchief flat on the table in front of you.

B Fold Corners A and B into the center of the handkerchief. The corners should just touch in the center of the handkerchief, as shown.

C Grasp the handkerchief at Points X and Y. Fold these two edges of the handkerchief into the center so that Points X and Y touch. You'll notice that the handkerchief is getting thinner in width with each fold.

D Repeat the folding actions as you did in Steps B and C. Then, continue folding the edges of the handkerchief into the center until the folded handkerchief is about 3" wide.

E Fold the right-hand half of the handkerchief over on top of the left-hand half. The handkerchief should now be about 1-1/2" wide.

F Fold the bottom end of the handkerchief about 1" toward your right, as shown. This forms a tab-like protrusion which is labeled T in the illustration.

G Beginning at the bottom of the handkerchief, roll it up tightly so that the tab (T) protrudes from the bundle. Roll up the entire length of the handkerchief until it forms a tight little package.

H The handkerchief should now look like this. Tuck the top "free" end of the handkerchief into the left-hand side of the rolled hank. (This is the side opposite the "tab.") You may use a blunt stick or other object to tuck this end down between the folds if you wish.

I When the handkerchief is properly rolled, it forms a tight little bundle which will not unroll until time for the production.

METHOD

1 With the handkerchief folded and rolled into this compact bundle, you are now ready for the production. Secretly get the bundle in your hand. (A good idea is to have the bundle hidden behind some prop on your table and to pick it up as you set down some other prop used in the preceding trick in your show.) When you pick up the bundle, grasp the protruding tab (T) and hold it firmly in the crook of your thumb. Relax your hand so that it appears normal to the audience. Keep the back of your hand to the spectators so that no one can see the hidden bundle.

2 If the handkerchief is held in your right hand, turn your right side toward the audience. Make a grabbing motion in the air to your left with your right hand. As you do this, straighten out your fingers and snap your wrist sharply. This action will cause the bundle to unroll and open out quickly. You now have the handkerchief held at one corner by the crook of your right thumb.

3 Quickly bend your right fingers inward and grasp the end of the handkerchief between your first and second fingers as shown.

4 Straighten out the fingers of your hand as you turn the hand palm up. The handkerchief is seen by the audience held at one end between the first and second fingers of your right hand. This completes the production sequence.

MARK WILSON'S CYCLOPEDIA OF MAGIC

COMMENTS AND SUGGESTIONS

The folding and rolling of the silk handkerchief described here is a basic method used by magicians for making a handkerchief into a compact self-contained bundle. It has many other applications that you will use as you progress to more advanced effects.

HANDKERCHIEF VANISH

In order to vanish the handkerchief, you must first construct a "pull." This is a clever device used by magicians that will enable you to cause the handkerchief to completely disappear in a startling manner.

SECRET AND PREPARATION

For the body of the pull, you can use either a hollow rubber ball or a small plastic bottle.

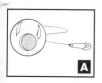

A For the ball pull, you must obtain a hollow ball that is small enough to be concealed in your hand, yet large enough to contain the handkerchief. Cut a small hole about 1" wide in the ball. This hole must be large enough for you to easily stuff the hand-kerchief into the ball. Then, attach a length of strong, black, round elastic on the other side of the ball, directly opposite the hole. Fasten a safety pin securely to the free end of the elastic.

B For the bottle pull, obtain a small plastic bottle which will easily hold the handkerchief. (The best bottle is the kind with a snap-on or twist-on cap in which the bottom is as large as the top. These are often used as containers for pills. If you don't have one around the house, you can buy it from the pharmacist at your local drugstore.) Make a small hole in the bottom of the bottle. Tie a large knot in one end of the elastic. Then, thread the other end through the mouth of the bottle and out the hole on the bottom. The knot will keep the end of the elastic from going through the hole, thus attaching it to the bottle. Tie a safety pin to the free end of the elastic.

NOTE: You may construct either pull you wish, or you may find some other suitable container, such as the small plastic cans which come with some types of camera film, etc. In any event, the pull must be small enough so that it can be comfortably held in your fist. Just remember that if the pull is too large for your hand, your audience will see it and the trick will be spoiled.

C After you have completed making the pull, fasten the safety pin to one of the rear loops of your pants or skirt. Allow the elastic to run beneath the next two or three belt loops so that the pull will hang on your left side near the seam of your pants or skirt. When performing the vanish, you must wear a coat or jacket so that the pull will be hidden from view.

METHOD

1 Assume that you are wearing the pull on your left side and have just produced the handkerchief from the air as described in the preceding trick. You are now prepared to vanish the handkerchief. Notice in the illustration, as you produce the handkerchief, your left hand is momentarily hidden from the audience's view by your body.

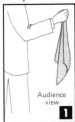

Audience view **1**

Back view

2

2 As you produce the handkerchief with your right hand, secretly grasp the pull with your left hand.

3 At this point, you should be giving your full attention to the handkerchief that is held in your right hand. At no time do you ever call attention to the hand containing the pull.

Audience view

3

Audience view

4

4 Turn your left side toward the audience as your left hand stretches the elastic attached to the pull. Your left hand should now be about 6" to 10" away from your body.

5 Place the handkerchief, which you are holding in your right hand, on top of your closed left fist. Use your right fingers to push the handkerchief into your closed left fist. Unknown to the audience, you are pushing the handkerchief into the pull as well.

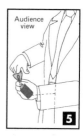

Audience view

5

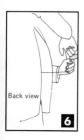

Back view

6

6 Here is a view of the action from the rear. The right fingers are pushing the handkerchief into the pull. Notice how the elastic runs from within your closed left fist, behind your left arm, and back inside your coat.

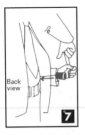

Back view

7

7 When the entire handkerchief has been pushed into the pull, relax the left-hand grip slightly. The pull will fly secretly out of your hand and be carried inside your coat.

NOTE: You will have to experiment a little in order to get the elastic to the proper length to ensure the maximum effect. The stretched elastic, when released, should cause the pull to go instantly inside the coat, while your left hand is held as if it still contained the handkerchief. During this action, your right index finger continues to pantomime the action of pushing the handkerchief into your closed left fist.

Audience view

8

8 Continue the action, pretending to pack the handkerchief into your left fist with your right index finger. As you do this, turn full front and extend both arms slightly away from your body without any jerking or unnatural motions. The audience is led to believe that the handkerchief is still held inside your left fist.

9 You may now open your left hand to show that the handkerchief has vanished without a trace. This should catch your audience totally by surprise. You may wish to pull up both your coat sleeves to prove that the handkerchief has not gone "up your sleeve."

Audience view

9

COMMENTS AND SUGGESTIONS

Remember to release the pull in a natural manner so as not to arouse any suspicion. If the release is accompanied by any jerking of the hands, the audience may suspect when the dirty work was done. Remember to keep your left hand motionless when you let go of the pull. Don't worry about it; the elastic will do the work. Now that you know the moves, you can begin to practice the whole routine until the actions blend together to form a smooth, relaxed sequence.

The pull and the variations of the principle on which it is based are all derived from a basic magic concept with many important applications. Now that you know the secret, you can devise many other ways to use this method of vanishing an object.

SERPENTINE SILK I

EFFECT

You display a colorful silk handkerchief that you twirl into a loose, rope-like configuration. You tie a knot in its center. Holding the handkerchief at one end, you cause the handkerchief to visibly untie itself right before the disbelieving eyes of the spectators.

SECRET AND PREPARATION

You will need a silk scarf or magician's silk handkerchief approximately 18" to 36" square and a spool of fine black nylon or silk thread. To prepare, attach one end of a 6' length of thread to one corner of the silk handkerchief. In the illustrations that follow, this corner has been labeled A and the free end of the handkerchief is marked B. The other end of the thread must be securely fastened to the top of your table (a small thumb tack works well). Fold the handkerchief and place it on your table, making sure that the thread is coiled next to the handkerchief, as shown in the illustration. You are now ready to present this classic mystery.

METHOD

1 Pick up the folded handkerchief and stand approximately 3' in front of the table edge. Grasp Corner A in your right fingers and allow the silk to unfold in front of you. The thread should now be hanging at your right side, below your right arm. Reach down and grasp the bottom of the handkerchief, Corner B, in your left hand and twirl the handkerchief into a loose, rope-like configuration, as shown. The thread now runs across the top of your right thumb and under your right arm to the table top.

2 Bring End A across and over End B, as shown. As you do this, move your right hand so that the thread is held in position under your right thumb.

3 With your left hand, reach through the loop formed by the handkerchief.

4 Grasp End A (and the thread) with the tops of your left fingers. Pull End A back through the loop.

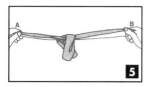

5 Slowly and steadily draw your hands apart, forming a loose knot in the middle of the handkerchief. The thread sewn to Corner A will be drawn through the knot and should now run over your right thumb, as shown.

6 Release Corner A and allow the handkerchief to hang from your right hand. If you have performed all the steps correctly, the situation will be as follows: The thread, which is attached to Corner A, runs up and through the knot in the handkerchief.

7 From there, it travels up and over your right thumb and under your right arm to the table.

8 Hold the handkerchief close to your body and move forward just enough to remove any remaining slack in the thread. By extending your right arm, the thread will begin to pull End A upward, as shown.

9 As you move your arm farther from the table, End A will be drawn into and completely through the knot, as shown.

10 By moving your body slightly forward, the thread will pull the rest of the End A portion of the handkerchief through the knot, causing it to visibly dissolve.

11 As soon as Corner A reaches your right fingers, immediately release Corner B, let it fall from your hand, and grasp Corner A.

12 You now hold the "untied" handkerchief by Corner A with Corner B hanging below, as shown.

COMMENTS AND SUGGESTIONS

It will appear to the spectators that the handkerchief has a life of its own and has wiggled out of its own knot. The position of the handkerchief at the end of the sequence leaves you all set to repeat the effect. This happens to be one of the rare cases in magic where repetition will help to build the mystery, but it is best to repeat the effect only once. At the conclusion, simply crumple the handkerchief and drop it on your table.

MARK WILSON'S CYCLOPEDIA OF MAGIC

SERPENTINE SILK II

You may wish to try the SERPENTINE SILK by this alternate method. Use a shorter length of thread with a small plastic bead tied to the free end. The end with the thread does not run to the table, as in the previous method. In this method, after the knot is tied the bead is secretly held under your right foot. The tying of the knot is the same as before, as is the action of the untying of the knot, except that this time you lift your arm instead of moving it forward. The benefit of this method is that you do not have to rely on a hookup to your table. With the bead-under-the-foot method, you can work the trick anywhere without fear of spoiling your setup. You will, however, need a bit more distance from the spectators, as the thread is more visible since it is not hidden by your body.

PHANTOM

EFFECT

You remove your pocket handkerchief and spread it open on the table in front of you. You then carefully fold over the four corners of the handkerchief, creating a small, temporary pocket or "ghost trap." Grasping an obviously empty handful of air, you tell the audience that you have actually captured a small phantom or ghost. When you pretend to place your mysterious little friend inside the miniature trap, the "ghost" takes on a solid, lifelike form which is clearly seen and heard through the fabric of the handkerchief. Yet, when you open the handkerchief, the invisible phantom has escaped, leaving the handkerchief quite empty!

SECRET AND PREPARATION

In this effect, you need a gentleman's pocket hand-kerchief with a wide hem. To prepare, cut a length of coat-hanger wire (or any similar thin, stiff wire) approximately 2-1/2" long. Carefully insert the wire into the hem of the handkerchief at one corner (Corner A in the illustrations). Now, sew the wire into place with a needle and thread. Fold the handkerchief and put it in your pocket. You will also need a common metal spoon. You are now ready to perform this excellent close-up mystery.

METHOD

1 To begin the presentation, remove the prepared hand-kerchief from your pocket and spread it open on the table in front of you. Corner D should be nearest you, pointing in your direction. Corner A, which contains the short length of wire, should be closest to the audience.

2 With your right hand, grasp Corner A and fold it up and over to the center of the handkerchief, as shown.

3 Grasp Corner B in your left hand and fold it over Corner A.

4 Grasp Corner C in your right hand and fold it over both Corners A and B so that it is even with the left edge of the handkerchief. You will notice that the three folded corners (A, B, and C) form a sort of pocket, with the opening of the pocket facing you at Corner D.

MARK WILSON'S CYCLOPEDIA OF MAGIC

5 With your right hand, reach out and pretend to grasp something from the air. State that you have just caught a "small invisible ghost." Be sure your audience realizes that your hand is quite empty and that you are merely pretending to hold something in your hand.

6 With your left hand, slightly raise the three folded corners (A, B, and C), opening the pocket just enough to insert your right hand as if to give the illusive spirit a place to hide. Now, while your hand is inside the pocket, grasp the secret wire that is sewn in Corner A and stand the wire upright, on its end.

7 As soon as the wire is secure in this position, remove your right hand from inside the pocket and release your hold on the handkerchief with your left hand. The wire will stand on its own accord due to the weight of the fabric. This creates the illusion of something being within the folds of the handkerchief. With your left hand, lift Corner D and fold it up and over the opening of the pocket, thus imprisoning the "ghost" inside.

8 The audience will see a definite form inside the handkerchief, which you claim to be your little friend, the ghost. To further convince them of its presence, place the palm of your hand directly on top of the handkerchief, allowing the secret wire to press against the middle of your palm. Then, with a slight downward pressure, move your hand in a circular motion, thus creating the very eerie illusion of a solid, round object inside the handkerchief.

9 The real convincer comes with this next move. Hold a spoon in your right hand. Hit the end of the secret wire several times with the back of the spoon. The noise created by the spoon hitting against the hidden wire will convince the spectators, not only visually but audibly as well, that you have really captured a small phantom.

10 To bring the mystery to its conclusion, set the spoon aside and quickly snap the handkerchief open, allowing the ghost to escape. Immediately show your hands and the completely empty handkerchief. Casually put the handkerchief in your pocket, leaving your audience totally baffled.

BROKEN-AND-RESTORED MATCH

EFFECT

You display a wooden kitchen match and give it to a spectator for examination. You spread out a pocket handkerchief on the table and place the match on the handkerchief near the center. You fold the four corners of the handkerchief over the match so it is hidden from view. You ask the spectator to grasp the match in both hands, through the folds of cloth, and break it into a number of pieces. Without any suspicious moves, you unfold the handkerchief, revealing the match completely unharmed and fully restored to its original condition!

        MARK WILSON'S CYCLOPEDIA OF MAGIC

SECRET AND PREPARATION

The secret to this mystery depends on the use of a certain type of handkerchief. It must be the kind that has a wide hem around the sides. This enables you to secretly conceal a duplicate match inside the hem. The spectators are never aware of the duplicate match.

NOTE: Toothpicks may also be used quite effectively in this trick instead of matches.

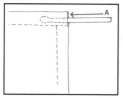

To prepare, carefully insert the match into the open end of the hem of the handkerchief. Push it just far enough inside so that it is completely hidden from view. In the illustrations, the corners of the handkerchief have been labeled A, B, C, and D, with the match inside the hem at Corner A. Fold the hand-

kerchief and place it in your pocket and have a box of duplicate matches handy for the presentation.

METHOD

Secret match **1**

1 Display the box of matches and open it, requesting that a spectator select one match to use in the trick. Remove your handkerchief (with the secret match hidden in the hem) and spread it on the table in front of you. Place the handkerchief so that the hidden match is in the lower right-hand corner (A), nearest you. Take the

match from the spectator and place it in the center of the handkerchief, as shown. Note that both matches are running parallel to one another at the start.

2 Fold Corner A up and over the center of the handkerchief, placing the secret match by the selected match. Notice that the selected match and the secret match are now perpendicular to each other. This way, it will be easy for you to distinguish which match is which, without having to see them. You can rely upon your sense of touch to tell them apart.

3 Fold the top left Corner C over the selected match and over Corner A, as shown.

4 Fold Corner B over Corners A and C as in the illustration.

5 Finally, bring Corner D over Corners A, B, and C, as shown.

6 Openly and deliberately grasp the secret match through the folds of the handkerchief and hold it between the thumb and fingers of both hands. You can be sure to grasp the secret match easily by simply "feeling" for the match that runs parallel to the edge of the table nearest you.

NOTE: The selected match remains within the handkerchief.

7 Hand the secret match to the spectator.

8 Instruct the spectator to break it several times through the fabric of the handkerchief. The spectator believes the match that was just selected and that you folded inside the handkerchief is the one being broken.

9 When the spectator is quite satisfied that the match has been completely destroyed, slowly and deliberately unfold each corner of the handkerchief, one at a time.

10 As you unfold Corner C with your left hand, keep your right hand over Corner A to conceal any possible bulge of the hem that might be caused by the pieces of the secret match. When you have completely opened the handkerchief, the spectators will be amazed to see that the broken match is now fully restored.

11 Immediately give the match to the spectator for examination. Hold up the handkerchief, shake it, and show it on both sides so that all can see that it is completely empty before you casually replace it in your pocket.

EGGS FROM NOWHERE

EFFECT

You call attention to a woven basket and a folded handkerchief resting on your table. Picking up the handkerchief, unfolding it, and displaying both sides, you show it to be quite ordinary. Folding the handkerchief in half to form a sort of pocket, you cause an egg to make a magical appearance inside and allow it to fall from within the folds of the handkerchief into the basket. The production continues, egg after egg, until the audience is sure that the basket is nearly full. Setting the handkerchief aside, you remove one of the eggs from the basket and break it into a glass to prove that it is genuine. Then, picking up the basket, you throw the contents into the air directly over the audience. To their surprise, and relief, the eggs have been magically transformed into a shower of confetti!

SECRET AND PREPARATION

A The items necessary for this effect are an opaque handkerchief (a bandanna is ideal), a medium-size basket, a gentleman's hat or a similar size box, and a plastic egg. This type of egg can be purchased from a novelty or "dime" store and is especially easy to find during the Easter season. The basket, hat, or box should be opaque, so that the audience cannot see through it. It should be deep enough to conceal a quantity of confetti and one real egg. You will also need confetti (or just tear some paper into small pieces), a glass, and some sewing thread which closely matches the color of the handkerchief.

B To prepare, drill a small hole in one end of the hollow plastic egg, as shown. Also, cut a piece of thread about 12" long. The exact length of the thread will depend upon the size of the handkerchief and the basket.

C Tie a short piece of toothpick to one end of the thread. Push the toothpick through the hole in the egg. The toothpick and the thread will be secured inside the egg, as shown. (You can also use transparent tape to secure the thread to the egg.)

D Sew the other end of the thread to the middle of the hem of the handkerchief.

E As shown here, the thread should be long enough to allow the egg to hang just below the center of the handkerchief.

F Fold the handkerchief and place it on the table next to the basket.

The thread should run from the handkerchief into the basket with the egg lying in the basket, as shown.

The basket should also contain a quantity of confetti and one real egg.

NOTE: The real egg should be down in the confetti to protect it from the plastic egg when it falls into the basket.

METHOD

1 To begin the presentation, pick up the handkerchief by the lower two corners (C and D) and display it on both sides. The egg remains concealed in the basket.

2

F Fold the handkerchief and place it on the table next to the basket. The thread should run from the handkerchief into the basket with the egg lying in the basket, as shown. The basket should also contain a quantity of confetti and one real egg.

NOTE: The real egg should be down in the confetti to protect it from the plastic egg when it falls into the basket.

3

METHOD

1 To begin the presentation, pick up the handkerchief by the lower two corners (C and D) and display it on both sides. The egg remains concealed in the basket.

4

2 Lay the handkerchief partially over the basket with the top hem (the hem with the attached thread) draped across the opening of the basket. The center of this hem, where the thread is attached, should be directly above the plastic egg in the basket.

5

3 Show that your hands are empty and grasp the handkerchief at Corners A and B, as shown.

6

4 Keep the top hem stretched tightly between both hands as you lift the handkerchief upward, away from the table and the basket. The thread will secretly draw the plastic egg out of the basket behind the handkerchief, as shown. Keep the handkerchief

7

8 The folded handkerchief should now be broadside to the audience. Raise the right-hand corners (C and D) slightly upward and gently shake the egg out of the handkerchief. The egg should fall into the basket and land safely on the confetti. You have just magically produced an egg from an empty handkerchief!

9 After the egg lands in the basket, toss the right-hand corners (C and D) of the folded handkerchief on the table in front of the bowl, leaving the two top corners (A and B) in your left hand.

10 Grasp Corner B in your right hand while continuing to hold the Corner A in your left and draw your two hands apart, as shown. Be sure the entire bottom edge of the handkerchief (C and D) is resting in front of the basket as you stretch the handkerchief open.

11 As you draw your hands apart, raise the top corners (A and B), secretly drawing the plastic egg out of the basket behind the handkerchief, ready to make a magical appearance.

12 Repeat Steps 5 through 7 to fold the egg inside the handkerchief as you did the first time. Tilt the handkerchief, and a "second" egg (really the same egg) falls out.

13 Follow the sequences as described from Step 9 through Step 12 for each egg you want to produce. When you wish to conclude the production portion of the trick, repeat the procedure only through Step 11. At this point, simply gather the handkerchief and place it aside, with the plastic egg concealed inside its folds.

14 Remove the real egg from the basket and display it as you pick up the glass in your other hand. Then, deliberately break the egg in the glass, proving it to be genuine.

15 For a conclusion, pick up the basket from your table and carry it toward the audience. They believe it is full of real eggs. Suddenly, toss the contents of the basket into the air above the audience, showering them with confetti! If you have followed all of the steps correctly and practiced the trick well before you present it, you will now have a very surprised and bewildered audience.

VANISHING GLASS

EFFECT

You openly exhibit an ordinary drinking glass. After covering the glass with a handkerchief, you lift it into the air. The audience can plainly see that the glass is under the handkerchief. Suddenly, you throw the bundle high above your head. Instantly, the glass vanishes, allowing the empty handkerchief to flutter into your hands.

SECRET AND PREPARATION

A To present this effect, you must have a magician's table with a "well," such as the one described on page 589 of this book. You will also need an ordinary drinking glass. The glass must fit comfortably into the "well" in your table.

B Cut a disc of plastic or cardboard just slightly larger than the mouth of the glass.

C You will need two matching hand-kerchiefs. (If possible, the handker-chiefs should have some kind of pattern or design on them.) Sew the disc to the center of one of the handkerchiefs.

D Cover the handkerchief and its attached disc with the duplicate handkerchief. Carefully sew the two hand-kerchiefs together around the edges with the disc sand-wiched between them. Put the glass on your table with the folded handkerchief next to it, and you are ready to perform.

METHOD

1 Pick up the glass and display it. Put the glass back on your table just in front of the well. Pick up the hand-kerchief. Snap it open so that the audience can see that it is apparently unprepared. Hold the handkerchief with the thumb and first fingers of each hand and position it behind the glass, as shown.

2 The next moves are critical. Place the handkerchief over the glass.

3 Be sure that the hidden disc goes over the mouth of the glass.

4 With the glass completely covered and the disc over the mouth of the glass, grasp the disc and the glass through the fabric of the handkerchief. Without lifting the glass, slide it backward until it is directly over the well in your table.

5 While still holding onto the disc, let the glass slide into the well. The disc will maintain the shape of the glass under the handkerchief.

6 Lift the handkerchief clear of the table and walk forward. The disc should be held lightly with your thumb and fingers so that it appears that the glass is still under the handkerchief.

7 Throw the handkerchief high into the air. The effect upon the audience is that the glass vanishes into thin air. Crumple the handkerchief and drop it on your table.

COMMENTS AND SUGGESTIONS

Having an object under a handkerchief or cloth after it has actually "gone" is an important basic principle of magic. The VANISHING GLASS effect is a classic example of the use of this principle. The secret disc concealed in the handkerchief leads the audience to believe that the glass is still there long after it has gone. This subtle method will be of great value to you in the performance of many effects. There is even an impromptu version of the VANISHING GLASS, which is described in the following pages.

VANISHING GLASS— IMPROMPTU VERSION

EFFECT

While seated at a table, you cover an empty glass with your pocket handkerchief. You raise the covered glass from the table and then throw the handkerchief in the air. The glass has vanished! You reach under the table, directly below the spot where the handkerchief landed, and reproduce the glass. The glass has apparently penetrated the table!

SECRET AND PREPARATION

You will need the same special handkerchief with the disc sewn in it as described in the VANISHING GLASS (see page 430). You will also need a glass with a mouth that is approximately the same size as the disc. The effect is even better when this trick is performed in an impromptu manner using an empty glass that is already on the table. For instance, you might use one after dinner or when you are seated with friends at a party.

METHOD

1 The presentation of this effect is exactly the same as in Steps 1 through 4 of the VANISHING GLASS; then instead of dropping the glass into the well on your table, you merely move the handkerchief back past the edge of the table and drop the glass into your lap!

2 Cover the glass with the handkerchief, being sure that the disc is properly positioned over the mouth of the glass. Pick the glass and the handkerchief up in your right hand, as shown.

3 As you hold the glass and handkerchief with your right hand, hold your left hand up, palm toward the spectators. Say, "As you can see, there is nothing in my left hand."

4 As you show your left hand, move the handkerchief and the glass back over the edge of the table so that the edge of the handkerchief is still touching the top of the table. As you display your empty left hand, drop the glass into your lap.

5 Holding the secret disc by the edges of your right hand, move the now empty handkerchief (as if it still covered the glass) back over the table.

6 Say, "And there is nothing under the handkerchief!" At the same time that you say this, throw the handkerchief up into the air. Catch it as it comes down and show the handkerchief on both sides. Then, drop it onto the table in front of you.

7 Show that both of your hands are empty and reach under the table. As you do, say, "The reason that you don't see the glass any more is because it has gone right through the table, like this." As your hands go under the table, with your right hand pick up the glass from your lap and carry it under the table to a spot directly beneath the crumpled handkerchief. With a pulling motion, apparently extract the glass from the table. Bring the glass out and set it on the table and put the handkerchief back in your pocket.

MARK WILSON'S CYCLOPEDIA OF MAGIC

CHAPTER 15
IMPROMPTU MAGIC

Here are some "quick tricks" that you can do anywhere at any time. Some are puzzles rather than tricks, others are more in the nature of stunts, but the majority are quite deceptive and will arouse interest among people who see them. In fact, that is the great purpose of this branch of magic; for once you have gained people's interest with something trivial and find that they want to see more, you can go into your regular routine with confidence since you know you already have a receptive audience.

JUMPING RUBBER BAND

EFFECT

NOTE: A, B, and C show the spectators' viewpoint. In all the illustrations, the fingers are pointing up.

A You place a rubber band around your first and second fingers.

B You close your hand into a fist.

C When you open your hand, the band magically jumps to your third and fourth fingers.

METHOD

All method illustrations are from the magician's viewpoint.

1 Place the rubber band around the bases of your first and second fingers on your left hand. If the band is too loose, you may put it around twice. Experiment with whatever rubber band you're using, so that you get the proper tension on the band. Your hand is toward the spectators, and your palm faces you.

2 Close your left hand into a fist, by bending your fingers into your palm. At the same time, secretly use the first finger of your right hand to stretch the rubber band so that the tips of all four left fingers can be inserted into the rubber band.

MARK WILSON'S CYCLOPEDIA OF MAGIC

3 This is how your hand now looks to you. (To the spectators, your hand will appear as in B.)

4 Straighten out your fingers and the band will automatically jump to a new position around your left third and fourth fingers.

REVERSE JUMPING RUBBER BAND

EFFECT

You make the rubber band jump back from your third and fourth fingers to your first and second fingers.

METHOD

1 Simply reverse the procedure used for the first jump.

2 After the band has jumped to your third and fourth fingers, fold your hand into a fist again. As you do, use the first finger of your right hand to stretch the rubber band.

3 Another way is to use your left thumb to stretch the band.

4 Then, when you close your left hand, secretly insert the tips of all four left fingers, as you did before.

5 When you straighten out your fingers, the band will jump back to your first and second fingers.

DOUBLE JUMPING RUBBER BAND I

EFFECT

You can double the mystery of this trick by magically making two rubber bands change places.

METHOD

1 Place one rubber band (a white one, for instance) around your left first and second fingers. Place a second, different-colored rubber band (say a blue one) around your left third and fourth fingers.

2 Before you close your hand into a fist, reach over with your left thumb and stretch the rubber band that is around the third and fourth fingers, as shown.

3 Use your right first finger to pull the band that is around the first and second fingers of your left hand, as shown.

4 Secretly place the tips of all four fingers into both rubber bands as you close your hand. The fingers of the left hand go into the opening indicated by the arrow.

5 At the same time that you insert the fingers of the left hand into the bands, release both the bands from your left thumb and from the first finger on the right hand. Your hand will look like this to you.

6 Call the spectators' attention to the fact that the white band is around your first and second fingers, and the blue band is around your third and fourth fingers. To the spectators, it looks like this.

7 Just straighten out your fingers. The bands will jump to the opposite fingers.

DOUBLE JUMPING RUBBER BAND II

EFFECT

The effect is the same as in the first version of the DOUBLE JUMPING RUBBER BAND described above; however, the method is slightly different.

METHOD

1 Place the two rubber bands on your fingers, as before.

2 With the first finger of the right hand, secretly stretch, or "nip," each of the bands away from the left hand.

3 Insert the second finger of the right hand into the loops formed by the right first finger and spread the loops open, using both right fingers.

4 Fold your left hand into a fist and insert the tips of the left fingers into the opening formed by the right fingers. To you, your hand looks like this.

5 Straighten out your fingers in the usual way, and the bands will change places.

MARK WILSON'S CYCLOPEDIA OF MAGIC

CHALLENGE JUMPING RUBBER BAND

The addition of an extra band to lock in the jumper is a clever touch that turns a simple trick into a very strong effect.

EFFECT

This can be used as a follow-up for either the JUMPING RUBBER BAND or the DOUBLE JUMPING RUBBER BAND. You explain that to make it impossible for the band to jump, you will encircle the tips of all of the fingers of your left hand individually with another rubber band.

METHOD

1 Place an additional rubber band around the tips of the fingers of your left hand, as shown in the picture.

2 Proceed in exactly the same way as you did before. Fold your hand into a fist and insert the tips of the fingers into the band that is to jump. Straighten out your fingers, and behold—another minor miracle—the band jumped just as before!

LINKING PAPER CLIPS

This is a most entertaining combination magic trick and puzzle. After you perform it, everyone will want to try it. If someone should figure it out, don't worry—they'll have as much fun with it as you do.

EFFECT

You show two paper clips and a dollar bill. You give the bill a three-way fold and use the clips to fasten the folds in place. As you pull the ends of the pleated bill, slowly but steadily the clips come closer together. You finish the pull with a sharp snap, as the clips fly from the bill and land on the table, linked together!

METHOD

The trick is almost automatic. It depends entirely upon the proper placement of the clips. Practice the setup until you can place the clips in position quickly and neatly, so observers will be unable to follow and will therefore find it difficult to duplicate the trick.

1 Start by holding the bill open between both of your hands.

2 Fold 1/3 of the length of the bill over to the right, as shown.

3 Place one of the paper clips over this fold to hold it in place, and push it down so it is snug against the top edge of the bill.

4 The clip should be positioned near the end of the folded portion of the bill, directly over the number that shows its value.

MARK WILSON'S CYCLOPEDIA OF MAGIC

5 Turn the bill completely around so that you are looking at the other side. Do not turn the bill upside down in the process; the clip should still be at the top, as shown.

6 Fold the left end of the bill over to the right, as shown in the illustration.

7 Put the other paper clip on the bill from the top, thus holding this end in place too. Clip together just the two front folds—those that are toward you.

8 The clip should be positioned near the end of the bill over its number value, as shown here.

9 If both clips have been properly placed, the bill should look as shown in this view.

10 Firmly grip both ends of the bill near the top and start to pull them apart. As the bill unfolds, the clips will start moving together, still pinned to the bill.

11 When you reach the point where the clips are practically on top of each other, give the ends of the bill a sharp tug.

12 The bill will open out and send the paper clips sailing across the table, linking them as they go!

COMMENTS AND SUGGESTIONS

The trick is particularly effective with jumbo clips that are longer and wider, so the linking can be followed easily. With ordinary paper clips, only a slight tug is needed; otherwise they may fly clear across the table as they link. If they go off the edge, the effect will be weakened.

With practice, placing the clips in position becomes a simple and rapid process. If using small clips, you can put two on the top edge and another pair on the bottom edge. The tug will shoot them in opposite directions, and each pair will be found linked.

LINKING PAPER CLIPS WITH RUBBER BAND

EFFECT

Here is a clever addition to LINKING PAPER CLIPS. In this effect, the two clips mysteriously link themselves and also link to a rubber band that was previously looped around the bill. This little twist not only takes the effect one step further, it also creates a very puzzling finish for LINKING PAPER CLIPS.

METHOD

1 Follow Steps 1 through 4 as described in LINKING PAPER CLIPS, placing the first clip over the folded portion of the bill, as shown.

2 Loop a rubber band of the size shown around the right end of the bill. The rubber band should be slightly longer than the width of the bill so that a portion of the band hangs below the bottom edge of the bill.

3 Fold back the right end of the bill and attach the second paper clip, as you did in the original routine. If both clips and the rubber band have been properly placed, the bill should look like this.

4 Firmly grip both ends of the bill and pull them apart. The rubber band will remain looped around the bill with the paper clips linked to it in a chain, as shown.

COMMENTS AND SUGGESTIONS

It is a good idea to practice this a few times until you understand why it works as it does. Once you understand the way it works, concentrate on placing the paper clips and the rubber band in exactly the same position every time you perform the trick. You can then succeed in baffling spectators without fear of making a mistake in the handling of the props.

BAG-TAG ESCAPE

EFFECT

You display what appears to be a typical baggage tag and give it to the nearest spectator to examine. A second spectator is given a length of string to examine. The tag and the string prove to be normal in every respect. You proceed to thread the string through the small hole in the tag. You give one end of the string to each spectator to hold. With the tag hanging in the center of the string, you cover the string and the tag with a pocket handkerchief. Reaching beneath the handkerchief, you "magically" remove the tag from the center of the string without damage to either! The spectators are left holding the now empty string suspended between them with no explanation for the mystery they have just witnessed.

SECRET AND PREPARATION

For this trick you will need to construct some small tags from cardboard. Filing-card stock is best. The tags should be cut so that they measure approximately 3" x 1 1/2" in size. Shape the tags by cutting off the two top corners at a 45° angle and punch a hole in the center of the top edge of each of the tags, as shown. The result will be a tag that closely resembles a standard baggage tag in every respect except one. Most standard tags are heavily reinforced around the small hole so that they will not tear when fastened to some object. This slight difference is what makes the entire effect possible. You will also need a piece of string about 2' long, which you place on the table along with one of the tags. Place an ordinary handkerchief in your left pocket and a duplicate tag in your right coat sleeve so that it is out of view of the spectators.

METHOD

1 To begin the presentation, ask for the assistance of two spectators. Hand one of the spectators the tag for examination and the other spectator the length of string. When they are satisfied that everything is unprepared, thread the string through the small hole at the top of the tag, as shown in the illustration.

2 Give one end of the string to each spectator, leaving the suspended tag imprisoned on the string.

3 Remove your handkerchief from your pocket, show it to be completely empty, and cover the tag and the center of the string, as shown. Be sure the handkerchief is spread open enough to provide the cover necessary to conceal your hands beneath it. Reach under the handkerchief with both hands and grasp the tag near the hole at the top.

4 Carefully and quietly tear through the tag to the hole. Remove the torn tag from the string.

NOTE: You may find it helpful to raise both hands slightly upward, thus lifting the handkerchief away from the tag. This will prevent the spectators from seeing the motion of what is actually taking place.

5 With the fingers of your right hand, secretly insert the torn tag into your left coat sleeve.

6 Exchange hand positions so that your left hand can withdraw the duplicate tag from your right sleeve, as shown.

7 Now for the startling climax. Bring both hands into view along with the duplicate tag. Ask the spectators to look beneath the handkerchief to see if you actually removed the tag from the string, as it appears. You may then offer the tag, the string, and the handkerchief for examination.

LIFESAVERS®
ON THE LOOSE!

EFFECT

You display an ordinary shoelace and hand it to a spectator for examination. Reaching into your pocket, you remove a new package of Lifesavers candy and give it to another spectator to open. A number of the Lifesavers are then threaded onto the shoelace, and the ends of the lace are handed to two spectators to hold. Removing the handkerchief from your pocket, you cover the Lifesavers dangling in the middle of the lace, concealing them from view. Reaching under the handkerchief, you magically remove the imprisoned Lifesavers, leaving the now empty shoelace suspended between the two spectators.

METHOD

1 The only items required for this effect are an ordinary shoelace or a length of string, and a package of Lifesavers or some similar candy with a hole in the center. To begin the presentation, hand the shoelace to a spectator for examination while you introduce the package of Lifesavers to another spectator to open.

2 Pick up one of the Lifesavers and thread it on the shoelace, as shown.

3 With the candy suspended from the center of the lace, thread the remaining Lifesavers on the shoelace by running both ends of the lace through the holes in the candy, as shown.

4 Give both ends of the shoelace to a spectator to hold; or give one end of the lace to one spectator and the other end to another spectator to hold. Either way, have the spectator(s) hold the ends far apart to allow enough space to drape your handkerchief over the suspended Lifesavers.

5 Remove your handkerchief and cover the Lifesavers, as shown. Be sure to spread open the handkerchief along the shoelace to provide enough cover for your hands when you place them underneath.

6 Reach under the handkerchief with both hands.

7 As soon as your hands are out of view, grasp the bottom Lifesaver between both hands and break it in half, as shown.

8 Try not to break it into little pieces, as these can be difficult to conceal in your hand and may also fall to the floor during the presentation and spoil the trick.

9 Hold the broken pieces so that they are concealed in your curled right fingers. Allow the loose candy to slide from the shoelace into your left hand.

10 With your right hand still concealing the broken pieces, lift the handkerchief away from the shoelace, revealing the loose Lifesavers in your left hand.

11 Place the handkerchief back in your pocket along with the broken pieces, and the mystery is complete.

® Lifesavers is a registered trademark of Lifesavers, Inc.

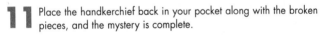

COMMENTS AND SUGGESTIONS

This is truly an ideal impromptu mystery. All of the items are ordinary and easily obtainable. Just be sure to thread enough Lifesavers on the string, and no one will miss the broken one—the real secret of this clever mystery.

MARK WILSON'S CYCLOPEDIA OF MAGIC

CORDS
OF FANTASIA

EFFECT

You borrow two finger rings from spectators. Handing one of the spectators a pencil, you display two shoelaces. These laces are secretly tied around the pencil. Both rings are threaded onto the shoelaces and held in place with an overhand knot. Under these conditions, even with the spectator holding onto the ends of the laces, you cause the rings to magically "melt" through the cords, leaving the rings, pencil, and laces intact!

SECRET AND PREPARATION

All you will need are a pencil, a pair of shoelaces, and the two finger rings. All of the props are quite unprepared, and this clever effect can be presented at any time and any place that these common items can be obtained.

METHOD

1 Begin by borrowing two finger rings from spectators. Have one spectator hold the pencil by the ends. Drape the two shoelaces over the pencil, as illustrated. From this

point on, we will refer to these as Lace A and Lace B.

2 While the spectator holds the pencil, grasp both strands of Lace A in your left hand and both strands of Lace B in your right. Tie a single overhand knot, as shown.

3 Pull the knot up tight and ask the spectator to release the grip on the pencil. Turn the laces so that they are now parallel to the floor and the pencil is held by the laces in an upright position. Pull the laces tight on the pencil so that the pencil does not slide out. Hand the ends of the laces to the spectator.

4 Call attention to the two borrowed finger rings and thread them onto the laces. Thread one ring on each side of the pencil, as shown. Be sure to put both strands of Lace A through one ring and both strands of Lace B through the other.

5 You are ready to tie the rings in place. To do this, take one of the B ends and one of the A ends. Tie those ends in a single overhand knot, as shown. You will notice that when you tie this knot, you are crossing an A end with a B end. It makes no difference which of the two A ends or which of the two B ends you have chosen to tie. Just be sure that you end up with one A end and one B end paired on each side of the pencil, as shown.

6 Pull this new knot up tight. The rings will be jammed against the pencil. Hand the ends back to the spectator so that the spectator is now holding the entire affair, as shown.

7 With your right hand, grasp the knot on the pencil, as shown. With your left hand, hold the pencil near the bottom and prepare to slip it free of the knot.

8 With your right hand firmly holding on to the knot, pull the pencil out of the laces with your left hand.

9 Thread the pencil through the rings. Note that the right hand, which still holds the knot firmly, has been eliminated from this illustration for clarity.

10 Ask the spectator to pull on the ends of the laces. At the same time, release your grip on the knot held by your right hand. The illusion is perfect. The rings seem to melt right through the laces!

11 The spectator is left holding only the two laces; the rings are on the pencil. Immediately allow the spectators to examine everything and return the rings to their owners with your thanks.

SUCKER TORN-AND-RESTORED NAPKIN

EFFECT

Displaying two napkins, you announce that you are going to "teach" the spectators how to perform a trick. One napkin you crumple into a ball and show how you secretly palm it in your left hand. You explain that this is a "secret" napkin, which none of the spectators is supposed to know about. You tear the other napkin into a number of pieces. Now for the secret. You demonstrate exactly how you cleverly switch the torn napkin for the secret napkin. You even open up the secret napkin to show how the torn pieces have supposedly been restored. The spectators, believing that they know how the trick is done, are warned by you that, if they should ever perform the trick, never to let anyone see the torn pieces in their hand. You explain that if that should ever happen, they would need to restore those pieces by magic. With that, you open the torn pieces, revealing that they too have been restored into a whole napkin! It is then that the spectators realize that they have been taken in by you all along.

SECRET AND PREPARATION

A To perform this highly entertaining effect, you will need three identical paper napkins. In this illusion, the napkins are numbered 1, 2, and 3. To prepare, spread open two of the napkins (1 and 2) and place one napkin (2) on top of the other napkin (1). Crumple the third napkin (3) into a ball and place it at the bottom center edge of the open napkins, as shown.

B Starting at the top edge, roll the two open napkins down into a "tube" around the third napkin.

METHOD

1 To begin, pick up the tube in your right hand near the center. Hold the tube so that End B is on top. Hold the third napkin (3) through the other two napkins (1 and 2). With your left hand, grasp the edges of the tube and start to unroll the open napkins (1 and 2) with your right hand. You should be able to feel the third napkin (3) inside as you unroll the tube. When the napkins are completely opened, secretly roll the inner crumpled napkin (3) into your right fingers, as shown, so that it is hidden from the spectators.

MARK WILSON'S CYCLOPEDIA OF MAGIC

2 Separate the two open napkins, taking one napkin (1) in your left hand and the other napkin (2) in your right. Announce to the spectators that you are going to teach them how to perform a trick.

3 Explain that one of the two napkins (1) is a secret napkin and must be concealed in your left hand until the proper moment. As you say this, with your left hand crumple the left-hand napkin (1) into a ball. Hold it in the curled fingers of your left hand, the same as the third napkin (3) in your right hand (of which the spectators are totally unaware). Explain to the spectators that this secret napkin must be secretly palmed in your left hand at all times as you perform the trick.

4 Explain that the trick begins when you tear the whole napkin (2) into a number of pieces, which you proceed to do. Roll these torn pieces into a small ball.

5 Here's how your hands should look from your point of view. The napkin (2), between the tips of your thumbs and fingers, is the torn one; the napkin (1) in your left hand is the secret napkin that the spectators know about; and the napkin (3) in your right hand is the one only you know about.

6 As you are finishing, roll the torn pieces (2) into a ball and secretly add to them the whole napkin (3) in your right hand.

7 Show both napkins (2 and 3) together as if they were just the torn pieces. As you display the supposedly torn pieces—really the torn pieces (2) and the third whole napkin (3)—turn your right hand so the spectators can see that it is quite empty. This is a very important part of the trick. It convinces the spectators that everything is on the level, so that they will not suspect there is a third napkin.

8 Pretend to roll these pieces (Napkins 2 and 3) into a smaller ball. As you do, secretly draw the torn pieces (2) downward, behind your right fingers with your right thumb. This leaves only the whole napkin (3) at the tips of your right fingers.

9 Transfer only the whole ball (3) to the tips of your left fingers, as if it were the torn pieces.

10 The spectators think that you have merely placed the torn pieces, which they just saw you crumple into a ball, into your left fingers. Here is the spectators' view of this action.

11 Explain that when they (the spectators) perform this trick for their friends, they should have a coin in their right pocket to use as a sort of magic wand. With your right hand, reach into your right pocket and bring out the coin. When you do, leave the torn pieces (2) in your pocket.

MARK WILSON'S CYCLOPEDIA OF MAGIC

NOTE: The spectators will not suspect anything because you have offered a logical reason for placing your hand in your pocket. This is a very important lesson to be learned by all magicians: There must be a reason for every move you make. Otherwise you will arouse suspicion and, more than likely, spoil the entire effect.

12 At this point, the spectators still believe that the torn pieces are held at the tops of your left fingers and the secret whole napkin is hidden in the curled fingers of the same hand. Actually, both of these napkins (1 and 3) are whole.

13 Tell the spectators that the real reason for getting the coin is to direct attention away from your left hand so you can execute the switch. Explain that when your right hand reaches into your pocket, the spectators' eyes follow it, leaving your left hand free to do the dirty work.

14 Openly demonstrate this dirty work (the switch). Slowly draw your left thumb and fingers down into your left hand.

15 Bring the supposedly torn pieces (3) along.

16 Move your thumb over to the secret napkin (1).

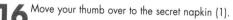

17 With the aid of your third and little fingers, raise this napkin (1) up to the tips of the fingers. Execute this series of moves slowly and deliberately with the palm of your left hand toward the spectators, to show them exactly how the switch is made.

18 Explain that at exactly the same time the switch is being made in the left hand, you remove the coin from your pocket with your right hand. Wave the coin over the napkin(s) and replace it in your pocket.

19 State that all that remains is to open the secret napkin and show it restored, and do just that.

20 Caution the spectators that they must always be very careful not to accidentally show the torn pieces concealed in their hands as they unfold the napkin, "as that would be very embarrassing." There is one thing, however, they can do to save themselves if that should ever happen.

21 "The only thing you can do in that case is to restore the torn pieces." As you say this, open up the napkin (3), which the spectators believe to be the torn pieces, and show it to be completely restored! It is then that the spectators will realize you have baffled them once again!

22 Pick up both napkins (1 and 3) and hold one in each hand. Show both of your hands to be unmistakably empty as you toss the completely restored napkins to the spectators.

JUMPING MATCH

EFFECT

During a casual encounter with a group of friends, you announce that you have discovered a surefire method of checking your own pulse. After removing two ordinary, wooden kitchen matches from your pocket, you place one across the palm of your left hand. You explain that this match will serve as the counter. The second match is slipped under the first. For this demonstration, it will serve as the transmitter. As the spectators watch the counter, it is seen to bounce rhythmically as if counting out your heartbeats. Suddenly it stops, then beats erratically, creating a humorous finish to this puzzling feat. The spectators are handed the matches for examination and are challenged to try to duplicate the test. Of course they can't, and the two matches will keep them busy for days in vain attempts to make the experiment work.

SECRET AND PREPARATION

Use large, wooden kitchen matches for this effect. They are not prepared in any way; therefore, they can be borrowed. The secret to this experiment lies in your unseen manipulation of the transmitter match.

METHOD

1 Place the first, or counter, match across your left palm, as shown. Position the end of this match so that it is resting against the side of your first finger with the head of the match pointed toward you.

2 The second, or transmitter, match is held between the thumb and first finger of your right hand. Your second finger presses its nail against the back of the match, as shown.

3 If you exert pressure against the match with the nail of the second finger, and slowly and imperceptibly slide the match across the nail, the match will create the necessary unseen pulses.

4 Position the transmitter match under the counter match, as shown. Secretly slide your right second fingernail across the match as described in Step 3. The right-hand transmitter match will cause the left-hand counter match to jump in a rhythmic beat.

COMMENTS AND SUGGESTIONS

This fine pocket trick is completely impromptu and can be very mystifying, if done well. Large, wooden kitchen matches are best since they show up better and make the secret move easier to perform. Remember that the counter match won't jump unless your right second fingernail is pressing firmly against its match when you slide it across. Another patter theme for this effect is to explain that you have learned how to magically magnetize matches. Rub the first (transmitter) match several times on your sleeve or the tablecloth. Sure enough, when you hold the magnetized first match up against the second (counter) match, it vibrates and shakes as if it really were impelled by some strange, new power!

FLYING MATCH

EFFECT

You show an ordinary book of paper matches. The book is opened, and the matches, all still attached to the book, are counted for all to see. One match is removed from the book, and the matchbook cover is closed. You light the match, by striking it on the book, and then blow the match out. You make the burnt match vanish as you throw it toward the matchbook. When the matchbook is opened by a spectator, the burnt match is found inside, attached to the matchbook like the rest of the matches! As an added "convincer," the matches are counted, and the number is found to be the same as at the start of the effect.

SECRET AND PREPARATION

A Before you perform this clever trick, you open the matchbook and bend one match in the first row down at the base, as shown.

B Close the matchbook cover. The cover can't be tucked in because of the bent match, but don't worry about that yet. Take a second, loose match, strike it, and set the head of the bent match on fire. Quickly blow out both matches.

C Now you must hide the burnt match that is still attached to the book. Place your left thumb on top of the matchbook so that it completely covers the bent match. The illustration shows how to conceal the match with your left thumb and hold the matchbook closed at the same time. With this secret preparation completed, you are ready to perform.

METHOD

1 With the bent match concealed by your left thumb, open the cover to the matchbook with your right hand, and ask a spectator to watch closely as you count the matches in the book. Be sure to keep the bent match hidden, and don't let the spectator take the matchbook from you as you count. Just hold the matchbook so that it's easy for the spectator to see the matches, then bend each match slightly forward with your right fingers as you count them.

NOTE: It is best to have only ten to twelve matches remaining in the book when you perform this trick. This means there are fewer matches for you to count, and there is less of a chance that the spectator will see the bent match during the counting. In addition, the smaller number of matches makes the reappearance of the burnt match even more startling.

2 With your right fingers, remove one match from the first row. This must be a match that is located next to the hidden bent match. Put this match on the table and close the matchbook cover.

3 As you close the cover, hold the book up in front of you so that the back of the book is toward the spectators.

4 As your right fingers close the cover, your left thumb is under the bent match and pushes it upward into the matchbook.

5 Immediately close the matchbook and tuck in the cover. The entire sequence takes only a few seconds and is hidden from the spectators, who see only the back of the matchbook.

6 Pick up the match you placed on the table (the one you just removed) and strike it on the matchbook. Let only the head of the match burn and then blow it out. Put the matchbook near the center of the table. Now for the magic!

7 Pretend to pick up the match on the table with your right hand. Your right fingers really only cover the match. You slide your right hand back toward yourself.

8 As you do this, the match is secretly swept off the table and falls into your lap.

9 Hold up your right fingers, as if they contain the match. Done correctly, the illusion of picking up the match is perfect.

10 Apparently throw the burnt match (from your really empty hand) toward the closed matchbook. Show that your right hand is empty.

11 Have the spectator pick up the matchbook and open it. Inside the spectator will find what appears to be the original match, now burnt and firmly attached to the matchbook.

12 As a final "convincer," have the spectator count the matches. The spectator will find the number of matches to be the same as at the start of the trick!

COMMENTS AND SUGGESTIONS

The vanish of the match, its reappearance in the matchbook, and the fact that the match is burnt and attached to the matchbook—all add up to an outstanding close-up mystery.

DOTS MAGIC WITH PADDLE MOVE

After you become known as a magician, you will often be asked to perform while you are seated at a table. The following effect teaches you a sleight, the Paddle Move, that is ideal under these very conditions.

EFFECT

You display a clean table knife. After polishing both sides of the blade with your napkin, you attach three red dots, one at a time, to the top surface of the blade. As you attach each dot, three identical dots appear on the opposite side of the knife, one at a time, as if in sympathy with the first three dots. You hand the knife to a spectator seated near you and ask that the person verify the existence of the duplicate set of dots. Upon retrieving the knife, you remove the top three dots from the blade and, magically, the bottom three dots vanish in sympathy. Suddenly all six dots reappear, three on each side of the knife blade. You remove the dots, one at a time, from the top of the blade. As you remove each dot, the corresponding dot on the bottom vanishes in perfect synchronization. With the table knife as clean as it was in the beginning, it is again handed to a spectator for examination.

SECRET AND PREPARATION

A The small, circular dots needed for this effect are available at your local stationery store. They are self-adhering and come in several colors. Red has a high visibility and is therefore recommended for the trick, but any color will do. (If you wish, you can even cut dots out of gummed paper, but the pressure-sensitive commercial dots can be much more easily attached and removed for this particular routine.) The dots selected should measure about 1/4" in diameter.

B For practice purposes, prepare the table knife by placing three of the dots on one side of the blade, as shown. Turn the blade over so that the blank side is face up.

C The next step is the classic turn, entitled the Paddle Move. After you have learned it, you will be able to show the blank side of the blade twice as you turn the knife over in your hand, apparently showing both sides. This will leave the spectators with the impression that they actually saw both sides of the blade. This is the one sleight used in this entire routine. It is one of the most valuable principles in close-up magic.

D To perform the Paddle Move, pick up the knife between the thumb and first two fingers of your right hand by the handle, as shown. The blank side of the blade should be facing up. You will notice that the blade is facing away from you (pointing toward the spectators). It should be held at about waist level. You are about to turn the knife over so that the blade points toward you. To prevent the dots fastened on the bottom of the blade from being exposed, you must simultaneously revolve the knife between your thumb and first two fingers as you turn the knife over.

E Your right thumb rolls the knife handle with your thumb and fingers one half-turn to your left.

F At the same time, you rotate the blade over so that it points toward you.

G Rotate the blade back toward the spectators. At the same time, execute Steps E and F in reverse and roll the knife back (to your right) with your thumb and fingers so that the blank side is still up. Practice in front of a mirror until you can execute the move smoothly. When properly done, the blade will appear to be blank on both sides. When you have mastered the Paddle Move, you will be ready to present this most clever and entertaining effect.

H Before the performance, place six of the dots in your wallet (or an envelope). After you are seated at the dinner table and have the opportunity, secretly attach three of the dots to the underside of the blade of your knife. You are now ready to perform a minor miracle.

NOTE: The illustrations depicting the Paddle Move above, as well as those in the Method that follows, are from the magician's point of view, as the knife is held horizontally over the surface of the table.

METHOD

1 Stand up and display the knife to the spectators. Using the Paddle Move, show both sides of the blade to be empty. (Really, there are three dots on one side.) Wipe both sides of the blade, one side at a time (really the same side twice, using the Paddle Move), with your napkin to further create the illusion of a clean knife.

MARK WILSON'S CYCLOPEDIA OF MAGIC

2 Remove the three remaining dots from your pocket and set them on the table. Place one of these directly in the center of the blank side of the blade, as shown.

3 Display the dot and execute the Paddle Move to apparently show the opposite side of the blade. To the spectators, it will appear that a duplicate dot has magically appeared on the other side of the blade.

4 Return the knife to its original position and attach the second dot near the end of the blade, as shown.

5 Execute the Paddle Move again and apparently show the arrival of the second dot on the back of the blade.

6 Repeat Step 3 with the third and last dot, again showing the knife on both sides. The spectators will now be convinced that the blade of your knife has three dots on both sides. At this point, it actually does have three dots on both sides because of the three, secret dots you previously attached. Hand the knife to a spectator for examination.

7 As soon as the knife is returned to you, openly remove the three dots from the top of the blade and put them in your pocket.

8 Execute the Paddle Move and show that the three dots on the back of the blade have vanished as well.

9 Pick up your napkin and apparently wipe the blade clean. Under cover of this wiping action, turn the blade over. The spectators will be surprised to see that the three dots have reappeared on the knife!

10 By executing the Paddle Move, you can show that the dots have magically returned, not only to the top of the blade but to the back as well.

NOTE: At this point you are set up for the vanish of the dots, one at a time, since the blade now has three red dots on the top surface only. Simply repeat Steps 2 through 6 in reverse.

11 Begin by removing the center dot and executing the Paddle Move. It will appear as if the center dot vanished from the back of the knife as well.

12 Remove the dot closest to the handle and apparently show both sides, as before. This will leave you with one dot on the tip of both sides of the blade.

13 Remove the last dot and slowly show both sides of the knife. The blade will be clean of spots and may now be handed to the spectator for examination.

COMMENTS AND SUGGESTIONS

As mentioned earlier, the Paddle Move is a classic sleight with many important uses in magic. Study the illustrations and practice the move until you can do it smoothly and almost without thinking. You will have learned an extremely valuable sleight that you will perform in many different effects as you progress through the wonderful world of magic.

DOTS MAGIC—
IMPROMPTU VERSION

DOTS MAGIC, as just described, can also be performed in a completely impromptu situation when you do not have the commercial dots with you.

EFFECT

The effect is the same as in DOTS MAGIC WITH PADDLE MOVE, except that instead of dots, you cut or tear small squares of paper (a paper napkin works well) for use in the trick. The squares are attached to the knife by moistening them slightly using the tip of your finger to obtain a drop of water from your water glass and applying it to each square. The slightly dampened squares will adhere to the blade of the knife.

SECRET AND PREPARATION

If you have an opportunity to apply the three secret squares before the performance, you may utilize the same routine as described in DOTS MAGIC WITH PADDLE MOVE. If you do not have the time or opportunity to tear, moisten, and apply the three extra squares, just start the routine from Step 10, using a total of three squares for the trick.

METHOD

1 Openly attach the three squares to one side of the examined blade.

2 Using the Paddle Move, show that three more identical squares have magically appeared on the opposite side of the blade.

3 Turn the blade over to show that the spots have vanished. Then use the Paddle Move to show the other side blank.

4 After showing both sides of the blade blank (again using the Paddle Move), the three squares reappear.

5 Proceed with Steps 11, 12, and 13, as the squares are openly removed from the top side of the blade and vanish from the bottom side.

GLASS THROUGH TABLE

EFFECT

You state that you will cause a solid object to penetrate through the top of the table. With that, you place a coin on the table and cover it with a glass, mouth down. You cover the glass with two paper napkins, concealing both the glass and coin from view. You explain that, by mere concentration, you will cause the coin to "melt" through the top of the table. After several unsuccessful attempts, you explain that the reason for failure is that you forgot one of the most important parts of the experiment. You must first strike the top of the glass, giving the coin the momentum to penetrate the table. Suddenly, with a sharp downward motion of your hand, you smash the glass and the napkins flat on the table. When the napkins are lifted, the coin is still there, but the glass is gone! Immediately, you reach beneath the table and produce the glass.

MARK WILSON'S CYCLOPEDIA OF MAGIC

SECRET AND PREPARATION

The secret of this trick is based on a very clever principle. Due to the natural stiffness of the paper napkins, they will retain the form or shape of the glass even if the glass is not within them. This creates a very convincing illusion, making this mystery possible. The glass should be smooth-sided so it slides easily from within the napkins. It should also be slightly smaller at the base than at the mouth. A glass that is approximately 4" or 5" tall works well. In addition, you need a coin (a half-dollar is a good size) and two ordinary paper napkins.

METHOD

1 You must be seated at a card table or dining table to perform this close-up mystery. Also, it is better if the spectators are seated at the same table. With the glass, napkins, and coin lying on the table, tell the spectators that you will attempt to cause a solid object to pass through the top of the table.

2 Place the coin directly in front of you, about 12" from the edge of the table. Cover the coin with the glass, mouth down. Point out that the glass completely encloses the coin so that it is impossible for you to touch it.

3 Open both napkins, lay them on top of each other, and place them over the glass, as shown. Explain that the coin must be kept in the dark, so you will cover the glass with the napkins.

4 With both hands, pull the napkins downward around the glass. This makes the form of the glass clearly outlined through the napkins.

5 With one hand, grip the top of the glass through the napkins and place your other hand around the mouth of the glass. Then, twist the glass, as shown, drawing the napkins tightly against the sides of the glass. This helps to form the shape of the glass even more distinctly inside the paper napkins.

6 To reassure the spectators that the coin is still on the table, lift both the glass and the napkins together.

7 Once again, cover the coin with the glass and explain that through deep concentration you can cause the coin to penetrate through the table. All eyes will be fixed on the napkin-covered glass, waiting to see if the coin actually does as you say.

8 Pretend to concentrate for a few seconds. Then announce that you think the coin has done its work. With your right hand, lift the napkins and glass, revealing that the coin is still on the table. Act surprised, as if you actually expected the coin to be gone.

9 Pick up the coin in your left hand as you remark that something seems to be wrong. At the same time, move your right hand to the edge of the table, as shown, while holding the napkins and the glass. This motion of your right hand is completely natural, as it must move away to make room for your left hand, which picks up the coin. Your eyes, your gestures, your total attention should all be directed at the coin. This is misdirection!

10 Here is a side view of the right hand holding the napkin-covered glass at the edge of the table. Notice that the hand is actually resting on the table.

11 It is at this time that the secret move takes place. While the attention of the spectators is on the coin, the fingers of your right hand relax their grip on the glass through the napkins. The weight of the glass will cause it to slide from within the napkins into your lap.

12 The napkins retain the shape of the glass, creating the illusion that the glass is still there.

13 As the glass falls into your lap, raise your heels enough to bring your knees a bit higher than your lap. This keeps the glass in your lap, so it does not roll onto the floor.

14 Here is the spectators' view as the secret drop takes place. Notice how the left hand is forward, focusing attention on the coin.

15 Dropping the glass in your lap should take only a moment. As soon as the glass falls from the napkins, place the coin back on the table and cover it with the napkins (which apparently still contain the glass).

16 Explain that the trick failed because you forgot to strike the top of the glass. As you say this, raise your left hand above the glass.

17 Smash the napkins flat on the table with your left hand. When this is done fast and hard, the reaction from the spectators will be one of complete astonishment.

18 Act puzzled for a moment. Lift the napkins with your left hand, revealing the coin on the table. At the same time, your right hand grasps the glass in your lap and carries it beneath the table, as if reaching below the spot where you "smashed" the glass. Then bring your hand into view from beneath the table with the glass.

19 Place the glass on the table and say, "Now I remember how the trick is done! It's the glass that is supposed to penetrate the table, not the coin."

CHAPTER 16
MENTAL MAGIC

This type of magic is unique because it depends on the effect
created on the audience rather than the objects used.
Instead of making props vanish and reappear, you use them
in special tests to presumably read people's minds.

For practical purposes, it is best to inject a few mental effects
at different parts of your performance and watch for audience reactions. If those prove favorable, add others to your
program or play them up more strongly, until you strike the
right balance. Most mental effects depend upon some unsuspected secret that spectators are apt to overlook. It is your
job to see that they do exactly that. Never refer to a mental
effect as a "trick." Call it a "test" or an "experiment" and, in
most cases, treat it rather seriously. If you find that somebody
is watching you too closely, don't try to work your way out
of it. Just put the blame on other people. Say that they are not
"projecting" the right thoughts. That makes it look all the more
genuine and gives you a chance to switch to another test.

THREE-WAY TEST

Reading a person's mind is surely a most effective way of demonstrating your magical powers. In this ESP experiment, you show your ability to predict and control the minds of three spectators. This effect requires a little closer study than most magic tricks, but it is well worth the sensational impact of your magical mind reading.

EFFECT

A In this mental effect, you demonstrate three different experiments in extrasensory perception. In the first experiment, you correctly determine the exact amount of change in a spectator's pockets.

B In the second test, you receive a mental impression of an object that a spectator is thinking of before the spectator picks it up.

C In the last experiment, you correctly predict which of three figure drawings a spectator will select from the table. With a small pad and pencil on your table, you are ready to begin.

METHOD

First, explain that you are going to demonstrate three different forms of ESP. To do this, you need three spectators to assist you, one person for each test. Continue by asking the members of the audience to assemble four or more small objects from around the room and to place them on the table in front of one of the spectators.

1 These can be any objects, as long as they are all different. Let's assume that the four items gathered are an ashtray, a pen, a matchbook, and a paper clip.

2 Pick up a pad of paper and tear off three of the blank sheets. On one sheet of paper, draw a circle; on the second, draw a square; and on the third, draw a triangle. Place these slips face up in a row in front of one of the spectators

3 Say to another one of the spectators, "Reach into your pocket or purse and bring out all of the small change you have there." Tell the spectator not to count it but to keep it held tightly in a closed fist.

4 You are now ready to begin the actual experiments. Explain that the first experiment is a test of clairvoyance, which is the ability to see hidden objects.

5 Pick up the pad and pencil and hold it so no one can see what you write. To the "money" spectator, say, "I am now going to write down my impression of the amount of change in your hand." Obviously, you can't write this amount, because you don't know it yet! Instead, draw a circle on the slip of paper.

6 Tear off the slip and fold it without letting anyone see what you have written. Say that you will call this first test, Test A, and that you will write the letter A on the outside of the slip. Instead, you really mark it with the letter C.

7 After you have marked the slip, place it where it will be out of view of the spectators. (Be careful not to let anyone see the letter C on the slip of paper.) A drinking glass or a coffee cup works well if it is the type you can't see through.

8 Another suggestion would be to turn an ashtray or saucer upside down on the table and place the slip under it. It's not important where you place the slip as long as the letter written on the outside cannot be seen by the spectators. Let's assume you place the slip in a coffee mug.

9 After the folded slip is in the mug, tell Person A to count the money out onto the table and leave it there for everyone to see. Let's say it comes to exactly $1.36.

10 You turn to the second person and say, "I'm going to try a test in telepathy with you. This means that I can mentally pick up an impression that you already have in your mind. To do this, I want you to concentrate on one of the four objects on the table, the object you are going to pick up in your hand. Tell me when you have decided on the one you want, but don't tell me which object, and don't pick it up until after I have written down my impression."

11 Instead of writing on the pad the name of one of the objects (because you don't know which one the spectator is thinking of), you write the amount of change that has been counted on the table from Test A, $1.36.

NOTE: Learning information from one test and secretly using it in the next test is called the One-Ahead Principle.

MARK WILSON'S CYCLOPEDIA OF MAGIC

12 Tear off this sheet and fold it. Tell the spectator that this is Test B and you will mark the slip with the letter B. But, instead of writing B, you mark it with the letter A.

13 Put this slip into the mug along with the other one.

14 Tell the spectator who was concentrating on an object to pick it up. Let's say this spectator picks up the matchbook.

15 Tell the third spectator that you will do an experiment in precognition. This means that you will predict a certain result before the spectator decides to do it.

16 Pretend to write a prediction on the pad, but really write down the object in Person B's hand, the matchbook.

17 Tear off the slip, fold it, and say you'll call this Test C. Instead of marking the slip with the letter C, you mark it with the letter B, as shown.

18 Place this slip into the mug along with the other two.

19 You must maneuver the spectator into selecting the slip of paper with the circle on it. This is called "Forcing," although the spectator believes it is a free choice. The force you will use here is called the MAGICIAN'S CHOICE.

20 Point out to the spectator that you have drawn a different figure on each of the three papers on the table. Ask the spectator to point to any one of the three slips. One of several situations will arise.

21 First Situation: If they point to the circle, say, "Please pick up the slip that you have selected and hold it in your hand."

22 When the spectator does this, you pick up the other two slips and tear them up, saying, "We will not need these, so I'll tear them up."

23 Second Situation: If the spectator points to the square or the triangle, you pick up the one the spectator pointed to.

24 After picking up the spectator's choice, you say, "Fine, I'll tear this one up and that leaves only two."

25 Ask the spectator to pick up either one of the remaining slips of paper. Either one of two things will now happen.

26 The spectator may pick up the paper with the circle on it.

MARK WILSON'S CYCLOPEDIA OF MAGIC

27 If that happens, then you pick up the one remaining slip on the table and tear it up, saying, "OK, the circle is the one you selected, so we won't need this one either."

28 The spectator may pick up the paper without the circle on it.

29 If that happens, you say, "OK, you tear up that slip, which leaves just the one on the table." Of course, the one that is left is the circle.

30 Once you have successfully "forced" the circle, you are ready for the payoff. Pick up the mug and dump the slips onto the table. Ask each spectator to take the slip that has the appropriate letter on it, and open it. When each slip is opened, all three of your tests prove to be correct!

COMMENTS AND SUGGESTIONS

This is a very strong trick. It can be performed anywhere. All you need are a pencil and some pieces of paper. There is no sleight of hand or special skill needed. However, it is a trick that must be studied thoroughly and practiced until you can remember easily which part comes next, which letter to write on each slip, etc. After you have mastered it, you will be able to baffle your friends with one of the finest "mind-reading" mysteries in the entire Art of Magic.

MAGAZINE TEST

Among mental mysteries, those in which a spectator does all the work can be rated among the best, for this apparently makes it impossible for the performer to inject any element of trickery. In fact, there are tricks in which the magician does nothing more than guide the spectator's actions. The MAGAZINE TEST is one such trick. You will find, however, that it does involve a small bit of work on your part, but this is mostly done beforehand. Hence, no one even knows about it, making the trick all the more effective.

EFFECT

Displaying a sealed envelope and a current issue of a well-known magazine, you explain to the audience that, prior to your appearance, you wrote one word on a white card and sealed it in an envelope. This envelope you now hand to one of the spectators in the audience. Ask a second spectator to join you on stage in order to demonstrate your ability to "see into the future." You hand the magazine to the second spectator along with a pencil or felt-tipped pen. In order not to influence the spectator's choice of a word from the magazine, ask this person to hold the magazine behind their back and to mark a page at random with a bold X. After you take back the now closed magazine you ask the first spectator to tear open the envelope you provided at the start and to read the predicted word. When the magazine is opened to the marked page, the audience is surprised to see that the intersecting lines of the X are directly through the identical word.

MARK WILSON'S CYCLOPEDIA OF MAGIC

SECRET AND PREPARATION

A Select a current issue of a magazine. Turn to any right-hand page located near the center of the magazine and draw a large X on the page. Make the mark so that the two lines of the X cross over a single word, as shown. From this point on, this word, "news," will be referred to as the force word.

NOTE: You should try marking the magazine page behind your own back before trying this trick. In fact, several trials are advisable in order to see just what a pair of crossed lines will look like when a spectator goes through the same procedure. Then, when you are ready to prepare the magazine that you intend to use in the test, you can copy one of your previous attempts, giving the lines slight curves or an irregular appearance to make them look authentic. Never have them cross exactly in the center of the forced word. Hit near one end, or just above or below, yet close enough so everyone will agree on that word.

B Print the force word across the face of a white card and seal the "prediction" in an opaque envelope.

C The final step is to prepare a pen or pencil to prevent the spectator from actually making a mark on the magazine. Be sure that this pen or pencil matches the one you used to mark the page. The best pen to use is a felt-tip one. Let it sit without the cap on until the tip is dried out. A ballpoint pen, which is out of ink, also works well. If a pencil is used, dip the tip in clear varnish and allow it to dry overnight. This will prevent the pencil from making a mark.

METHOD

1 Display the sealed envelope with the force word written on the card inside. Have a member of the audience hold the envelope. Pick up the magazine and demonstrate for the audience how you would like a spectator to mark the magazine page. Tell the spectator to thumb through the magazine while holding it behind their back. Once the spectator has selected a page, demonstrate how to fold the left-hand pages of the magazine to the rear. This ensures that the spectator will mark on a right-hand page of the magazine.

2 When you are sure that the spectator understands the proper procedure for marking the magazine, give them the prepared pen or pencil. Have the spectator hold the magazine behind their back, select any (right-hand) page, fold the other (left-hand) pages out of the way, and mark the page with a large X. The prepared pen or pencil will ensure that no mark is actually made.

3 Have the spectator close the magazine before bringing it out from behind their back. Take the pen or pencil and the magazine from the spectator. Put the pen or pencil away in your pocket as soon as you have finished this phase of the trick.

4 Call attention to the sealed envelope that is being held by a member of the audience. Emphasize that the envelope was given to the spectator before the magazine was marked! Have the person holding the envelope tear it open and call out the word written on the card inside.

5 Give the magazine back to the spectator who marked the page and have them look through the pages until the marked page is located. When it is found, have the spectator call out the word that is indicated by that mark. It will match the force word that was written on the prediction card!

CURIOUS COINCIDENCE

When performing mental marvels, always remember that your main purpose is to create an effect in the minds of your audience, not to display skill or spring some quick surprise. In short, method is a secondary factor in any mental test and should be played down to such a degree that no one will suspect that trickery is underway. That is the case with the effect that follows. Though the procedure is extremely bold, it will be free of suspicion if you adopt a matter-of-fact delivery.

EFFECT

Four identical pairs of papers bearing the names of past famous magicians are shown, along with two ordinary paper bags. You take one complete set of papers, put it in a bag, and give it to a spectator. You place the other identical set of papers in the remaining bag, which you hold. You and the spectator each remove one of the folded papers from the bags and exchange your choices with each other. When you open the papers and read them aloud, they match. This is repeated three more times with amazing results. The papers match perfectly each time.

SECRET AND PREPARATION

For this amazing trick, you will need two ordinary paper bags and two matching sets of paper bearing the names of famous magicians. (Any names or words may be used, such as famous singers or actors, presidents, or cities. Just use whatever best suits your act.) Make up two identical sets of papers. Write the names of the four magicians on the papers before folding each of them into quarters. Secretly prepare one set of papers as shown. The Dunninger paper is left unprepared. The Thurston paper has one corner folded up. The Houdini paper has two corners folded, and the Kellar paper has three folded corners. With the papers secretly prepared in this manner, you can tell at a glance which paper bears what name. This is your key to the trick; you will be using these prepared papers during the effect.

METHOD

1 To perform the effect, place the unprepared set of papers into one bag and give it to the spectator to hold. Place the prepared set of papers in the other bag and hold it in your left hand.

2 Instruct the spectator to remove one of the folded papers from the bag. You do likewise from the bag you are holding. As soon as you remove your paper, you will be able to tell at a glance which name is written inside because of the folded key corner(s). In the illustration, the paper with two folded corners, the "Houdini" paper, has been removed.

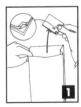

3 Once you have removed a folded paper from your bag, place the paper in full view on the table.

4 By now, the spectator has had time to remove a paper from the bag. Caution the spectator not to open the paper yet.

5 Take the spectator's folded paper. Instruct the spectator to pick up your paper from the table and open it.

6 While the spectator is unfolding your paper, you open the other paper. Because of your corner-fold system, you already know what name appears on the paper held by the spectator. If you are not holding the matching paper, then you miscall the paper you hold. This means that if the paper you hold says "Kellar," as in the illustration, you say, "Houdini." There will be amazement that the paper held by the spectator matches the one you just announced. After you have miscalled the paper you hold, fold it back up and place it aside on the table.

7 Repeat the entire process with the three remaining pairs of papers. If by chance, the two of you remove identical papers, then you have an actual miracle. If not, simply miscall each paper as described in Step 6. The effect will work perfectly due to your corner-fold key. A little practice will show you how clever an effect you can make of this simple principle.

COMMENTS AND SUGGESTIONS

It is important that the slips not be examined or compared until after the effect is over. Keep the used slips in a confused pile on the table so that the spectators can't mentally pair up the slips at the trick's conclusion and discover one of your miscalls. Try this one a few times and you will be amazed at the startling effect it has on the spectators.

MILLION TO ONE

EFFECT

You show the spectators ten small cards with a large spot printed on the face of each card. These cards are placed on the table in a long, straight row so that they alternate face up and face down. In this arrangement, the spectators can see five of the red spots and five of the red backs. You ask one of the spectators to think of the color blue. As soon as that is acknowledged, you ask the same person to call out a number between one and ten. With the number selected, you quickly point to the card that corresponds to the spectator's choice. To the complete surprise of your audience, this card proves to be the only blue card in the row.

SECRET AND PREPARATION

The cards may be made from index cards or any type of stiff white cardboard. Use crayons or marking pens to color each card. Eight of the ten cards are alike. They all have a red spot on the face and red-colored backs.

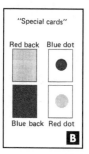

"Special cards"

Red back   Blue dot

Blue back   Red dot

B

B The two remaining cards are prepared differently. One card has a red spot on the face, but the back is colored blue. The other special card has a red back and a blue spot on the face.

C Arrange the ten cards in a stack. The top (uppermost) card is a regular card, face up. The second card from the top is also regular, face down. The third card is the special blue-backed card, face up. The fourth card is the other special card with the blue dot, face down. The fifth card is regular, face up. The sixth card is regular, face down. The seventh card is regular, face up. The eighth card is regular, face down. The ninth card is regular, face up. The last card, the tenth card, is regular, face down.

METHOD

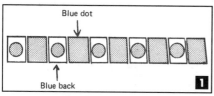

Blue dot

Blue back

1

1 Using your left hand, hold the cards in the prearranged order. With your right hand, deal the ten cards, starting at the top of the packet, onto the table from left to right.

This means that the cards alternate face up and face down and that the two special cards will be in the third and fourth positions from your left.

2 After you have placed the cards on the table, ask a spectator to concentrate on the color blue. Then, have that person call out any number between one and ten. You now proceed to force one of the two specially prepared (blue) cards on the spectator.

3 After hearing the spectator's number, count the cards. Here is the procedure for whatever number the spectator calls:

NUMBER ONE—Begin with the card at the left end and spell, "O, N, E," arriving at the third (blue-backed) card.

NUMBER TWO—Begin at the left end and spell, "T, W, O," arriving at the third (blue-backed) card.

NUMBER THREE—Count, "One, Two, Three," from the left arriving at the third (blue-backed) card.

NUMBER FOUR—Count, "One, Two, Three, Four," from the left, arriving at the fourth (blue-spotted) card.

NUMBER FIVE—Begin at the left and spell, "F, I, V, E," arriving at the fourth (blue-spotted) card.

NUMBER SIX—Begin at the left and spell, "S, I, X," arriving at the third (blue-backed) card.

NUMBER SEVEN—Have the spectator count from the right end of the row, arriving at the fourth (blue-spotted) card.

NUMBER EIGHT—Have the spectator count from the right end, arriving at the third (blue-backed) card.

NUMBER NINE—Begin at your left end and spell, "N, I, N, E," arriving at the fourth (blue-spotted) card.

NUMBER TEN—Begin at your left end and spell, "T, E, N," arriving at the third (blue-backed) card.

4 After you have finished the spelling or counting, emphasize the fact that the spectator was given a free choice of any card. (Or so the spectator thinks!) Turn the chosen (forced) card over to show that the opposite side is blue.

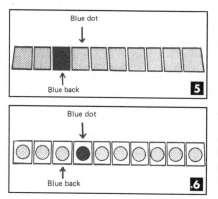

5 If the selected card is the blue-backed (third) card, turn all the cards that are face-up cards face down to show that all have red backs except the chosen card.

6 If the selected card is the blue-spotted (fourth) card, turn all the cards that are face down, face up to show that all have red spots except the chosen card.

7 This final turning of the cards serves to convince the spectators that the cards are all identical except for the one card that the spectator selected, and to conceal the fact that you are using one more specially prepared card. After this turnover, gather up all the cards, being careful not to expose the remaining special (blue) card among the rest.

COMMENTS AND SUGGESTIONS

Carry the ten cards in their prearranged stack in a separate pocket so that you can remove the cards and place them on the table in a smooth, unhurried fashion. Practice placing the cards on the table until you can do it in a natural, relaxed manner. This effect can be presented either as a demonstration of ESP or as a magic trick. Never repeat this trick, or you will give away the principle used to force the special card.

GYPSY MIND READER
(PSYCHOMETRY)

The subject of "psychometry" is based on the theory that objects belonging to a person, particularly those that the person carries around, can be identified as belonging to the person even when they are removed from the owner. For years, this was an old Gypsy custom, depending on guesswork or trickery. Today, many people, including some professors, regard psychometry as a form of extrasensory perception (ESP). As such, it belongs in a program of mental magic. The test about to be described is one of the best of that type.

EFFECT

Five plain white envelopes are distributed among the audience. Each recipient is asked to place a small article into the envelope and seal it. A spectator gathers up the envelopes and thoroughly mixes them before handing them back to you. You openly place the envelopes into a clear glass bowl. Explain to the audience that the little-explored subject of "psychometry" is based on the theory that, by handling articles belonging to a person, it is possible to gain a mental impression of the actual person even though the articles are sealed in an envelope. In order to demonstrate the validity of this theory, you pick up one of the envelopes and hold it to your forehead. Without hesitation, you announce that the article inside the sealed envelope belongs to a young lady. You open the envelope and allow the article to fall into your open palm. After closing your hand around the item, you proceed to describe the owner in minute detail, apparently from the vibrations received from the article. Finally, you walk among the spectators and are mysteriously led to the surprised young lady.

This demonstration is repeated using the four remaining envelopes and the objects they contain with the same unfailing accuracy.

NOTE: Properly performed, this effect is one of the strongest mental feats available. Some professional magicians have built their entire reputation based on this presentation. Again, it is important that you present the effect as entertainment, assuring your audience that it is merely a magician's demonstration of the phenomenon of psychometry.

SECRET AND PREPARATION

Light pencil dot

A

A You will need a number of plain white envelopes. Letter-size envelopes, measuring approximately 3-1/2″ × 6-1/2″, are perfect for this effect. Four of the five envelopes are prepared by placing a small pencil dot in a different corner of each of the envelopes. The dots are put on the flap side of the envelope, one in each of the four corners. They are made in pencil, lightly, so as not to be noticed by the spectators.

B

B Each of the four corner dots represents a different spectator. The fifth envelope is left unmarked. Stack the five envelopes so that the dots are arranged, clockwise from top to bottom, running one through five, as shown.

METHOD

1 Holding the envelopes in this prearranged stack, pass them out to the spectators, moving from left to right through the audience. All you have to do is remember who gets each envelope.

2 After returning to the stage, instruct the five spectators to place a small object into their envelope, seal it, and pass it to a sixth spectator. This person is asked to thoroughly mix up the envelopes and then to hand them back to you.

3 Drop the envelopes into a clear glass container. As you remove the first envelope, turn it flap side up and locate the coded dot. You now know to whom this envelope belongs.

4 Hold the envelope to your forehead and slowly reveal whether the object belongs to a man or a woman. You might say, "I'm getting a very strong vibration from this envelope. Yes, the article inside must belong to a gentleman in his late twenties or early thirties."

5 At this point, tear open the envelope and allow the article to fall into your hand. After discarding the envelope, close your fingers around the item and begin to reveal details regarding this person's appearance (which you can see from the stage, or better yet, which you remember from when you handed out the envelopes).

6 During this reading, start moving down into the audience and, as if being led by the vibrating force of the object in your hand, dramatically locate the owner.

7 Repeat the demonstration with the four remaining objects. When you have finished, the audience will be left with a profound mystery that is quite different from any other effect on your program.

CENTER TEAR

This is without a doubt one of the simplest yet cleverest of all methods for learning the contents of a short message, a word, or a number written by a spectator. Properly performed, it is so deceptive that your audience will have no idea that trickery is involved. As a result, some members of the audience may be ready to accept the trick as a display of actual mind reading. Naturally, you should disclaim such power; at the same time, keep the secret to yourself, thus adding to a very perplexing mystery.

EFFECT

You give a spectator a square slip of paper and a pencil, telling the person to write a name, a number, or even a brief message in the center. This is done while your back is turned. The spectator folds the paper in half and then in quarters, so that you cannot possibly see the writing. You tear up the folded slip. The pieces are openly dropped into an ashtray and burned. Yet you learn the spectator's message and reveal it!

SECRET AND PREPARATION

A To prepare for this trick, you will need to place a book of matches in a pocket on your left-hand side. You will also need to have an ashtray handy.

B Cut out a small slip of paper approximately 3" square. Draw a circle about 1-1/4" wide in the center of one side of the paper, as shown.

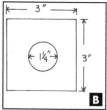

METHOD

1 Give the paper to a spectator with instructions to write a word or a short message within the "magic circle." Make sure that the spectator understands that you are not to see what is written on the paper.

2 When the message is complete, ask the spectator to fold the paper in half so that the writing is within the fold.

3 Have the spectator fold the paper once again, so that it is in quarters.

4 Take the folded slip from the spectator. You can look at the packet and easily see which corner is actually the center "magic circle" of the piece of paper.

NOTE: Practice folding the paper yourself until you can instantly spot the right corner.

5 When you have located the center corner of the paper, hold the folded packet so that the "magic circle" is in the upper right-hand corner, facing you. With the packet held in this manner, tear it in half. This tear should leave the "magic circle" undamaged.

6 Once you have torn the packet in half, place the pieces of paper in your left hand behind the pieces in your right hand. Hold all the pieces in your left hand. The "magic circle" should be at the top of the packet, and it should be nearest your body.

7 Rotate the packet a quarter turn to the right and grasp it between both hands. The "magic circle" is still facing you, held by your right thumb and first finger. Holding the packet in this position, tear it in half once more.

8 Again, place the left-hand pieces behind the right-hand pieces. Then, take all the pieces in your right fingertips. The "magic circle" is still facing you and is directly under your right thumb.

9 Hold all the pieces in your right hand, between your thumb and fingers. Now, position your right hand over the ashtray. Drop all of the pieces of paper except the "magic circle," which is held directly under your thumb, into the ashtray. As you release the pieces, use your thumb to slide the piece of paper containing the "magic circle" back toward the middle joints of your fingers.

10 You secretly hold the "magic circle" concealed in your right fingers. The rest of the pieces of paper have fallen into the ashtray. The audience is unaware that you hold this paper (which contains the message) in your hand.

11 With the "magic circle" safely hidden in your right hand, use your left hand to reach into your pocket and take out the book of matches. Use both hands to remove a match, strike it, and set fire to the pieces of paper in the ashtray. Place the matchbook on the table with your right hand and use your left hand to hold the lighted match.

12 While the spectators are concentrating on the burning pieces of paper, drop your right hand below the table and use your right thumb to secretly open up the "magic circle" hidden in your right fingers. As soon as you have read the message, quietly crumple up or refold the paper. As the paper continues to burn, pick up the book of matches and place them and the "magic circle" in your right pocket. Concentrate deeply on the rising smoke before you reveal the words of the message!

COMMENTS AND SUGGESTIONS

The most important thing to remember is that your right hand, while it secretly holds the center portion of the paper, must be held completely relaxed and natural. When you drop your right hand below the table to open up the paper and read the message, ask the spectators to focus their attention on the burning pieces of paper and the smoke as you casually glance at the message.

This is another classic method that is used not only by magicians but also by fraudulent spirit mediums and psychics. Its great strength lies in that it uses only ordinary objects. With the proper buildup, this simple effect can be made into a "real" miracle!

SPECTRUM PREDICTION

Prediction effects form an important phase of mentalism and should be included on nearly every program. Moreover, where predictions are concerned, one good test definitely calls for another, because the more predictions you fulfill the less chance there is that luck has anything to do with it. Any good prediction may puzzle the spectators; but if you follow one with another, or even hit three in a row, people will really be bewildered. However, simply repeating the same prediction time after time is not the right policy. Some spectators lose interest when the same trick is repeated; others are apt to watch for a weak point and may be just sharp enough to spot it. So the answer is to have some special type of divination in reserve, differing from the rest in regard to objects used as well as method. The SPECTRUM PREDICTION meets both those qualifications.

EFFECT

You display eight brightly colored squares of cardboard and spread them out on the table so that everyone can see that each square or chip is a different color. You write a prediction on a piece of paper that you fold and give to a spectator to hold. The colored chips are gathered together by a spectator and wrapped in your opaque handkerchief. This same person is asked to reach into the folds of the handkerchief and withdraw a single chip. This done, the prediction is unfolded and read aloud. You are proved to be correct!

SECRET AND PREPARATION

A From a stationery or art supply store, obtain eight different colors of cardboard; or you may use colored construction paper, or even white cardboard that you have colored with paint, crayons, or ink. The colors you use are unimportant, but use easily recognizable colors such as yellow, blue, green, red, orange, purple, black, and white. In any event, make eight 1" squares, all of a different color. You also need to cut eight more squares that are all the same color. For the purpose of explanation, let's assume that these additional squares are all red. You therefore have eight different colored squares and eight squares that are all red.

B You will also need two identical pocket handkerchiefs. Handkerchiefs made with a colored pattern work best. (Bandannas are good.) Place one on the other and sew them together, as shown by the dotted lines.

C You will notice that Point X is the center of the handkerchief. The stitching along Lines XY and XZ form a hidden pocket that can be opened at AB. Sew two small beads at the A and B corners. These beads will enable you to find the pocket opening quickly. (The beads are optional, but they do help greatly in locating the secret pocket at the proper time.)

D Place the eight red squares in the hidden pocket. Grasp Corners A and B and shake out the handkerchief. Place the prepared handkerchief in your coat pocket with Corners A and B on top, where you can grasp them easily so that the extra, secret squares will not fall out when you remove the handkerchief.

E Along with the eight squares of different colors, place a small pad of paper and a pencil on the table.

METHOD

1 Call the spectators' attention to the colored squares. Pick up the pad and, without letting the spectators see what you are writing, write, "You will select the color red." Tear the prediction from the pad and fold it so that it cannot be read by the spectators. Hand the folded slip to one of the spectators to hold.

2 With your right hand, reach into your coat pocket and grasp the prepared handkerchief by the small beads that are sewn into the Corners A and B. Withdraw the handkerchief, show it on both sides, and gather all of the corners together, forming a bag, as shown.

3 Have the spectator pick up the colored squares from the table. You are holding the handkerchief by the corners in your right hand. With your left thumb and first finger, release Corner D and allow the spectator to drop the squares into the handkerchief. These squares do not go into the secret pocket.

4 Shake the impromptu bag, mixing the colored squares inside. Release Corner A and allow the spectator to reach inside and remove a single square. The spectator will be reaching inside the hidden pocket that contains only red squares. Be sure the spectator removes only one of the squares.

5 Once the spectator has the red square, simply bunch up the handkerchief and put it back in your pocket, squares and all.

6 Ask the spectator to unfold the slip of paper. Again, you have proven your magical powers. Your prediction proves to be exactly correct!

COMMENTS AND SUGGESTIONS

The success of this trick depends upon handling the handkerchief in a natural, casual manner, so as to avoid suspicion. Since the handkerchief is a common article, it seems nothing more than a mere adjunct to the prediction.

For that reason, it is comparatively easy to focus attention on the colored squares at the outset and the prediction slip at the finish, leaving the spectator with one red square and the prediction.

If you have an ordinary handkerchief resembling the special double handkerchief, you can use it in some previous effect in which it plays an innocent part. Place it in your pocket afterward. When you bring out the double handkerchief for the SPECTRUM PREDICTION, everyone will suppose it to be the same one that you used before. It is also a good plan to have eight extra squares of some color other than red, so that if you perform the prediction for the same group of people on another occasion, you can force a different color.

PING-PONG PRESTIDIGITATION

Here is a comedy trick in which you let everyone in on the secret of the effect except for one person—the spectator who assists you on stage. This is the only person who is deceived by your magical methods, creating a situation that develops into good fun for everyone.

EFFECT

You display three pairs of different colored ping-pong balls. One pair is white, one pair is red, and one pair is blue. You drop all six balls into a paper bag and invite two spectators to assist in the effect. The spectator on your left is asked to reach in the bag—without looking—and remove any ball. No matter which ball is withdrawn, the other spectator is able to reach into the bag and remove the matching ball without looking inside the bag. The selected balls are replaced, and the trick is repeated over and over again with the same improbable results.

SECRET AND PREPARATION

What the first spectator doesn't know is that everyone else, including the other spectator, can see the colored balls all along through a secret "window" in the side of the bag! Because of the secret window, everyone sees how the trick works, except for the spectator on the left who is unaware throughout the presentation that the bag is cleverly gimmicked.

A To prepare, obtain an ordinary brown paper bag, about the size of a standard lunch bag. Cut a hole in the side of the bag, as shown. The position of the hole should be such that it is completely hidden from view by the bottom portion of the bag when the bag is folded flat. This way, the bag can be freely shown on both sides and handled quite casually before it is opened to begin the effect.

B Glue or tape a piece of transparent kitchen wrap (clear plastic) over the hole so that the balls will not fall out of the bag during the presentation. The construction of the bag is complete. As you can see, a sort of window has been formed in the bag, allowing you to see into the bag quite easily.

C Purchase six ordinary ping-pong balls. Prepare the three pairs of balls by painting or coloring them in three brightly contrasting colors. Permanent-ink marking pens also work well for coloring the balls and can be purchased at most stationery stores. Instead of ping-pong balls, you can use lightweight plastic or rubber balls. These can be obtained at department or toy stores. Be sure they are all the same size and are made of the same material, so that it is impossible to distinguish one color from another without looking at them.

METHOD

1 Invite two spectators to help you. Position yourself between them, facing the audience. Display the balls and call attention to the fact that there are three pairs of different colored balls. Pick up the bag and display it—folded flat—so that everyone (especially the spectator on the left) can see that it is quite ordinary. Open the bag so that the window faces the audience (and not the spectator on your left) and openly drop the six balls into the bag. The audience will immediately see that the bag is gimmicked. They will begin to see why, as you continue.

2 Ask the spectator on your left to reach into the bag—without looking—and remove one ball. Tell the spectator to keep it concealed, so that no one else knows its color. Be sure to hold the bag so that the window is facing away from this person, who must not see that the bag is prepared.

3 After the spectator removes the ball, swing your body to the right and ask the other spectator to concentrate very hard, to reach into the bag, and to try to remove the matching colored ball. Be sure to hold the bag so that the window faces this person, who of course will catch on immediately. It is a simple matter for the spectator to remove the correct ball, as it will be the only ball inside the bag without a matching color.

4 Once the second spectator has removed the ball, have both openly display the two selected balls to the audience. Since the spectator on your right has removed the correct ball, the two balls will match in color.

5 Have both spectators replace the balls in the bag and perform the effect a few more times. Each time the trick is successful, the reaction of the spectator on your left will become more and more humorous. Because this person is unaware of the secret window, there will be no way to explain this seemingly impossible series of coincidences.

COMMENTS AND SUGGESTIONS

At the end of the trick, you should humorously reveal the secret to the puzzled spectator by "accidentally" turning the window side of the bag toward that person as you reach out to shake hands. Thank both of the spectators for being such good sports as they rejoin the audience.

This is a good trick to work at a party, when you are waiting for more people to arrive before you begin your regular show. After the spectator on the left has been utterly baffled, you suggest that next time, they can play the part of the spectator on the right. When some newcomers arrive, you repeat the trick, inviting one of them to serve as the spectator on your left. Your former victim, now the spectator on your right, has the pleasure of seeing how nicely the trick works. This procedure can be repeated with other new arrivals, making an excellent prelude for your show.

NOTE: You must be careful, in presenting tricks of this nature, that you don't offend or insult the intelligence of the spectator who is unaware of the working of the effect. Present the trick in a warm, humorous style so that the spectator does not get annoyed.

ENVELOPE STAND

With mental tests, it is a good idea to use props only if they make the presentation more direct and more effective. When such devices actually aid in the deception, without the spectators realizing it, the effect is even better. This is especially true of the ENVELOPE STAND.

EFFECT

You display an attractive pasteboard stand with five numbered envelopes arranged on it. You announce that one of the sealed envelopes contains a dollar bill and the rest are empty. A spectator is given a free choice of any envelope. When the chosen envelope is opened, it is found to contain the dollar bill. It appears as if you have been able to influence the decision of the spectator.

SECRET AND PREPARATION

A Actually, all five envelopes are empty. The stand is constructed in such a way as to deliver the bill into any selected envelope. Construct the stand

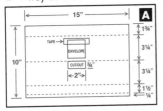

as shown. Use a piece of cardboard about 10" x 15" (depending upon the size of the envelopes). Cut out a hole in the center of the back of the stand. Tape the lower portion of an envelope that you have cut in half to the back of the cardboard just below the opening.

B Fold the cardboard as shown by the dotted lines so that the half-envelope is hidden inside the triangular body of the stand.

MARK WILSON'S CYCLOPEDIA OF MAGIC

C This illustration shows the completed stand. Notice the turned up "lip" located on the front edge of the stand. This ledge prevents the envelopes from slipping off the stand.

D Arrange five numbered envelopes on the face of the stand. Secretly place a folded dollar bill out of sight in the half-envelope.

E This is a view from the rear. Notice how the dollar bill protrudes slightly from the hole behind the center envelope. The top edge of the bill extends 1/4" or so from the hole and cannot be seen from the front side of the stand.

METHOD

1 To perform the trick, display the stand and call attention to the five numbered envelopes displayed on the stand. (Small coin or pay envelopes work best.) Announce that before the trick, you placed a dollar bill in only one of the envelopes. Predict that the envelope with the dollar will be chosen at random by a spectator. Select a spectator. Allow this person to choose any envelope. Give the spectator the opportunity to change their choice.

2 Remove all envelopes not chosen from the stand.

3 Place the selected envelope, in this case Number 4, directly in front of the secret hole in the stand.

4 Here is the rear view of the stand at this point in the routine. Notice how the bill in the half-envelope protrudes slightly from the hole in the stand.

5 Remove the selected envelope from the stand with the thumb and fingers of your right hand and, as you do, secretly grasp the upper end of the hidden bill with your right fingers. Hold the dollar bill firmly behind the selected envelope as you remove the envelope from the stand. Be sure not to expose the bill hidden behind it.

6 Casually transfer the envelope (and the hidden bill) to your left hand. The left thumb holds the bill against the back of the envelope. This move gives the spectators a chance to see that both of your hands are empty. With your free right hand, tear off one end of the sealed envelope. Be sure not to prematurely expose the bill.

7 Insert your right first and second fingers into the envelope and appear to remove the bill from inside. Actually, you pull the bill out from behind the envelope using your right thumb. Display the folded bill, held between the thumb and fingers of your right hand.

8 Unfold the bill and show it to be authentic before you pick up the other four envelopes. Tear these envelopes in half to show that they are all empty—or better yet, have the audience open and examine them. You may reward your spectator with the dollar as a souvenir if you wish. In any event, hand the remains of all of the envelopes to your audience for inspection.

CHAPTER 17

BETCHAS

In magical parlance, the term "betcha" is short for "I'll bet you!"—which means that you, as the magician, would be willing to bet a spectator that you can do something that they can't. Of course, you don't have to make a bet to prove your point. You can go right ahead and do it, just for the fun of it. People appreciate that because, if they have a good time watching magic, they will want to see more.

Actually, a Betcha is more of a puzzle than a trick. Practically every Betcha has some neat twist that gives it audience appeal; and some, if done smoothly and fairly rapidly, may even become tricks in their own right. Although you show the audience exactly what is done, the moves may be too complex for them to follow. So instead of learning "how it's done," they only become all the more puzzled.

The best plan is to "warm up" with a few Betchas—getting people to try some trifling tricks for themselves, which will put them in a mood to appreciate the real magic that you show them later.

IMPOSSIBLE PENETRATION

EFFECT

You display two rolled-up dollar bills. You place a bill in the crook of each of your thumbs, one bill in each hand. By grasping the ends of the bills with the thumbs and second fingers of the opposite hands, you are able to separate your hands, causing the bills to apparently pass magically through one another. The real mystery is that the spectators are unable to duplicate the feat.

METHOD

1 Roll two dollar bills into tight cylinders and hold the bills in the crooks of your thumbs, as shown.

2 Rotate your hands in opposite directions, so that you can take the left-hand bill with the right thumb at A and the right second finger at B. At the same time, your left hand grasps the right-hand bill with the left thumb at D and the left second finger at C.

3 Held correctly, your hands should look like this. To the spectators, the illusion of the linking of your fingers and the bills is perfect.

4 Rotate your hands in opposite directions, as you pull your hands apart.

MARK WILSON'S CYCLOPEDIA OF MAGIC

5 The bills will free themselves and appear to magically pass through each other.

COMMENTS AND SUGGESTIONS

This effect can also be done with two corks, short pencils, or any small objects of the correct shape and size. Whatever you use, it's a very deceptive quickie. It may also be done as a puzzle. In this case, you repeat the trick over and over as the spectators try to duplicate it. Each time, do the penetration a little slower. Finally, someone will get it and start to fool the other participants. Present it this way at the next party you attend and see how much fun you will have!

IMPOSSIBLE KNOT

Tricks of the "Do As I Do" type are always effective, and this is one of the best. All you need are two ropes, each about 3' in length; one is for yourself, the other for a spectator. With a little practice and one simple, secret move, you can baffle spectators time after time—to the point where they will actually fool themselves!

EFFECT

You hold a length of rope with one end in each hand, and you invite a spectator to do the same with another piece of rope. Stating that it would be impossible to tie a knot in a rope without letting go of at least one end, you proceed to drape the rope over your arms, forming a series of simple loops and twists. This is done slowly, without letting go of the ends, so the spectator can copy every move you make with the rope. Still holding both ends, you shake the rope from your arms, and a knot magically appears in the center. No knot is found in the spectator's rope, even though everyone is sure the spectator has copied your every move exactly.

METHOD

1 Hold the rope near the ends between the thumb and first finger of each hand with the rope hanging below, as shown.

2 Bring your right hand inward (toward you) and drape the rope over your left wrist, as shown.

3 Draw the right end of the rope downward and beneath the hanging loops. This divides the hanging loop into two sections, left and right.

4 Insert your right hand (still holding the right end) through the left section of the loop; and, in the same continuous action, bring your hand back through the right section of the loop, nipping the rope at Point A, as shown.

5 Without releasing either hand, move your right hand back to the right, bringing the nipped rope with it. Point A is now resting on the back of your right wrist.

NOTE: This is the only part of this excellent magical puzzle that is difficult to illustrate. Just try it with the rope in your hands, until you hold the rope as shown in Step 5. Another way to describe Step 4 is that your right hand, still holding its end, goes into the loop and picks up Point A on the back of your right wrist. Point A is then pulled out through the loop to form the setup shown in Step 5.

6 Move your right hand level with your left and pull the rope taut so it forms the crisscross pattern between your wrists, as shown. Note that in the illustration a new spot is indicated on the rope, Point B. Point B is just below the end held by your right hand. Relax the tension on the rope and tilt both hands forward and downward, so the outside loops, which are pressed against your wrists, begin to slide over the tops of your hands.

7 You are now ready for the secret move. As the rope begins to fall off your wrists, your right hand prepares to secretly release its end and grasp the rope at Point B, as described in Step 8.

8 As the loops slide completely over and off your hand, draw your hands apart. At the same time, release the right end of the rope with your thumb and first finger, and secretly grasp Point B with your other three fingers. Because of the tossing movement of the loops as they fall off your wrists, the spectators are completely unaware of this small move that is the whole secret of the trick.

9 As you draw your hands apart, the right end of the rope will automatically pull through the little loops, forming a knot in the center of the rope.

10 Your right thumb and first finger immediately regain their original grip on the end of the rope, so all looks the same as the knot is formed.

COMMENTS AND SUGGESTIONS

All through the routine, you should emphasize that you never release the ends of the rope. Yet a knot still appears in the rope. That makes this an IMPOSSIBLE KNOT. Practice the moves until they become smooth and natural. When you present the effect, do each move very slowly, step-by-step, so the spectators can follow them easily. Your purpose is to show the spectators exactly how to do it—except for the final toss where you secretly release the right end of the rope, enabling you to produce a knot where everyone else fails. Although they copy your moves with ropes of their own, they will always miss at the vital point, making the trick more baffling each time it is repeated.

DO-IT-YOURSELF KNOT

To show the baffled spectators how "easy" the IMPOSSIBLE KNOT really is, you form the preliminary loops with your own rope. You then hand the ends to the spectator before the spectator tosses the rope. When the spectator takes the rope from your hands, the spectator still finds that a knot has mysteriously appeared!

METHOD

1 Simply go through all of the preliminary Steps 1 through 5 of the IMPOSSIBLE KNOT, to the point where you have the two ends projecting from each hand with the loops still around your wrists.

2 Extend your hands and invite the spectator to take the ends of the rope, one end in each hand, and draw them apart. When the spectator does, the knot will make its puzzling appearance!

COMMENTS AND SUGGESTIONS

The neat feature here is that the secret move is not necessary. The mere transfer of the ends to the spectator, before you toss the rope off, sets up the formation of the knot. You can further emphasize that the ends of the rope are never released, just as with the IMPOSSIBLE KNOT.

Having shown the spectator how easy it is, you can revert back to the original IMPOSSIBLE KNOT routine. The spectator will again find it impossible to form a knot.

Here, you can offer further help by having the spectator go through the preliminary moves with a rope. You then say to the spectator, "I think you've got it!" Now you take the ends and take the rope from the spectator's hands to show the knot. Give the spectator back the rope, and tell the spectator to start again now that it is obvious that the spectator can do it. But when the spectator tries, there is failure as usual! This is a great party trick. Just have a number of ropes handy, as everyone will want to try it!

TURNED-UP GLASSES

EFFECT

You place three glasses in a row on the table and announce that you will turn over two glasses at a time, and that in three moves you will have them all facing mouth up. Without hesitation, you proceed to do just as you said. At the end of the third move, all three glasses are mouth up. This seems easy enough to accomplish; yet every time the spectators try to duplicate your actions, something goes wrong. They always finish with the three glasses mouth down! No matter how often you repeat the effect, the spectators are unable to arrive at the same result as you and are left totally puzzled as to the reason why.

METHOD

1 Arrange the three glasses in the position shown here. Cups A and C are mouth down at both ends of the row, and Cup B is mouth up between them. With the cups in this position, the stunt is really quite easy to accomplish. What the spectators do not realize is that when you let them try it, the three glasses are not in this same starting position, although it seems that they are.

2 To perform the feat, turn your hands thumbs down and grasp the two glasses at your right (B and C) and turn them over, as shown.

3 The arrangement of the glasses should now appear as shown in the illustration. This completes move number one.

4 Again, start thumbs down and grasp the two glasses at both ends of the row (Cups A and C) and turn them over as well.

5 The cups should be positioned as shown here. This completes move number two.

6 Finally, grasp the two glasses at the right (B and C) and turn them over, just as you did in move number one.

7 This completes move number three. All three glasses are now mouth up. You have performed the stunt, as you said you would, in only three moves.

8 Now for the dirty work. To position the cups for the spectator to try, simply turn over the center glass, as shown. Remember, when you performed the stunt you started with one up and two down—and that will work. But one down and two up will not! Therefore, with the cups arranged as shown here, the spectator never will be able to perform the feat with the same results as you.

9 If the spectator follows the series of moves exactly as you did, the spectator will be left with the three glasses facing bottoms up, as shown here.

10 By turning over the center glass when all three are in this position, you regain your original position, and your moves are ready-made.

11 Then turn down the center glass, leaving the end ones up, and the spectator is doomed to failure once again.

COMMENTS AND SUGGESTIONS

If you perform the stunt too many times, it is possible that your spectators will begin to catch on to the fact that you are changing the arrangement of the cups. It is usually best to do it just once; then let others try and fail. Give another quick demonstration later, but let others worry in the meantime. Use discretion in determining how many times to perform it for the same spectators. You can vary your moves, starting with the two at the left instead of the right, if you wish, but speed is the factor that counts. People are then less likely to note the difference at the start, thanks to your casual turnover of the middle glass.

RUBBER BAND RELEASE

Here is a stunt that you can perform quite easily, yet no one else is able to duplicate it.

EFFECT

You display an ordinary rubber band, twirling it between the first fingers of each hand. You proceed to touch the tips of your right thumb and first finger to the tips of your left thumb and first finger. Even though the tips of your fingers remain touching, the rubber band instantly drops to the table. Yet, when the spectator tries to duplicate the stunt, the rubber band remains trapped between the thumbs and forefingers. No matter how many times you repeat the feat, no one else is able to perform it.

METHOD

Fingers and thumbs touch

1 Begin by displaying the rubber band looped over the tips of your two first fingers, as shown.

2 Rotate your fingers around each other, as shown by the arrows, keeping the rubber band lightly stretched between your fingers.

3 Stop twirling the band and move both thumbs so that they touch the tips of the first fingers of the same hand. The band is now held between both hands, as shown.

4 Here is the key move. Rotate both hands a quarter turn in opposite directions, so that you are able to touch the tip of your left first finger to your right thumb and the tip of your right first finger to your left thumb, as shown. As you do this, continue to hold the tips of the fingers of each hand together, as shown in Step 3.

NOTE: This quarter-turn move, as you continue to hold the band between your fingers, is the whole secret of the mystery. Later, when the spectators try to duplicate your moves, they will neglect to hold the fingers and thumbs of each hand together and to execute the quarter turn. They will probably just touch both thumbs together and both first fingers together instead. Or, even if they touch the first fingers of each hand with the thumbs of the other hand, the trick is still impossible unless they hold the band in place, as shown in Step 4.

5 To release the band, spread your thumbs and first fingers apart, as shown.

6 The band will drop freely to the table.

7 This very puzzling stunt is quite difficult to figure out without being shown the proper procedure. Give the band to a spectator and encourage the spectator to attempt to duplicate your moves. The spectator will most surely be unable to do so, because the spectator will fail to touch the proper fingers together and make the correct moves in order to release the band from the fingers.

COMMENTS AND SUGGESTIONS

Experiment with the rubber band until you fully understand the release positions of the fingers. When you can perform the routine smoothly and without hesitation, you will be ready to present the stunt. This deceptive little maneuver will cause a stir among your friends and keep them busy for some time.

KNOT IN HANDKERCHIEF

EFFECT

Here is a quick and easy challenge that can be performed anywhere with any handkerchief. You wager that you can tie a knot in a handkerchief without letting go of either end in the process. With that, you offer the handkerchief to anyone who wishes to try their luck before you attempt the seemingly impossible task yourself. It soon becomes quite apparent that no one is able to perform the feat under those conditions. When all have tried and failed, you cleverly perform the stunt with ease and grace.

METHOD

1 Hold the handkerchief at opposite corners and twirl it in a rope-like fashion between your hands. Place it on the table directly in front of you.

2 In order to meet the terms of the challenge, before you pick up the handkerchief cross your arms, as shown.

3 Lean forward until you can grasp one end of the handkerchief in each hand.

4 With one end of the handkerchief held tightly in each hand, simply uncross your arms. As you do, the ends of the handkerchief will be drawn through your arms, creating a single knot in the center of the handkerchief—without releasing the ends!

5 Immediately toss the handkerchief to your spectators, as they will, no doubt, want to try the stunt themselves and later perform this Betcha for their friends.

CHAPTER 18

SPONGE SORCERY TRICKS

SPONGE SORCERY, performed with sponge balls or sponge cubes, is a distinctive type of magic. Originally, magic tricks evolved around common objects such as cards, coins, and matches because they were "natural" objects to carry or borrow for magical purposes.

Then magicians began carving sponge balls out of rubber sponges. As different weights, textures, and compressibility of synthetic sponges emerged, sponge sorcery became increasingly popular. Today, sponge balls have a fairly solid look, causing spectators to overlook their compressibility. Sponge balls are also easier to manipulate than their predecessors.

SPONGE SORCERY

EFFECT

The performer magically causes three sponges to appear, multiply, and vanish in an entertaining and amusing manner. They even seem to multiply in the hands of a spectator!

SECRET AND PREPARATION

Before the performance, place three sponges in your right pants pocket and one sponge in your left pants pocket.

METHOD

Sponge balls are used in the following illustrations. To practice and present your routine, you may substitute sponge cubes in place of the balls, as shown.

A SPONGE APPEARS

1 With the four sponges located in your pants pockets, as described, casually place your hand in your right pants pocket. Grasp one of the sponges in the finger-palm position (see FINGER-PALM VANISH page 256) and remove your hand, holding the sponge secretly. Reach into the air and produce it at the tips of your right fingers. You can also produce the sponge from the spectator's coat lapel, from behind the spectator's ear, or any other appropriate place.

2 As you display the first sponge in your right hand, position it in readiness for the FINGER-PALM VANISH, by placing it on your open hand at the base of the second and third fingers, as shown. The left hand lies casually, palm down, on the table.

3 In one smooth, flowing movement, bring both hands together, turning them over as you do. This is done on the pretense of gently tossing the sponge from your right hand into your left hand. But instead of actually tossing the sponge into the left hand, it is secretly retained in the second and third fingers of the right hand, in the finger-palm position.

4 Move your right hand away (with the sponge), as you close your left hand into a loose fist. The first finger of your right hand should casually point toward your left fist, as shown in the illustration.

5 Pause for a moment and then make a crumpling motion with your left fingers, as if to cause the sponge to "dissolve" in your hand. Open your left hand to show that the sponge has vanished.

NOTE: What you have just done is the basic FINGER-PALM VANISH with a sponge. Practice it with the sponge until it becomes smooth and convincing. When done correctly, the spectators should not suspect that you really retain the sponge in your right hand.

FLIGHT TO THE POCKET

7 Explain to the spectators that often, when a sponge vanishes, it manages to reappear in your right pocket. Reach into your right pants pocket (being careful not to flash the vanished sponge that is now concealed in your right fingers) and grasp one of the two sponges that are left in that pocket.

8 Openly remove this sponge from your pocket, keeping the first sponge finger-palmed. Display it in your right fingertips. Again, be careful not to let the spectators see the sponge finger-palmed in your right hand, as you display the other sponge. The effect is that you vanished a sponge from your left hand and caused it to reappear in your pants pocket.

GUESS WHICH HAND

9 Upon completing the Flight to the Pocket, you now hold one sponge at your right fingertips and one sponge secretly in the finger-palm position of the same hand. Openly place the sponge from your right fingertips into the palm of your left hand, as shown.

10 Close your left hand into a fist and hold it palm up in front of you, as shown. Close your right hand and hold it palm down next to your left fist. The spectators still believe that only one sponge is being used and that it is in your left hand.

11 Strike both fists together several times and hold your hands crossed at the wrist, as shown. Explain how this seems to have a strange effect on the location of the mischievous sponge. With that, ask the spectator which hand the sponge is in.

12 The answer will probably be, "In your left hand." No matter which hand the spectator says, uncross your hands and open your left hand, revealing that the sponge is still there.

MARK WILSON'S CYCLOPEDIA OF MAGIC

13 State that it really didn't matter which hand was chosen; the spectator would have been correct in either case. With that, turn your right hand palm up and open the fingers, revealing the other sponge. It appears that the strange effect you spoke about has caused one sponge to multiply into two.

SPECTATOR'S DOUBLES

14 Place the left-hand sponge on the table and hold the right-hand sponge in position for the FINGER-PALM VANISH.

15 Pretend to place the sponge in your left hand. Actually you execute the FINGER-PALM VANISH, secretly retaining the sponge in your right hand. Remember that each time you perform this vanish, your left hand should be closed in a loose fist as if it actually contained the sponge.

16 Without hesitation, move your right hand toward the sponge lying on the table. Be careful not to expose the sponge finger-palmed in your right hand.

17 As your right hand arrives above the sponge on the table, secretly place the finger-palmed sponge directly on top of the sponge on the table.

18 By drawing your right hand along the table, the sponges will roll toward the tips of your right fingers, where they can be picked up together as one sponge. Because of the soft texture of the sponges when they are pinched together slightly, this will appear to be just one sponge.

19 As you display the two sponges as one at the tips of your right fingers, ask the spectator to open their right hand and hold it palm up above the table.

20 Place the sponge(s) in the spectator's hand as you state, "Here, you hold this sponge in your hand while I hold the other." At this point, everyone thinks that you still hold one sponge in your left hand and that you are merely giving the spectator the other sponge to hold, when actually you are giving the spectator both sponges.

21 Instruct the spectator to close their fingers around the sponge and to squeeze it tightly so it would be impossible for you to remove it without their knowledge. Be sure you maintain a firm grip on the two sponges until the spectator's fingers are completely closed around them. Then, and only then, should you remove your fingers from the fist.

22 Explain that you intend to cause the sponge that you are holding to travel invisibly from your hand into the spectator's closed fist.

23 Again, make a crumpling motion with your left fingers and open your hand to show it is empty. Ask the spectator if anything happened. Whatever the answer, tell the spectator to open their hand, revealing the two sponges.

TRANSPOSITION IN YOUR HANDS

24 Take both sponges from the spectator and place them on the table in front of you about 12" apart. Turn your hands palm up and openly place the back of your hands on top of the sponges, as shown. This is the starting position for the next series of moves.

NOTE: Steps 25 through 36 are a clever sequence of moves designed to confuse and amaze the spectators.

25 Raise your right hand, turn it over, and pick up the sponge that was beneath it with the tips of your right thumb and finger.

26 Without lifting your left hand from the table, rest the sponge in the palm of your left hand. Close your hand into a fist over your right fingers and the sponge. As you do this say, "The right sponge goes in your left hand." Withdraw your right fingers, actually leaving the sponge in your closed left hand.

27 Raise your left fist off the table and pick up the sponge that was beneath it with the tips of the right fingers. Close your right fingers into a fist around the sponge. Hold your right fist next to your left fist as you say, "And the left sponge goes into the right hand."

28 You now hold one sponge in each hand, as shown in the illustration.

29 Open both hands together revealing the two sponges, one in each hand. So far, no magic has happened! State that you will now do the same thing again. Unknown to the spectators, this trial run is a very important part of the mystery that is about to take place. By first executing this series of moves without any magic, you condition the spectators to expect the same results next time.

30 Again, place both hands on top of the two sponges in the starting position for the same series of moves.

31 Again, raise your right hand, turn it over, and pick up the sponge beneath it in the tips of the right fingers (just as you did in Step 25).

32 Rest the sponge in the palm of the left hand and close your left fingers over your right fingers and the sponge. Again you say, "The right sponge goes in the left fist." This time, however, instead of leaving the sponge in your left fist, as you withdraw your right hand secretly retain the sponge between your right thumb and fingers. Be sure to keep your right fingers together so that the spectators cannot see the sponge between them.

33 Immediately move your right hand away from your closed left hand, secretly carrying the sponge in your right hand, as shown. Direct your complete attention toward your left hand, as if it really contained the sponge. As your right hand moves away, draw your right thumb inward, moving the sponge slightly deeper into your hand, where it will not be seen by the spectators.

34 Raise your left hand and, with your right fingers, pick up the sponge that lay beneath it. When you pick up the left-hand sponge, secretly add the palmed right-hand sponge to it (just as you did in Step 18).

35 Close your right hand into a fist around the two sponges. Hold your right fist next to your left fist, as shown. To the spectators, you have apparently just repeated Steps 24 through 28, and they think that you now hold one sponge in each hand.

36 Make a crumpling motion with your left fingers and open your left hand to show that the sponge has vanished. Slowly open your right hand, revealing both sponges! It appears as though one sponge has jumped invisibly from your left hand into your right hand!

IMPOSSIBLE PENETRATION

NOTE: If you have been sitting at a table as you perform the trick, you must now stand up for the next portion of the routine. Steps 37 through 44 are shown from the spectators' viewpoint. (You should have an extra sponge in your left pocket before beginning Step 37.)

37 After Transposition in Your Hands, place one sponge on the table and keep the other sponge in your right hand, in position for the FINGER-PALM VANISH.

38 Execute the FINGER-PALM VANISH, pretending to place the sponge in your left hand, but actually retaining it finger-palmed in your right hand.

39 Hold your closed left hand in a loose fist, as if it actually contained the sponge, and casually move your right hand (with the finger-palmed sponge) away. Again, be sure to direct your complete attention toward your left fist.

40 Place your left hand (which supposedly contains the sponge) into your left pants pocket, as you explain that your clothes are made of a special material.

41 With that, move your right hand (which secretly holds the other sponge) in front of your left pants pocket. Your left hand is still inside your pocket. With your right hand, press the sponge against your pants leg next to where your left hand is inside your pocket.

42 Inside your pocket, your left thumb and fingers grasp the sponge through the fabric and hold it between the folds of the cloth so that it is concealed from view by the material. As soon as the sponge is in position, move your right hand away from in front of your pants leg. The pinched section of the fabric will look like a fold in the cloth.

43 Immediately begin a back-and-forth rubbing motion with your left fingers. At the same time, relax your grip on the sponge through the fabric. This will cause the sponge to slowly emerge into view as though it were penetrating right through the cloth.

NOTE: This illusion is very effective. Don't worry if the sponge is not completely hidden in the folds of the fabric before you remove your right hand. It will just appear that the penetration of the cloth started when you first placed your right hand on your pants leg.

44 When the sponge emerges almost totally into view, grasp it in your right hand and pull it away from the pocket. At the same time, with your left hand, secretly secure the sponge already in that pocket in the finger-palm position. While all the attention is on the sponge in your right hand, remove your left hand from your pocket with the new secret sponge.

SPECTATOR'S HAND REVISITED

45 There are now three sponges in play, although the spectators are aware of only two. One sponge is on the table, another is held at the tips of your right fingers, and the secret sponge is finger-palmed in your left hand.

46 Call attention to the sponge in your right hand. While the spectators are looking at it, with your left hand, pick up the sponge on the table and add the secret sponge to it.

47 With your left hand, display the sponge that was on the table and the secret sponge as one, holding them with your left thumb and fingers. At this point you actually hold three sponges (one in your right hand and two in your left). To the spectators, it appears that you hold only one sponge in each hand.

48 Transfer the two sponges in your left hand to your right hand, placing them directly on top of the sponge in your right fingers. Say, "Now I would like you to hold these two sponges."

49 Move your right hand (which now holds the three sponges) toward the spectator and ask the spectator to open their hand to take the sponges from you.

50 Place all three sponges in the spectator's hand. Instruct the spectator to close the fingers around them. Tell the spectator to squeeze their fist tightly to make sure that you cannot remove them. Again, remember to wait until the spectator's hand is completely closed before releasing your grip on the sponges.

51 Once the spectator has a firm grip on the sponges, reach into your right pants pocket and remove the fourth sponge from your pocket. Openly display the sponge as you say, "You may be wondering how all this is happening. Well, the secret is that I have a third sponge that nobody knows about."

---

52 With that, execute the FINGER-PALM VANISH, pretending to place the sponge into your left hand, but actually retaining it in the finger-palm position in your right hand.

53 Casually drop your right hand to the table and move your closed left fist next to the spectator's hand.

54 Make the crumpling motion with your left fingers and open your hand to show it empty. Instruct the spectator to open their hand, revealing all three sponges. It appears that the third sponge has flown invisibly from your fingers into the spectator's hand.

TWO IN THE HAND, ONE IN THE POCKET I

55 After the Spectator's Hand Revisited, there are four sponges in use, although the spectators are only aware of three. The next sequence begins with the three sponges in a horizontal row in front of you and the fourth sponge held secretly in your curled right fingers.

56 With your right hand, pick up the sponge at the right end of the row, and execute the "two-as-one" pickup, as in Steps 17 and 18. In your right hand, you now hold two sponges together as one.

57 Place the two sponges in the palm of your left hand and close your left fingers around them as you say, "One in the hand."

58 Withdraw your right hand from your left fist. Pick up another of the sponges on the table with your right hand, as shown.

59 Move your right hand toward your left fist. Open your left fingers just enough to place the sponge in your left hand. Say, "Two in the hand." Close your left fingers around the three sponges and withdraw your right hand from your left fist.

60 Pick up the remaining sponge in your right hand.

61 Openly place the last sponge in your right pants pocket. Say, "And one in the pocket." As your hand reaches in your right pants pocket, do not leave the sponge in your pocket. Instead, hold it in the finger-palm position and remove your hand from your pocket, secretly carrying the sponge along. The spectators will believe that you merely placed the sponge in your pocket.

62 Ask the spectator, "How many sponges are in my hand?" The answer will be, "Two." Open your left hand, revealing three sponges, as you remark, "Maybe I went too fast. I'll do that again."

TWO IN THE HAND, ONE IN THE POCKET II

63 With your left hand, place the three sponges in a horizontal row on the table as in Step 55. The fourth sponge is secretly held in the curled fingers of your right hand.

64 As before, execute the "two-as-one" pickup with the sponge on the right, as in Step 56.

65 Place the two sponges as one in your left hand and close your left fingers into a fist around them, as in Step 57. Say, "One in the hand."

66 Withdraw your right fingers from your left fist and pick up another sponge with your right hand, as in Step 58.

67 Open your left fingers just enough to place the sponge into your left fist, as you did in Step 59. Say, "Two in the hand."

68 Pick up the remaining sponge in your right fingertips, as in Step 60.

69 Say, "And one in the pocket." Openly place this sponge into your right pants pocket, the same as in Step 61, but this time, leave the sponge in your pocket.

70 Withdraw your right hand from your pocket and gesture toward your fist. Make the gesture in such a way that the spectators can see that your right hand is quite empty. Do not call special attention to your right hand, merely show it in an open and casual manner, so that there is no question that it is empty.

71 As you gesture ask, "How many in the hand?" The answer will probably be, "Two." The spectators are so baffled by this time, however, that there is no predicting what they will say! In any event, open your left hand revealing all three sponges. Now say, "Let's try just once more."

TOTAL VANISH

Now for a smashing climax to the routine!

72 At this time, there are only three sponges remaining. With your left hand, place them on the table in a row, as you did before.

73 Begin again, just as you did before, by picking up the sponge on the far right with your right thumb and fingers. Rest this sponge on the palm of your open left hand.

74 Close the fingers of your left hand around the sponge and the fingers of your right hand. Your right fingers retain their grip on the sponge. Say, "One in the hand." Your right fingers continue to hold the sponge in your closed left hand.

75 Instead of leaving the sponge in your left hand, secretly retain the sponge in your right fingers, as you withdraw your right hand from your left fist.

76 To keep the sponge concealed from view during this procedure, as you withdraw your hand move your right thumb slightly inward, rolling the sponge behind your right fingers, out of sight.

77 Without hesitation, move your right hand toward the next sponge and execute the "two-as-one" pickup, as in Step 17.

78 With the two sponges held together, as one, in your right hand, open your left fist just enough to place your right fingers into your hand. Say, "Two in the hand." Once again, your thumb secretly draws both sponges out of view behind your right fingers.

79 At the same time, you withdraw your right fingers from your left hand and close your left hand into a loose fist.

80 Without pausing, pick up the remaining sponge in your right hand. Do not execute the "two-as-one" pickup. Just keep the two palmed sponges behind your fingers and openly pick up the third sponge, holding it at the fingertips of your right hand.

81 Immediately, place your right hand into your right pants pocket. Say, "And the last sponge goes in the pocket." Leave all three sponges in your pocket.

82 Remove your right hand from your pocket. With your right hand, gesture toward your left fist so that the spectators can see that your right hand is quite empty.

83 Ask, "How many in my hand?" By now, the spectators will probably answer, "Three," thinking that they know what is going to happen. Whatever number is given, say, "No, actually they are all gone, because that was the end of the trick." With that, open your left hand to show that all three sponges have vanished, bringing the routine to a startling climax!

COMMENTS AND SUGGESTIONS

It is generally good policy to avoid handling sponges either too boldly or too cautiously. A quick thrust of the hand excites suspicion, and so does a tight squeeze of the sponge itself when the performer is actually giving the spectator two as one. A casual in-between course is best, particularly when done in an unhurried manner. In fact, the correct preliminary procedure will do much toward dispelling suspicion on the part of the spectators.

If a sponge is held lightly at the fingertips, with absolutely no pressure, no one is apt to regard it as compressible; and, later, when two are shown as one, correct pressure of the thumb and fingers can give the double ball a distinctively single appearance. While a natural, unhurried motion of the hand is sufficient to cover the deception, larger loads depend upon fuller compression for complete concealment.

When practicing, it is a good idea to break the routine down into smaller units. Learn each phase before you go on to the next. SPONGE SORCERY is undoubtedly one of the finest close-up tricks in magic. Each effect in this routine can be performed separately; and as you will see when you perform it for your friends, the entire routine is constructed in a logical progression, building to a perfect climax—truly a masterpiece of magic!

CHAPTER 19
CUP-AND-BALL TRICKS

Unquestionably, CUPS AND BALLS is one of the oldest routines in the Art of Magic. It was first performed in antiquity by jugglers who embellished their usual juggling routines with sleight of hand. In the Middle Ages, jesters and minstrels performed their share of magic along with jugglers, and in many instances, CUPS AND BALLS had become their mainstay. The trick was so successful that it remained virtually unchanged during the next 400 years.

Since the Middle Ages, however, the routine has been simplified and modernized to suit the needs of today's close-up magicians. So the descriptions that appear in the following section may prove amazing even to our predecessors!

CUPS AND BALLS

This classic of magic deserves a top rating, for although it dates back to ancient times, it has maintained its popularity throughout the centuries. Even though it is among the oldest of magical effects, it always seems new. The following routine gives the appearance of requiring great skill, yet actually the basic moves are comparatively simple. This is because CUPS AND BALLS combines misdirection with the element of surprise so that the spectators never know what to expect next.

EFFECT

On the table before you are three empty cups and three small colored balls. You position the three balls in a horizontal row and place a cup, mouth down, behind each ball. You place one of the balls on top of the center cup and stack the remaining two cups on top of the first, imprisoning the ball between them. Upon lifting the stack of cups as a group, the ball is found to have mysteriously penetrated through the center cup and now rests on the table. This baffling process is repeated with the two remaining balls until all three balls have magically gathered beneath the stack of cups. Then you vary your procedure by causing a single ball to vanish from your hand and appear beneath the center cup on the table.

Next, you place a ball beneath each cup. You then mysteriously cause the ball under the center cup to vanish and join the ball under the right-hand cup. From there, it vanishes once again and reappears with the ball under the left-hand cup. You place the three balls in your pocket, one at a time, only to find that they have once again appeared beneath the cups on the table. This procedure is repeated once more, when suddenly you reveal the surprise appearance of three full-size lemons, one beneath each cup.

SECRET AND PREPARATION

A You will need to acquire the proper type of cups in order to perform this routine effectively. The cups should nest within each other easily and leave enough space between each cup to permit the concealment of a ball between them. (See Comments and Suggestions.) You will also need four small identical balls of the appropriate size to be used with the cups. The only other props you will need are three ordinary lemons, or three small potatoes, or three small rubber balls. The primary requirement for these props is that each can fit easily inside one of the cups.

B To set up the apparatus for the start of the routine, place one of the cups mouth down on your table and put a ball on top of it. Nest the other two cups on the first, concealing the ball between the first and second cups.

C Turn the entire stack mouth up and drop the three remaining balls into the top cup of the stack. Throughout the presentation, the spectators should only be aware of three balls. The primary secret of the entire routine is the hidden fourth ball.

D At the start, have the three lemons in your right pocket. The lemons are not used until the final phase of the routine, but it is a good idea to practice with them in position so that you become used to their presence as you practice.

NOTE: To make CUPS AND BALLS easy to learn, the routine has been broken down into separate phases. Learn each phase before proceeding to the next. Practice the entire routine from start to finish, until each portion becomes smooth and natural.

METHOD
PHASE 1—PENETRATION

All of the illustrations in this phase are from the spectators' viewpoint.

1 Stand at the table with the spectators across from you. Pick up the cups with your left hand and tip the three balls from the top cup of the stack onto the table. With your right hand, arrange the balls in a horizontal row. The stack of nested cups is held in your left hand so that the bottom of the cups slants toward the table and the mouth of the cups tilts slightly up toward you, as shown. This angle is important in order to prevent the spectators from seeing into the cups during the performance of the following steps.

2 With your right hand, draw the bottom cup from the stack downward, as shown.

3 In one continuous flowing motion, turn the cup, mouth down, and place it on the table behind the ball at the right end of the row.

4 Remove the second cup from the stack in the same manner.

5 Place the second cup, mouth down, on the table behind the center ball.

NOTE: You can now see why the cups must be tilted slightly toward you since this cup is concealing the fourth ball. If this step is executed in a smooth, unbroken motion, the fourth ball will be carried along inside the cup to the table, unnoticed by the spectators.

6 Grasp the last cup in your hand.

7 Place the last cup, mouth down, behind the ball at the left end of the row.

NOTE: It is important that the placement of the individual cups on the table be executed at the same exact pace so as not to attract attention to the center cup.

8 The three cups, mouth down, are now on the table, with the extra ball secretly under the center cup. The three visible balls are positioned in front of the cups, as shown.

9 You are now ready to execute the first trick, Penetration. Pick up the right-hand ball and place it on top of the center cup.

10 Lift the right-hand cup and nest it over the center cup, imprisoning the ball between the two cups, as shown.

11 Pick up the left-hand cup and add it to the stack.

12 With your right first finger, tap the top cup of the stack and say, "I'll make the first ball penetrate the cup."

13 Without hesitation, lift the entire stack of cups with your left hand, revealing the ball on the table beneath them. To the spectators, it will look as if the ball you placed on the center cup penetrated the solid bottom of the cup and landed on the table!

14 Holding the three cups together in your left hand, turn your left palm up so that the cups are positioned just as they were in Step 1.

15 Repeat the same series of moves that you used in Steps 2 through 7. Remove the bottom cup and place it, mouth down, on the table to your right. Remove the second cup (which now contains the secret ball) and set it, mouth down, over the ball that just penetrated the cup in the previous sequence. Unknown to the spectators, there are now two balls under this cup, instead of one. Place the last cup, mouth down, behind the left-hand ball. The situation should be as shown here.

16 You are now ready to execute the second penetration. Pick up the ball in front of the center cup and place it on top of the center cup.

17 Nest the other two cups, one at a time, over the center cup and the ball, just as you did in Steps 10 and 11.

18 Tap the top cup once with your right finger and say, "Now I'll make the second ball penetrate the cup."

19 Immediately lift the stack of three cups, revealing the two balls beneath them. To the spectators, it appears as if the ball on the second cup penetrated through the cup to join the other ball beneath it.

20 Once again, turn your left palm up, holding the cups in the basic starting position as in Step 1.

21 Repeat the same sequence again (Steps 2 through 7), placing the cups, one at a time, mouth down on the table. Be sure to place the second cup containing the secret ball over the two balls, which have already penetrated through the cup.

22 Repeat the same series of moves (Steps 8 through 13) to penetrate the last ball. Pick up the ball and place it on top of the center cup.

23 Nest the other two cups over the ball and tap the top cup to make the ball magically penetrate the cup.

24 Lift the stack to reveal all three balls on the table, beneath the center cup.

NOTE: Before continuing, be sure you have mastered the first phase of the routine. When you can perform it smoothly and with confidence from start to finish, you are ready to move on to the second phase.

PHASE 2—INVISIBLE FLIGHT

All of the illustrations in Phase 2 are from the spectators' viewpoint.

25 While holding the stack of cups in your left hand in the basic starting position, arrange the three balls on the table in a horizontal row before you. Place the three cups, one at a time, mouth down, behind the three balls, as shown here. The secret ball will once again be carried along, unnoticed, inside the center cup to the table.

26 With your right hand, pick up the ball in front of the center cup and display it briefly on your right fingers in readiness for the FINGER-PALM VANISH (see page 256).

27 Apparently transfer the ball to your left hand using the FINGER-PALM VANISH. The spectators will believe that you have merely placed the ball into your left hand. Actually, the ball is secretly retained in the fingers of your right hand.

28 Casually lower your right hand and make a tossing motion with your left hand, as if to throw the ball invisibly from your left fist into the center cup.

29 With your left hand, lift the center cup and roll the ball slightly forward to reveal its magical arrival.

30 Set the center cup on the table, mouth down, behind the center ball. This is a very important phase of the routine, as it allows you to get the secret ball out of the cups and into your hand where you can use it to execute the next series of impossibilities described in Phase 3.

31 Still holding the secret ball in the finger-palm position in your right hand, pick up the ball in front of the cup on the right with the tips of your right thumb and fingers, as shown.

PHASE 3—ANY CUP CALLED FOR

The illustrations are from the spectators' and from your viewpoint, as indicated.

32 Here is a view of this action from your point of view. Notice how the visible ball is held between the thumb and first finger, while the secret ball is still concealed in the curled fingers. As you pick up the ball, your left hand grasps the right cup near the mouth, as shown.

33 Tilt the cup back toward you, leaving the rear edge of the cup resting on the table. At the same time, allow the visible ball to roll alongside the secret ball in your curled fingers.

34 Without hesitation, slip both balls well under the front edge of the cup, as shown.

MARK WILSON'S CYCLOPEDIA OF MAGIC

35 Here is a view of this action from the spectators' point of view. The spectators will believe that you are placing only one ball under the cup.

36 As you hold the balls under the cup, tilt the cup down and withdraw your fingers, leaving both balls beneath the cup.

37 Without pausing, pick up the ball in front of the center cup with the tips of your right thumb and fingers, just as you did with the first ball in Step 31. At the same time grasp the center cup, which is in position to apparently repeat the previous series of moves—as when you placed the ball(s) under the right cup.

38 Here is the situation as seen from your point of view. Notice how the ball is held against the second and third fingers with your thumb.

39 Tip the center cup back on its edge and move your right fingers and the ball under the front edge of the cup, as shown.

40 As soon as your fingers are well beneath the cup, remove your thumb from the ball and hold the ball with your right fingers, as shown. Withdraw your hand, secretly carrying the ball along. As you withdraw your hand from beneath the cup, be sure to tilt the back of your hand toward the spectators, so no one will see that you still hold the ball in your fingers instead of leaving it under the cup.

41 Immediately lower the front edge of the cup to the table as you remove your fingers and the ball from beneath the cup. The spectators believe that you merely placed the second ball under the center cup.

42 Without hesitation, move your right hand (still concealing the ball) to the last visible ball. Pick this up with your right thumb and fingers (just as you did in Step 31), as your left hand grasps the cup.

43 You are now going to repeat Steps 32 through 36 with the third cup. With your left hand, tip the third cup back on its edge and place both balls under the cup, "as one," as shown in this illustration from your point of view.

44 Here is the same action as seen from the spectators' point of view. To the spectators, it should appear as if you are merely placing a single ball under the third cup, just as you did with the other cups.

45 Lower the front edge of the cup, allowing it to drag both balls from your fingers as you withdraw your hand.

46 As soon as your fingers clear the front edge of the cup, set the mouth of the cup down, flush with the top of the table.

MARK WILSON'S CYCLOPEDIA OF MAGIC

47 At this point, the spectators believe that you have simply placed one ball under each of the three cups. Actually, as the illustration shows, you have two balls under both end cups and nothing under the center cup.

48 State that you will cause the ball under the center cup to vanish and appear beneath whichever end cup the spectator wishes. Assuming the spectator chooses the right-hand cup, slowly tip over the center cup, allowing your spectators to see that the ball you placed under that cup has vanished. Leave the center cup on its side on the table, as shown.

49 Tip over the selected cup (in this case, the right-hand cup) to reveal the mysterious arrival of the missing ball, apparently joining the ball already under that cup.

50 With your right hand, pick up one of the two balls and display it at the base of your curled fingers in readiness for the FINGER-PALM VANISH. As you display the ball, make some comment about how difficult it is to keep track of that particular ball.

51 With that, apparently transfer the ball into your left hand, executing the FINGER-PALM VANISH. Actually, the ball is secretly retained in your right fingers, as shown.

52 Your left hand (which the spectators believe contains the ball) makes a tossing motion toward the left cup. As you "toss" the ball, open your left hand and show that the ball has vanished. At the same time, your right hand drops casually to your right side, carrying the secret ball with it.

53 With your empty left hand, tip the left cup over and reveal the missing ball to complete the sequence.

NOTE: After mastering this phase, combine the first three phases into a smooth routine. When you have accomplished this and feel confident of all of the moves, you will be ready to learn Phase 4.

PHASE 4—REPEAT PRODUCTION

All of the illustrations in Phase 4 are from the spectators' viewpoint.

54 After the conclusion of Phase 3, rearrange the three visible balls in a horizontal row and place one cup, mouth down, over each ball, as shown. The secret ball is still concealed in the curled fingers of your right hand.

55 With your left hand, lift the cup on the right.

56 Without pausing, turn the cup mouth up and transfer it to your right hand, which contains the secret ball.

MARK WILSON'S CYCLOPEDIA OF MAGIC

57 Without hesitation, pick up the ball that was under the cup with your left fingers. At the same time, release your grip on the palmed ball in your right hand and allow it to secretly roll into the cup, as shown.

58 In a smooth, unbroken motion with your right hand, turn the cup mouth down and place it on the table in its former position. If the action of setting the cup down is done properly, the ball will remain hidden in the cup as the mouth of the cup comes to rest on the table.

59 At this point, you have apparently lifted the right-hand cup, picked up the ball that was under it, and replaced the cup on the table. Really, you have secretly loaded the fourth ball into the cup.

60 Once the cup is on the table, openly transfer the ball from your left hand to your right hand.

61 Place your right hand in your pocket, apparently leaving the ball there. Actually, you secretly retain the ball in the finger-palm position and remove your right hand from your pocket with the ball concealed in your right fingers.

NOTE: Steps 55 through 61 are the key moves in Phase 4. The spectators will be convinced that the first cup is empty and that the ball is now in your pocket.

62 Repeat this same sequence of moves (Steps 55 through 61) with the center cup, secretly loading the extra ball into the cup as you apparently place the visible ball in your pocket.

63 Once again, repeat the sequence (Steps 55 through 61) with the last cup, up to the point where your hand is in your pocket, apparently leaving the ball there.

64 The situation at this point should look as shown in the illustration. Unknown to the spectators, there is one ball under each cup, and the extra ball is in your pocket. The spectators think you have placed all three balls, one at a time, in your right pocket. Really, you have secretly loaded the balls back under the three cups. You could stop now by merely revealing the "return" of the three balls. However, don't make that revelation quite yet. Continue to Phase 5.

NOTE: The next series of moves is based on the same secret loading process that you have just learned. Practice the moves thoroughly, until you can load each cup quickly and smoothly without undue attention to your right hand.

PHASE 5 — LEMON SURPRISE

65 When your right hand is in your pocket in Step 64, release the ball and grasp one of the three lemons, curling your fingers around it as far as possible. Remove your hand from your pocket, secretly holding the lemon, and let your hand fall casually to your side. Be sure to use a lemon (or potato or small rubber ball) that can be totally concealed from view as you hold it in your hand, as shown.

66 As your right hand secretly holds the lemon, grasp the cup on the right with your left hand in readiness to lift it from the table. Then, as you lift the cup to reveal the ball beneath it, bring your right hand up from your side, making sure to keep the back of your hand to the spectators. The surprise appearance of the ball under this cup will draw the eyes of the spectators to the table.

67 In the same motion, turn the cup mouth upward with your left hand and place it in your right hand, as shown here from your viewpoint. Be sure the fingers and the back of your right hand completely cover the top of the cup, so that the spectators cannot see between your hand and the mouth of the cup.

68 This illustration shows the action from the spectators' point of view. It is very important that you practice these critical moves in front of a mirror in order to observe the spectators' view of the presentation, as well as your own.

69 As soon as you transfer the cup to your right hand, move your left hand to the table and pick up the now visible ball. At the same time, allow the lemon to drop unseen into the cup.

70 From your point of view, this loading action looks like this. Be sure to keep the mouth of the cup tilted toward you during this procedure.

71 As you lift the ball from the table with your left hand, swing the cup mouth down and place it on the table with your right hand, as shown. The important point here is to execute this movement smoothly and quickly, keeping the lemon well within the cup and out of sight of the spectators.

72 Openly transfer the ball from your left hand to your right hand and place it in your right pocket. While your hand is in the pocket, grasp another lemon in readiness to load the next cup.

73 Repeat the exact same sequence (Steps 65 through 72) with the center cup. Just go back to Step 65 and repeat all of the steps through Step 72 with the second cup, ending with a lemon secretly loaded under the cup and your right hand in your pocket, grasping the third lemon.

74 Repeat Steps 65 through 72 with the third cup, ending with a lemon secretly loaded under it as well.

75 When the last ball is placed in your pocket, leave it there and remove your empty right hand. The three cups now each conceal a lemon beneath them. The spectators believe that you merely placed the three balls back into your pocket and that the cups are now empty.

MARK WILSON'S CYCLOPEDIA OF MAGIC

76 To bring the routine to its startling and spectacular conclusion, ask a spectator if there is a ball under any of the cups. No matter what the answer is, lift the cup the spectator points to, revealing the lemon beneath it! The appearance of the first lemon will catch your spectators completely off guard.

77 Without hesitation, quickly lift the other two cups, one at a time, revealing the other two lemons.

COMMENTS AND SUGGESTIONS

CUPS AND BALLS is probably the oldest and certainly one of the most popular tricks in magic. The necessary props (three cups and four balls) may be purchased at any good magic supply company. For practice purposes, and even for your first performances, a practical set of "cups" may be made from paper cups. The heavy paper kind is best (the type used for coffee or other hot beverages). These cups are strong and usually have a slightly recessed bottom. The cups can be decorated by painting them an attractive color, if you wish.

A professional set of balls may be made of cork or hard rubber. Sometimes a cork ball with a knitted or crocheted cover is used. You may also make your first set of balls as well. Balls made from sponge rubber are excellent for practice. They are quite easy to make and equally easy to handle during the presentation.

Though the basic moves are relatively simple, they should be practiced until they become almost automatic, in order to perform a convincing routine. Any hesitation on your part may detract from the effect, as the whole purpose is to keep just enough ahead of the spectators so that they are constantly wondering what will happen next. In placing the balls beneath the cups, or pretending to do so, the moves must be natural and identical to one another. Once your actions become automatic, the vital moves will begin to feel more casual and less conspicuous, and therefore less likely to arouse suspicion. Another reason for continued practice is that of gaining self-confidence. When first performing the CUPS AND BALLS, you may wonder just why the routine deceives people. This is particularly true when you load the lemons at the finish. Having watched the small balls jump from cup to cup, spectators become so caught up with the action of the balls on the table that they are never ready for the unexpected appearance of the lemons.

CUPS AND BALLS is especially suited for performing while seated at a table, but it can be worked just as well when standing at a table. Any points of individuality that you may add to the routine will most likely prove helpful. Some performers like to vary it by using either hand to turn over a cup, even though the hand may have a ball palmed at the time. Just think of CUPS AND BALLS as your trick, to be done the way you like it most. Once you have mastered CUPS AND BALLS, you will be able to present one of the finest and most respected effects in the Art of Magic.

CHAPTER 20
MAKE-AT-HOME MAGIC

When magicians speak of "building their acts," they may mean two different things. In some cases "building an act" means that the magician is selecting which tricks to use for a particular program. In other cases, "building an act" means the actual construction of the magic apparatus to be used in a show. Instead of selecting the tricks a magician intends to do, the magician goes to the workshop and actually builds them. Every magician needs a workshop, even if it is only a desk drawer containing old playing cards, envelopes, and construction paper. For more ambitious projects, you will require a well-equipped home workshop.

"Build-it-yourself" projects are covered in this section, which includes simple working plans and the magical effects that can be presented with the completed pieces. They have all been chosen because they are easy to build and effective when used in a performance. If you feel that you require a very special apparatus, you can have it built to order or buy it ready-made.

AFGHAN BANDS

EFFECT

You show the audience a wide strip of cloth material that has been glued end-to-end to form a continuous loop of fabric. By tearing the loop lengthwise twice, you divide the circle into three separate rings of cloth. One of these rings is handed to a spectator, another is set aside, and the third ring you proceed to again tear lengthwise down the middle. As you do this, you instruct the spectator to tear their ring of cloth in the same manner. As one would expect, you end up with two separate rings of cloth. The spectator, however, somehow manages to create a linked chain of two rings.

You offer to give the spectator another chance and hand over the remaining single loop of cloth. As the spectator tears it down the middle, the audience anticipates that the circle will again become two linked rings. The final surprise, however, comes when the loop suddenly transforms into one large, continuous circle of cloth, twice the size that it was at the start!

SECRET AND PREPARATION

The cloth chosen for this effect must be a type that will tear easily. All woven fabrics tear in a straight line, but knits must be cut; so if you must purchase fabric, be sure it is a woven one. A lightweight cotton such as percale tears easily, is inexpensive to buy, and is available in many attractive colors and patterns. An excellent choice that will cost you nothing is to use strips cut from the remnants of worn bed sheets, which are usually made from percale. Special glues for fabrics are available where you buy the fabric, or you may sew the ends of the strips together.

A After you have found a material that works well, cut a strip of cloth 36" long by 6" wide. At one end, cut two slits about 2-1/2" long, dividing the end of the strip into three 2" wide bands. We will refer to these new bands as A, B, and C.

B Give Band A a full twist (360°) and glue it to the opposite end of the cloth strip as shown. Be sure to allow about 1/2" overlap of gluing surface. Next, glue Band B directly to the other end of the strip without twisting it as shown. Give Band C a half twist (180°) before gluing it to the opposite end of the loop.

C The next step is to cut one slit about 2" long in the exact center of each band. Each slit must pass through the glue joint. Study the illustrations for the correct location of these three slits. You are now ready to present the AFGHAN BANDS.

METHOD

1 Holding the glued joints and the twists concealed in your right hand, display the loop of cloth to your audience. Call attention to the fact that the fabric is formed into one continuous loop.

2 Tear Band C away from the main loop (the dotted lines in the illustration show the path of the tear) and drape it over your right arm, concealing the twist in the crook of your elbow.

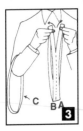

3 Tear the main loop again, separating Bands A and B, as shown. Give Band A to the spectator and keep Band B for yourself. Call attention to the narrow slit in the middle of both bands and instruct the spectator to tear Band A lengthwise into two parts while you do the same with your Band B.

4 Band B, the unprepared section, will result in two equal and separate rings after the tear is completed.

5 As the spectator completes the tearing of Band A, the audience will expect the same result which you achieved. It comes as quite a surprise when the spectator ends up with two linked loops, as shown.

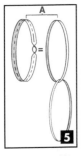

6 Explain that, since there is still one loop remaining, you will give the spectator another chance. Remove Band C from your right arm and instruct the spectator to tear it down the middle as before. The climax comes when Band C transforms into one large loop right in the spectator's own hands!

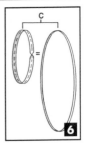

COMMENTS AND SUGGESTIONS

The AFGHAN BANDS can also be performed using strips of paper instead of cloth. The preparation is identical except that, instead of tearing the loops, you must cut them with a pair of scissors.

UTILITY CONE

Here is a clever utility prop which you can construct out of paper. Construction paper and newspaper both work well, depending upon what props you will be using in the cone. If you use construction paper, you may wish to decorate it with a suitable design to help conceal the glued edges of the secret pocket. When you have completed the construction of the UTILITY CONE, you will have a very useful device which you can use to vanish things like a handkerchief, a card, stamps, and many other flat or comparable items.

EFFECT

You display a sheet of newspaper. You fold the paper into the shape of a cone and place a silk handkerchief (or other item) in the cone. Immediately, the cone is opened up and shown on both sides. The handkerchief has completely vanished.

SECRET AND PREPARATION

A Obtain two identical pages of newspaper. Square the two pages together and place them so the identical sides are showing and the long edges of one side of the sheets are nearest you.

B Make the first fold in both of the papers.

C Make the second fold in the papers following the dotted line as shown.

D Make the third fold in the papers following the dotted line as shown. The cone, folded with both papers, should look something like this.

E Carefully unfold the two pieces of paper. Spread the papers out on the table in exactly the same position as in Step A. Pick up the top sheet of paper and carefully cut out Section X (indicated by the dark shading in the illustration) from this sheet. Once this is done, discard the rest of this page.

F You now have one complete sheet of paper and one extra piece, Section X, which matches a portion of the complete sheet. Glue this matching extra, triangular Section X on top of its identical portion of the full-size page. Glue it along the two long edges only, as shown. You have created a secret, hidden pocket in the newspaper page. If you place an object into the open top of the pocket, it will be hidden inside.

METHOD

1 To perform the vanish, pick up the specially prepared newspaper page from your table. Hold the page with both hands so that the secret pocket faces the audience. Your right hand is positioned over the mouth of the secret pocket holding it closed, as shown. Use both hands to refold the paper along the original fold lines. When you have completed the folding, the opening to the secret pocket should be located at the mouth of the cone on the very inside fold of the paper. Position the cone so that the secret pocket is on the side of the cone nearest you.

MARK WILSON'S CYCLOPEDIA OF MAGIC

2 Hold the body of the cone in your left hand. Insert your right fingers into the mouth of the cone and open the secret pocket. Do this in a casual manner, as if you are merely straightening up the cone a bit.

3 After you have opened the secret pocket, remove your right hand from within the cone. Then, with your right hand, pick up the handkerchief from your table. Use your right fingers to push the handkerchief all the way down into the secret pocket.

4 Once the handkerchief is securely inside the secret pocket, close the top opening of the pocket and hold it shut, pinching the top edges together between your right thumb and fingers.

NOTE: Position your right hand with the fingers inside the cone and your thumb on the outside.

5 Without removing your right hand from this fixed position, use your left hand to open out the piece of paper.

6 Once this is done, you should be holding the open sheet of paper with both hands by the two upper corners. Your right hand continues to hold the top of the secret pocket closed after the paper has been fully opened out. It will appear as if the handkerchief has vanished.

7 You may now release the left hand and show the paper on both sides with your right hand. When doing this, be sure that you have a firm grasp on the mouth of the secret pocket. You do not want to risk dropping the paper on the floor.

COMMENTS AND SUGGESTIONS

If you wish, you may crush the paper into a ball before you casually throw it aside. This action serves to convince your audience that the paper is unprepared. Pay very little attention to the paper once the vanish has been done. Always handle the page of newspaper as if it were totally unprepared. There are many uses for the UTILITY CONE. It makes an ideal magic prop because it appears to be so ordinary, just a sheet of paper!

DOUBLE-WALLED BAG

As the title of this next item might suggest, this is not a trick itself. Rather, it is a magical prop which can be very useful to you as a utility piece of equipment for switching one item for another or when used as a complete vanish for small objects. The strong point of this special bag is that it can be torn open after completing an effect to show that it is empty.

SECRET AND PREPARATION

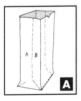

A Begin with two identical paper bags. The brown lunch-bag size available at any grocery store is perfect. Cut one of the bags along the dotted line, as illustrated. Save Part B and discard Part A.

B Spread Part B flat on the table and apply glue along the three edges, as shown.

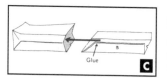

C Carefully slide Part B into the unprepared bag and align the top edges of both bags. Now, press the glued edges of Part B to the bottom and sides of the unprepared bag. The edges of Part B are glued to the same matching parts of the inside of the unprepared bag.

D As far as the audience is concerned, you now have an ordinary-looking paper bag; actually, however, you have added an undetectable secret pocket.

E Before you use it in a trick, fold the bag flat. When you are ready to use it, just pick up the flat bag and open it. This helps give the audience the impression that it is just an ordinary paper bag. At the conclusion of the effect, you can tear away the unprepared side so that the spectators can see clearly into the bag. Make sure to keep the prepared side closed by holding it at the top edge with your hand. Some of the many uses of the bag will be explained in the effects that follow.

DOUBLE-WALLED BAG—
VANISH

EFFECT

If you have constructed the DOUBLE-WALLED BAG properly, you should have no trouble in causing an item to vanish from within the bag.

METHOD

Secret pocket

1 Let's suppose you are going to vanish a dollar bill. To do this, pick up the bag from your table and open it, with the secret-pocket side toward you. Hold the bag with your left hand. Your left thumb should be located on the outside of the bag, your left first finger is inside the secret pocket, and your other three fingers are in the main compartment of the bag. This means that the mouth of the secret pocket is open. Keep the open bag tilted slightly away from the audience so that they do not see the double wall.

2 Pick up the dollar bill with your right hand. Place the bill in the secret pocket of the bag.

3 With your left hand, place the bag on your table in full view; position the bag so that the secret pocket is toward the rear.

4 When you are ready to make the bill vanish, pick up the bag, grasping the rear (secret pocket) side with your left hand so that the secret pocket is held closed.

NOTE: When you pick up the bag, your left fingers grasp both the rear side of the bag and the extra flap of the secret pocket. You now hold the secret pocket closed between your left thumb and fingers.

5 Use a magical gesture to make the bill vanish. Grasp the front, unprepared edge of the bag with your right hand. Pull down with your right hand, tearing the unprepared side of the bag open down the center, exposing the empty interior. The dollar bill you placed inside the bag has vanished.

6 After showing the empty bag, crumple it up and place it aside on the shelf behind your magic table or just toss it offstage. Handle the bag naturally, but be careful not to expose the bill which is hidden inside the secret pocket.

DOUBLE-WALLED BAG—TRANSFORMATION

EFFECT

In addition to being able to vanish an object from within the special bag, you can also transform one object into a completely different one. The handling of the bag in both routines is practically identical.

SECRET AND PREPARATION

For explanation purposes, assume that you wish to transform a silk handkerchief into a playing card. Place the playing card into the main body of the bag. Fold the bag flat and lay it on your table.

METHOD

1 Pick up the bag, open it, and hold it with your left hand at the top just as you did in Step 1 of the VANISH so that the secret pocket is to the back.

NOTE: The secret pocket is open and facing your body.

2 With your right hand, pick up the silk from your table and place it into the secret pocket of the bag.

3 Place the bag on your table so that the secret pocket is still to the back, exactly as you did for the VANISH sequence.

4 When you are ready for the transformation, pick up the bag with your left hand, as you close the secret pocket with your left thumb and fingers. This is exactly the same as in Step 4 of the VANISH routine.

5 Reach into the bag with your right hand and remove the card you secretly placed there earlier. Show the card to the audience and place it on your table.

6 Grasp the front edge of the bag with your right hand and tear the bag open just as you did for Step 6 in the VANISH trick. The bag appears to be empty. The silk handkerchief has magically turned into a playing card!

COMMENTS AND SUGGESTIONS

If the item which is present in the main body of the bag is flat, such as a playing card, fold the bag flat prior to the performance. If the object is bulky, such as an orange, you will have to leave the bag standing open on your table. If you use a heavy object inside the bag, it is best that you perform the routine with the bag sitting on your table until after this object has been removed from the bag in Step 5. You can then pick up the bag and proceed to tear it open to show the interior.

SUN AND MOON

Here is a mystery which is sure to please any audience. It is a comedy effect, and it centers around the apparent destruction of two sheets of tissue paper. One sheet is white, the other is any contrasting color. Let's suppose that the other color is red.

EFFECT

You show two sheets of tissue, front and back. Then, you fold them into quarters and tear out the centers. You place the torn sheets, along with their centers, in a paper bag for their magical restoration. You make a magical gesture at the bag, and, when the papers are removed, they are restored except that the center portions are transposed! Undaunted, you place the "mismade" tissues back into the bag. This time, you hold the bag very still as you make the magic. The sheets of tissue are removed again from within the bag and opened up. This time, they are completely restored to their original state. The bag is torn open to show it to be empty, and the papers are passed around for examination.

SECRET AND PREPARATION

A You will need six sheets of tissue (three white and three red), about 1' square is a good size. The first pair of papers, consisting of one white sheet and one red sheet, are unprepared.

B The second "mismade" pair of tissues (one white, one red) have circles of the opposite color tissue pasted on them in the center on both sides.

C To prepare the "mismade" tissues, carefully tear out or cut four circles of the same size (two red and two white) out of other "matching" pieces of tissue.

D Glue these circles, one on each side, in the center of the sheet of the opposite color.

E The third pair of tissues, like the first pair, are unprepared.

F The paper bag is really the special DOUBLE-WALLED BAG which you have already learned to construct.

G Fold the first pair of unprepared tissues into quarters. Do the same with the second, "mismade" pair of tissues.

H Put both these folded separate packets together and place them into a DOUBLE-WALLED BAG. Do not put these papers into the secret pocket. Place them into the larger section of the bag.

I Fold the bag flat. This will conceal the presence of the papers which are secretly hidden inside. Fold the bag and place it on your table. Put the remaining (ungimmicked) pair of tissues on the table beside the paper bag.

METHOD

1 Pick up the two papers, holding one in each hand. Say, "Here are two sheets of tissue. One is white; one is red."

2 Continue by saying: "I shall place the tissues together, fold them into quarters, and tear out the center portions."

3 As you say this, tear the center corner out of the tissues in a quarter circle as shown.

NOTE: When tearing the circles, try to make the torn centers approximately the same size as the center portions you pasted on the second pair of tissues. You may have to practice tearing the tissues a few times before you can do this action automatically.

4 Once you have removed the centers, open up the tissues and the centers. Display them to the audience.

5 Refold the tissues into quarters and put them, along with the center portions, into the bag. As you do this, place them all into the secret pocket. Close the bag and shake it. Announce that, by making a magic gesture and by shaking the bag, you will cause the tissues to restore themselves.

6 Reach inside and remove the "mismade" pair of tissues from the bag. Place the bag on the table with the interior facing away from your audience.

7 Open the "mismade" tissues to show your mistake. The papers are restored, but the centers are switched around.

8 Act surprised as you look at the papers, wondering what went wrong. Place the tissues together and refold them into quarters. Hold the folded papers as shown in the illustration.

9 "It seems I have made a terrible mistake. Wait a moment! Perhaps I can correct the situation." As you say this, tear the centers out of the tissues, as shown.

10 Pick up the bag and place the torn tissues, and their centers, into the secret pocket. Say, "I know what happened. I shook the bag when the magic was happening and the papers got a little mixed up."

11 Holding the bag very still, make a magical gesture at the bag. Then, tear open the bag to reveal the remaining pair of untorn tissues. Be careful not to expose the extra tissues hidden in the secret pocket.

12 Toss the torn bag aside before you unfold the two tissues. Now, unfold the two papers as you say, "Things seem to have worked out for the best." You can hand both tissues to the spectators for examination if you wish.

COMMENTS AND SUGGESTIONS

This trick will be very well received if you play it in a tongue-in-cheek fashion. The only thing you have to worry about is when you tear open the bag. Be careful not to expose the secret pocket or its contents. This classic comedy effect gives you an opportunity to add as much acting as you wish to emphasize your mistake when you display the "mismade" tissues.

TAKE-APART VANISH

EFFECT

You display a dove or small rabbit and openly place the animal into an attractive wooden box. Instantly, the box is taken apart, piece by piece, allowing the spectators to view all sides of the now dismantled container. Impossible as it seems, the animal has mysteriously vanished from within the box without a trace.

SECRET AND PREPARATION

To perform this astonishing vanish, you will need to construct a specially gimmicked wooden box. This box works on the same principle as a number of large stage illusions. The quality of the finished product will depend upon your ability as a craftsperson. If you take your time in the construction of the prop, however, you will probably be using this vanish in your act for many years.

CONSTRUCTION

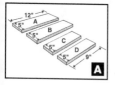

A From a sheet of 1/2" plywood, cut two pieces that measure 5" × 12" (labeled A and B in the illustrations) and two more pieces that are 5" × 9" (labeled C and D).

B You will also need three 10" × 13" pieces of 1/2" plywood labeled E, F, and G. One of these pieces (G) has a 7" × 10" opening cut in the center, leaving a 1-1/2" border around the opening.

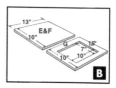

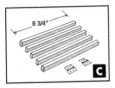

C Cut five strips of 1/4" square soft pine 8-3/4" long. This type of wood can be purchased at most arts and crafts shops or obtained at any lumber yard. You will also need two 1-1/2" butt hinges which can be purchased inexpensively at any hardware store. (The illustration shows this type of hinge.)

ASSEMBLY

The assembly of the apparatus is quite simple. Take care, however, in fitting the parts together to guarantee the proper working of the equipment and to ensure the overall attractiveness of the prop.

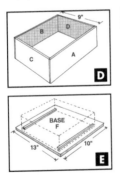

D Begin by constructing the rectangular frame of the box, as illustrated, using Parts A, B, C, and D. Be sure that A and B overlap the ends of C and D so that the inside of the frame is 9" wide.

E Attach two of the 1/4" strips to the top surface of Part F, which serves as the removable bottom for the rectangular frame constructed in Step D. To ensure exact alignment, center the frame on top of the board (F) and position the two strips along the inner walls of the frame, as illustrated. Then, fasten these strips to the baseboard with wood glue and finishing nails. If done correctly, the frame should fit easily over the baseboard with the two strips serving to hold the frame in position during the presentation.

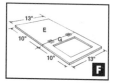

F To construct the lid of the box, butt the long ends of E and G together and attach the two hinges, as illustrated here. When E is hinged over, on top of G, the two boards should align evenly on all sides.

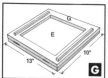

G Turn the unit over and attach two 1/4" strips to the underside of Part G, as shown here. To ensure their exact alignment, follow the same procedure outlined in Step E.

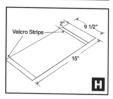

H The basic construction is now complete except for the addition of a secret cloth bag which is attached to the lid of the box. The bag should be constructed from a strip of strong, black material approximately 15" long by 9-1/2" wide. Cut a strip of Velcro to fit across the full width of the cloth. (Or you may use snaps or a zipper.) Velcro can be obtained in fabric stores and in the notions section of department stores. You will notice that the Velcro strip consists of two pieces of ribbon with fuzzy nylon loops which stick together. Each half of the Velcro strip has a different texture. Sew one side of the strip of Velcro across the width of the cloth approximately 2" from one end. Then, sew the corresponding side of the Velcro strip (the one with the different texture) even with the edge of the opposite end of the cloth, as shown.

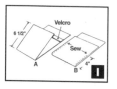

I Fold the cloth over, as shown, and press the Velcro strips together. This fold will form a bag approximately 6-1/2" deep and 9-1/2" wide. Next, sew the two layers of material together along the sides of the bag. However, only sew about 4" up from the fold which forms the bottom of the bag.

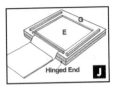

J Place the lid of the box on the table, bottom side up, so that Part G of the lid is facing up. Position the bag so that its upper edge lies over the hinged side of G as shown. Place the remaining 1/4" strip of wood on top of the edge of the bag and secure the wood strip and the bag to Part G with glue and finishing nails as shown here. This strip must be properly positioned to ensure the centering of the lid on the rectangular frame. The construction of the box is now complete, and you are ready to assemble the components into the finished product.

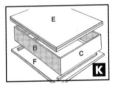

K Place the baseboard F on your table with the 1/4" strips facing up. Next, set the open frame on top of the baseboard; then, place the lid E on top of the frame.

L Be sure that the bag hangs inside the frame and the hinges are nearest to the audience, as shown.

M If everything fits together well, paint the equipment in a decorative manner. Now you are ready to present this most baffling vanish.

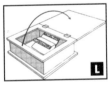

METHOD

1 As you display the rabbit (or other small animal or object) to the audience, step to your table and open the lid of the box. The lid should open away from you in the direction of the audience, as shown in Step L. Carefully place the rabbit into the black bag and press the Velcro strips together. This done, close the lid as if to prevent the rabbit from escaping.

2 You are now ready to vanish the rabbit by showing all sides of the box as you take it apart. Although this procedure can be executed by the magician alone, the handling of the apparatus is easier and much less risky if you utilize the aid of an assistant. With your assistant standing at your left, open the lid, Part E, completely so that the audience can see its top surface. Then, grasp Part G by the back edge with your left hand and lift the entire lid assembly off the frame, as shown. This will pull the bag, and the animal, out of the frame, concealing it behind Part E. The spectators have now seen both sides of the lid, which you give to your assistant to hold. Be sure not to let the audience catch a glimpse of the hidden bag as you hand the lid to your assistant.

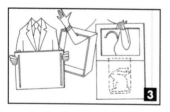

3 Direct your attention to the rectangular frame. Lift it slowly from the baseboard as though it contained the rabbit. Slowly move forward, and then suddenly spin the frame between your hands showing that it is empty. Hang the empty frame over your assistant's free arm and once again direct your attention back to the table. Pick up the baseboard by tilting it toward the audience and hold it as though you were concealing something behind it. Take a few steps forward and then slowly turn the board over with a smile. The total vanish of the rabbit will leave the audience contemplating this mystery for a long time to come.

BUNNY BOX

EFFECT

In this trick, you vanish an attractive box which contains a rabbit or other small animal. You will find the BUNNY BOX an excellent effect to perform for children as they are always delighted to see tricks with furry animals.

SECRET AND PREPARATION

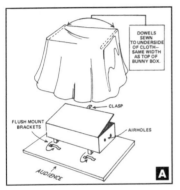

Construct the box out of 1/4" pine or plywood to a size which suits the rabbit you wish to vanish. You will need to add some hardware to the box so that the lid can be locked shut. Then, mount two metal hooks on the underneath side of the box. Position the two corresponding brackets on the plywood tray so that the hooks on the bottom of the box fit into them exactly. The box may now be hooked to the tray. Drill a few air holes in the ends of the box so that your livestock can get plenty of air. Paint the box one color and the tray another, but select colors that match the rest of your props so that the entire affair will blend nicely with your other props.

Prepare the double cloth by sewing two dowels between the double cloth. The dowels must correspond with the top outside edges of the box. By grasping the dowels and stretching them tightly between your hands, you retain the form of the livestock box beneath the cloth.

METHOD

1 Show the box and place it on the tray held by your assistant so that the hooks attach firmly to the brackets. Gently place the bunny into the box. Close the lid and fasten it securely before covering the box with the prepared cloth.

2 Use both hands to spread the cloth over the box and tray. Place the cloth over the box so that the dowels are located directly over the edges of the box.

3 For this phase of the trick, timing is critical. With both hands, grasp the two dowels through the cloth as if you were picking up the box. Hold one dowel in each hand and stretch the cloth between the dowels, as shown, to retain the form of the box.

4 Lift the dowels upward as you turn to face the audience. At the same time that you lift the cloth (and the secret dowels), your assistant tips the front edge of the tray upward and takes one step back. The box, attached to the tray, swings to a position hidden by the bottom of the tray.

5 Step forward as you hold what appears to be the box under the cloth (really just the dowels). The audience's attention will be entirely on you. This gives your assistant the opportunity to exit, secretly carrying the box and bunny or other livestock hidden on the rear side of the tray.

6 Step toward the audience holding the cloth with the box apparently underneath. Toss the cloth into the air to cause the box and the bunny to vanish!

COMMENTS AND SUGGESTIONS

When you vanish the box and the bunny, grasp the cloth by one corner as it falls and snap it out sharply. You may now drape the cloth over one arm as you take your bow. This small addition of business is possible because of the flexibility of the cloth containing the dowels. To see the magician drape the cloth over one arm before taking a bow not only creates an attractive picture, it also serves to convince the audience that the cloth is unprepared.

PRODUCTION BOX

EFFECT

On your magician's table rests what appears to be an ordinary shoe box. You pick up the box and show it inside and out, proving it to be quite empty. Replacing the box on your table, you pick up the lid and allow the spectators to clearly see it on both sides as well. It is just what it appears to be: an ordinary cardboard lid to a shoe box. Placing the lid on the box, you pick up the container and display it to the audience. Upon lifting the lid, you reach into the previously empty box and remove a small live animal (or any other item of similar size), much to the delight of the astonished spectators.

MARK WILSON'S CYCLOPEDIA OF MAGIC

SECRET AND PREPARATION

The following is a simple but effective method to produce a live dove or other small animal. The items you will need for this effect are: a shoe box complete with lid, some black felt, a table, and, of course, the animal (let's assume it's a dove) to be produced.

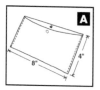

A The first step in construction of the PRODUCTION BOX is to sew together a cloth bag made of strong black felt. Let's assume you will be using a standard shoe box with a lid that measures 12" × 6" × 3/4". (The size of the lid determines the size of the bag you will make.) In this case, the bag should measure approximately 8" × 4". Cut an 8" square

piece of felt and fold it in half. Sew up the ends of the folded square to form an 8" × 4" bag or pouch that is open at the top and large enough to contain a live dove. Sew a small dress snap in the center of the opening at the top of the bag, as shown.

B Cut a length of strong, clear mono-filament fishing line or heavy thread. This line should be threaded through the lip of the lid and then sewn to the top corners of the bag, as in the illustration.

C The exact length of the line must be determined through experimentation. The end result, however, should center the load bag on the back of the lid, as shown.

D Carefully load the dove into the bag and close the snap to prevent it from escaping. Then, rest the lid of the box near the back edge of your table with the inside of the lid facing up. The bag containing the dove should be suspended below the table top, as shown. Position the empty shoe box in front of the lid, and you are ready.

METHOD

1 Begin by picking up the empty shoe box and displaying it on all sides. Make sure to give the audience a clear view of the inside of the box.

2 Replace the box on your table and pick up the lid. This is done by tilting the lid forward before lifting it clear of the table. The load bag will be lifted unseen into position behind the lid, as shown.

3 Keeping the inside of the lid facing the audience, lower the lid directly in front of the shoe box, allowing the load bag to secretly slip inside the box. Now, stand the lid on its edge using the shoe box as a support.

4 Release your grip on the lid and show that your hands are empty. Then, lift the lid just enough so you can rotate the lid completely over and place it on the box. Be careful not to raise the lid too high when you rotate it as that would lift the load bag out of the box where it would be seen by the audience.

5 Pick up the covered box and display it freely on all sides. Then, place the box back on your table and raise the back of the lid with your left hand, as shown. With your right hand, reach into the box, open the snap, and remove the dove from the bag.

6 To conclude the production, bring the dove into view and then close the lid of the box and take your bow.

COMMENTS AND SUGGESTIONS

The above principle may be applied to any size box. Simply adjust the dimensions of the load bag to fit the concealment area behind the lid.

It is a good idea to practice this production before a mirror and watch your angles. You will find that by reversing the procedure, a very effective vanish can also be presented with the same equipment.

MAGIC TABLE

If you intend to perform on a stage or for larger groups, you should have a MAGIC TABLE. The following plans explain how you can easily and inexpensively build your own table in a style that is ideal for this purpose. It is attractive, simple to build, and folds flat for traveling or storage between shows.

CONSTRUCTION

A The entire table is constructed from thick plywood and 1" × 2" clear pine stiffeners. Begin by cutting one piece of plywood 36" × 12" and another 36" × 10-3/4".

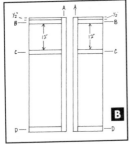

B Take the 12" width and add the 1" × 2" stiffeners, as shown. Attach the long stiffener A flush with the right side of the panel. Be sure to set the wooden stiffener marked B 1/2" below the top edge of the panel, as illustrated. Position the stiffener C 12" below stiffener B. Stiffener D should be flush with the bottom edge of the panel. Next, install the stiffeners on the 10-3/4" width. Stiffener A is attached to the left side of the panel. Stiffeners B, C, and D are attached as they were on the first panel. When finished, sand the panels smooth to prepare for painting.

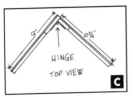

C Butt the end of the 10-3/4" panel next to the outer back edge of the 12" panel.

MARK WILSON'S CYCLOPEDIA OF MAGIC

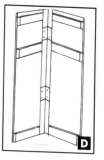

D Attach two hinges to the stiffeners, as indicated. Notice that both sides of the screen-like table base now measure 12". This hinging arrangement provides an automatic stop when opening the panels, but allows them to be folded flat for storage.

E In order to build the top and storage shelf, you will need to cut a piece of 1/2" thick plywood 18" long by 12" wide and an additional piece 10" square, as in Figure E.

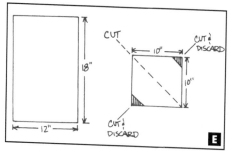

The larger of the two pieces is utilized as the top of your table. The 10" square must now be cut diagonally in order to form two triangular sections. One of these will serve as the rear shelf and rests on top of the C stiffeners.

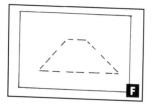

F The second triangular section must be glued to the underside of the tabletop, as illustrated in Figure F. This will insure the proper positioning of the top into the screen-like uprights. Now, sand these parts thoroughly, and you will be ready for the final assembly.

REAR VIEW

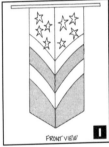

FRONT VIEW

G You will need four small "screen door" fasteners to hook the entire arrangement together. Two of these are mounted to the tabletop with the eyes positioned in the uppermost stiffener, A, as illustrated. As you can see from this diagram, these fasteners hold the top to the panels. The triangular piece fastened to the underside of the top prevents the panels from closing unexpectedly.

H This hook-and-eye arrangement is also used to secure the triangular shelf into position on top of the B stiffeners as shown in Step G.

I After you have positioned the fasteners and are satisfied with the rigidity of the equipment, you can begin to decorate the table. The first step is to paint the back side of the screen, the underside of the top, and the small triangular shelf "flat black." When these parts are dry, cover the top surface of your table with black felt and trim the edges with silver (or some other bright color) braid. The front surfaces of the screen can be decorated in any motif that you feel is attractive and suitable to your style of performance.

BLACK ART WELL

This title graphically describes a very useful addition to your magic table. Simply stated, a BLACK ART WELL is an "invisible hole" in the top of your table which enables you to vanish an object.

CONSTRUCTION

A Cut a piece of 1/2" thick plywood into a rectangular shape measuring 12" × 18". Add a triangular section measuring 10" on each of the right-angled sides to the bottom of this new top, in the same manner as you did with the regular top in Step F of the MAGIC TABLE.

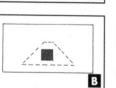

B Cut a 3" square hole through both layers of your new top, as illustrated.

C Sand the top smooth on all sides. Then, paint the entire unit "flat black."

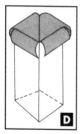

D You must sew up a square black velvet bag. This bag should measure 3" square and at least 7" deep, as shown. Also, be sure that the soft (napped) side of the velvet is on the inside surface of the bag.

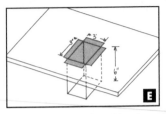

E Pull the bag up through the hole in your tabletop and staple it into position, as illustrated. At this point, the well should measure 6" deep.

F It is now necessary to cover the entire tabletop with a piece of matching velvet measuring 12" × 18". This is best accomplished by gluing the fabric directly to the plywood top.

G Allow the adhesive to dry thoroughly, and then carefully cut out the excess material above the well with a sharp razor blade.

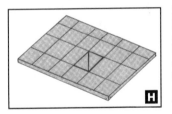

H In order to conceal the edges around the well, stretch brightly colored braid across the top, as shown here. You can attach this braid to the edges of the table by using small carpet tacks or staples. When you have completed the above, trim the edge of the top with a strip of matching braid.

I All that is left is to mount the two hooks to the underside of the completed top as described in the MAGIC TABLE.

CHAPTER 21
MAGICAL ILLUSIONS

In magical terms, an illusion is any trick or effect involving a human being, most notably an appearance, vanish, or transformation. The term has been extended to include large animals and sizable objects as well.

Two important factors to consider when including illusions in a show are expense and portability. It is unwise to spend time and money building illusions unless you feel sure you can use them often enough to make it worthwhile. Similarly, it is a mistake to make an act too big for the places you expect to play or to run up extra costs for transporting your equipment. Such points have been considered in designing the illusions that appear in this section. All are inexpensive to construct and light to carry, so, if you plan to perform before large audiences, you can't go wrong on either count!

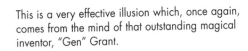

ARABIAN TENT ILLUSION

This is a very effective illusion which, once again, comes from the mind of that outstanding magical inventor, "Gen" Grant.

EFFECT

You call the audience's attention to a stack of heavy cardboard sheets. You display each part and begin to fit them together one at a time. The spectators soon realize that you are building a small tent. With the four walls standing intact, you position the roof, completing the structure. Almost instantly, you lift the roof, revealing the magical appearance of an assistant from within the tent!

SECRET AND PREPARATION

A very inexpensive and practical way to build this illusion is out of heavy cardboard. If you decide, after presenting the effect, to incorporate the illusion as a permanent part of your show, you can rebuild the equipment using wooden frames made of 1" by 2" pine covered with colorful light-weight canvas.

A If you plan to use cardboard as your building material, it must be strong and sturdy. You can buy new cardboard at wholesale paper supply houses or from companies that manufacture large cardboard cartons. Also, moving and storage companies usually have large cardboard boxes for sale. On the other hand, you may wish to build your first illusion from materials that cost little or nothing. In this case, obtain a large cardboard box or shipping carton in which large items such as refrigerators are shipped.

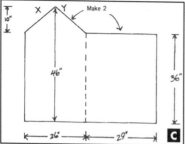

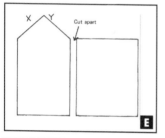

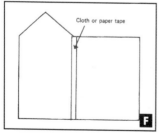

B The only other items you will need for this illusion are some strong paper or cloth tape to make the hinges that hold the various parts together and, if you wish, some paint and brushes to decorate the final prop.

C After you have obtained your materials, cut out two identical pieces from the cardboard, as shown here. If your cardboard is not exactly the dimensions shown here, don't worry. The parts just need to be large enough to hide your assistant as you perform the routine, as outlined above.

D Fold the two parts where indicated by the dotted line in Figure C.

E If you find that the board is too stiff to make a clean fold, it may be necessary to cut the piece in two, as shown in Figure E.

F Hinge the pieces back together with a wide band of paper or cloth tape. When you have them completed, these parts make up the four walls of your tent.

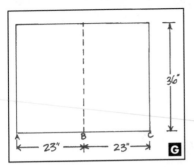

G Next, cut out one piece of board, as shown here. This is the roof of the tent. It must also be folded, as indicated by the dotted line. If necessary, cut and hinge the two parts with tape, as suggested in Steps E and F.

H Be sure that the two sides of the roof (A to B and B to C) are the same size and that they are each approximately 2″ longer than the top of the tent's walls (X and Y) on which the roof will rest after you have assembled the tent.

I Check to see that all parts fit well to make up the completed tent. Then decorate the tent to fit the patter theme that you will use for the trick (circus tent, haunted house, doll house, etc.).

J This type of cardboard will take paint very well so don't hesitate to use it. Any slight warping that may occur can be cured by bending the part in the opposite direction to the warp. However, if you paint both sides of the board, the possibility of warping is minimized. You can also use contact paper or colored paper to decorate this illusion.

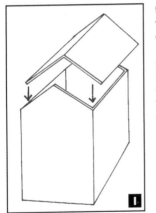

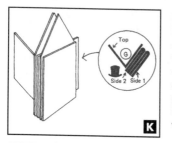

K After you complete the construction and decoration, stand the roof on end like a twofold screen. Fold the two side pieces flat and lean them against the left side of the roof, as shown. Your assistant must be secretly positioned behind the roof section, as illustrated by the circle in the overhead view, shown in Figure K.

NOTE: In these pictures, and in all those that follow, your location is indicated by the top hat and your assistant's location by the letter G.

METHOD

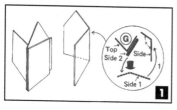

1 After the curtain opens, explain that you are going to do a little magical construction. Take the first folded part (one of the sides of the tent), open it out and allow the audience to see it on all sides. Position this piece as illustrated in the circular insert picture.

2 The piece indicated by the dashes in the picture is the side you show the audience during the middle of Step 1. Also, when you study the insert drawing, you will see that the back of this side is left open when you place it in position on the floor. There is a very important reason for this, as you will see. Also note that the longer side of Side 2 is pointing directly at the audience.

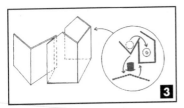

3 Immediately pick up the second folded section (the other side) and display it to the audience. Turn and position it exactly as illustrated here.

4 It is at this precise moment that your assistant moves secretly from behind the roof into the tent, as shown in the insert drawing. As you can see from the encircled diagram in Step 3, the arrangement of the top and the two sides masks this move from the audience.

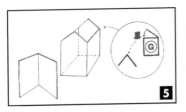

5 Quickly walk around the tent, circling to your left. As you pass the rear panel, openly close the gap in it, as if you were merely straightening the sides. Cross on the right of the tent, pick up the roof section, and display it.

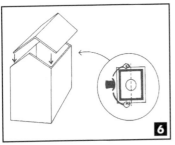

6 After showing the roof to the audience, set it in place on top of the tent. (Be careful not to move the sides and expose the presence of your assistant inside.)

7 Make a magical gesture toward the tent, and then suddenly lift the roof section. At the same time, your assistant should stand up, magically appearing.

8 During the applause, hinge open the front panel and allow your assistant to step forward for a bow.

HAUNTED HOUSE

EFFECT

You call attention to the stacked sections of a miniature house with weird decorations and hooded figures peering from windows with broken shutters. You state that this is a replica of a haunted house that is waiting for a ghost to rent it, so that strange manifestations can take place within its musty walls and beneath its ramshackle roof. You decide to play the part of a ghost by putting on a sheet. Thus attired, you set up the walls and finally pick up the roof and put it in place. Continuing your ghostly act, you walk around the house, then make weird gestures and suddenly raise the roof. To the audience's amazement, who pops up but you! Then, stepping from the house, you grab the ghost before it can get away. When the sheet is whisked clear, the ghost proves to be your assistant, who takes a bow along with you.

SECRET AND PREPARATION

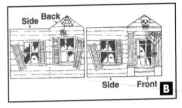

Side Back

Side Front **B**

A The equipment for this startling effect is the same as used in the ARABIAN TENT ILLUSION, previously described. The only change required will be in the decoration of the parts.

B This is an appropriate design for the walls of the house.

C Paint the roof to look like worn shingles, as shown here.

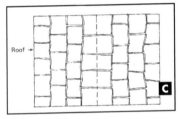

Roof → **C**

D You will need two identical white sheets. The size of the sheets is determined by your height and by your assistant's height. Be sure to make the ghost costumes long enough to touch the stage floor, so that your feet do not show. The eye holes should be cut as shown. You should also pin the sides of the sheets together and sew the material so that it forms makeshift sleeves as well.

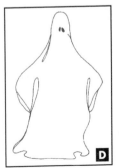

D

E Arrange the parts of the ghost's house exactly the same as in the ARABIAN TENT ILLUSION at the start. Your assistant should be wearing the ghost sheet and be standing behind the roof, as before. Drape the duplicate sheet over your arm and make your entrance.

METHOD

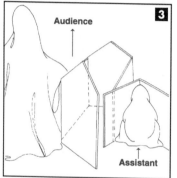

1 Call attention to the vertical stack of parts on stage. Unfold the sheet and cover yourself completely. Make sure the eye holes line up properly. Then lift the first section (the back and left side of the house) from the stack as in Step 1 of the ARABIAN TENT ILLUSION.

2 Display and position the second side (the front and right side of the house), just as in Step 2.

3 The illustration here gives you a back view of the situation at this point in the presentation.

4 After the second side is in place, circle the illusion to your left and end up standing directly behind your concealed assistant.

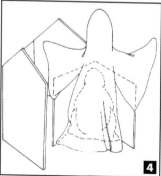

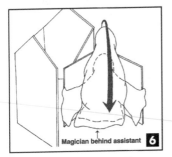

Magician behind assistant 6

5 It is very important at this point in the illusion that you don't look down and give away the presence of your assistant to the audience. You are about to make the most critical move in this presentation, and any hesitation will mean failure.

6 Stoop down behind your assistant and the folded roof, as shown. Keep your arms at your sides, for as soon as you are out of sight, your assistant grasps the outer edges of the roof, as illustrated. The audience will believe that those are your hands, since they are completely unaware of the concealed duplicate ghost.

7 Quickly crawl into the house, as shown here. (This is the same secret move your assistant made in the ARABIAN TENT ILLUSION.)

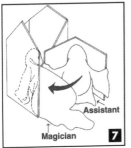

Assistant

Magician 7

8 As soon as you are inside the house, your assistant immediately stands up, picking up the roof, as shown here.

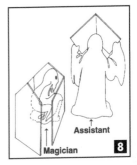

Assistant

Magician 8

9 You and your assistant must practice this maneuver until it blends into one flowing motion. When done correctly, this move is so deceptive that the audience believes that you never left their sight.

MARK WILSON'S CYCLOPEDIA OF MAGIC

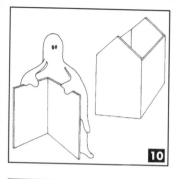

10 The ghost (really your assistant) now displays the roof in your place.

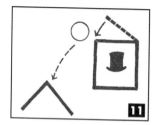

11 Your assistant then sets the roof back down on the floor, slightly away from the house. Circling to her left, the assistant closes the rear gap in the back wall of the house.

12 Next, your assistant places the roof into position on the house.

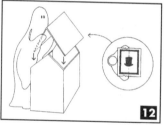

13 Steps 10, 11, and 12 of this routine are a slightly different sequence from their counterparts in the ARABIAN TENT ILLUSION routine.

14 Making one more circle around the haunted mansion, your assistant prepares to lift the roof. During the time it takes the assistant to complete this circle, you carefully remove your ghost costume, taking care not to hit the sides of the house.

15 As soon as your assistant lifts the top, you stand erect. If you have executed the illusion properly, the audience will react with utter disbelief. During the applause, quickly step out of the house from the back, so as not to reveal your ghost costume in the house.

16 Now unveil your assistant! This second surprise will boost the reaction so that you may both take the bows.

COMMENTS AND SUGGESTIONS

Much depends on how you play your part as the ghost when presenting this striking illusion. If you have the sheet handy at the start, you can put it on immediately and begin a weird pantomime. But you can also have the sheet hanging over the second wall, so that you can put the first side of the house in position before you come to the sheet and decide to play the ghost.

Also, your assistant must copy your gestures exactly, so the audience will be held in suspense until the climax. By taking time to parade around the assembled house, your assistant can give you ample opportunity to dispose of your ghost costume. There is definitely no need to hurry, for if spectators suspect that someone is going to appear from the house, the one person they won't expect is you. So the longer the suspense, the stronger the climax.

VICTORY CARTONS ILLUSION
"GEN" GRANT

For a quick and surprising way to produce a person from nowhere, this is ideal because of its surprising magical effect, its portability, and its inexpensive cost. In addition, it can be set up in a matter of moments and worked on any stage or platform where your audience is located in front, making it a valuable feature for your magical program.

EFFECT

You display two large cardboard boxes. Both boxes are folded flat and held upright by your assistant. The tops and bottoms of the boxes have been removed so that actually the boxes are rectangular tubes which fold along their seams. You take the first box from your assistant and open it up into a square. Obviously, nothing of any size could be concealed inside since the box has been folded flat from the beginning. The second box is then also opened. To prove even more convincingly that it, too, is completely empty, you and your assistant show the audience a clear view through the ends of the box. The second box, which is slightly larger than the other, is then placed over the first box. The two nested boxes are now revolved to show the audience all sides. It seems impossible that anything could be concealed within the cardboard containers. Yet, upon your command, a person makes an appearance from within the boxes!

SECRET AND PREPARATION

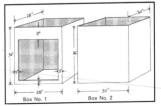

All you need are two large cardboard boxes of the size shown and the proper amount of rehearsal with your assistants. As you can see from the dimensions on the illustration, one of the boxes must be slightly larger so that it will fit over the other box. We will call the inner or smaller box No. 1 and the larger box No. 2. You can make two boxes from corrugated paperboard or any lightweight material. The sides are held together with heavy paper or cloth tape. The boxes are both 36" high. The smaller box is 28" square, and the larger is 30", as shown. Neither box has a top or bottom, so actually they are rectangular tubes. The smaller box has an opening cut in one side. The opening is 24" high by 20" wide with a 3" lip around the sides and bottom and a 9" lip at the top. The audience is never aware of this opening. The boxes must fold flat as shown.

METHOD

1 Fold both boxes flat and stand them on end with the prepared box (No. 1) nearest the audience. The secret opening in Box No. 1 must face to the rear. Box No. 2 is directly behind it. Your assistant should stand at the right side of the cartons, supporting them in their position. Step 1 shows the "backstage" view with the proper position of the two containers at the start. Unknown to the audience, a second assistant is crouched behind the two cartons, as shown.

MARK WILSON'S CYCLOPEDIA OF MAGIC

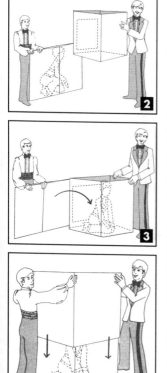

2 To begin the presentation, call attention to the two flattened containers. Lift the front box (No. 1) and open it up into a square, as shown. Be sure to keep the secret opening to the back so that the audience cannot see it.

3 Place the box (No. 1) in the position illustrated, so that it overlaps the left edge of the other box (No. 2) which is still held by your assistant. As soon as Box No. 1 is open and on the floor, the person crawls from behind the other, still flat box (No. 2) through the secret opening into the open Box No.1. Because the boxes overlap, the movement of your second assistant from behind the closed box (No. 2) into the open box (No. 1) will not be seen by the audience. Your position at the left of the open box (No. 1) will also help to hide your assistant's movement from any spectators watching from that side. Your other assistant's body helps hide any movement from the right side.

4 After your assistant enters the open box (No. 1), your first assistant immediately lifts the other box (No. 2) and hands it to you. This action must be done smoothly, with perfect coordination between you and your assistants. With the help of your first assistant, open Box

No. 2 and tilt it on its side, allowing the audience to see completely through the box. Then, slide Box No. 2 over the prepared box (No. 1) which now conceals your assistant.

5 With the aid of your assistant, revolve the nested cartons one complete turn to show the audience all sides of the cardboard containers. Since the outer container conceals the cutout portion of the inner box, everything appears quite normal. Be sure to keep the bottoms of the boxes on the floor as you turn them so that you do not expose your assistant's feet.

6 Upon your command, your assistant quickly stands up, apparently having magically appeared inside the two empty boxes! You and your first assistant now help the second assistant out of the box by holding on beneath the arms as the assistant jumps out of the box. (See Comments and Suggestions.) Your first assistant can now carry the equipment safely off stage as the audience applauds this startling illusion.

COMMENTS AND SUGGESTIONS

Although the construction and the presentation are comparatively simple, this illusion must be carefully rehearsed until you can perform it in a brisk, straightforward manner. Coordination and timing, on your part and on the part of both of your assistants, are vital. Any hesitation at the wrong moment may arouse the audience's suspicion. The same applies to too much haste. As an example of proper timing, your assistant should begin to enter the smaller box (No. 1) while you are adjusting it to its proper position overlapping the other, still flat box (No. 2). In this way, if your assistant accidentally hits Box No. 1 while entering it, the motion will be attributed to your handling of the box. The quicker your assistant enters Box No. 1, the better. Your other assistant can then immediately pick up the larger box with less chance that anyone will guess its real purpose, which was to conceal the assistant behind it. You can then slow down the pace while showing the large box (No. 2) as the real work has been accomplished. Revolving the boxes is very effective because, when the spectators think back later, they will be sure that each box was shown clear through and all around at the start.

MYSTERY OF
THE MAGICAL MUMMY I

EFFECT

You unfold an attractive piece of cloth measuring approximately 6' by 8'. A male assistant, standing to your left, picks up the left top corner of the loose material and stretches it tightly between the two of you. On your command, your assistant rolls himself up in the cloth and turns his body so that the material is wrapped tightly around him. You walk quickly around the mummy-like figure and then grasp the loose end of the cloth. With a broad flourish, you unroll the fabric from the body. When the cloth falls free, the audience is surprised to see a female assistant standing in place of the male assistant!

SECRET AND PREPARATION

A The only prop you will need is a piece of cloth 6' x 8'. If you are presenting this illusion in your home, you can use a blanket or a sheet. For stage use, however, an attractive, opaque piece of fabric is best.

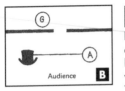

B This first version is the method for presenting the effect in your home. Select a room in the house where there is a door or archway located approximately in the center of a wall, as shown here. The female assistant should hide behind this wall and to the right of the door, as illustrated. Your male assistant, who, by the way, should be close to the same height as the female assistant, stands to your left with the folded cloth over his arm. The spectators must be located in front of you, so that the door is obscured by the cloth when you and the assistant hold it up between you, as shown in Step 1 that follows.

METHOD

In the circular inserts, your location is indicated by a top hat, your female assistant is indicated by a G, and your male assistant is shown as A.

1 Take the cloth and open it to your left. Your male assistant (A) grasps the fabric by the top left corner and stretches it between the two of you, as shown. This action must place the archway directly behind the cloth, as illustrated in Step B above. Also, be sure that the bottom edge of the fabric touches the floor.

2 As soon as the cloth is in position, your female assistant (G) leaves her hiding place and positions herself directly behind the cloth.

3 Steps 3 and 4 are the important secret moves in this illusion. On your command, the male assistant openly steps around the left edge of the cloth and stands behind the fabric, as shown. The two of you must keep the cloth tightly stretched while he moves.

4 As your male assistant moves out of sight behind the cloth, your female assistant takes a new position between the male assistant and the cloth, as shown here. The male assistant allows her room in this area by extending his left arm and taking an unseen step backward. In the meantime, the female assistant grasps the side of the cloth with her right hand at Point X, as shown in the illustration. The male assistant's left hand should curl the top corner of the cloth inward just prior to the female assistant's move in order to conceal his own hand from the audience's view.

5 Together, Steps 3 and 4 take only a second or two and must be executed without hesitation. The flow of action should continue smoothly into the following steps.

6 As soon as the female assistant (G) takes hold of the cloth, the male assistant (A) quickly and secretly exits through the arch.

7 Simultaneously, the moment the male assistant is out of sight through the door, the female assistant begins to wrap herself in the cloth until she is standing next to you.

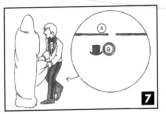

8 At this point, the audience thinks that the male assistant simply stepped behind his edge of the fabric and wrapped himself in the cloth.

9 Now walk around the mummy and grasp the loose end of the cloth. At this point in the presentation, the audience does not anticipate the final result, so you should play it up to the fullest.

10 Start to unwrap the figure, slowly at first, then gradually increase your tempo until the female assistant is about to be revealed. With a flourish, whip the remaining cloth away and dramatically play up the magical appearance of the female assistant.

MARK WILSON'S CYCLOPEDIA OF MAGIC

COMMENTS AND SUGGESTIONS

For an added climax, the male assistant can do a "run around" and make a surprise appearance in the audience. A "run around" means that as soon as the assistant is out of sight through the doorway, he literally runs through (or outside) the house by some route that the spectators cannot see and secretly enters the audience. If the physical setup of the house is right, the assistant may have time to actually sit down in the audience. The viewers are concentrating on the action "on stage" and will not notice this new arrival. Then the male assistant can loudly lead the applause until he is discovered by the now doubly amazed spectators!

MYSTERY OF
THE MAGICAL MUMMY II

EFFECT

The effect in this variation is identical to that of the first version; however, this is the presentation designed for use on stage or in a theater. Therefore, the placement of assistants and the sight line controls must be changed. We will assume that you are now completely familiar with the first version and move directly into the description of this new method.

SECRET AND PREPARATION

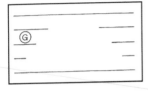

This onstage version must be performed in a theater with vertical legs (side curtains), as shown in the illustrations. The right center "leg" will serve as a replacement for the doorway used in the first method. The female assistant hides behind this leg, as shown.

METHOD

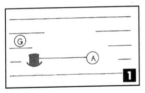

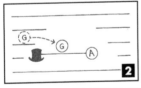

NOTE: All illustrations are from the overhead point of view in order to diagram the moves more clearly.

1 Stretch the cloth between you and your male assistant (A). It is important that you stand so that your body and the cloth mask the onstage edge of the right center leg, as illustrated. This will protect the female assistant's unseen entrance from the curtain to her new position behind the cloth in Step 2.

2 As soon as the cloth is stretched, with its bottom edge resting on the stage floor, the female assistant secretly moves into position behind the cloth.

3 At this point, the male assistant steps behind the cloth in the same manner as in the first version.

4 The female assistant immediately takes her position between the male assistant and the cloth, as shown, and substitutes her own grip on the top corner of the cloth for that of the male assistant, as before.

5 The male assistant makes a quick exit into the wings, as illustrated.

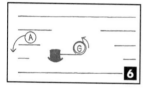

6 At the same time the male assistant is making his unseen exit, the female assistant starts to wrap herself in the cloth. In the meantime, the male assistant makes a rapid, but hidden, journey around the outside of the theater (or through a hallway, etc.) so that he will be ready for his magical reappearance from behind the audience.

7 When the female assistant has utilized approximately one-half of the material, carry the right end of the cloth in and around her, as shown. This will serve to position you away from the wings.

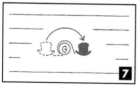

8 Now unwrap the figure, until your female assistant is magically revealed.

9 During the audience's surprised reaction, point dramatically to the rear of the theater as your male assistant makes his unexpected appearance by running down the aisle among the members of the unbelieving audience!

CURIOUS CABINET CAPER

EFFECT

A tall, slender, attractive cabinet is revealed in the center of the stage. You and your assistant spin the equipment so that the audience can see it on all sides. You open the front and the back doors which allows the spectators a clear view through the cabinet. You even walk through the empty cabinet. Then, you and your assistant close the doors. Instantly, the front door bursts open, revealing the magical appearance of your second assistant!

SECRET AND PREPARATION

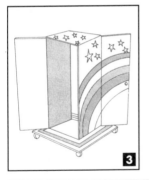

A This effective production is quite easy to build. The cabinet should measure approximately 2-1/2' square by 6' tall and rest upon a castered platform 5' square. The doors hinge open from diagonal corners, as illustrated. In order to save weight, the cabinet may be made of 1/4" thick plywood with vertical framing underneath to prevent sagging with the assistant's weight.

B After the construction is complete, decorate the cabinet in a style that blends with the theme of your presentation.

METHOD

For simplicity and clarity, the first assistant is not shown in the illustrations. All of the appropriate actions for that person can be clearly followed from the written description.

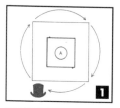

1 The second assistant is loaded into the cabinet offstage. On your cue, the illusion is wheeled rapidly to the center of the stage. You and your assistant then spin the cabinet, showing all sides.

2 Your first assistant opens the back door. Immediately, the second assistant moves secretly from inside the cabinet to a new position behind this door, as shown.

3 Almost simultaneously, you walk around to the back of the illusion and quickly step through the cabinet, pushing the front door open toward the audience as you exit.

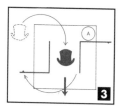

4 Your first assistant has moved forward and is now standing at attention to the left of the front door.

5 You are standing to the right and pointing out the empty interior of the illusion. Your second assistant is hidden behind the open back door.

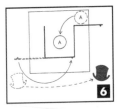

6 This next step is important. Since both you and your first assistant are standing to the front of the illusion, the proper timing in closing the doors is essential. You close the front door first, as your assistant moves to close the back door. The time it takes for your first assistant to get into position will create the fraction of a second necessary for your second

assistant to step back into the cabinet. If these moves are properly timed, the effect will be that both doors are closed simultaneously.

7 You and your first assistant step away from the cabinet. Your second assistant flings open the front door, making a magical appearance to the audience!

MUMMY'S CASKET

EFFECT

A tall, slender cabinet decorated to resemble an Egyptian mummy casket is wheeled onstage by your assistant. All sides of the equipment are shown to the audience prior to opening the front and back doors. The casket contains a cloth-wrapped mummy covered with the dust of ages past. Your assistant carefully removes this relic as you step through the cabinet brushing away the imaginary cobwebs. The audience can see completely through the casket as you walk through it. Together, you and your assistant reposition the mummy inside the casket and close the doors. Once again, you revolve the equipment to prove to the audience that the mummy is safely sealed inside its tomb. Suddenly, the doors are opened, revealing the startling transformation of the mummy into another one of your assistants dressed in the ancient style of Egypt.

SECRET AND PREPARATION

A The equipment and the method are basically the same as in the CURIOUS CABINET CAPER (see page 81). The only difference is in the decoration of the equipment and the additional task of constructing a replica of an Egyptian mummy. There are several ways in which to construct the mummy. The best method, but unfortunately the most difficult, is to build a wire form in the shape of a person approximately 5'3" tall and then completely wrap the finished form in wide surgical gauze. The second method is to sew up a cloth dummy of the same height as your assistant and stuff this large doll with lightweight foam rubber. Wrap the dummy figure with gauze as before. The last, and least desirable, method is to simply cut out an outline of the figure in 1/4" thick plywood. Wrap this silhouette with gauze as in the first two descriptions. Remember, whichever method you choose, to keep the figure as light as possible. Also, lightly spray the completed figure with black or gray paint to "age" it. Attach a thin piece of wire to the top of the

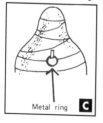

Metal ring **C**

mummy's head, as shown.

B The wire should be of the proper length to suspend the figure from a hook fastened to the inside top of the casket, as shown in Step 3 of Method.

C A metal ring should be sewn to the back of the mummy in the position diagrammed.

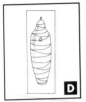

D This ring will enable the figure to be hung on the back of the door from a hook screwed into the panel, as shown here.

E To present the illusion, hang the mummy from the top of the head inside the casket. Place your second assistant in the cabinet standing behind the suspended figure, as shown in this diagram. Then, close both doors and have your first assistant wait for your cue.

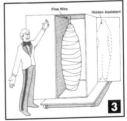

METHOD

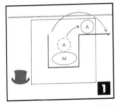

1 After you have verbally introduced the illusion to your audience, your first assistant wheels the equipment onstage so that it stands to your left. Together, you revolve the cabinet. Your first assistant steps back and opens the rear door. Your second assistant shifts to a new position behind this door, as shown.

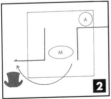

2 As soon as the back door is open, your first assistant moves back into position near the front of the equipment. Simultaneously with this forward movement, you open the front door.

3 Here is the audience's view at this point.

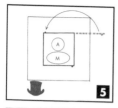

4 Your first assistant reaches into the cabinet and removes the wrapped figure. This clears the way for you to walk into and through the empty cabinet as you did in Step 3 of the CURIOUS CABINET CAPER (see page 614).

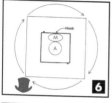

5 As you exit from the front, turn and help your first assistant in repositioning the mummy in the casket. As soon as the figure is secure, close the front door. Your first assistant moves directly to the rear. Your second assistant has moved back into the casket by the time your first assistant closes the back door.

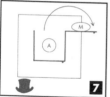

6 Revolve the cabinet in order to assure your audience that the mummy is still inside. During this rotation, your second assistant unhooks the mummy from the top and fastens it by the ring on the back door, as illustrated.

7 Your first assistant moves to the rear and opens the back door as before. This time, however, the mummy swings into concealment behind the back door.

8 As soon as your first assistant has opened the back door completely, you swing the front door wide open. The transformation of the mummy into your second assistant will shock the audience into applause.

WHO'S THERE?

This is the modern equivalent of one of the popular cabinet illusions featured in big-time magic shows that worked on full-size stages in large theaters. It usually required several assistants to move a cabinet around so that the magician could open the door and show that it was empty. Here, the illusion has been reduced to simply a door, a frame, and a curtain—making the illusion easy to do and light to handle. The effect is nearly the same, but it is enhanced by the simplicity of the equipment.

EFFECT

Standing on stage is a full-size door mounted in a thin door frame. Your assistant opens the door, revealing a curtain hanging across the threshold. Drawing the drape aside, your assistant walks through the door and around its skeleton framework. The audience can see that the doorway is quite normal and totally unprepared. Without hesitation, the assistant redraws the curtain and closes the door so that everything is exactly as it was originally. Immediately a loud knocking sound is heard coming from the other side of the door. The assistant swings the door open and there you stand, making your first appearance onstage in a startling and amazing manner.

SECRET AND PREPARATION

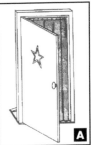

A The equipment necessary to present this illusion is quite simple and easy to construct. As you can see from the illustrations, the door is mounted in a simple frame, which in turn is anchored securely to a thin platform for sturdiness. An opaque curtain is hung from a rod at the top of the frame where it will not

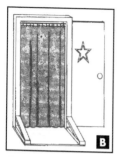

B

interfere with the opening and closing action of the door. The curtain must be long enough so that it touches the surface of the platform. This will prevent the spectators from seeing behind or under the curtain when the door is open.

B Here is a backstage view of the doorway. The angle brackets support the apparatus in its upright position and keep the framework from moving about when the door is open.

METHOD

1 At the start, the door should be in its closed position with the curtain drawn closed also. You should be standing on the back edge of the platform, behind the center of the curtain, as shown from this top view.

2 To present the illusion, your assistant (G) steps to the front of the framework and opens the door to its maximum capacity, as shown. You should still be concealed by the closed curtain at this point in the presentation.

3 Here is the audience's view of the situation at this point. You can now see why it is important that the curtain is long enough to touch the platform.

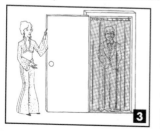

1

2

3

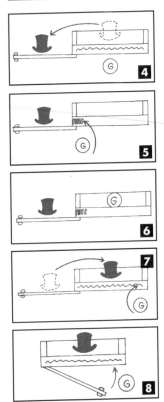

4 As soon as the door is completely open, quickly and quietly move to a new position behind the open door, as shown. At that same time, your assistant crosses in front of the framework to a position in front of the closed curtain. Practice exact timing with your assistant so that both moves are perfectly synchronized, thus eliminating any hesitation in the presentation.

5 Your assistant immediately draws the curtain open, as illustrated.

6 From the spectators' point of view, the doorway appears to be quite empty. Your assistant immediately walks through the open doorway and turns to face the audience, proving that everything is just as it appears. Be sure that your assistant does not glance in your direction. After a brief pause, the assistant walks back through the threshold and closes the curtain.

7 At this point, you return quickly to your former position behind the curtain.

8 During your move, your assistant walks from in front of the curtain to the edge of the open door and closes it.

As soon as you hear the door click shut, pull the curtain open and begin to knock loudly on the back of the door.

MARK WILSON'S CYCLOPEDIA OF MAGIC

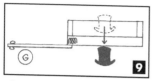

9 With this cue, your assistant swings the door open.

10 You immediately step through the doorway in a grand gesture, making your magical appearance on the stage.

TIP-OVER TRUNK

EFFECT

You and your assistant show and revolve an attractive trunk. All sides are displayed to the audience. The trunk is even tilted on its side, permitting a clear view of the top. In this position, the lid is raised, giving the spectators an opportunity to view the trunk's empty interior. Closing the lid, you and your assistant return the trunk to its original upright position. Immediately the top of the trunk bursts open, revealing the magical appearance of another one of your assistants!

SECRET AND PREPARATION

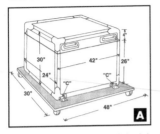

A The dimensions of the trunk shown here are for instructive purposes only. You will notice that two hinges, indicated by the letter C, hold the trunk to the platform by its bottom front edge. This allows you and your assistant to "tip" the trunk over (hence the name) on the base and, at the same time, keep the trunk in place on the platform. The two handles mounted on the front edge of the lid make it convenient for you to open the lid while the trunk is tipped on its side. The casters fastened to the four corners of the base permit the easy rotation of the trunk during the performance.

B In this illustration, you can see that the trunk actually has no bottom. The shaded area represents the top surface of the platform. The upright panel, marked A, is mounted permanently to the top surface of the platform and held in this position by Sections B1 and B2 which are also permanently attached to the platform and to Panel A. These end pieces (B1 and B2) are cut into a pie-wedge shape in order to allow the bottom back edge of the trunk to pass over them during the "tipping" action. A length of webbing (or lightweight chain) is attached to the lid as illustrated

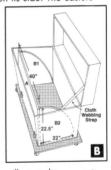

to prevent the lid from falling too far back and shearing the hinges when the lid is open.

C When the trunk has been tipped over on its side, as in Figure 3, the upright Panel A becomes the bottom of the trunk. The magician is then free to lift the lid, as illustrated, and allow the audience a clear view into the trunk's empty interior.

METHOD

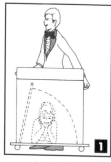

1 With your second assistant concealed in the trunk, the entire affair is rolled on stage so that it stands between you and your first assistant. The two of you now revolve the trunk, showing all sides.

2 With the front now facing the audience, you and your first assistant grasp the handles at the back and tip the trunk forward on its base. Be sure to keep the lid closed as you tip the trunk or the audience will see the false bottom swinging into position. When the trunk is on its side, swing the lid open and allow the audience to see that the inside of the trunk is empty.

3 This is a "backstage" view and shows how your assistant is hiding behind the false bottom (A). Depending upon the line of sight of your audience, you and your first assistant should stand next to the open trunk, one on each side, to hide the two end supports (B1 and B2) which also conceal your second assistant.

4 Close the lid and set the trunk upright on its base. Step in front of the trunk, turn, and clap your hands. On this cue, your second assistant stands erect, pushing open the lid which flies back into the hands of your first assistant.

NOTE: In order to give your assistant a graceful exit from the trunk, it will be necessary for you and your other assistant to vault your second assistant out in a strong, sweeping motion so that the second assistant lands on both feet to conclude the dramatic magical appearance.

COMMENTS AND SUGGESTIONS

"Box Jumpers" is an interesting term that is used by professional illusionists. A Box Jumper is the assistant who helps the magician by conveniently appearing, vanishing, being divided into two or more parts and then becoming magically restored, and so on during the illusion show. You can see from the "exit" your second assistant makes from the TIP-OVER TRUNK just how these talented people acquired that unusual nickname.

SUSPENSION ILLUSION

For centuries, tales were told of Hindu fakirs who could levitate themselves and remain suspended in midair for hours or even days. Such exaggerated reports caused the magicians of Europe and America to devise their own methods of presenting this fanciful effect. Unfortunately, in its ultimate form, the illusion was costly, difficult to transport, and could only be presented on a fully equipped stage in a large theater. In contrast, the version about to be described is inexpensive, portable, easy to set up, and can be presented on practically any stage that has drapes and on which the "angles" (line of sight) are those normally found in a theater.

EFFECT

You call the audience's attention to a thin board resting on two small, sawhorse-like supports. These supports are positioned at the ends of the board and elevate it to a height of approximately 3'. This equipment is standing in the middle of the stage, and the audience can see the basic simplicity of the arrangement. Your assistant enters and sits comfortably on the board. With your aid, your assistant is positioned horizontally on the board. Walking behind and leaning over your assistant's body, you apparently hypnotize your assistant. The arms fall limply over the side of the board, and the eyes close. Carefully placing the arm next to the body, you move to the feet and slowly remove the sawhorse from beneath this end of the board. Magically, and with only the support of the single sawhorse, your assistant remains suspended as if being held in balance by an unseen force. Passing your hands under the suspended assistant, you carefully remove the last sawhorse. The audience is stunned to see that the sleeping assistant is now "floating on air" with no other support than your will!

Again, you pass your hands under and over the assistant's suspended figure, proving to the audience that the assistant is truly "levitated." Quickly replacing the supports beneath the board, you snap your fingers and awaken your assistant, who then bows to the applauding spectators.

SECRET AND PREPARATION

NOTE: Since this is one of the true classics of magic, it is important that you construct this illusion with care. Any skimping or make-do arrangements will only spoil a great effect.

A Figure A tells the whole story. Except for the 12" × 54" × 3/4" plywood board, the entire structure is made up of hardened steel 2" wide by 1/4" to 1/2" thick. The board is fastened to the top extension arm by two heavy angle brackets (A and B), as illustrated. After construction, paint the entire unit "flat black." Trim the edge of the board with a 5" fringe, as illustrated. This fringe conceals the steel support directly under the board. You will also require an attractive carpet that can be

thrown over the floor supports of the apparatus, and two lightweight sawhorses that are the correct height to apparently support the board. In fact, the board is always supported by the secret device located behind the curtain. Paint these supports white (or leave them their natural light color of unfinished wood) in order to create the contrast necessary to help divert the spectators' eyes from the board. If the black felt-covered board is also trimmed with black fringe, the audience, many times, will leave the theater with the impression that the assistant was only supported by the two white sawhorses.

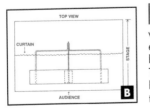

B You will also require a curtain directly behind the illusion, as shown in the top view. The support arm for the board must extend through the curtain, as shown. The brighter the color of this curtain, the better. The object here is to create a brilliant area behind your assistant, giving the audience the impression of a clean separation.

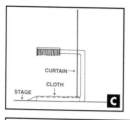

C The equipment is positioned onstage as shown in this side view. You will notice that the support arm extends through the center slit in the backdrop. The floor supports extend under the bottom edge of the curtain and are disguised with the small carpet.

D Place the two sawhorses under the ends of the board as in Figure D. The effect will be as illustrated.

METHOD

1 Introduce your assistant to the audience and have the assistant sit on the center of the board. Take hold of the assistant's ankles and position the feet near the left end support.

2 Walk around the front side of the equipment and help your assistant in leaning back until the assistant is resting flat on the board with the neck just above the sawhorse support at that end.

3 Move around the head end of the board until you are standing behind the assistant and the board. The hidden arm of the equipment will be next to your left wrist.

4 The following move will help establish separation between the assistant and the curtain. Lean over and apparently hypnotize your assistant. As the eyes close, have the assistant drop the right arm limply off the board. This diversion gives you an excuse for moving back to the front in order to replace the arm.

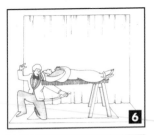

5 After repositioning the arm, move to the end of the board supporting the head. Reach under it, remove the sawhorse, and set it aside.

6 Step around behind your assistant at the head of the board and pass your hands over and under the suspended figure.

7 Move back around to the front and cross over to the foot end of the equipment. Gently slide the last sawhorse from beneath the board, leaving the assistant apparently suspended in the air!

8 Pass your hands over and under the suspended figure.

9 Quickly, replace the foot support. Then, cross over to the other side and slide the second sawhorse under the head. Snap your fingers as if to awaken your assistant and help the assistant stand up as you take your bows.

YOUR FUTURE IN MAGIC

Magic itself can shape your future. The study and practice of magic develops versatility, the ability to handle emergencies while under pressure, the gift to recognize coming trends, and perhaps most importantly, the skill to appear before and speak to groups of people— a definite asset in almost any career you may choose.

Interest in magic has expanded so rapidly that it has become an adjunct not only to professions, but to social life as well. Anyone versed in magic will find it helpful in making contacts in almost any line. Moreover, the demand for magic has increased so greatly that it can be turned into profit as a sideline. There is no longer any need to serve as an apprentice to learn the magic trade. You can start as a semiprofessional, if you go about it in the right way.

To begin, you must learn to do magic well. By studying this course, you have already made progress in that direction. More importantly, you should learn magic comprehensively. Many phases of magic, particularly misdirection and showmanship, apply to small tricks as well as large. Anything you learn from one trick may be applied to another. Also, by trying your hand at different magic tricks, you'll find those that suit you best. Just remember that the audience's reaction is what matters most.

Harry Houdini originally billed himself as the "King of Cards" but dropped the title when he found that his escape act created a sensation. Today, such a change in repertoire is easier than ever. In fact, it may be too easy. So many good tricks are available that many magicians switch from one type to another without giving any a fair trial. This can prove a waste of time as well as money, so it should be strictly avoided. Try to make your work progressive by adapting each new effect to your own particular style. Get people talking about you and the way you do your magic rather than about the tricks you perform. That will enable you to find your place in magic according to your own individuality.

Where you go from there will be largely up to you. Once you have a working pattern and style, you can decide whether to regard magic as a fascinating hobby, a form of social contact and enjoyment, a profitable sideline, or an outright profession. New fields are constantly developing within the magic industry. The demand for new tricks has attracted inventors and stimulated the manufacture of special apparatus. Magic dealers are increasing steadily. So if you have talents in any of these fields, a future in magic is certainly worthy of consideration.

The choice is yours, so make the most of it!

GLOSSARY

ACCORDION PLEAT: Method of folding a handkerchief or paper, in much the same manner as the bellows of an accordion are designed to expand and contract.

BOW KNOT: Specialty rope-tie with magical applications, similar to the type of knot used when tying one's shoes.

BRIDGE-SIZE DECK: A deck of cards slightly smaller than a poker deck, measuring 2-1/4" wide. Bridge-size cards are frequently used and give the magician an advantage in certain tricks because of their smaller width.

CARD DISCOVERY: The climax or end of many card tricks during which the spectator's card is revealed or produced in a "magical" manner.

CARD LOCATION: Any method that allows the magician to find or locate a selected card after it has been returned to the pack.

CLASSIC-PALM POSITION: Method of hiding a small object by gently squeezing it in the palm of your hand.

CLOSE-UP MAGIC: Magic tricks that can be performed at close quarters to an audience. Card and coin tricks, among others, are generally referred to as Close-Up tricks.

COIN FOLD: Method of folding a coin in a piece of paper, yet being able to secretly remove it without the spectators' knowledge.

COIN ROLL: Classic manipulation of a coin rolling across the back of a performer's hand.

CONTROL: Any method (usually unknown to the audience) that allows the performer to move a particular card or cards to a specific location in the pack. This term is used extensively in this book. In almost every instance, it refers to the return to the pack of the selected card by the spectator and the magician's ability to "control" the placement of the card and its location within the deck (top, bottom, etc.).

CORING: Procedure of removing the center strands found in some types of cotton rope to make the rope more pliable and easy to work with.

DO-AS-I-DO EFFECT: Any trick in which a spectator is asked to follow the actions of the magician.

DOUBLE OR MULTIPLE CUT: Dividing the deck into more than two stacks and then reassembling the deck.

DOUBLE-WALLED BAG: A paper bag used to vanish or change objects, thanks to a secret compartment made by gluing part of a second bag inside the first.

FACE: The face of a card shows its value and suit.

FACE CARDS, PICTURE CARDS, OR COURT CARDS: All of the jacks, queens, and kings.

FALSE CUT: Any cut that leaves the deck in the same order as it was before the cut.

FALSE SHUFFLE: Any shuffle that leaves the deck in the same order as it was before the shuffle.

FINGER-PALM POSITION: One of the many methods of concealing a coin or other small object by holding it with the fingers and keeping the hand in a natural position.

FLASH: Allowing the spectator to briefly see the face of any card.

FLOURISH: A display of skill with the cards. Flourishes are usually not tricks, although they can become important parts of some effects. Examples of flourishes are Fanning the Pack, the Ribbon Spread, One-Hand Cuts, etc.

FORCE: Causing a spectator to select a particular card or cards when the spectator thinks the choice was freely made.

FREE CHOICE: Legitimately free selection of a playing card from a deck.

GENIE CARD: Specially printed card, about the size of a business card, used to perform many special close-up tricks. The card depicts a Genie rising in a wisp of smoke from a lamp.

GIANT CARD: An extra-large card that is usually four times larger than a regular poker-size playing card.

GIMMICK: Any secret device used to perform a trick. The audience is usually not aware of a gimmick.

GLIMPSE: Secretly noting a card while holding or shuffling the pack.

HALF-CARD: The basic secret to all Genie Card routines. The Half-Card, which depicts the top part of the Genie drawing, is placed on top of a packet of full-size Genie Cards, and held in place with a rubber band.

IMPROMPTU EFFECT: Effects that are done on the spur of the moment, without advance preparation, and generally with everyday objects.

INDICATOR CARD: A playing card used to identify the location, value, or suit of a different card, usually selected by the audience. Also called a Key Card.

INSTANT MAGIC: Magic tricks, "Betchas," and other stunts that can apparently be performed on the spur of the moment.

KEY CARD: Any card that can be used as a locator card.

LAPPING: The act of apparently picking an object off a table, yet secretly allowing it to drop into your lap.

LOCATOR CARD: Any card that can be used as a key to find some other card in the pack. An example of a locator card is a short card.

MAGIC LOOP: Double-stick cellophane tape, which has a sticky surface on both sides, is useful in many magic effects, particularly if the audience is unaware of its presence. If you wish to do tricks that call for double-stick tape and do not have any on hand, you can easily make your own by forming a Magic Loop. This is done by taking a piece of regular, single-side tape and forming it into a loop with the sticky side out. Place this on whatever surface you want to apply the tape to, and by pressing the loop flat, you will have formed the equivalent of a piece of double-stick tape.

MASTER MOVE: Method of sliding one Genie Card from a packet in order to achieve most Genie Card routines.

MECHANIC'S GRIP: A method used for holding the deck in the left hand for dealing. The left first finger extends around the front of the deck.

MISDIRECTION: Distracting the audience's attention from one place to another during crucial portions of the magic presentation.

MOVE: A "move" may be either secret, in which case it is a sleight, or some movement of the cards that the spectators can see such as cutting the deck.

ONE-WAY DECK: A picture-back deck in which the back patterns may all be arranged so that they face one way. After a card has been selected, the deck is merely turned around so that when the card is returned, its picture is facing in the opposite direction and then can easily be found.

PADDLE MOVE: A type of manipulation used to apparently show both sides of a two-sided object, yet the audience actually sees the same side at all times.

PALM: General term used to describe hiding small objects in the hand. There are several subcategories and types of palms.

PATTER THEME: The basis for any story, real or imaginary, used during the performance of magic.

PENETRATION: One of the many subcategories of magic tricks, specifically, the apparent ability to pass one solid object through another.

POKER-SIZE DECK: A deck of standard-size playing cards, measuring 2-1/2" wide.

PREARRANGED DECK: A deck that has been set up or arranged in some special order before the performance.

PRESTIDIGITATOR: Another term for "magician." Its most literal translation, from French, means "fast fingers."

RELEASE: The magical separation of one or more items that seem hopelessly intertwined or bound together.

REVERSED CARD: Any card that is face up in a face-down pack (or face down in a face-up pack).

ROLL DOWN: Advanced coin manipulation in which a stack of coins is single-handedly spread between the fingers of one hand.

ROPE COILING: Loosely wrapping rope into a bundle.

ROUTINING: Combining two or more individual tricks into a "flowing" performance pattern. For example, a rope routine may be a five-minute act made up of six or seven individual rope tricks, yet the tricks flow smoothly from one to another.

SANDWICHED CARD: Any card that is placed, or located, between two other pre-designated cards.

SELF-WORKING TRICK: Any trick that can be performed with little, if any, secret "moves" or sleight-of-hand maneuvers.

SINGLE CUT: Removing a packet of cards from the top of the deck, placing it beside the lower portion, and then completing the cut by placing the lower portion on top of the upper portion.

SLEIGHT: A secret move done with the cards that is not known to the spectators, such as Double Lift, Glide, etc.

SLEIGHT OF HAND: General term describing any magic trick whose method relies on skilled manipulation of the fingers and/or hand.

SPOT CARDS: Any card from ace through ten in any suit.

SPRING: Describes action of objects as they are rapidly passed from one hand to another. Usually used in connection with playing-card manipulations.

STANDARD DEAL: Cards are drawn off, one at a time, face downward, and placed on the table. Each card goes on the card that was dealt before it. This reverses the order of the cards.

STOCK: Any portion of the pack containing cards that have been set up in a special order.

TOP OF DECK: When the deck is face down, the uppermost card or portion of the deck.

TRANSPOSITION: The apparent, invisible transfer of an object from one place to another.

TREY: Another name for a three.

TRICK: General definition for all types of individual magic.

TURN-UP DEAL: The cards are dealt singly from the top of the face-down deck, but they are turned face up as they are dealt. This does not reverse the order of the deck.